THE STRUGGLE FOR THE SOUL OF TEACHER EDUCATION

D1596170

The Struggle for the Soul of Teacher Education is a much-needed exploration of the unprecedented current controversies and debates over teacher education and professionalism. Set within the context of neo-liberal education reforms across the globe, the book explores how the current struggles over teaching and teacher education in the US came about, as well as reflections on where we should head in the future. Zeichner provides specific examples of work that moves teacher education toward greater congruency between ideals and practices, while outlining the basis for a new form of community-based teacher education, where universities and other program providers, local communities, school districts, and teacher unions share responsibility for the preparation of teachers. Ultimately, Zeichner problematizes an uncritical shift to more practice and clinical experience, and discusses the enduring problems of clinical teacher education that need to be addressed for this shift to be educative.

Readers are sure to gain insight on transforming teacher education so it more adequately addresses the need to prepare teachers capable of providing a high-quality education with access to a rich and broad curriculum, and culturally and community responsive teaching for everyone's children.

Kenneth M. Zeichner is the Boeing Professor of Teacher Education at the University of Washington, USA.

The Critical Social Thought Series

Edited by Michael W. Apple, University of Wisconsin—Madison

THE STRUGGLE FOR THE SOUL OF TEACHER EDUCATION

Kenneth M. Zeichner

Routledge
Taylor & Francis Group

NEW YORK AND LONDON

First published 2018
by Routledge
711 Third Avenue, New York, NY 10017

and by Routledge
2 Park Square, Milton Park, Abingdon, Oxon, OX14 4RN

Routledge is an imprint of the Taylor & Francis Group, an informa business

© 2018 Taylor & Francis

The right of Kenneth M. Zeichner to be identified as author of this work has been asserted by him in accordance with sections 77 and 78 of the Copyright, Designs and Patents Act 1988.

Library of Congress Cataloging in Publication Data
A catalog record for this book has been requested

ISBN: 978-1-138-06408-9 (hbk)
ISBN: 978-1-138-06409-6 (pbk)
ISBN: 978-1-315-09807-4 (ebk)

Typeset in Bembo
by Saxon Graphics Ltd, Derby

This book is dedicated to my beautiful grandchildren:
Elana, Ezra, and Margo.

CONTENTS

SERIES EDITOR INTRODUCTION

In *Educating the "Right" Way* (Apple, 2006) and *Can Education Change Society?* (Apple, 2013), I spend a good deal of time on the ways in which education has been and is now a significant site of struggle for both retrogressive and progressive movements. Unfortunately, it is these more retrogressive movements who are often in the driver's seat in educational reform currently.

We should not be surprised that education has once again become a focal point of concerted criticism. This is not new. Whenever there is significant turmoil in society, economic worries, a loss of cultural stability and a feeling that "all that is solid melts in the air," and more—all of this has very often led to a focus on educational theories, policies, and practices as both a major cause of our social and well as educational problems and a major source of possible solutions.

This is particularly the case now. Neoliberals have pushed for privatization, the use of corporate models and logics, and competition in everything educational. Neoconservatives have urged a restoration of "real knowledge" and "tradition." Authoritarian populist religious conservatives have lamented the "loss of God" in our schools and daily life. And they have exerted pressures at all levels of education to bring back conservative religious understandings to the central place that they supposedly once had. And new managerial impulses that stress reductive forms of measurement, accountability, and audit as the only way to judge success in schools have had powerful effects as well (Apple, 2006).

All of these movements have had very real effects not only on education in general. They have been and are equally powerful in one of the most significant areas of education, that of teacher education. One of the things that provides support for these tendencies is the lamentable fact that we live in a time of increasing disrespect of teaching and teachers. All too often there seems to be an underlying assumption that the act of teaching is somehow "easy," that it doesn't require an extensive amount of varied skills, both intellectual and interpersonal, and that therefore it can be done by almost anyone. Nothing could be farther from the truth. If anything, a robust and critically reflective teacher education, both pre-service and in-service, is required now more than ever.

This is exactly the argument that *The Struggle for the Soul of Teacher Education* takes up. Kenneth Zeichner's aim in this fine book is something almost everyone who cares deeply about the quality of teacher education should share. As he says, "The emphasis in this book is on transforming US teacher education so it more adequately addresses the need to prepare teachers capable of providing a high-quality education with access to a rich and broad curriculum, and culturally and community responsive teaching for everyone's children." But Zeichner doesn't stop there. He goes beyond this more general aim to include an even more ambitious agenda. This is perhaps best summed up when he discusses why he employs the word "soul" in the book's title. As he says:

> My use of the terminology "the struggle for the soul" in the title of this book indicates my efforts to analyze the rules, standards, systems of reasoning, and assumptions that underlie current debates about teacher education in the US. In using this language, I assert that the debates over teacher education are, in fact, debates about the meaning of children, families, communities, teachers, the processes of teaching and learning, the ways that classrooms are managed, public schooling, and the place of teachers in the communities in which they work. Teacher education in this sense is a process of shaping the souls of teachers with regard to these issues.

Clearly Zeichner understands the real depth of the problem. But let me be clear about something else. Kenneth Zeichner is not a romantic about the current dominant models of teacher education, many of which are under attack by conservatives. His criticisms of many current models are thoughtful and well argued. Yet, one of the things that sets this book apart from many others that I know is Kenneth Zeichner's ability not only to offer cogent critiques of the accepted and emerging positions and programs increasingly dominating teacher education, but also to provide equally cogent alternatives to them. I know of no other book that does these multiple tasks in such a cogent and forceful way.

He argues for and describes more community-based and democratic approaches to teacher education. These are public, not privatized, models. They are socially committed, connected to the realities of real people in real schools, equitable, and workable. They go a long way toward solving the pressing problems of preparing teachers for a truly and proudly multicultural society and preparing teachers with the knowledge, skills, dispositions, and values so necessary to be successful in the real conditions and challenges that teachers will actually face.

For years, Kenneth Zeichner has been one of the most talented, articulate, and socially committed writers on teacher education in the world. Yet this is not adequate to describe his work. He is also one of the very best practitioners and builders of socially conscious teacher education programs in the world. This combination is on full and rich display in *The Struggle for the Soul of Teacher Education*. Those who follow Zeichner's work know that he has repeatedly made significant contributions to the debates over teacher education (see, e.g., Zeichner, 2009; Liston & Zeichner, 1991). But in this book he surpasses even those past achievements, challenging accepted positions, challenging many of the reforms that have been proposed, and showing a way forward in creating a teacher education that is worthy of its name.

Michael W. Apple
John Bascom Professor
Curriculum and Instruction
and
Educational Policy Studies
University of Wisconsin, Madison

References

Apple, M. W. (2006). *Educating the "right" way: Markets, standards, God, and inequality* (2nd edition). New York: Routledge.

Apple, M. W. (2013). *Can education change society?* New York: Routledge.

Liston, D., & Zeichner, K. (1991). *Teacher education and the social conditions of schooling.* New York: Routledge.

Zeichner, K. (2009). *Teacher education and the struggle for social justice.* New York: Routledge.

INTRODUCTION

The Teacher Education Landscape: Then and Now

In the last two decades, there has been unprecedented controversy and debate about teacher education in the US among policymakers and the general public. Although controversy over teacher education is not new, these recent debates are different from what occurred in the past. They differ both in their level of intensity and in the efforts that have been made by policymakers, philanthropists, and other private investors to support the disruption of the current system through deregulation and the construction of an alternative one (Wilson, 2014).

Formal teacher education programs began in the US in the early part of the nineteenth century. During this period, and for much of the history of teacher education in the US, a variety of options have been available to individuals seeking to become elementary or secondary teachers. For much of the time, most individuals entered teaching through what now would be referred to as "alternative routes" (Fraser, 2007). These included programs offered by academies, seminaries, high schools, normal schools, and teacher institutes in the nineteenth century, and later by teachers' colleges, community colleges, and colleges and universities (Fraser, 2007; Lucas, 1999; Mattingly, 1975).

Many individuals entered teaching during the early period without any significant preparation and, in many parts of the country, the passing of a local exam (often based solely on mastery of subjects to be taught) qualified individuals to teach. From the beginning of the twentieth century, there was growth in teacher certification based on the successful completion of a teacher education program rather than examinations, and teacher licensing became centralized at the state level (Sedlak, 2008).

Universities began their involvement in preparing teachers in the later part of the nineteenth century. By 1960, almost all teachers entered teaching after completing a college or university program. Despite the entry of universities into teacher preparation and the growing number of universities that became involved, for the first three decades of the twentieth century, university programs only prepared a minority of the nation's teachers (Fraser, 2007). It was only for a relatively brief period of time (1960–1990) that colleges and universities had a virtual monopoly on preparing teachers (Fraser, 2007).

Since the 1990s, there has been a tremendous increase in non-college and university programs, including for-profit programs. More and more individuals are entering teaching through completion of a non-college or university program, sometimes with very little preparation before assuming full responsibility for a classroom of students (Zeichner & Hutchinson, 2008). These "early-entry" teachers most often teach students in communities highly impacted by poverty (Peske & Haycock, 2006). A growing number of these non-college or university programs have been developed by privately run charter school networks to provide teachers for their schools (Stitzlein & West, 2014).

Despite the growth in non-college or university programs, most teachers in the US still enter teaching through a 4-year or 5-year undergraduate or fulltime post-baccalaureate college or university program (National Research Council, 2010). In some parts of the country, though, nearly as many teachers enter the field through an "alternative" program (Feistritzer & Haar, 2008).[1]

In addition to the non-college or university programs (independent programs) that operate independently of existing colleges and universities—such as the Relay Graduate School of Education, TEACH-Now, and iteachTEXAS—other alternative programs initiated outside of colleges and universities, like Teach for America, have partnered in preparing teachers with either colleges and universities or independent programs. Additionally, some teacher education programs are run by community colleges, either on their own or in partnership with a college or university.

A final type of teacher education program that exists in the US today is the new hybrid teacher education programs that are jointly developed by school districts and various partners such as nonprofits, universities, and community groups to prepare teachers to teach in specific school districts (Guha, Hyler, & Darling-Hammond, 2016). Teacher residency programs and "grow your own" (GYO) (Skinner, Garreton, & Schultz, 2011) programs are two examples of these programs.

Controversies in Teacher Education

Struggles within Higher Education

From the beginning of the involvement of universities in preparing US teachers, there has been severe criticism of university teacher education, and teacher education faculty in universities have struggled for a long time to gain legitimacy both within the university environment and with public school educators (Clifford & Guthrie, 1988; Goodlad, 1990; Labaree, 2004). During the twentieth century, as teacher education programs became established in colleges and universities, and despite the efforts of the federal government to focus universities on the practical arts of agriculture, engineering, and teacher training to serve the needs of the society when it established land grant universities (Palmer, 1985), the point of view persisted that a sound liberal arts education, complemented by an apprenticeship in a school, was the most sensible way to prepare teachers for their work. Since the 1930s, and continuing today, it has been argued based on this assumption that teacher education programs in colleges and universities provide an intellectually inferior and unnecessary education.

One of the earliest critics of university teacher education was Abraham Flexner, who was also noted for his role in critiquing medical education. In his widely cited study of US and European universities in 1930, Flexner lodged a number of criticisms of university teacher education that have continued to be raised by critics over the years. These included assertions that the mastery of subject matter is the most important thing in the education of a teacher and that university education courses interfere with this goal. Flexner, like many who followed him, criticized education courses for their allegedly intellectual superficiality, education students and their professors for their meager educational resources, and educational scholarship for its insignificance. Accepting the value of a few areas of study he considered to be legitimate, such as educational philosophy and comparative education, Flexner argued that all the rest of what teachers needed to learn beyond a sound liberal education could be gained through an apprenticeship in a school.

> Why should not an educated person, broadly and deeply vested in educational philosophy and experience, help himself from that point on? Why should his attention be diverted during these pregnant years to the trivialities and applications with which common sense can deal adequately when the time comes?
>
> *(Flexner, 1930, pp. 99–100)*

Since Flexner's critique of university teacher education, a number of highly visible and controversial analyses have articulated the same themes. These include Lynd's (1953) *Quackery in the Public Schools*, Bestor's (1953) *Educational Wastelands*, Koerner's (1963) *The Miseducation of American Teachers*, Conant's (1963) *The Education of American Teachers*, Mitchell's (1981) *The Graves of Academe*, Kramer's (1991) *Ed School Follies*, and Chubb's (2012) *The Best Teachers in the World: Why We Don't Have Them and How We Could*.

Several different strategies were pursued over the years to address these criticisms. They included investment by foundations to provide more opportunities for arts and sciences faculty to play a greater role in preparing teachers by funding postgraduate programs requiring significant arts and science faculty involvement, such as Master's of Arts in teaching (MAT) programs. MAT programs were started at many research universities following the initiation of the model at Harvard (Coley & Thorpe, 1986). Beyond the implementation of new programs more tied to arts and sciences faculty, there has also been advocacy and financial support for what is referred to as the "all-university" approach to teacher education where arts and sciences faculty from throughout the university play a role in program governance (Stiles, 1958).

Finally, another approach to limit the control of programs by college and university departments, schools, and colleges of education is to place a statutory limit on the number of education credits that can be included in a teacher education program. In 1987, Texas was one of the first states to pursue this strategy by limiting Education credits in a teacher education program to 18 semester hour credits, including six credits of student teaching (Simms & Miller, 1988).

One response by education schools to these criticisms from arts and sciences faculties is the emergence of efforts to push for greater autonomy for education schools within universities, where they, like law schools and medical schools, would have more control over their activities, budgets, and systems for evaluating and rewarding faculty. *A Design for a School of Pedagogy* (Smith, 1980) and the National Network for Educational Renewal's support for establishing "Centers of Pedagogy" (Patterson, Michelli, & Pacheco, 1999) are examples of this attempt to create spaces within universities where teacher education is the priority.

Another response by education schools and states to these criticisms has been to raise standards for entry and completion of teacher education programs. Despite continuing criticisms of low standards in college and university programs, there is a consensus among scholars who have examined the evidence on this issue that there is wide variation in the rigor and quality in all types of teacher education programs. There is some evidence that the general increase in teacher education admission, completion, and program accountability standards has resulted in an improvement in the academic quality of graduates from college and university programs (Goldhaber &Walch, 2014).

Criticism From the Schools

In 2004, Tom Payzant, then superintendent of the Boston schools, gave an invited address at the annual meeting of the major teacher education organization in the US, the American Association of Colleges for Teacher Education. In his lecture, "Should teacher preparation take place at colleges and universities," Payzant (2004) criticized existing teacher education programs for not supplying urban districts with teachers who were successful and stayed in their jobs over time. He warned his audience of college and university faculty and administrators that unless they engaged in serious reform soon, he and other urban superintendents would look elsewhere for their teachers, including even preparing some of them themselves. It later became known that Payzant had already begun efforts in 2003 to develop a teacher residency program with several local partners to prepare teachers specifically for Boston public schools.

The Boston Teacher Residency program (BTR) is one of dozens of clinically oriented teacher residency programs nationally that prepare teachers for specific school districts and in which districts partner with a variety of higher education and community partners in the preparation process (Guha et al., 2016).

In 2010, the major national accreditation body for teacher education programs in the US, The National Council for the Accreditation of Teacher Education (NCATE) issued a report that called for major changes in teacher education that would make practice the center of preparation programs (NCATE, 2010). Since then, there has been much activity both within and outside the higher education teacher education community to shift teacher education more into schools and focus more on what are seen as "practical teaching skills," and less on what is defined as "educational theory."

Although there are extreme examples of new startup programs boasting that educational theory has been marginalized in their curriculums and uncritically glorifying practice (e.g., Gastic, 2014; Schorr, 2013; TNTP, 2014), most programs that have made clinical experiences more central to the teacher education curriculum have done so without this kind of anti-theory rhetoric. "Clinically-rich" or "clinically-oriented" teacher preparation has become the new slogan in the field and significant national reform efforts based on this concept have emerged.

Another aspect of the movement toward practice in US teacher education has been a new incarnation of a long-term desire to articulate the practices that teachers should learn to enact in their preparation programs. This newer version of "practice-based teacher education" (e.g., Forzani, 2014; Grossman, 2011) is much more developed and sophisticated than earlier "practice-based" versions of teacher education (Charters & Waples, 1929; Gage & Winne, 1974; Sykes, Bird, & Kennedy, 2010). It is articulated in relation to the particular subjects that are being taught, and does not seek to reduce teaching to mere mastery of a set of techniques. This focus on practice within a vision of teachers as intellectuals who must learn how to exercise their judgment in the classroom and teach in culturally responsive ways is not always clearly evident in the practice-based literature (Zeichner, 2012), but much of the recent work to help teacher candidates learn how to enact what are considered to be core or high-leverage practices falls into what Feiman-Nemser (1990) referred to as the teacher-as-decision-maker (vs. competency-based) strand of what she terms the technological orientation to teacher education.[2]

The Reemergence of "Alternative" Teacher Certification in the 1980s

After the virtual monopoly of colleges and universities on US teacher education from about 1960–1990 (Fraser, 2007), beginning in the early 1980s there was an increase in both non-college and university programs (including for-profit programs), and in new, more flexible college and university programs that made it easier for individuals to switch into teaching from another career and for individuals who were not able to attend classes within a traditional college and university schedule to do so. Some of these programs reduced the requirements from those that existed in college and university programs, while others held teacher candidates to the same level of requirements, but did so in more flexible ways (Darling-Hammond, 1992). In some of these programs ("early-entry") individuals became teachers of record after a short pre-service preparation period of a few weeks and completed most of the program while teaching fulltime.

There were a number of reasons for the reemergence of these "alternative" programs and for their continued growth. First, similar to Flexner's belief discussed earlier that much of what individuals need to learn to be teachers can be learned on the job in an apprenticeship with an experienced teacher, the factor that is most often cited as reason for states establishing alternative routes into teaching has been the need to fill teaching vacancies in critical shortage areas. These include real or projected shortages in particular fields such as mathematics, science, and special education, and shortages in hard-to-staff schools in remote rural and urban school districts. The rationale has been that teachers prepared through alternative routes would allegedly be better equipped and presumably do a better job of teaching and stay longer than the emergency licensed teachers that were then filling many positions. Hawley (1990) labeled this rationale for alternative programs as the "last resort rationale."

Another reason alternative routes to teaching were approved by states was to draw individuals into teaching who might not otherwise choose to become teachers. For example, there was and continues to be a desire to use alternative certification programs to attract more people of color into teaching, so the nation's teaching force will better reflect the diversity of pupils in the schools. There has also been a desire to draw more mature individuals with varied life experiences into teaching, a population that was quite different from the typical college and university student population. Also, alternative programs were seen as a way to bring more men, career changers, and retired military personnel into teaching who, it was argued, would not otherwise consider a career in teaching.

Some advocates of alternative certification programs expressed dissatisfaction with college and university programs for allegedly failing to supply teachers who were willing to teach in the schools that most needed them and/or for the poor quality of the teachers they prepared (Haberman, 1986). It was felt by some that college and university programs added to the inequitable access to fully certified teachers and teachers teaching in the fields of their expertise (Eubanks & Parish, 1990). Others such as Bliss (1990) argued that alternative programs could serve as a catalyst for the reform of college and university programs. Finally, Wisniewski (1986) argued that the development of new alternative routes to teaching provided an opportunity for researchers to test the efficacy of different approaches.

One irony in all of this is that until recently most of the alternative programs that have emerged since the 1980s have been developed and run by universities (Feistritzer & Haar, 2008). It has only been in the last decade or so that non-college and university programs, and the hybrid programs like teacher residencies, have begun to expand their presence.

Current Efforts to Disrupt Teacher Education

> Teacher Preparation is shaping up to be the next frontier for entrepreneurs. Growing attention from Federal and state policymakers and newly available capital from large philanthropic sources such as the Schusterman and Gates Foundations are attracting attention from entrepreneurs looking to break the lock that universities have on preparing teachers.
>
> *(Stacey Childress, CEO, New Schools Venture Fund, 2016)*

Historically, federal teacher education policy and the philanthropic community invested in strengthening the quality of college and university teacher education programs. The National Teacher Corps, which existed from 1965–1981—a huge investment to improve the quality of teaching in high-poverty rural and urban communities (Sykes & Dibner, 2009)—is a prime example of this federal commitment to improving college and university teacher education.

Similarly, the philanthropic community (e.g., Carnegie Corporation and Ford Foundation) have historically promoted and supported innovation in these programs. The $100-million-plus "Teachers for a New Era" project (2001–2009), funded by a consortium of foundations led by Carnegie, is one of the most recent examples of foundations' efforts to strengthen college and university teacher education.

Recently, however, it has become clear that the philanthropic community has turned away from building capacity in the current college and university system of teacher education, and toward funding alternative providers and programs. Major conferences and the national media have been flooded with speeches, papers, and opinion pieces that question the very idea of a system of teacher education dominated by colleges and universities (e.g., Keller, 2013; Vedder, 2011). Levine (2010) claimed "there is a growing sense among critics that it would be more fruitful to replace university-based teacher education than attempt to reform it" (pp. 21–22).

Similarly, the federal government in the last 15 years or so has implemented policies that have encouraged states to deregulate teacher education and to open investment opportunities for non-university providers. For over two decades, there has been a steady call from policymakers, philanthropists, venture capitalists, and the media for further deregulating teacher education, closing down allegedly poor-quality programs and creating more market competition (Chubb, 2012; Finn & Kanstoroom, 1999; Hess, 2009). In response to this call to "disrupt" the dominant higher-education-based system of teacher education, many new non-higher-education providers (both nonprofit and for-profit have emerged.

About this Book

All the chapters in this book were written during the presidency of Barack Obama, when there was a strong push to "disrupt" university dominance in teacher education and to support the creation of new non-university startup programs through federal teacher education policy and resource distribution. As I write this introduction, the US is in the early days of a new Republican administration with Donald Trump as president. In the first few weeks of the Trump administration, there has been a sharp shift in the direction of federal teacher education policy in the area of teacher education accountability. This shift has been part of a general effort by the Trump administration and leading Republicans in Congress to roll back what they consider to be the over-regulation of the Obama era across the board. Two sets of education regulations, the Elementary and Secondary School Act (ESSA) and teacher education accountability, were targeted for deregulation among multiple other areas in other federal agencies.

Among the first actions of the new administration related to teacher education was to push for the removal of a set of controversial accountability rules for teacher education programs that were promulgated by the Obama administration in October, 2016 under the Higher Education Act.[3] These rules were opposed by most of the teacher education community and other groups. They created a rating system for teacher education programs throughout the US that could have resulted in the withholding of federal funds to teacher candidates in universities housing programs that failed to meet the federal standards.

Although it is not clear at this point in the Trump administration what specific initiatives will be taken with regard to teacher education, there are some clues in Trump's appointment of a champion of "school choice" as secretary of education, Betsy DeVos. DeVos has advocated for choice and voucher programs in K–12 education and has made many derogatory statements over the years about the quality of public education. Her appointment was strongly opposed by many educators and civil rights groups, including the two major teacher unions.

Trump's first budget proposal that would affect the 2018 fiscal year also provides some clues. This proposal calls for a $9 billion (13 percent) cut in the federal education budget, including a cut of $2.25 billion in the part of the federal elementary and secondary school education act (ESSA) that is concerned with recruiting, preparing, retaining, and supporting educators—particularly in "high-need" schools (Title 2, Part A). Trump's budget proposal also eliminates the $43 million Teacher Quality Partnership Program that has funded the creation of model teacher education programs to prepare teachers to work in "high-needs" districts. Many of the newer hybrid teacher residency programs have been funded through this program.[4]

While calling for these cuts in funding to public education and teacher education, Trump has proposed a $168 million increase in funds for charter schools—which already receive over $300 million annually in federal funding—and the allocation of $250 million for a new private school choice program. The Trump budget also calls for a new $1 billion for Title 1 of ESSA that would be used for "choice," (i.e., money that would follow students wherever they choose to go to school).

Although it is not certain currently which of his proposals will be approved by Congress, or if the Trump administration will even last long enough for the enactment of his proposals, given all of the investigations and scandals that have plagued his presidency in its early days, it is clear that if the Trump administration continues, that shifting federal funds to support private and religious education will be a priority. Also, Secretary DeVos has been closely involved in her past in supporting online education and for-profit education. When she gets around to focusing on teacher education, I expect that the role of these institutions in teacher education will expand with federal help.

It is also not clear at this time how states will respond to the recent elimination of the federal teacher education accountability rules by Congress. Although it has been claimed by some (e.g., Arnett, 2017) that many states will continue with their plans to implement the federal rules even though they no longer exist, I believe that it is likely that states will continue to vary greatly in how they approach teacher education accountability.

In addition to the changes that will be brought to teacher education by the Trump administration, it is important to remember the more general point that teacher education and the contexts that surround it continue to change on an ongoing basis. Even before the end of the Obama presidency, there were changes to the programs, organizations, and policies discussed in this book. For example, The New Schools Venture Fund, which is discussed in Chapter 3, decided not to continue funding programs in teacher education after their new director Stacey Childress arrived. Much of the preparation and many of the related programs that they had funded such as Relay, Urban Teachers, Teach for America, Deans for Impact are now funded by others such as the Schusterman and Gates Foundations. These teacher education programs continue to change and evolve. For example, at the time that some of these chapters were written Relay offered only one fast-track pathway to teaching and has since added a residency option where teacher candidates work under the guidance of a mentor teacher before assuming full responsibility for a classroom.

Also, the legislation that was created by the New Schools Venture Fund and is discussed in Chapter 3 (The GREAT Act), failed to gain approval in two Congressional sessions and was eventually inserted into Title 2 of ESSA in its recent reauthorization. Although many of the elements of the original conception of teacher preparation academies were maintained in the final version passed by Congress, the Trump budget proposal calls for cutting the funding to all of the teacher preparation funding in this section of ESSA.

Finally, while it is important to be conscious of the fact that programs, organizations, and policies continue to change, it is also critical that we maintain suspicion of claims about innovation and reform in teacher education. Throughout the modern history of teacher education in the US we have seen issues like reflection, professional development school partnerships, "clinically rich" programs, and now teacher residency programs become slogans that attract much attention and external funding. When these slogans are adopted by programs, it gives the appearance that significant and substantive change has taken place. This appearance of innovation and significant change often turns out however, to be merely the illusion of change because the changes take place only on the surface while the underlying program substance and relations of power, knowledge, and coherence remain the same (e.g., Duffy, 1994; Zeichner, 2014). Counts (1935) reminded us of the difference between appearance and reality in teacher education reform and my intention in this book is to address both levels in my analyses.

Responding to the Controversies in Teacher Education

I have seen three general responses to the controversies in US teacher education. The first is an effort to defend the current system dominated by college and university programs and not to admit that there are any serious weaknesses in current programs. I call this the position of the *defenders*. A second position calls for "disrupting" or "blowing up" the current system through deregulation and replacing it with a new system based on investments in programs largely based in schools and run by districts or nonprofits and for-profits. I call this approach that of the *reformers*, based on the way in which advocates of deregulation and greater market competition have referred to themselves. Finally, a third position regarding the future of US teacher education is to recognize the weaknesses in the current system and to address them, while maintaining the largely public nature of teacher education in the US. I refer to this approach as that of the *transformers*.

The emphasis in this book is on transforming US teacher education so it more adequately addresses the need to prepare teachers capable of providing a high-quality education with access to a rich and broad curriculum, and culturally and community responsive teaching for everyone's children. The *reformers* have declared the college and university dominated system of teacher education to be "an industry of mediocrity" (Keller, 2013) and most current programs (1.0 programs) as obsolete. They identify the new entrepreneur developed programs that they seek to expand as 2.0 programs and tout them as the future for the field. In this book, I argue that neither 1.0 or 2.0 programs are adequate for the preparation of teachers capable of providing a high-quality education to everyone's children.

In recognizing the strengths and weaknesses in both 1.0 and 2.0 programs, I argue that we need a new, more community- and school-centered model for programs in which colleges and universities, districts, teacher unions, and local communities share in the responsibility for preparing culturally and community responsive teachers to teach everyone's children—a type of teacher education program I call Teacher Education 3.0.

In Chapter 1, I discuss the changes in the last 40 years of teacher education in the US that have resulted from two very different strategies for improving the preparation of teachers. These changes have resulted in substantial inequities in the distribution of fully prepared teachers who teach in the areas of their expertise. The affordances and limitations of promoting greater deregulation and privatization vs. investing in strengthening the dominant college and university teacher education system are discussed. I argue for investing in reinventing college and university programs while being open to the growth of high-quality alternatives to these programs.

In Chapter 2, I discuss recent developments in US teacher education in relation to the global neo-liberal project. My focus is on how changes experienced in different ways throughout the world have played out in the US. I pay particular attention to four issues: the commodification of teacher education; the defunding of public K–12 and higher education; hyperrationality (rationality beyond the bounds of reasonableness); and attacks on multiculturalism in teacher education. This chapter concludes with a call for the development of greater democratic professionalism in teaching and teacher education where university teacher educators collaborate more deeply than they have to date with schools and local communities in the preparation of teachers, and become a part of broader alliances that are working for greater humanity and social justice in different realms of social and economic life.

In Chapter 3, César Peña-Sandoval and I trace the ways venture philanthropy and the ideas of educational entrepreneurship and disruptive innovation shaped teacher education policy under the Obama administration. In doing so, we focus on the role of one of the most influential venture philanthropy organizations, the New Schools Venture Fund, in shaping federal legislation that encouraged expansion of the kind of entrepreneurial programs they funded. Much of this activity took place under the radar and out of public view. Our purpose in illuminating the ideas and processes pushing teacher education toward greater deregulation and market competition is to bring a greater level of transparency to private influences on public policy on teacher education and to promote greater public discussion and debate about alternative solutions to current problems.

In Chapter 4, Hilary Conklin and I analyze how research has been misrepresented through the processes of "knowledge ventriloquism" and "echo chambers" to support policies and programs that would reduce the role of colleges and universities in preparing teachers and support the expansion of non-university programs. We also examine the print media's role in reproducing a narrative of failure about college and university programs and uncritical acceptance of a narrative of success about new entrepreneurial programs and the organizations that promote them—attention that has served to inflate the public perception of these organizations and programs beyond what is warranted by the available evidence.

We focus on examples of knowledge ventriloquism and echo chambers at work: the misuse of Arthur Levine's 2006 study of teacher education in the US; the role of the National Council on Teacher Quality in creating a narrative of failure about college and university teacher education; the continual celebration of the alleged wonders of the Relay Graduate School of Education; and the misrepresentation of research on pathways into teaching in a 2012 Congressional hearing on alternative teacher certification. Following these cases, we offer several specific recommendations for raising the quality of debates in teacher education, including better communication between researchers and stakeholders, using only research that has been vetted to inform debates, and genuinely exploring different policy options for teacher education.

Chapter 5 is presented in a different format from the other chapters. It was written as a policy brief for the National Education Policy Center at the University of Colorado and has been left in its original form with no references embedded in the text. In this brief, following a survey of historical and contemporary trends in US teacher education, I examine the evidence supporting the efficacy of five of the most well-known independent teacher education programs that are not associated with any colleges or universities. These are: Relay Graduate School of Education, Match teacher residency, iTeach, TEACH NOW, and the High Tech High internship program. I examine both internal and external evidence that addresses the impact of these programs on teacher quality, teacher retention, and student learning. I conclude from the analysis that there is no credible evidence supporting the claims of success that have been made about these programs. I also conclude that two of the programs, Relay and Match, contribute to the inequitable distribution of professionally prepared teachers and to the stratificaton of schools based on the social class and racial composition of its students. I conclude the brief by offering several specific recommendations for state and federal policymakers based on my analysis.

In Chapter 6, Katie Payne, Kate Brako, and I argue that teacher education needs to make a fundamental shift in the epistemology of teacher education programs challenging current approaches to the issue of whose knowledge and expertise counts in the education of new teachers. Using tools afforded by cultural historical activity theory (CHAT) and deliberative democracy theory such as knotworking, boundary zones, horizontal expertise, and third space, we argue that by recasting who is considered an expert, and rethinking how teacher candidates and their college and university teacher educators cross institutional boundaries and collaborate and learn from local communities and schools, teacher education programs can invent better solutions to enduring problems of teaching and teacher education. We then provide examples of these more democratic approaches to teacher education from teacher education programs across the US, including some of our own work at the University of Washington.

In Chapter 7, Marisa Bier and I examine the current push toward making clinical experiences a more central focus in teacher education programs. We begin with a discussion of some of the enduring problems of clinical teacher education. These include the lack of coordination between coursework and clinical experiences, the uneven quality of mentoring, the under-resourcing of clinical experiences, the marginal status of both school-based and university-based mentors, and the lack of a carefully articulated clinical curriculum. We then discuss examples of current attempts to make teacher education more practice-centered in all three major types of teacher education programs (early-entry, college-recommending, and hybrid) including some of the work that we both have been involved in at the University of Washington.

In Chapter 8, Michael Bowman, Lorena Guillen, Kate Napolitan, and I discuss research that we conducted together on the impact of the community teaching strand in our elementary and secondary teacher education programs at the University of Washington. In this work, which used Peter Murrell's (2001) conception of "community teachers" as a lens for expressing the culturally and community responsive teachers we sought to prepare, we employed local community members as mentors of our teacher candidates and co-planned the learning activities that composed the strand with two leaders of a local community-based organization.

Three different conceptions of the nature and purpose of teacher-family-community relations frame the analysis: *involving* families and communities, *engaging* families and communities, and *working in solidarity* with families and communities.

Three primary research questions are explored in the chapter: What do teacher candidates (TCs) learn through their participation in the community teaching strand (CTS)? To what extent, and how, do TCs bring community teaching into their classrooms during the program and as first-year teachers? What programmatic features encouraged and/or constrained TC learning from the community mentors?

Following a discussion of several of the different kinds of teacher candidate-community mentor encounters we designed, we discuss the teacher candidate learning and practice outcomes we found as well as a number of tensions that arose in the programs in our attempt to implement engagement and solidarity approaches to working with families and communities in a teacher education program. Finally, the implications of this work for teacher education are discussed.

In Chapter 9, Jesslyn Hollar and I contrast the approaches to improve teaching quality through teacher education in the Canadian province of Alberta—which has consistently performed well on international comparisons of student learning and equity in student learning like the Program in International Student Assessment (PISA)—to the approaches taken in the US, a country that has performed less well than the average country in these same comparisons.

In doing so, we draw on a study we conducted on policies and practices related to teaching and teacher education in Alberta (Zeichner, Hollar, & Pisani, 2017) and on analyses of US teacher education policy and practice. Using

Hargreaves and Fullan's (2012) framework, which contrasts policies and practices that reflect an emphasis on building professional or business capital, we conclude that policies in Alberta have focused on developing the professional capital in teaching and on maintaining strong public schools, while recent US policies have emphasized the development of business capital in teaching and on the privatization of public education. For example, Alberta requires all teachers to become certified before becoming teachers of record fully responsible for classrooms. There are no fast tracks to teaching in the province. Teachers are highly regarded by the society and well compensated. In Alberta, resources are focused on promoting teacher learning and development, as opposed to testing and external accountability. Alternatively, in the US there has been a strong push by policymakers and philanthropists to expand the number of fast-track preparation programs. This has created a situation where more and more students living in communities highly impacted by poverty are taught by uncertified teachers learning on the job or teaching outside of the fields of their expertise. Also in the US, policies have focused on building and maintaining expensive accountability systems for students, teachers, and schools rather than on supporting teacher learning and development.

The difference in performance between education systems in the US and Alberta cannot be explained by the differences in education policies and practices alone. In addition to the educational policies that distinguish the two education systems, Alberta has implemented a variety of policies that have provided social and economic supports to its people, such as universal access to high-quality healthcare and childcare subsidies to low-income families. The US has failed to provide many families living in poverty with these social and economic supports.

In Chapter 10, I argue that many 1.0 and 2.0 teacher education programs that claim to prepare teachers to teach for social justice have failed to enact in their practices key values they want teachers to carry to their classrooms. To support my argument, I examine two issues where I believe many teacher education programs often do not practice what they preach and where they undermine their goals: the importance of culturally responsive teaching and their approach to whose knowledge counts in the education of teachers and in teaching. For example, both 1.0 and 2.0 programs largely ignore the issue of preparing teachers to work with students' families and to learn about and use the resources and expertise in their students' communities. Also, both 1.0 and 2.0 programs often ignore the cultural and linguistic capital brought to teacher preparation by teacher candidates and contradict in their programs the idea that culturally and linguistically responsive teaching is important in teaching. Following these critiques of dominant trends in 1.0 and 2.0 programs, I outline a vision of Teacher Education 3.0 and provide ideas for how both 1.0 and 2.0 programs can better reflect in their practices the noble ideals related to democracy and social justice they espouse.

It is my hope that the ideas in these ten chapters will support the creation of more genuine debates about different options for the future of teacher education in the US at the levels of both policy and practice. Part of this process of engaging in more productive debates requires an unmasking of the diversity in commitments and values that are hidden by the use of general terminology such as reflection, partnerships, practice, and teacher residency programs. To contribute to this process has been one of my central goals in writing this book.

A Note on the Title

My use of the terminology "the struggle for the soul" in the title of this book indicates my efforts to analyze the rules, standards, systems of reasoning, and assumptions that underlie current debates about teacher education in the US. In using this language, I assert that the debates over teacher education are, in fact, debates about the meaning of children, families, communities, teachers, the processes of teaching and learning, the ways that classrooms are managed, public schooling, and the place of teachers in the communities in which they work. Teacher education in this sense is a process of shaping the souls of teachers with regard to these issues.[5]

Kenneth M. Zeichner
Seattle, Washington
April, 2017

Notes

1 I use the term alternative program to refer to programs other than the fulltime undergraduate and graduate programs noted above. These include both programs where the standards of these fulltime programs are maintained and the structure and delivery modes are altered to make them more accessible and those programs where standards have been lowered (Darling-Hammond, 1992).
2 Liston and Zeichner (1991) refer to the technological orientation as part of a social efficiency tradition in teacher education.
3 https://www.ed.gov/news/press-releases/education-department-releases-final-teacher-preparation-regulations
4 http://blogs.edweek.org/edweek/teacherbeat/2017/03/trumps_proposed_budget_cuts_hi.html; http://www.npr.org/sections/ed/2017/03/16/520261978/trumps-budget-blueprint-pinches-pennies-for-education; https://www.americanprogress.org/issues/education/news/2017/03/17/428598/trump-devos-budget-dismantle-public-education-hurting-vulnerable-kids-working-families-teachers/
5 For discussion of shaping the souls of teachers see Ball's (2003) discussion of performativity and Popkewitz's (2017) analysis of the shaping of teachers' souls in Teach for America. Green, B., Reid, J.A., & Brennan, M. (2017). Rethinking practice: Struggling for the soul of teacher education. In T.A. Trippestad, A. Swennen & T. Werler (Eds). *The struggle for teacher education* (pp. 17–38). London: Bloomsbury.

References

Arnett, T. (April, 2017). Trump may have stepped back regulations on teacher preparation, but many states are moving forward. *The 74*. Retrieved April 12, 2017 from https://www.the74million.org/article/arnett-trump-may-have-stripped-back-regulations-on-teacher-preparation-but-many-states-are-moving-forward

Ball, S. (2003). The teacher's soul and the terrors of performativity. *Journal of Education Policy, 18*(2), 215–228.

Bestor, A. (1953). *Educational wastelands*. Urbana, IL: University of Illinois Press.

Bliss, J. (1990). Alternative teacher certification in Connecticut: Reshaping the profession. *Peabody Journal of Education, 67*(3), 35–54.

Childress, S. (2016) Fifteen years of educational entrepreneurship. In F.M. Hess & M.Q. McShane (Eds). *Educational entrepreneurship today* (pp. 11–34). Cambridge, MA: Harvard Education Press.

Charters, W. W., & Waples, D. (1929). *The commonwealth teacher training study*. Chicago: University of Chicago Press.

Chubb, J. (2012). *The best teachers in the world: Why we don't have them and how we could*. Palo Alto, CA: Hoover Institute Press.

Clifford, G. Joncich, & Guthrie, J. W. (1988). *Ed school: A brief for professional education*. Chicago: University of Chicago Press.

Coley, R. & Thorpe, R. (1986). *The M.A.T. model of teacher education and its graduates: Lessons for today*. Princeton, NJ: Educational Testing Service.

Conant, J. (1963). *The education of American teachers*. New York: McGraw Hill.

Counts, G. (1935). Break the teacher training lockstep. Reprinted in M. Borrowman (Ed.) (1965). *Teacher education in America: A documentary history*. (pp. 218–223) New York: Teachers College Press.

Darling-Hammond, L. (1992). Teaching and knowledge: Policy issues posed by alternative certification for teachers. *Peabody Journal of Education, 67*(3), 127–154.

Duffy, G. (1994). Professional development schools and the disempowerment of teachers and professors. *Phi Delta Kappan, 75*(8), 596–600.

Eubanks, E., & Parish, R. (1990). Why does the status quo persist? *Phi Delta Kappan, 72*(3), 196–197.

Feiman-Nemser, S. (1990). Teacher preparation: Structural and conceptual alternatives. In W. R. Houston (Ed), *Handbook of research on teacher education*. New York: Macmillan.

Feistritzer, E., & Haar, C. (2008). *Alternative routes to teaching*. Upper Saddle River, NJ: Pearson.

Finn, C., & Kanstoroom, M. (July, 1999). *Better teachers, better schools*. Washington, DC: Thomas B. Fordham Foundation.

Flexner, A. (1930). *Universities: American, English, and German*. Oxford: Oxford University Press.

Forzani, F. (2014). Understanding "core practices" and practice-based teacher education: Learning from the past. *Journal of Teacher Education, 65*, 357–368.

Fraser, J. W. (2007). *Preparing America's teachers: A history*. New York: Teachers College Press.

Gage, N., & Winne, P. (1974). Performance-based teacher education. In K. Ryan (Ed.), *Teacher education* (pp. 146–172). Chicago: University of Chicago Press.

Gastic, B. (2014). Closing the opportunity gap: Preparing the next generation of effective teachers. In R. Hess & M. McShane (Eds), *Teacher quality 2.0: Toward a new era in education reform*. Cambridge, MA: Harvard Education Press.

Goldhaber, D., & Walch, J. (2014). Gains in teacher quality. *Education Next, 14*(1). Retrieved from http://educationnext.org/gains-in-teacher-quality/ on June 10, 2015.

Goodlad, J. (1990). *Teachers for our nation's schools.* San Francisco, CA: Jossey-Bass.

Grossman, P. (2011). A framework for teaching practice: A brief history of an idea. *Teachers College Record, 113*(12), 2836–2843.

Guha, R., Hyler, M. E., & Darling-Hammond, L. (2016). *The teacher residency: An innovative model for preparing teachers.* Palo, Alto, CA: Learning Policy Institute. Retrieved on January 3, 2017 from https://www.learningpolicyinstitute.org/sites/default/files/product-files/ Teacher_Residency_Innovative_Model_Preparing_Teachers_REPORT.pdf

Haberman, M. (1986). Alternative teacher certification. *Action in Teacher Education, 8*(2), 13–18.

Hargreaves, A., & Fullan, M. (2012). *Professional capital: Transforming teaching in every school.* New York: Teachers College Press.

Hawley, W. D. (1990). The theory and practice of alternative certification: Implications for the improvement of teaching. *Peabody Journal of Education, 67*(3), xxx.

Hess, F. (2009). Revitalizing teacher education by revisiting our assumptions about teaching. *Journal of Teacher Education, 60*(5), 450–457.

Keller, B. (October, 2013). An industry of mediocrity. *New York Times.* Retrieved from www.nytimes.com/2013/10/21/opinion/keller-an-industry-of-mediocrity.html?_r=0 on 10/20, 13

Koerner, J. (1963). *The miseducation of American teachers.* Boston: Houghton Mifflin.

Kramer, R. (1991). *Ed school follies.* New York: Free Press.

Labaree, D. (2004). *The trouble with ed schools.* New Haven, CT: Yale University Press.

Levine, A. (2010). Teacher education must respond to change in America. *Phi Delta Kappan, 92*(2), 19–24.

Liston, D., & Zeichner, K. (1991). *Teacher education and the social conditions of schooling.* New York: Routledge.

Lucas, C. (1999). *Teacher education in America: Reform agendas for the twenty-first century.* New York: St. Martin's Press.

Lynd, A. (1953). *Quackery in the public schools.* Boston: Little, Brown.

Mattingly, P. (1975). *The classless profession: American schoolmen in the nineteenth century.* New York: New York University Press.

Mitchell, R. (1981). *The graves of academe.* Boston: Little, Brown, and Co.

Murrell, P. C., Jr. (2001). *The community teacher: A new framework for effective urban teaching.* New York: Teachers College Press.

National Council of Accreditation for Teacher Education. (NCATE). (2010). *Transforming teacher education through clinical practice: A national strategy to prepare effective teachers.* Washington, DC: National Council of Accreditation for Teacher Education.

National Research Council (2010). Preparing teachers: Building evidence for sound policy.www.nap.edu/catalog/12882/preparing-teachers-building-evidence-for-sound-policy

Palmer, J. (1985). Teacher education: Perspective from a public university. In C. Case & W. A. Matthes (Eds), *Colleges of education: Perspectives on their Future* (pp. 51–70). San Francisco, CA: McCutchan.

Patterson, R. S., Michelli, N. M., & Pacheco, A. (1999). *Centers of pedagogy: New structures for educational renewal.* San Francisco, CA: Jossey-Bass.

Payzant, T. (2004). Should teacher education take place at colleges and universities? Invited Address presented at the Annual Meeting of the American Association of Colleges for Teacher Education, Chicago, IL.

Peske, H., & Haycock, K. (2006). *Teaching inequality: How poor minority students are shortchanged on teacher quality*. Washington, DC: Education Trust.

Popkewitz, T. (2017). *Teacher education as struggling for the soul: A critical ethnography of making a difference*. New York: Routledge.

Schorr, J. (2013). A revolution begins in teacher prep. *Stanford Social Innovation Review*, *11*(1). Retrieved from http://ssir.org/articles/entry/a_revolution_begins_in_teacher_prep

Sedlak, M. (2008). Competing visions of purpose, practice, and policy. In M. Cochran-Smith, S. Feiman-Nemser, & J. McIntyre (Eds), *Handbook of research on teacher education*. (3rd ed) (pp. 855–885). New York: Routledge.

Simms, R. & Miller, J. (1988). Assault on teacher education in Texas. *Journal of Teacher Education*, *39*(6), 17–20.

Skinner, E. A., Garreton, M. T., & Schultz, B. (2011) (Eds). *Grow your own: Grassroots change for teacher education*. New York: Teachers College Press.

Smith, B. O. (1980). *A design for a school of pedagogy*. Washington, DC: US Government Printing Office.

Stiles, L. (1958). The all-institution approach to teacher education. *Phi Delta Kappan*, *40*(3), 121–124.

Stitzlein, S., & West, C. (2014). New forms of teacher education: Connections to charter schools and their approaches. *Democracy & Education*, *22*(2), 1–10.

Sykes, G., & Dibner, K. (March 2009). *Fifty years of federal teacher policy: An appraisal*. Washington, DC: Center for Education Policy. Retrieved from http://eric.ed.gov/?id=ED505035 March 19, 2010.

Sykes, G., Bird, T., & Kennedy, M. (2010). Teacher education: Its problems and some prospects. *Journal of Teacher Education*, *61*(5), 464–476.

TNTP (2014). *Fast start: Training better teachers faster with focus, practice and feedback*. Retrieved from http://tntp.org/assets/documents/TNTP_FastStart_2014.pdf August 10, 2014.

Vedder, R. (September, 2011). Who should educate the educators? *Chronicle of Higher Education*. Retrieved from http://chronicle.com/blogs/innovations

Wilson, S. (2014). Innovation and the evolving system of U.S. teacher preparation. *Theory into Practice*, *53*, 183–195.

Wisniewski, R. (1986). Alternative programs and the reform of teacher education. *Action in Teacher Education*, *8*(2), 37–44.

Zeichner, K. (2012). The turn once again toward practice-based teacher education. *Journal of Teacher Education*, *63*(5), 376–382.

Zeichner, K. (2014). The politics of learning to teach from experience. In V. Ellis & J. Orchard (Eds), *Learning to teach from experience: Multiple perspectives* (pp. 257–268). London: Bloomsbury.

Zeichner, K., & Hutchinson, E. (2008). The development of alternative certification policies and programs in the United States. In P. Grossman & S. Loeb (Eds), *Alternative routes to teaching: Mapping the new landscape of teacher education* (pp. 15–29). Cambridge, MA: Harvard Education Press.

Zeichner, K., Hollar, J., & Pisani, S. (2017). Teacher policies and practices in Alberta. In C. Campbell, K. Zeichner, A. Liberman, & P. Osmond-Johnson (2017). *Empowered educators in Canada: How high performing systems shape teaching quality* (pp. 13–85). New York: Wiley.

1

THE STRUGGLE FOR THE SOUL OF TEACHING AND TEACHER EDUCATION IN THE US

Kenneth M. Zeichner

Currently, there is an intense debate that is taking place in many parts of the world about the kind of teaching and teacher education that should define education in the twenty-first century. In this chapter, I outline the main ideas at issue in these debates in the US and offer my analysis of how we should seek to resolve the current controversies and the jurisdictional challenge that colleges and universities are now facing to their authority to offer teacher education programs (Grossman, 2008). The debates that I describe are concerned with the most basic questions about teaching and teacher education, such as the nature of the role for which we are preparing teachers, who should prepare them, when and where this preparation should take place, and what should be the content of the preparation program.

Over the 40 years since the founding of the *Journal of Education for Teaching*, there have been many challenges to the college and university-based system in the US. What exists now is the result of the ascendance worldwide of an effort to privatize public services including education and teacher education and the growing influence of philanthropy and venture capitalists on public policy in education (Zeichner, 2010a; Zeichner & Peña-Sandoval, 2015).

Historically, the central issues underlying debates about the best approaches to teacher education stem from different assumptions and convictions about the purposes of public education, the teaching and learning process, and the teacher's role (Labaree, 1997). In the current debates, two different visions of the role of teachers and teacher preparation are being advocated. On the one hand, some propose building or maintaining a professional teaching force and a system of teacher education that prepares teachers for professional roles and teaching careers (Darling-Hammond & Bransford, 2005). Others believe that it is too costly to build and maintain a professional teaching force to teach everyone's children and have advocated preparing teachers of "other people's children" as technicians to implement the teaching scripts with which they are provided, in the belief that the preparation these teachers receive and the subsequent scripting of instruction will lead to improvements in pupils' standardized test scores.

Initial teacher education in this view (usually referred to as "teacher training") should be very brief and take place mainly on the job. There is little expectation that these teachers will have teaching careers, and the system is designed to make it possible for these temporary teachers to be replaced in a few years by other narrowly trained teachers who also will leave the classroom in a few years (Rosen, 2003).

While these same debates are going on in many parts of the world (e.g., Moon, 2007), I will concentrate here on how they are being enacted in the United States, which has a teaching force of approximately 3.6 million teachers who teach in about 90,000 schools (US Department of Education, 2011b). Approximately 1,400 colleges and universities are authorized to offer teacher education programs in the US and increasingly a variety of other non-profit and for-profit programs, including school districts themselves, are running programs that currently prepare about one-third of the new teachers in the nation each year (National Research Council, 2010).

The Landscape of Teacher Education in the US

For most of the formal history of teacher education in the US, a variety of pathways into teaching have existed both inside and outside colleges and universities. At one time or another since the mid-nineteenth century when formal teacher education began, a variety of institutions such as secondary schools, seminaries, academies, normal schools, teacher institutes, teacher colleges, community colleges, and colleges and universities have all played important roles in educating the nation's teachers (Fraser, 2007). Throughout the nation's history, most teachers have entered teaching through what might now be referred to as "alternative routes" including a substantial number of teachers who were prepared in school district-based teacher education programs. Fraser (2007, p. 92) has noted "by 1914 virtually every city in the US with a population of 300,000 or more and over 80% of those over 10,000 maintained their own teacher preparation program as part of the public school system."

It was for only a relatively brief period of time in the US (approximately 1960–1990) that colleges and universities held a virtual monopoly in teacher education. Since the 1990s, there has been a tremendous increase in non-college and university-sponsored teacher education programs including new for-profit programs (Baines, 2010; Holland, 2003). More and more individuals are entering the teaching force through non-university-sponsored routes into teaching, sometimes with very little or no preparation at all before assuming full responsibility for a classroom of students (Grossman & Loeb, 2008).

Despite the growth in these non-university programs, most teachers still enter teaching through 4- to 5-year undergraduate programs or 1- to 2-year postgraduate programs. It is estimated that 70–80 percent of teachers still enter the profession through college and university programs (National Research Council, 2010). In some parts of the country though, nearly as many teachers enter the field through non-college and university pathways (Feistritzer & Haar, 2008), and in at least one state (Florida), school districts are required to have their own teacher education programs (Emihovich, Dana, Vernetson, & Colon, 2011). In Texas, in each year since 2007, two for-profit online teacher education programs, "A+ Texas Teachers" and "iteachTEXAS," have produced far more teachers than any other teacher education program in the state (Smith & Pandolfo, 2011).

Gaps in Schooling and Criticism of University Teacher Education

Currently in the US, as in many other countries in the world, there are serious gaps in opportunities to learn, school completion rates, and academic achievement for different segments of the population. For example, in addition to the growing inequalities in access to the resources and environments that help individuals live their lives with dignity (Duncan & Murnane, 2011), there continues to be a crisis of inequality in public schools that denies many children living in poverty and "children of color" a high quality of education, despite the good work of many dedicated and talented teachers. A number of gaps in educational opportunities and outcomes have persisted despite all of the reform efforts that have taken place in schools. These include inequalities: in achievement as measured by standardized tests in reading and mathematics (Rothstein & Wilder, 2005); in secondary school graduation rates (Hall, 2007); in increased segregation of students according to their race, ethnicity, and social class background (Orfield & Lee, 2005); in inequitable public funding for schools in different areas between and within districts (Carey, 2004); in unequal access to advanced courses that provide the gateway to college (National Centre for Education Statistics, 2000); in unequal access to a broad and rich curriculum that educates students to understand and to think critically (Kozol, 2005); and in the disproportionate assignment of students of color and English learners to special education classes with limited educational opportunities (Artiles, Harry, Reschly, & Chinn, 2002; Hawkins, 2011). These inequities have served to widen the gaps between students who learn to be thinkers and authentic problem-solvers and those who are forced to learn out of context and to interact with knowledge in artificial ways (Rose, 2011).

There is also, as there is in much of the world, an inequitable distribution of fully qualified teachers. Currently, we have a situation in the US where there are serious inequities between the kinds of preparation provided for teachers who work in different communities. Most of the teachers who enter the teaching force through one of the "fast track" programs in which novices are fully responsible for a classroom teach in poor urban and rural communities of color (Darling-Hammond, 2004; Lankford, Loeb, & Wyckoff, 2002; Peske & Haycock, 2006). These "early-entry" teachers who complete most of their preparation while serving as teachers of record are not found in public schools for the middle and upper middle classes teaching the children of many of the advocates of deregulation.

Although the research on the effects of different pathways to teaching is not conclusive (e.g., Constantine, Player, Silva, Hallgren, Grider, & Drake, 2009; Decker, Mayer, & Glazerman, 2006; Helig & Jez, 2010; National Research Council, 2010), there is some evidence of a "learning loss" by pupils as underprepared beginning teachers of record are catching up with teachers who completed all of their preparation for an initial teaching license prior to becoming responsible for classrooms (Zeichner & Conklin, 2005). It is clear though, given the high turnover of teachers in the most poverty-impacted schools (e.g., American Federation of Teachers, 2007; Lankford et al., 2002), that schools staffed by many early-entry teachers have become dependent on a constant supply of early-entry teachers who stay for a few years and then leave. The current teacher education system does not help these communities to develop the capacity to access a more experienced teaching staff and to lessen their dependence on inexperienced and underprepared teachers. Given the documented importance of teacher experience in teaching quality (e.g., National Commission on Teaching and America's Future, 2010), this is a serious problem of injustice for many poor communities.

Because of some econometric studies that have shown a low correlation between teacher experience and/or degrees and student test scores, some critics have made an absolute claim that neither experience nor schooling beyond the bachelor's degree makes any difference in teacher effectiveness. Rose (2011, p. 36) criticizes these claims based on the limited nature of the studies on which they are based.

> On the face of it, this is a remarkable assertion. Can you think of any other profession from hair styling to firefighting to neurosurgery … where we wouldn't value experience and training. … The problem is that the studies for the most part deal in simple aggregates and define experience and training in crude ways. Experience is defined as years on the job, and it is no surprise that years alone don't mean much. … What people do with their time on the job is crucial, becomes the foundation of expertise. As for the question of post-baccalaureate work, the same principle applies. What kind of training? Where? What was the curriculum? The quality of supervision? … To discount experience and training in blanket fashion is not only wrong-headed but also undercuts attempts to create better working conditions for teachers, more robust professional development, and opportunities for career advancement.

Government and Foundation Responses to the Problems of Teacher Education

There have been two major responses by the US government and private foundations to the enduring problems of teacher education over the last 40 years.

The first response has involved efforts to build an effective system of teacher education in the country within colleges and universities. Since the mid-1960s, the federal government has invested in strengthening the college and university system of teacher education through competitive grants that were administered directly in Washington DC or through the states. Programs like the "Teacher Quality Partnerships" program, which funds partnerships in teacher education between schools and universities, are examples of how the federal government has attempted historically to improve the quality of the teacher education system in the US by injecting targeted resources into college and university education schools to promote innovative practices (Sykes & Dibner, 2009).

Additionally, several private foundations, notably the Carnegie Corporation and the Ford Foundation, have historically invested substantial amounts of money to improve the quality of teacher education in the US, especially for schools highly impacted by poverty. The $60 million-plus "Teachers for a New Era" project led by the Carnegie Corporation from 2001 to 2009, which sought to reform teacher education programs around a small set of core design principles (e.g., teaching is an academically taught clinical practice), is the most visible of recent foundation efforts to transform American teacher education (Carnegie Corporation, 2006).

The second and more recent response has involved efforts greatly to reduce the role of, or to dismantle, the college and university system of teacher education. In part, because of a widespread perception of the unwillingness of college and university teacher educators to improve, there has been a shift away from investing in the improvement of the current system that is dominated by college- and university-based teacher education toward efforts to break up the system and try to replace it with greater market competition. Arthur Levine, a former president of Teachers College, Columbia University, and now president of a large private foundation that supports education, has argued that

> The private sector sees teacher education and professional development as a low-cost, high-volume field with the potential for significant profits. Higher education is viewed as high in price, low in technology use, inefficient and weak in leadership. These perceived weaknesses make it a superb investment prospect.
>
> *(Levine, 2010, p. 21)*

This belief that creating a competitive market for the preparation of teachers will lead to the greatest quality is also occurring in many other countries, often promoted by governments or development agencies such as the World Bank and USAID (Klees, 2008; Furlong, Cochran-Smith, & Brennan, 2009; Robertson, 2005; Tatto, 2006).

Consistent with the current fervor in the national media to criticize university education schools in the US as obstacles to "real reform" (e.g., Hartocollis, 2005;

Kristof, 2006; Will, 2006), and teacher education programs as barriers to entry to teaching (Corcoran, 2009), both the Bush and Obama administrations and several influential private foundations have promoted the deregulation of teacher education and the growth of non-university providers of programs (Zeichner, 2010a). One clear example of this is an "Innovation in Education" competition sponsored in 2010 by the US Department of Education, in which $263 million was awarded on a competitive basis to promote innovation in various sectors of education. The only teacher education projects that were funded in this competition were two of the major non-university providers of teachers, "Teach for America" ($50 million), and the "New Teacher Project" ($20 million), as well as the nonprofit-situated "Boston Teacher Residency Program" ($4.9 million). None of the projects that were submitted by college and university teacher education institutions were funded.

Another example is the "Race to the Top" competition sponsored by the US Department of Education (Crowe, 2011) that provided a record amount of funding for school reform to states. Significantly, one of the criteria in evaluating Race-to-the-Top proposals was whether states had legislation in place that allowed non-university providers of teacher education to operate within their borders. These two examples demonstrate the ironic stance of the Obama administration in promoting looser standards for teacher education while at the same time advocating for higher standards in K–12 education (elementary and secondary schooling).

Currently, college and university teacher education is not seen as worthy of significant investment either by the federal government or by many of the private foundations, and both are pouring money into supporting alternatives to university pathways and to pathways that lessen the role of universities even when they are involved.

> As interest in TFA and other non-traditional programs has increased, funder interest in schools of education as a mechanism for bolstering the supply and quality of teachers has lagged.
>
> *(Suggs & deMarrais, 2011, p. 35)*

Major conferences and the national media have been flooded with speeches and papers that wonder if a college and university system of teacher education is a good idea (e.g., Payzant, 2004; Vedder, 2011). Levine (2010) has claimed that "there is a growing sense among the critics that it would be more fruitful to replace university-based teacher education than to attempt to reform it" (pp. 21–22).

Confirmation of the low regard for university teacher education by many policymakers and mainstream media outlets can be found in the current situation where national rankings of university teacher education programs are conducted annually by *US News and World Report* working in partnership with The National

Council on Teacher Quality (NCTQ). NCTQ is an advocacy group biased against university teacher education that was founded to promote alternatives to the current college and university system of teacher education (Ravitch, 2012). The lack of investment in college and university teacher education has had many serious consequences for university-based teacher education and, ironically, has deepened the inability to innovate in many programs that are most in need of reform.

The local media all over the country have taken up in an uncritical way the narrative of derision about the alleged failure of university teacher education that is being promoted by groups like the New Schools Venture Fund and Democrats for Education Reform, which are shaping teacher education policy in the Obama administration and in the US Congress. For example, on October 7, 2011 the *Seattle Times* lead editorial "Refocusing the Teacher Quality Debate" praised the main element in Secretary Duncan's plan for teacher education accountability that requires the value-added evaluation of teacher education institutions, and then reprinted the following comment made by a teacher educator in an online forum.

> A growing chorus of critics including prominent education professors are amplifying concerns about weaknesses in teacher-prep programs. The director of teacher education at the Harvard Graduate School of Education was quoted on a New York Times online forum as saying that of the nation's 1,300 graduate teacher training programs only about 100 were doing a competent job. The rest could be shut down tomorrow, said Harvard's Kay Merseth.
>
> *(A.13)*

This type of derogatory depiction of university teacher education programs has been repeated over and over again in local newspapers around the country. It does not matter that there are not 1,300 graduate teacher education programs in the country or that Duncan's (2011) assertion in his blueprint that "only 50% of current teacher candidates received supervised clinical training" (p. 5) is not true for college and university programs because current state teacher licensing requirements would not allow it. It seems that people can say whatever they want or call things whatever they want and their assertions are taken at face value. When the National Council on Teacher Quality issues a report on university-based teacher education, it is covered by the national media (e.g., Levin, 2011) as if it has been vetted through an independent peer-review process. It does not seem to matter that these reports have not been reviewed independently.

Along with the lack of investment by the federal government and foundations and the increased regulation of college and university teacher education programs by the federal education department and states, which further undermine the ability to innovate in college and university programs, most states continue to substantially reduce their level of financial support to public universities where most of the nation's teachers continue to be prepared (Newfield, 2008). This lack of access to federal government and private foundation money and the continued deep cuts in state support for public universities have made it extremely difficult for university-based teacher education programs to operate, let alone innovate.

Additionally, new punitive forms of accountability have been brought into teacher education even though they have been questioned by many leading experts in assessment. The most controversial of these reforms, which is the major element in the Secretary of Education's new blueprint for teacher education (Duncan, 2011), is to evaluate and rank teacher education programs in universities based on the standardized test scores of the pupils taught by their graduates (Zeichner, 2011). This is equivalent to evaluating medical schools according to how many patients are cured by doctors who graduated from different medical schools or, at another level, holding business schools accountable for the terrible state of the economy in the country or holding medical schools accountable for the undisputed problems in our health care system. All of the cautions that have been raised by assessment experts about using student test scores to evaluate teacher quality (e.g., Economic Policy Institute, 2010), and the additional problems that are raised by trying to use this same method to link student test scores to teachers and then back to their teacher preparation programs have been ignored by policymakers (Zeichner, 2011). Louisiana and Tennessee, two states that have already attempted to link student performance back to teacher education programs, and that also have among the worst public school performance records in the nation, have suddenly become exemplars for reforming teacher education program accountability (Baker, 2011).

There are other more reasonable and valid ways to strengthen the accountability system in teacher education, including more rigorous and mandatory national accreditation of programs; higher quality classroom observation-based assessments during clinical experiences; the development of a high-quality exit performance assessment that includes a student learning component; and higher standards on state teacher licensing exams (Darling-Hammond, 2010b; Pecheone & Chung, 2006; Zeichner, 2011). For example, in response to the undisputed problem of high variability in the quality of classroom observation-based assessments during clinical experiences, Pianta (2011, p. 4) calls for:

> Requirements by states and federal agencies that direct, valid assessments of teacher performance be included as part of teacher preparation and certification systems. Direct assessments actually sample real teaching behaviors as they are experienced by students (observations or student surveys) while valid assessments have demonstrable links to student achievement and other outcomes.

In addition to identifying weak and strong teachers and teacher education programs, it is also important that an accountability system for teaching and teacher education support the improvement of weak teachers and programs.

Even the strongest supporters of the use of value-added accountability, such as Harris (2011), have stated that there is little evidence that the use of this approach has improved teaching and learning.

While it is true that both professional accountability through accreditation mechanisms and bureaucratic accountability through state program-approval policies have failed to close down or improve some weak programs, the solution to this situation, in my view and in the opinion of the National Research Council Panel on Teacher Education (National Research Council, 2010), is to study and redesign the system, not to destroy it.

Support for non-university providers of teacher education programs continues to increase and both nonprofit and for-profit independent providers of teacher education (including the *New York Times* and the American Museum of Natural History) are opening up many new programs across the country. The current dominant view among policymakers and the public is that the US needs to greatly reduce the role of universities in teacher education and move toward shorter, more "practical," and more clinically based programs. It is argued that bringing a "wider range of expertise and competition" into the preparation of teachers will promote innovation and raise the overall quality of teacher education programs (Democrats for Education Reform, 2011). Despite these noble proclamations of intent, there is a lot of money to be made by private investors if teacher education in the US is transformed into primarily a competitive market economy.

Some of the newer non-university state-approved programs like A+ Texas Teachers advertise "fast, affordable, and easy access" to the teaching profession while other non-university-sponsored programs provide a more substantive preparation for teaching (Grossman & Loeb, 2008). One of the more recent aspects of this movement to privatize what has largely been a public teacher education system in the US is an effort to open charter teacher education programs like the "Relay Graduate School of Education" that began in New York State to prepare teachers for charter schools (Gonen, 2011). In return for what they claim are higher standards (e.g., program completion is dependent on demonstrating the ability to raise student test scores), these charter schools for preparing teachers want to be exempted from the many state regulations governing teacher education programs in colleges and universities. A bipartisan-sponsored bill was introduced in June 2011 into the US Congress to support the development of more charter teacher education programs across the country that would compete with college and university programs, but would not be subject to many of the accountability requirements as college and university programs (Riley, 2011). Not surprisingly, the "New Schools Venture Fund," a nonprofit organization that invests money in education given by individual and institutional investors, has provided a strong lobbying effort on behalf of the bill (Zeichner & Peña-Sandoval, 2015).

Hess (2009) of the American Enterprise Institute has articulated a view that is shared by many others (e.g., Fraser, 2002; Walsh, 2004) when he proposed decoupling the preparation of teachers from institutions of higher education rather than calling for reinvesting in such programs. Hess and many others want to create a system where teacher preparation is controlled by local school districts. He advocates:

> A shift from the assumption that teacher preparation and training should necessarily be driven by institutions of higher education toward a more variegated model that relies on specialized providers, customized preparation for particular duties, and a just in time mindset regarding skill development and acquisition. Abandoning the default role for colleges and universities creates new opportunities. Rather than struggle to connect college-based education programs with site-based mentors or to boost the quality of practice teaching, new models might provide new providers or district-based operations to host training in more client-friendly locales and to import academic expertise, input and structure as they deem useful.
>
> *(p. 456)*

Two Forms of Teacher Education and Two Visions of the Teaching Role

Currently, there are two general approaches to teacher education in the US despite all of the specific program variations that exist (e.g., selectivity in admissions, curriculum variations). First, there are college-recommending programs, where all of the initial teacher preparation is completed before individuals assume full responsibility for a classroom as "teachers of record." On the other hand, there are "early-entry" or "direct entry" programs where much of teachers' initial education is completed by individuals while they are fully responsible for a classroom of students.

The encouragement of alternatives to university hegemony over teacher education is not necessarily a bad thing. There is a wide range in quality in both early-entry programs and college and university-recommending programs (Grossman & Loeb, 2008; Zeichner & Conklin, 2005) and the introduction of different models can potentially stimulate innovation and help improve all types of teacher education programs. Despite the improvements that have been made in recent years in many college and university-based teacher education programs, there is clearly a need for further and significant changes in many of these programs (e.g., National Council of Accreditation for Teacher Education, 2010).

It is also the case, as pointed out by Wilson and Tamir (2008), that there are progressive elements in the critiques of university-based teacher education that address the failure of these programs overall in preparing enough teachers who choose to teach in, are successful in, and stay in schools serving students living in poverty. There is greed and self-serving behavior as well as a genuine commitment to greater justice for those who are currently not served well by our public schools within both university and non-university teacher preparation. There is a big difference, though, between providing multiple pathways into teaching and seeking to dismantle the college and university system of teacher education that continues to prepare most of the nation's teachers.

It is important to note that many of the early-entry alternatives that currently exist are often closely linked with a mostly technical view of the role of teachers and with efforts to erode teachers' autonomy and collegial authority. Contrary to the many recommendations internationally to recognize teaching as complex and demanding intellectual work involving specialized knowledge and skills (Gopinathan, Tan, Yanping, Devi, Ramos, & Chao, 2008), the focus in some of the new programs is on preparing teachers to serve primarily as "educational clerks" who implement scripted teaching strategies and curriculum instead of on preparing teachers as well-educated professionals who, in addition to their technical expertise, have also acquired adaptive expertise so that they are able to exercise their discretion and judgment in the classroom to adjust their teaching to meet the varied needs of their students (Zeichner & Ndimande, 2008).

This trend to prepare teachers primarily as technicians and to minimize the financial cost of their preparation can also be seen very clearly in other countries such as the widespread use of para-teachers in India (Kumar, Priyam, & Saxena, 2001), "plasma" teachers in Ethiopia (Dahlstrom & Lemma, 2009) and in the growing emphasis on teachers as implementers of tightly structured teaching scripts in others (Compton & Weiner, 2008).

It is important to point out that the difference between a view of teachers as professionals and teachers as technicians is not whether teachers are taught to use a particular set of teaching skills that are based on research, professional consensus, or in some cases (e.g., Lemov, 2010) on observations of the practices of good teachers. Both the teacher-as-technician and teacher-as-professional orientations should provide teachers with the tools and skills that they need to be effective in supporting student learning.

The difference between these two views is that the teacher as a professional view goes beyond providing teachers with teaching and management skills and also seeks to ensure that teachers have extensive knowledge about the social and political contexts in which they work including the "funds of knowledge" (Gonzales, Moll, & Amanti, 2005) in the communities in which their students live, and of the many elements connected to teaching, such as assessment, learning and development theory, and theories about how languages are acquired. A professional preparation for teachers also seeks to help teachers learn how to exercise their judgment in the classroom and adapt what they do to meet the continually changing needs of their students; to learn how to learn in, and from, their practice so that they continue to become better teachers throughout their careers and are active participants in school renewal (Darling-Hammond, 1999; Kennedy, 1987). Both perspectives value the importance of having deep knowledge of the content to be taught.

The Future for Teaching and Teacher Education

The role of alternative pathways into teaching has long been a part of teacher education in the US, and research on different models of teacher preparation supports the need for different pathways into teaching that provide access to teaching for individuals at different stages of their lives and in different life circumstances. However, it is clear from research, as I pointed out before, that there is a great range in quality in both college and university programs and those offered by other providers (National Research Council, 2010), and that there are weak programs of all kinds that should be improved or closed.

Research has begun to provide a clearer understanding of the characteristics of effective teacher education programs that prepare teachers to promote student learning in the most economically challenged urban and rural areas of the country (Boyd, Grossman, Hammerness, Lankford, & Loeb, 2008; Darling-Hammond, 2006; Grossman & Loeb, 2008). The presence of a clear and common vision of good teaching and of learning that permeates all coursework and field experiences is an example of one of these characteristics (Darling-Hammond, 2006). The goal should be to support strong teacher education programs and to improve or close down weak programs, whether they are sponsored by universities or others.

Problems with Disinvesting in University Teacher Education

There are several major problems with the current lack of significant investment in strengthening college- and university-based teacher education while pouring substantial resources into promoting other models. The first issue is the question of capacity. Despite the exponential growth of various alternative pathways into teaching since the 1980s, as noted above, colleges and universities continue to prepare between 70–80 percent of teachers in the US (National Research Council, 2010; US Department of Education, 2011a). It is doubtful, given a teaching force in the US of over 3.6 million teachers, that an alternative system can be developed by advocates of greater competition and markets in teacher education that would not include significant involvement of colleges and universities (Fallon, 2010).

In the current policy environment in the US, attracting and preparing academically talented individuals and preparing them for teaching is a central element in debates about how to improve schooling (e.g., Barber & Mourshed, 2007). However, as Paine (2011) has pointed out, this element of education reform has often been translated into an emphasis on attracting academically talented individuals with a de-emphasis on the content of teacher preparation. Paine comments on the 2010 McKinsey study that builds on its widely cited 2007 report referenced above.

McKinsey's follow-on study (Auguste, Kihn, & Miller, 2010) is intriguing both by what it does in terms of addressing the question of teacher education and what it doesn't do. In *Closing the Talent Gap*, the authors ground the discussion of improving the teaching profession in the larger argument about achieving high performance (of schools and systems). Yet far more of the report is focused on issues around entry to teaching (recruiting the right people) and far less on what preparation actually should entail. A key thrust of the 2010 McKinsey report is that the 'top third+' strategy is worthy of emulation, as top performing countries (Singapore, Finland, and South Korea are the cases highlighted in the report) use this approach. There is a relative lack of discussion of the content of initial teacher education, and no substantive interrogation of what rigorous teacher preparation entails (pp. 6–7).

This almost exclusive focus on attracting the "best and the brightest" into teaching, even for a few years, through early-entry programs like the New Teacher Project and Teach for America, will not help solve the problem of providing all students in the US with a fully prepared and effective teacher. As Grossman (2008) states: "We will never be able to recruit all of the teachers we need from the ranks of elite college students" (p. 13).

Second, there is also a legitimate question that should be raised about the capacity of resource-strapped school districts to handle the increased responsibilities of a more school-based system of teacher education without the infusion of additional resources (Sykes, Bird, & Kennedy, 2010). Shifting teacher education to be more school based without building the capacity in schools for handling their increased role in initial teacher preparation will result in a situation like that which occurred in the UK where a shift to school-based preparation merely served to reproduce the status quo.

> Experience in schools simply becomes an opportunity to receive or become acculturated to the existing practices of the setting with an emphasis on the reproduction of routinized behaviors and the development of bureaucratic virtues such as compliance.
>
> *(Ellis, 2010, p. 106)*

Third, following the pattern in countries that lead the world today in student educational performance, preserving and strengthening the role of colleges and universities in the preparation of a professional teaching force of career teachers is critical (Tucker, 2011). Colleges and universities can potentially make important and unique contributions to the education of professional teachers to help them learn how to use research-based teaching and assessment practices; to situate their teaching in relation to the historical, political, and institutional contexts in which they work; to learn how to learn in and from their practice; to exercise their judgment in the classroom to adapt their teaching to the changing needs of their students; and to be active participants in ongoing school renewal (Darling-Hammond, 1999; Goodlad, 1990). The solution to the problems of college- and university-based teacher education is to redesign and strengthen the system, not to abandon it.

No country in the world today that has been successful in international comparisons of student achievement has achieved its success by relying heavily on a market-based economy in teacher education (Darling-Hammond, 2010a). Despite the success of some charter schools, the overall poor track record of privatization and the spread of charter schools at the K–12 level (e.g., Clark, Gleason, Clark Tuttle, & Silberberg, 2011; CREDO, 2009) does not bode well for the similar effort that is now underway to deregulate greatly the teacher preparation in the US.

Finally, underlying much of the movement to privatize public schooling and teacher education is a belief that the major cause of the problems of inequities in schooling that I have alluded to is bad teachers and bad teacher education programs. The current US Secretary of Education has asserted that most college and university programs have done a mediocre job in preparing teachers based on his linking the inequities in public schooling for students largely with ineffective teachers (Duncan, 2009). A previous Secretary of Education had argued that participation in a teacher education program should be optional (Paige, 2002).

There is the mistaken belief that if only we could fire the bad teachers and close the bad teacher education programs and turn public schooling and teacher education over to market competition, all will be fine. This narrative ignores the overwhelming evidence that links inequities in schooling to inequities in the broader society, such as the inequitable access to housing, nutritious food, jobs that pay a living wage, health care, early childhood care, and so on (Anyon, 2005; Berliner, 2006; Rothstein, 2004).

Noguera (2011, p. 9) challenges the wisdom of policies that assert that the opportunity and learning gaps for students living in poverty can be eliminated by school interventions alone.

> It has become fashionable for policymakers and reformers to criticize anyone who points to poverty as an obstacle to learning and higher achievement. Loudly proclaiming "no excuses," these reformers proclaim that large numbers of ineffective classroom teachers, not poverty, are the real obstacles to improving educational outcomes for poor children. While it is absolutely the case that poor children need dedicated, passionate, and effective teachers and principals to be successful, there is no evidence that even the best schools can overcome the effects of poverty on their own.

Despite a clear need to improve university teacher education, these programs are as responsible for the crisis of inequality in public education as business schools are for the collapse of the US economy and the growing inequalities in the broader society, such as access to jobs that pay a living wage, housing, nutritious food, and quality early childhood and health care.

University Teacher Education Responds

Despite the indisputable problems that have existed in university teacher education in the US that have been pointed out by both external critics and education school faculty themselves (e.g., Goodlad, 1990; Levine, 2006; Holmes Group, 1995), the improvements that have been made in many university programs over time (Darling-Hammond & Bransford, 2005) and the existence of a number of exemplary programs (Darling-Hammond, 2006), there is a growing movement in college and university-based teacher education in the US today to respond to some of the enduring problems that have undermined its effectiveness. These responses include: (a) to move the pre-service preparation of teachers closer to practice so as to conduct some of the instruction of new teachers (e.g., methods courses) in the kinds of settings in which teacher candidates will later teach and (b) to strengthen the clinical component in teacher preparation by investing in building the capacity of schools to serve as sites for clinical teacher education and experienced teachers to serve as effective mentors (National Council of Accreditation for Teacher Education, 2010). There are a growing number of examples of a new, more connected and school-based, form of college and university teacher education where responsibility for teacher preparation is shared across schools, universities, and sometimes local communities (Zeichner, 2010b; Zeichner, Payne, & Brayko, 2015).

There has also been a growth in hybrid programs (e.g., urban teacher residencies) that are centered in a rigorous clinically based education for teaching under the supervision of an experienced teacher that offer the potential to utilize the strengths of both university and school-based teacher educators (Berry, Montgomery, Curtis, Hernandez, Wurtzel, & Snyder, 2008). Carefully structured and well-supervised clinical experience, like that which exists in the education of other professionals, is absolutely essential for the education of teachers no matter what pathway into teaching is taken (Ball & Cohen, 1999).

We know a great deal from existing research about the kinds of investments that should be made to provide this kind of experience for all novice teachers such as careful selection of clinical placements, the preparation and ongoing support for mentors and schools that serve as clinical training sites, and the development of more rigorous evaluations of the success of these efforts in the practices of teacher candidates and in their ability to promote student learning upon completion of their pre-service preparation (NCATE, 2010). We also know from research about the negative consequences of not providing a strong and well-supervised clinical experience for teachers before they enter the workforce (e.g., Valencia, Martin, Place, & Grossman, 2009).

Conclusion

Currently, we have a situation in the US where there are serious inequities between the kinds of teacher education that is provided for teachers who work in different communities. As mentioned earlier, most of the teachers who enter the teaching force through one of the "fast track" or early-entry programs in which novice teachers are fully responsible for a classroom teach in poor urban and rural communities of color (Corcoran, 2009; Darling-Hammond, 2004; Peske & Haycock, 2006). These underprepared teachers who complete most of their preparation for teaching while serving as teachers of record are not found teaching students in public schools from the middle and upper middle class.

Addressing the serious inequities in educational opportunity and outcomes that continue to plague our public schools will require a significant investment in redesigning the college and university system of teacher education in the US, so that it becomes more clinically based and more focused on the specific contexts for which teachers are being prepared (Zeichner & Bier, 2013). This new system must more effectively integrate college and university expertise with the expertise and knowledge that exists in successful schools and in local communities to prepare the professional career teachers that everyone's children deserve (Zeichner, 2009, 2010b).

There is no reason to believe from the poor performance of deregulation and markets in any other sector of society, or from the experience of other countries with strong records of student achievement in their public schools that have created strong and well-funded university systems of teacher education (Tucker, 2011), that the current trend to dismantle college and university-based teacher education and replace it with a market economy will result in anything positive for the nation. Continuing on this path will only serve to widen the inequalities in public education that now exist between different segments of the population.

References

American Federation of Teachers. (2007). *Meeting the challenge: Recruiting and retaining teachers in hard-to-staff Schools.* Retrieved from www.aft.org/sites/default/files/hardtostaff_2007.pdf

Anyon, J. (2005). *Radical possibilities: Public policy, urban education and a new social movement.* New York: Routledge.

Artiles, A., Harry, B., Reschly, D. J., & Chinn, P. C. (2002). Over-identification of students of color in special education: A critical overview. *Multicultural Perspectives,* 4(1), 3–10.

Auguste, B., Kihn, P., & Miller, M. (2010). *Closing the talent gap: Attracting and retaining top-third graduates to careers in teaching.* London: McKinsey.

Baines, L. (2010). *The teachers we need vs. the teachers we have.* Lanham, MD: Rowman & Littlefield.

Baker, B. (2011). *Rating ed schools by student outcome data?* Boulder, CO: National Education Policy Center. Accessed October 1, 2011. http://nepc.colorado.edu/blog/rating-ed-schools-student-outcome-data

Ball, D. L., & Cohen, D. (1999). Developing practice, developing practitioners: Toward a practice-based theory of professional education. In L. Darling-Hammond & G. Sykes

(Eds), *Teaching as the learning profession: Handbook of policy and practice* (pp. 3–32). San Francisco, CA: Jossey-Bass.

Barber, M., & Mourshed, M. (2007). *How the world's best performing school systems come out on top*. London: McKinsey.

Berliner, D. (2006). Our impoverished view of educational research. *Teachers College Record, 108*(6), 949–995.

Berry, B., Montgomery, D., Curtis, R., Hernandez, M., Wurtzel, J., & Snyder, J. (2008). *Creating and sustaining urban teacher residencies: A new way to recruit, prepare and retain effective teachers in high needs districts*. Washington, DC: Center for Teacher Quality, The Aspen Institute.

Boyd, D., Grossman, P., Hammerness, K., Lankford, R. H., & Loeb, S. (2008). Surveying the landscape of teacher education in New York City: Constrained variation and the challenge of innovation. *Educational Evaluation and Policy Analysis, 30*(4), 319–343.

Carey, K. (2004). *The funding gap: Many states shortchange low income and minority students*. Washington, DC: The Education Trust.

Carnegie Corporation. (2006). *Teachers for a new era: Transforming teacher education*. New York: Carnegie Corporation.

Clark, M., Gleason, P., Clark Tuttle, C., & Silberberg, M. (2011). *Do charter schools improve student achievement? Evidence from a randomized study*. Washington, DC: Mathematica Policy Research.

Compton, M., & Weiner, L. (Eds). (2008). *The global assault on teaching, teachers and their unions*. New York: Palgrave Macmillan.

Constantine, J., Player, D., Silva, T., Hallgren, K., Grider, M., & Drake, J. (2009). *An evaluation of teachers trained through different routes to certification*. Washington, DC: US Department of Education.

Corcoran, S. P. (2009). Human capital policy and the quality of the teacher workforce. In D. Goldhaber & J. Hannaway (Eds), *Creating a new teaching profession* (pp. 29–52). Washington, DC: Urban Institute Press.

CREDO (Center for Research on Education Outcomes). (2009). Multiple choice: Charter school performance in sixteen states. Stanford, CA: Stanford University. Accessed December 21, 2010. http://credo.stanford.edu.

Crowe, E. (2011). *Race to the top and teacher preparation: Analyzing state strategies for ensuring real accountability and fostering program innovation*. Washington, DC: Center for American Progress.

Dahlstrom, L., & Lemma, B. (2009). Critical perspectives on teacher education in neo-liberal times: Experiences from Ethiopia and Namibia. *SARS, 14*(1–2), 29–42.

Darling-Hammond, L. (1999). The case for university teacher education. In R. Roth (Ed.), *The role of the university in the preparation of teachers* (pp. 13–30). New York: Routledge.

Darling-Hammond, L. (2004). Inequality and the right to learn: Access to qualified teachers in California's public schools. *Teachers College Record, 106*(10), 1936–1966.

Darling-Hammond, L. (2006). *Powerful teacher education*. San Francisco, CA: Jossey Bass.

Darling-Hammond, L. (2010a). *The flat world and education*. New York: Teachers College Press.

Darling-Hammond, L. (2010b). *Evaluating teacher effectiveness: How teacher performance assessments can measure and improve teaching*. Washington, DC: Center for American Progress.

Darling-Hammond, L., & Bransford, J. (Eds). (2005). *Preparing teachers for a changing world.* San Francisco, CA: Jossey Bass.

Decker, P. T., Mayer, D. P., & Glazerman. S. (2006). Alternative routes to teaching: The impact of Teach for America on student achievement and other outcomes. *Journal of Policy Analysis and Management, 25*(1), 75–96.

Democrats for Education Reform. (2011, January 12). Ticket to teach [blog post]. Retrieved from http://edreform.blogspot.com/2011/01/ticket-to-teach.html

Duncan, A. (2009). Teacher preparation: Reforming an uncertain profession. Address given by the US Secretary of Education, Teachers College, Columbia University.

Duncan, A. (2011). *Our future, our teachers: The Obama administration plan for teacher education reform and improvement.* Washington, DC: US Department of Education.

Duncan, G., & Murnane, R. (Eds). (2011). *Whither opportunity? Rising inequality, schools, and children's life chances.* New York: Russell Sage Foundation.

Economic Policy Institute. (2010). *Problems with the use of student test scores to evaluate teachers.* Washington, DC: Economic Policy Institute.

Ellis, V. (2010). Impoverishing experience: The problem of teacher education in England. *Journal of Education for Teaching, 36*(1), 105–120.

Emihovich, C., Dana, T., Vernetson, T., & Colon, E. (2011). Changing standards, changing needs: The gauntlet of teacher education reform. In P. Earley, D. Imig, & N. Michelli (Eds), *Teacher education policy in the US* (pp. 47–69). New York: Routledge.

Fallon, D. (2010). A golden age for teacher ed. *Phi Delta Kappan, 92*(2), 33–35.

Feistritzer, E., & Haar, C. (2008). *Alternative routes to teaching.* Upper Saddle River, NJ: Pearson.

Fraser, J. (2002). A tenuous hold. *Education Next.* Retrieved from www.aei.org

Fraser, J. (2007). *Preparing America's teachers: A history.* New York: Teachers College Press.

Furlong J., Cochran-Smith, M. M., & Brennan, M. (Eds). (2009). *Policy and perspectives in teacher education: International perspectives.* London: Routledge.

Gonen, Y. (2011). Charters get own education graduate school. *New York Post.* Retrieved from http://nypost.com/2011/02/15/charters-get-own-education-graduate-school/

Gonzales, N., Moll, L., & Amanti, C. (Eds). (2005). *Funds of knowledge: Theorizing practices in households, communities, and classrooms.* New York: Routledge.

Goodlad, J. (1990). *Teachers for our nation's schools.* San Francisco, CA: Jossey-Bass.

Gopinathan, S., Tan, S., Yanping, F., Devi, L., Ramos, C., & Chao, E. (2008). *Transforming teacher education: Redefined professionals for 21st century schools.* Singapore: Singapore Institute of Education and the International Alliance of Leading Education Institutes.

Grossman, P. (2008). Responding to our critics: From crisis to opportunity in research on teacher education. *Journal of Teacher Education, 59*(1), 10–23.

Grossman, P., & Loeb, S. (Eds). (2008). *Alternative routes to teaching: Mapping the new landscape of teacher education.* Cambridge, MA: Harvard Education Press.

Hall, D. (2007). *Graduation matters: Increasing accountability for high school graduation.* Washington, DC: Education Trust.

Harris, D. (2011). *Value-added measures in education.* Cambridge, MA: Harvard Education Press.

Hartocollis, A. (2005). Who needs education schools? *The New York Times,* 24–28.

Hawkins, M. (2011). *Social justice language teacher education.* Bristol: Multilingual Matters.

Helig, J. V., & Jez, S. J. (2010). *Teach for America: A review of the evidence.* Boulder, CO: University of Colorado, Education and the Public Interest Center.

Hess, F. (2009). Revitalizing teacher education by revisiting our assumptions about teaching. *Journal of Teacher Education, 60*(5), 450–457.

Holland, R. G. (2003). *To build a better teacher: The emergence of a competitive education industry*. Westport, CT: Praeger.

Holmes Group. (1995). *Tomorrow's schools of education*. East Lansing, MI: Holmes Group.

Kennedy, M. (1987). Inexact sciences: Professional education and the development of expertise. *Review of Research in Education, 14*, 133–167.

Klees, S. (2008). A quarter century of neoliberal thinking in education: Misleading analyses and failed policies. *Globalisation, Societies, and Education, 6*(4), 311–348.

Kozol, J. (2005). *The shame of the nation: The restoration of apartheid schooling in America*. New York: Crown.

Kristof, N. (2006, April 30). Opening classroom doors. *The New York Times*. Retrieved from http://query.nytimes.com/gst/fullpage.html?res=9B02E0D9103FF933A05757 C0A9609C8B63

Kumar, K., Priyam, M., & Saxena, S. (2001). The trouble with para-teachers. *Frontline, 18*(22). Retrieved from www.frontline.in/static/html/fl1822/18220930.htm

Labaree, D. (1997). Public goods, private goods: The American struggle over educational goals. *American Educational Research Journal, 34*(1), 39–81.

Lankford, H., Loeb, S., & Wyckoff, J. (2002). Teacher sorting and the plight of urban schools: A descriptive analysis. *Educational Evaluation and Policy Analysis, 24*, 37–62.

Lemov, D. (2010). *Teaching like a champion*. San Francisco, CA: Jossey-Bass.

Levin, T. (2011, July 21). Training of teachers is flawed study says. *New York Times*. Retrieved from www.nytimes.com/2011/07/21/education/21teaching.html

Levine, A. (2006). Educating school teachers. *The Education Schools Project*. Retrieved from www.edschools.org/pdf/Educating_Teachers_Report.pdf

Levine, A. (2010). Teacher education must respond to changes in America. *Phi Delta Kappan, 92*(2), 19–24.

Moon, B. (2007). *Research analysis: Attracting, developing and retaining effective teachers: A global view of current policies and practices*. Paris: UNESCO.

National Center for Education Statistics. (2000). *Mapping the road to college: First-generation students math track, planning strategies and context of support*. Washington, DC: National Center for Education Statistics.

National Commission on Teaching and America's Future. (2010). *Who will teach: Experience matters*. Retrieved from http://nctaf.org/wp-content/uploads/2012/01/NCTAF-Who-Will-Teach-Experience-Matters-2010-Report.pdf

National Council of Accreditation for Teacher Education. (NCATE). (2010). *Transforming teacher education through clinical practice: A national strategy to prepare effective teachers*. Washington, DC: National Council of Accreditation for Teacher Education.

National Research Council. (2010). *Preparing teachers: Building evidence for sound policy*. Washington, DC: National Academies Press.

Newfield, C. (2008). *Unmaking the public university*. Cambridge, MA: Harvard University Press.

Noguera, P. (2011). A broader and bolder approach uses education to break the cycle of poverty. *Phi Delta Kappan, 3*, 8–14.

Orfield, G., & Lee, C. (2005, July 13). *Why segregation matters: Poverty and education inequality*. Los Angeles, CA: The Civil Rights Project, UCLA. Retrieved from https://www.civilrightsproject.ucla.edu/research/k-12-education/integration-and-diversity/why-segregation-matters-poverty-and-educational-inequality/?searchterm=why%20segregation%20matters

Paige, R. (2002). *Meeting the highly qualified teacher challenge: The second annual report on teacher quality*. Washington, DC: US Department of Education.

Paine, L. (2011). Exploring the interaction of global and local in teacher education: Circulating notions of what preparing a good teacher entails. Keynote Address presented at the First Global Summit on Teacher Education. Beijing: Beijing Normal University.

Payzant, T. (2004). Should teacher education take place at colleges and universities? Invited address presented at the Annual Meeting of the American Association of Colleges for Teacher Education, Chicago, IL.

Pecheone, R., & Chung, R. (2006). Evidence in teacher education: The Performance Assessment for California Teachers (PACT). *Journal of Teacher Education, 57*(1), 22–36.

Peske, H., & Haycock, K. (2006). *Teaching inequality: How poor minority students are shortchanged on teacher quality.* Washington, DC: Education Trust.

Pianta, R. C. (2011). *Teaching children well: New evidence-based approaches to teacher professional development and training.* Washington, DC: Center for American Progress.

Ravitch, D. (2012, May 24). What is NCTQ (and why you should know). *Washington Post,* The Answer Sheet. Retrieved from www.washingtonpost.com/blogs/answer-sheet/post/ravitch-what-is-nctq-and-why-you-should-know/2012/05/23/gJQAg7CrlU_blog.html

Riley, B. (2011, August 11). Innovation and entrepreneurship in education. *News + Ideas.* San Francisco, CA: New Schools Venture Fund. Retrieved from www.newschools.org/blog/why-we-need-great-colleges-of-education

Robertson, S. (2005). Re-imagining and rescripting the future of education: Global knowledge economy discourses and the challenge to education systems. *Comparative Education, 41*(2), 151–170.

Rose, M. (2011). The mismeasure of teaching and learning: How contemporary school reform fails the test. *Dissent* (Spring, 2011), 32–38.

Rosen, A. (2003). For-profit teacher education [Transcript]. *Chronicle of Higher Education,* Colloquy Live. Transcript retrieved from http://chronicle.com. colloquyliveon6/9/2003

Rothstein, R. (2004). *Class and schooling: Using social, economic and educational reform to close the black–white achievement gap.* New York: Teachers College Press.

Rothstein, R., & Wilder, T. (2005). The many dimensions of educational inequality across races. Paper presented at the 2005 Symposium of the Social Costs of an Inadequate Education. New York City: Teachers College Columbia University. Retrieved from www.tcequity.org

Smith, M., & Pandolfo, N. (2011). For-profit certification for teachers is booming. *New York Times.* November, 27 National Edition, p. A33A.

Suggs, C., & deMarrais, K. (2011). *Critical contributions: Philanthropic investment in teachers and teaching.* Atlanta, GA: Kronley & Associates.

Sykes, G., Bird, T., & Kennedy, M. (2010). Teacher education: Its problems and some prospects. *Journal of Teacher Education, 61*(5), 464–476.

Sykes, G., & Dibner, K. (2009). *Fifty years of federal teacher policy: An appraisal.* Washington, DC: Center on Education Policy.

Tatto, M. (2006). Education reform and the global regulation of teachers' education, development and work: A cross-cultural analysis. *International Journal of Educational Research, 45,* 231–241.

Tucker, M. (2011). *Surpassing Shanghai: An agenda for American education built on the world's leading systems.* Cambridge, MA: Harvard Education Press.

US Department of Education. (2011a). Preparation and credentialing of the nation's teachers: *The Secretary's eighth annual report on teacher quality*. Washington, DC: US Department of Education.

US Department of Education, National Center for Education Statistics. (2011b). *Digest of education statistics, 2010*. Washington, DC: US Department of Education, National Center for Education Statistics.

Valencia, S., Martin, S., Place, N., & Grossman, P. (2009). Complex interactions in student teaching: Lost opportunities for learning. *Journal of Teacher Education, 60*(3), 304–322.

Vedder, R. (2011). Who should educate the educators? [blog post] *Chronicle of Higher Education*. Retrieved from http://chronicle.com/blogs/innovations/who-should-educate-the-educators/30362

Walsh, K. (2004). A candidate-centered model for teacher preparation and licensure. In F. Hess, A. Rotherham, & K. Walsh (Eds), *A qualified teacher in every classroom?* (pp. 223–254). Cambridge, MA: Harvard Education Press.

Will, G. (2006, January 16). Ed schools vs. education. *Newsweek*. Retrieved from www.newsweek.com

Wilson, S., & Tamir, E. (2008). The evolving field of teacher education. In M. Cochran-Smith, S. Feiman-Nemser, & D. J. McIntyre (Eds), *Handbook of research on teacher education* (3rd ed.), (pp. 908–935). New York: Routledge.

Zeichner, K. (2009). *Teacher Education and the Struggle for Social Justice*. New York: Routledge.

Zeichner, K. (2010a). Competition, economic rationalization, increased surveillance and attacks on diversity: Neo-liberalism and the transformation of teacher education in the US. *Teaching and Teacher Education, 26*(8), 1544–1552.

Zeichner, K. (2010b). Rethinking the connections between campus courses and field experiences in college- and university-based teacher education. *Journal of Teacher Education, 61*(1–2), 89–99. Published in Spanish in 2010 in *Revista Interuniversitaria de Formacion del Profesorado, 68*(24.2), 123–150 (Spain). Published in 2010 in Portuguese in *Revista Educação* (Brasil).

Zeichner, K. (2011). Assessing state and federal policies to evaluate the quality of teacher preparation programs. In P. Earley, D. Imig, & N. Michelli (Eds), *Teacher education policy in the United States: Issues and tensions in an era of evolving expectations* (pp. 75–105). New York: Routledge.

Zeichner, K., & Bier, M. (2013). The turn toward practice and clinical experiences in US teacher education. *Beitrage Zur Lehrerbildung* (*Swiss Journal of Teacher Education*), *30*(2), 153–170.

Zeichner, K. H., & Conklin, H. (2005). Teacher education programs. In M. Cochran-Smith & K. Zeichner (Eds), *Studying teacher education*. New York: Routledge.

Zeichner, K., & Ndimande, B. (2008). Contradictions and tensions in the place of teachers in educational reform: Reflections on teacher preparation in the US and Namibia. *Teachers and Teaching, 14*(4), 331–343.

Zeichner, K., Payne, K., & Brayko, K. (2015). Democratizing knowledge in university teacher education through practice-based methods: Teaching and mediated field experiences in schools and communities. *Journal of Teacher Education, 66*(2), 122–135.

Zeichner, K., & Peña-Sandoval, C. (2015). Venture philanthropy and teacher education policy in the United States: The role of the new schools venture find. *Teachers College Record, 117*(6). Retrieved from tcpress.org

2

COMPETITION, ECONOMIC RATIONALIZATION, INCREASED SURVEILLANCE, AND ATTACKS ON DIVERSITY

Neo-liberalism and the Transformation of Teacher Education in the US[1]

Kenneth M. Zeichner

> The principles of the market and its managers are more and more the managers of policy and practices in education.
>
> *(Bernstein, 1996)*

> No one will have the freedom to seek better teaching and stronger education until the intellectual stranglehold exerted by the teacher education cartel is broken.
>
> *(Holland, 2004)*

Today teacher education in many parts of the world is engaged in a major transformation. Although my perception of this situation is highly influenced by my experience with the US federal government's efforts under the Clinton, Bush Sr. and Jr., and Obama administrations to further privatize public education and de-professionalize the work of teaching (e.g., Baines, 2006a, 2006b, 2010; Raphael & Tobias, 1997), it is clear that what is discussed below is true in some form in many countries because of the wide influence of the neo-liberal, new managerial, and neo-conservative thinking that is guiding efforts to dismantle public education and teacher education in the US and elsewhere and promoting the spread of neo-liberal corporate capitalism (Bates, 2007; Carnoy, 1995; Compton & Weiner, 2008; Freeman-Moir & Scott, 2007; Grimmett, Fleming, & Trotter, 2009; Hypolito, 2004; Sachs, 2003). The promotion of these ideas has often taken place using liberal-humanist human rights discourses (e.g., "Education for All," "quality") that hide from view the consequences of taking up these ideas and mask other ways of thinking about the issues (Tamatea, 2010).

A variety of policies are continuing to emerge that seem directed at taking control of education away from teachers and teacher educators, and eliminating—under efficiency arguments—the very mechanisms that can help teachers to effectively increase education quality (the professional character of teaching with all that it brings, such as a deeper knowledge of the subjects they will teach, a deeper knowledge of how to teach those subjects to an increasingly diverse population, critical thinking, cognitive growth, among others).

(Tatto, 2007a, p. 13)

There have been several major trends occurring in initial teacher education programs throughout the world that will be discussed in this chapter in relation to the US. These include the commodification of the work of preparing teachers and making teacher preparation subject to market forces, excessively prescriptive accountability requirements from government bodies and accreditation agencies that seek to control the substance of the teacher education curriculum, consistent and painful cuts in the budgets of public institutions including those charged with the education of teachers, and attacks on efforts to educate teachers to teach in socially just ways such as preparing them to engage in multicultural or anti-racist education (Duthilleul, 2005a, 2005b; Furlong, Cochran-Smith, & Brennan, 2009). I will conclude with some reflections about the future for teacher education in the US and propose a direction for responding to these trends.

Although references will be made throughout the discussion to how these trends exist in other countries, the focus in the analysis will be on the situation for teacher education in the US. Because of the differences in systems of schooling and teacher education and cultural traditions in different parts of the world (Steensen, 2006), both the analysis of the problems and the proposal for combating the negative effects of neo-liberalism in teaching and teacher education may not be appropriate in other countries.

The Commodification of Teacher Education

Many of the pressures on teacher education today are a result of the spread of neo-liberal ideas and policies about markets, privatization, deregulation, and the private vs. public good (Ball, 2004) from the world of elementary and secondary education into teacher education (Beyer, 2007; Dahlstrom, 2009; Hinchey & Cadiero-Kaplan, 2005; Kumashiro, 2010).[2] According to Robertson (2008) these policies have three central aims:

The redistribution of wealth upward to the ruling elites through (1) new structures of governance, (2) the transformation of education systems so that the production of workers for the economy is the primary mandate, and (3) the breaking down of education as a public sector monopoly opening it up to strategic investment by for profit firms.

(p. 12)

What we are seeing in the US is the tremendous growth of alternatives to traditional college and university-based teacher education that include many new for-profit companies and universities that have gone into the business of preparing teachers.[3] These alternatives (e.g., Kaplan, iteachTEXAS, the University of Phoenix and Laureate) have actively been supported by the federal government under both Republican and Democratic party administrations (a former secretary of education said in a major report on teacher quality that he thought participation in a teacher education program should be made optional)[4] and by state policies in certain parts of the country that have actively encouraged alternatives to college and university-based teacher education.[5] In 2001, $40 million non-competitive grants from the US Department of Education led to the founding of the American Board for the Certification of Teaching Excellence (ABCTE), which currently certifies teachers in 11 states based on two online examinations in content knowledge and professional knowledge. ABCTE does not require enrollment in a teacher education program or demonstration of teaching competence in a classroom for a teaching license.[6]

The federal government's current support of teacher residency programs that require a stronger role for schools and possibly communities in pre-service teacher preparation and that disrupt traditional and hierarchical university-based teacher education models is another example of governmental support of shifting teacher education programs more into schools and communities and away from universities (Howey, 2007). New York State has also recently aided the spread of non-university teacher education programs by empowering non-university providers like "Teach for America" to award master's degrees to teachers, thereby enabling them to meet the state requirement for earning a master's degree within the early years of their careers without having to enroll in a college or university-based program (Foderaro, 2010).

The current push by the US government to encourage deregulation and competition in initial teacher education is very similar to what has been happening for a number of years now in the UK and in other parts of the world (e.g., Furlong, Barton, Miles, Whiting, & Whitty, 2000). As Steensen (2006) points out though, in her analysis of neo-liberal influences on teacher education in Denmark and Sweden, the push toward markets and greater external controls in teacher education takes place differently in different parts of the world because of the interplay of local cultural traditions with the global trends that circulate from country to country. Thus, there is always a tension between the local and the global that determines the specific ways in which neo-liberal ideas influence both teaching and teacher education. Steensen's (2006) point is demonstrated by a recent collection of case studies of reforms in teaching and teacher education in 10 different countries (Tatto, 2007b). The case of Germany in this set of cases illustrates how global ideas have been borrowed and then transformed in some areas to help serve local interests (Blomeke, 2006). In other cases, such as in Ontario, Canada (Pitman, 2007), there is some evidence that global forces play a more powerful role. There is also of course much variation within certain countries in terms of how policies related to teaching and teacher education play out (Tatto & Plank, 2007).

One interesting development internationally in promoting alternatives to university-based initial teacher education is the founding in 2007 by Teach for America, a widely publicized pathway to teaching in the US in collaboration with its British clone "Teach First," of a program called "Teach for All." This program is designed to support the development of entrepreneurs in other countries who would like to develop a Teach for America/Teach First like program in their area.[7]

The encouragement of alternatives to university hegemony over teacher preparation in and of itself is not necessarily a bad thing. Colleges and universities have only had a monopoly on pre-service teacher education in the US during a very brief period, roughly 1960–1990. During all other times, there have always been multiple pathways into teaching including those that have not involved colleges and universities (Fraser, 2007). It is also the case that alternative non-university pathways to teaching sometimes have progressive elements and have been encouraged by some because of the failure of traditional university models to prepare teachers to be successful and stay in schools serving students living in poverty (Wilson & Tamir, 2008).

What is important to note about the alternatives being encouraged, though, is that they are often closely linked with a technicist view of the role of teachers and with efforts to erode teachers' autonomy and collegial authority. A number of scholars have carefully documented the transformation of the occupation of teaching in many parts of the world to what has sometimes been called "the new professionalism," which accepts the view that decisions about what and how to teach and assess are largely to be made beyond the classroom rather than by teachers themselves (e.g., Furlong, 2005; Robertson, 2000; Smyth, Dow, Hattam, Reid, & Shacklock, 2000; Tatto, 2007a). The same ideas that have resulted in the new professionalism for teaching have now entered the world of teacher education to try to ensure that teachers are prepared to assume their limited roles as educational clerks who are not to exercise their judgment in the classroom (e.g., Johnson, Johnson, Farenga, & Ness, 2005).[8] This trend can be seen very clearly in many countries such as the widespread use of parateachers in India (Kumar, Priyam, & Saxena, 2001) and "plasma" teachers in Ethiopia (Dahlstrom & Lemma, 2009) and in the growing focus on teachers as implementers of teaching scripts in many parts of the world (Compton & Weiner, 2008).

A Note on Teacher Professionalism

Evetts (2009) distinguishes between two views of professionalism that now exist in knowledge-based work such as teaching: organizational professionalism and occupational professionalism. Her argument is that organizational professionalism (similar to what is referred to above as the "new professionalism") has changed the meaning of professionalism in education to a situation where a discourse of control has come to overshadow in practice more traditional views of occupational professionalism based on collegial authority. On the one hand, administrators espouse an ideology of professionalism that suggests traditional forms of occupational professionalism and collegial authority. In reality, though, practice often reflects the greater external controls and surveillance that come with organizational professionalism.

> The appeal to the discourse by managers in work organizations is to a myth of an ideology of professionalism which includes aspects as exclusive ownership of an area of expertise, autonomy and discretion in work practices and the occupational control of the work. But the reality of the professionalism that is actually involved is very different. The appeal to the discourse of professionalism by managers in work organizations often includes the substitution of organizational for professional values; bureaucratic hierarchical and managerial controls rather than collegial relations; managerial and organizational objectives rather than client trust based on competencies and perhaps licensing; budgetary restrictions and financial rationalizations, the standardization of work practices rather than discretion; and performance targets, accountability, and sometimes increased political controls.
>
> *(p. 24)*

Apple (1996) discusses a third form of professionalism, "democratic professionalism." This is seen as an alternative to increased state control on the one hand, which erodes teachers' abilities to exercise their judgment in the classroom, and traditional occupational professionalism on the other hand, which may be unresponsive to the needs of students and communities (Zeichner, 1991). Sachs (2003) argues that the core aspect of democratic professionalism in teaching is an emphasis on collaborative and cooperative action between teachers and other education stakeholders in a manner that is not common with more traditional forms of occupational professionalism. It is this democratic form of professionalism that I see as the needed response to growing forms of occupational professionalism and excessive bureaucratic controls in teaching and teacher education.

The Nature and Consequences of Many Non-university Pathways to Teaching

There is evidence that many of the non–college and non-university programs in the US focus on meeting only the minimum standards set by governmental bodies (e.g., Baines, 2010)[9] and that the goal is to prepare "good enough teachers"[10] to teach children of the poor by obediently following scripted curriculum and instructional practices that are allegedly supported by research (to raise standardized test scores), but that in reality have lined the pockets of friends of the government who own the companies that make the materials.[11] This approach serves to widen the gap between who gets to learn to be thinkers and authentic problem solvers and those who are forced to learn out of context and interact with knowledge in artificial ways (Kozol, 2005).

These attempts to further de-professionalize teaching through scripting the curriculum and standardized tests at every grade level continue to ensure that spots will be available for the teachers produced by the growing number of teacher education programs outside of the formal tertiary education system. In many places, teacher professional development has become "product implementation" aligned with standards and standardized tests and is increasingly conducted by those employed by the testing companies and publishers who produce and sell the materials that are promoted by the government. Money that used to be available in schools for more teacher-initiated and controlled professional development, like action research groups and study groups, is largely disappearing from American public schools (Randi & Zeichner, 2004) and professional development has shifted from a professional model that focuses on the learning of individual teachers who identify their own learning needs to an institutional model that focuses on getting teachers to conform to institutional mandates (Young, 1998).

What is happening in public schools today has served to drive many good people out of teaching who are not willing to put up with the continued erosion of the dignity of public school teaching that is associated with these changes and actively undermines the goal of improving the quality of learning for all students (Goodnough, 2001; Ingersoll, 2003). Teachers have become easily replaceable technicians in the eyes of many policy makers. The continual openings for the products of the new alternative programs ensure higher profits for the investors in the new teacher education companies. There is a lot of money to be made if teacher education in the US can be privatized.

The solution to the teacher quality problem according to some is to deregulate teacher education and open the gates to individuals who have not completed a teacher education program prior to certification (e.g., Hess, 2009; Walsh, 2004) rather than to improve the conditions in public schools that are driving teachers out. Andrew Rosen, president of Kaplan College, which is part of one of the major for-profit teacher education companies to enter the US teacher education market in recent years, stated the following in an online conversation about teacher education that clearly illustrates this stance:

Teaching is less lucrative and is rife with work environment issues that many deem not to be worthy of investment. By reducing the barriers for bright-minded professionals, we can increase the population of qualified candidates.

(Rosen, 2003)

Many of these new alternative programs use a "learn while you earn" model where the teacher candidates are fully responsible for a classroom (usually of poor children of color) while they are completing their minimalist program.[12] The standards to get into these programs are often very low, sometimes only requiring "a heartbeat and a check that clears the bank" (Baines, 2006a, p. 327). The Education Trust has closely monitored the achievement test scores and other educational opportunities made available to various groups of learners in public schools. They have consistently found that if you are poor, and particularly if you are poor and a student of color (i.e., African American, Latino, Native American, Asian American), you are much more likely in many areas of the country to be taught by inexperienced teachers, teachers who have not completed a full-scale teacher education program, or teachers teaching outside of the fields in which they were prepared (Peske & Haycock, 2006; Also see Darling-Hammond, 2004; National Research Council, 2010).

Although most teachers going into teaching in the US still enter teaching through traditional college and university programs (National Research Council, 2010), in some parts of the US (Texas and California for example) nearly as many teachers enter through an alternative route, which is often one of the "fast track" programs that provide minimal preparation to teach (Feistritzer & Haar, 2008).[13] In these fast-track or "early-entry" programs most of the initial education for teaching takes place after teachers have become fully responsible for classrooms (Grossman & Loeb, 2008).

Defunding Public K–12 and Higher Education

A second aspect of current developments in US teacher education is the continuing cuts in state government financial support for public universities where the majority of teachers in the US are still prepared. Even before the recent crisis in the global economy, the states have had to address increased healthcare costs for the elderly, the building of prisons to house the minorities and other poor people whom the public schools have failed to educate, and to make up for the shortfalls in federal support for various programs in public elementary and secondary schools that the states are obligated by law to provide (for example programs for special education students),[14] they have reduced funding to public universities (Lyall & Sell, 2006; Newfeld, 2008). As the demands on university teacher educators have increased with expanding accountability requirements, their resources have gone down and highly rationalized corporate budgeting models such as activity-based budgeting have been introduced into public universities to manage the distribution of the diminished resources.

For example, in Wisconsin, state appropriations to the University of Wisconsin system's 13 campuses adjusted for inflation decreased by 22 percent or $223 million between 2000 and 2007. The public contribution to this so-called public university in Madison was reduced to approximately 19 percent of the total budget in 2007 (Clark, 2007). The rest of the money needed to run the university has had to come from research grants, private gifts, and student tuition. Another example of the defunding of public universities is at the University of Washington where, between 2009 and 2011, the university lost $132 million (33 percent) of its state support (Emmeret, 2010).

There is hardly any difference anymore between a public and private university in the US. This pressure to reduce the size of teacher education in universities by starving the education schools and universities that prepare teachers serves to support the growth of non-university programs and the corporatization of teacher education.

With regard to elementary and secondary school education, with the exception of a few energy-rich states,[15] state governments have for a number of years been facing huge budget deficits that, together with soaring energy costs, have resulted in continual cuts in the budgets of many school districts in the US that have affected the quality of educational programs and the availability of professional development for teachers. The budget situation was so bad in the largest school district in Wisconsin (Milwaukee Public Schools) that the school board came close a few years ago to dissolving the school district (Aarons, 2008; Borsuk, 2008; McNeil, 2008).

Hyper-rationality and Increased Accountability[16]

A third aspect of current developments in US teacher education is the increased and often excessive accountability demands that are placed on teacher education programs by state governments and national accrediting bodies. In just about every state, teacher education graduates are required to pass a series of standardized tests to enter and complete their programs and to demonstrate mastery of a set of detailed teaching and subject matter standards. Teacher educators are required in submitting their programs to states and sometimes also to a national accrediting body for approval to spend inordinate amounts of time preparing detailed assessment plans showing how each course in their programs is aligned with state standards, and performance indicators showing exactly what competencies student teachers are required to meet.[17]

There is nothing wrong *per se* with testing teachers in basic skills and content knowledge, or with holding teacher education institutions accountable to have performance-based assessment systems that determine that their students are prepared to successfully meet a set of agreed-upon standards of practice to receive an initial teaching license.[18] In fact, these kinds of data about what program graduates know and are able to do in classrooms not only can be valuable as sources of knowledge about program effectiveness, but can also become important sources for stimulating ongoing teacher education program renewal (Zeichner, 2005b).

The problem arises when those who accredit and approve programs take the process beyond the bounds of reasonableness to a point where the level of details teacher educators are required to produce for evaluators begins to interfere with the accomplishment of the goals of teacher educators, and is loosely if at all connected to actual program quality (Johnson et al., 2005).[19] This excessive level of bureaucratization of teacher education program approval was a major problem for competency-based teacher education in the 1970s (Zeichner, 2005a) and is once again becoming a concern.

As the associate dean for teacher education at my university in Wisconsin, I spent 3 months, several years ago, essentially full time, preparing the reports to our state education department on our teacher education programs so that the state could review our programs for their compliance with state certification laws. While some aspects of this work were valuable to us in better understanding the opportunities for our students to learn and what our students actually are learning in our programs, other aspects (e.g., aligning hundreds of arts and science classes across our campus with state content guidelines) were clearly less useful and marginally related to program quality. So while some forms of accountability for teacher education institutions are reasonable and necessary, in a growing number of states, current demands for teacher educators to rationalize their programs have gone beyond the realm of reasonableness and are beginning to interfere with teacher educators being able to accomplish their goals.

For example, recent studies in Maryland and California have shown that while teacher educators in some situations have been able to meet the increasingly prescriptive program approval requirements while still maintaining intellectual control over their programs (Kornfeld, Grady, Marker, & Ruddell, 2007; Rennert-Ariev, 2008), precious resources were spent in both of these cases on meeting requirements that teacher educators felt did not enhance the quality of their programs. These resources could have been used for other things that would have contributed to improving program quality, like strengthening school-university partnerships. Rennert-Ariev (2008), who conducted the study in Maryland, found the practice of what he called "bureaucratic ventriloquism" where "superficial demonstrations of compliance with external mandates became more important than authentic intellectual engagement" (p. 8). In many teacher education programs across the country, a clash has been created by current accountability demands between authenticity (doing what one knows is in the best interest of the learning of one's students) and performativity (doing what one needs to do to meet accountability demands even when one knows it is not in the best interest of one's students).

A whole new industry in electronic portfolios has emerged with these requirements, where a few companies (e.g., Live Text, Chalk & Wire) aggressively market portfolio systems to colleges and universities so that they can provide the necessary data to gain approval for their programs. These portfolio systems have emphasized the bureaucratic aspects of keeping track of student teachers' performance on standards and for the most part have failed to take advantage of the potential in portfolios to deepen teacher learning (e.g., Bullough, 2008). Several of the portfolio companies and the two companies that make most of the tests used nationally (ETS and NES) have come to sponsor parts of the annual meetings of the major national teacher education association in the US—The American Association of Colleges for Teacher Education (AACTE). When people walk into a plenary session at the AACTE conference, they are likely to see giant screens with the logo of one of the testing companies such as Educational Testing Service (ETS), the maker of most of the tests used in US teacher education programs, or of one of the companies that market electronic portfolio systems such as Live Text.

One extreme form of accountability expectations referred to as the "positive impact mandate" (Hamel & Merz, 2005) is being seriously pushed by policy makers in a number of areas in the country[20] and there are predictions by some that the "results-based" teacher education that will come from using the positive impact mandate will become the norm in the country in a few years. With this requirement, teacher education institutions will be evaluated and ranked based on the standardized test score results of the pupils taught by the graduates of the teacher education programs. This is analogous to evaluating and approving medical schools on the basis of how many of the patients of their graduates are helped by their medical care or get sicker. There are several reasons why the positive impact mandate is a bad idea even if one accepts the ability of value-added assessment to link pupil performance with individual teachers in a way that rules out other explanations for student test performance: (a) No other professional school is held accountable for the performance of its graduates after they have left the preparation program; (b) Even if one accepts the ability of value-added assessment to link student test performance with individual teachers in a manner that rules out other explanations of student test score differences, the costs involved in implementing this kind of assessment would divert enormous resources away from other teacher education activities that arguably would do a lot more to improve the quality of teacher preparation programs (Zeichner, 2005a, 2005b); and (c) there are serious technical and educational problems associated with the technique of using value-added assessment of curriculum-specific pupil test scores to evaluate teacher education programs. For example, Darling-Hammond and Chung Wei (2009) argue:

> In addition to the fact that curriculum-specific tests that would allow gain score analysis are typically not available in most teaching areas and grade levels, these include concerns that readily available tests do not measure many important kinds of learning, are inaccurate measures of learning for

specific populations of students (for example new English language learners and some special education students), and that what appear to be the "effects" of a given teacher may reflect other teachers and learning experiences, home differentials, or aspects of the school environment that influence teaching (e.g., curriculum choices, resources and supports, class sizes, whether a teacher is assigned out of field, etc.). Furthermore, value-added analyses have found that teachers look very different in their measured effectiveness depending on what statistical methods are used, including whether and how student characteristics are controlled, whether school effects are controlled, and how missing data are treated. In addition, effectiveness ratings appear highly unstable: a given teacher is likely to be rated differently in his or her effectiveness from class to class and from year to year. Thus, while value-added models may prove useful for looking at groups of teachers for research purposes, and they may provide one measure of teacher effectiveness among several, they are problematic as the primary or sole measure for making decisions about individual teachers or even teacher education programs.

(p. 54)

Several years ago, the lead story in our national education newspaper, *Education Week*, praised the state of Louisiana for implementing this system for its teacher education programs (Honawar, 2007). Louisiana spends close to the least amount of money on education, healthcare, and other social service systems in the country. Under the logic of the current government, though, the states that most support its policies (e.g., Texas, Louisiana, and Mississippi) are ranked higher in educational quality reports because of their compliance rather than because of the actual quality of their education systems. The states with the highest overall educational quality are often the ones least supportive of the accountability mandates (Zeichner, 2009).

All of this together—the requirements for extremely detailed information about institutional assessment systems, testing, and so on—have been forcing teacher educators to spend time on things that they do not believe will help them do their jobs better just to appear that they are doing what is expected to get approval for their programs. This is time and money that could alternatively be spent on actually improving their programs. Lots of time and money are currently being spent on things in US teacher education institutions that have no relation to improving program quality (Johnson et al., 2005).

Attacks on Multicultural Education

The final current elements of teacher education in the US are the attacks stemming from neo-conservative views about the proper content for a teacher's education. These attacks have focused on the increased emphasis on multicultural education in

American teacher education programs and on preparing teachers who can contribute to eliminating the achievement gaps between students from different racial, ethnic, and social class backgrounds that not only have persisted in elementary and secondary schools but that have grown larger under current government policies. These attacks equate a focus on social justice and multiculturalism with a lowering of academic standards and blame university teacher educators for the continued problems in educating public school students who are increasingly poor and of color. These attacks on multicultural education divert attention from the real influences on the problems in public schools—a variety of factors including the underfunding of public education, the lack of access to affordable housing, transportation, healthcare, and jobs that pay decent wages.

One example of the criticism of social justice and multicultural education efforts by external groups was a successful effort in 2006 to force the major national accrediting body in teacher education in the US (The National Council for Accreditation of Teacher Education) to drop the term "social justice" from its accrediting standards for teacher education programs (Wasley, 2006).[21]

A second aspect of the critique of education schools involves the construction of an oversimplified distinction between teacher-centered and learner-centered instruction and the creation of a caricature of teacher educators as advocates of an unrestrained form of learner-centered instruction. Multicultural education in teacher education programs is often equated with a lack of concern for academic standards (e.g., Greene & Shock, 2008). For example, in a report on teacher education in California done by the Pacific Research Institute for Public Policy, Izumi and Coburn (2001) quote Florida State University psychologist K. Anders Ericksson who describes college and university teacher educators as "radical constructivists" who act in extreme ways that few teacher educators would actually support.

> Radical constructivists recommend educational settings where students are forced to take the initiative and guide their own learning. Many radical constructivists even discourage the teacher from correcting students when their reasoning and ideas are invalid because such criticism may jeopardize their self-confidence in their independent reasoning and challenge their self-respect.
>
> *(p. 9)*

While all of these forces are operating on teacher education from the outside (cuts in resources, privatization, increased accountability, and attacks on multiculturalism), inside college and university teacher education programs, teacher educators everywhere are claiming to have programs that prepare teachers to teach for social justice, to provide everyone's children with a high-quality education, and to work against the forces that are leading to increased inequality and suffering in the world today (McDonald & Zeichner, 2009). Social justice teacher education has become a slogan like reflective teaching was in the 1980s and 1990s and it is hard to find a teacher education program in the US that does not claim to have social justice as a central part of their mission in preparing teachers.

The reaction of college and university teacher educators in the US to the outside forces of privatization, increased accountability, budget cuts, and attacks on multiculturalism has understandably been a defensive one, but has resulted in an oversimplification of the motives of external critics and a failure to acknowledge and address some of the weaknesses in the still dominant college and university system of pre-service teacher education (Wilson & Tamir, 2008). Currently news articles and academic papers are being published, and major addresses are being presented at important national conferences, questioning whether colleges and universities should continue to be involved in pre-service teacher education to the degree that they have historically in the US (e.g., Duncan, 2009; Hartocolis, 2005; Levine, 2006; *New York Times*, 2009; Payzant, 2004). Following is a brief overview of how I think teacher educators in the US should respond to the current situation in a way that will enable the US to do a better job of preparing a corps of teachers who will be prepared to provide a high-quality education to everyone's children.

The Future for Teacher Education in the US

From my perspective, college and university teacher educators should not seek to uncritically defend all college and university-based teacher education programs from external criticisms. It is very clear from research and observation that there is a wide range of quality in both traditional and alternative teacher education programs in the US (Cochran-Smith & Zeichner, 2005; Cochran-Smith, Feiman-Nemser, & McIntyre, 2008; Darling-Hammond, 2006), from those that are rigorous and high quality to those that should probably be shut down.

It is also not a question of determining the best single type of program from research studies because there is not currently a consensus about the desired outcomes for teacher education programs. For example, preparing teachers to obediently use scripted curriculum materials is a very different goal from that of preparing teachers to be reflective professionals who can exercise wise judgment in their classrooms and adapt their instruction to meet the changing needs of their students. Although research can potentially make important contributions to policy and practice in teacher education, decisions about policy and practice are inevitably mediated by moral, ethical, and political considerations, whether acknowledged openly or not (Zeichner, 2005a, 2005b).

Recent syntheses of research in teacher education in the US (e.g., Cochran-Smith & Zeichner, 2005; Cochran-Smith et al., 2008; Darling-Hammond & Bransford, 2005; National Research Council, 2010) have demonstrated the need for several things to happen to improve the quality of college and university-based teacher education, including an increased focus on preparing teachers to teach the diverse students who attend US public schools (e.g., English learners), forming closer connections between the campus-based components of teacher education programs and the schools and communities in which teacher candidates teach, greater engagement of arts and science faculty in teacher education programs, and so on. Research has also begun to illuminate the characteristics of pre-service teacher education programs that are effective in preparing teachers to teach a wide range of students in meaningful ways (e.g., Boyd et al., 2008; Darling-Hammond, 2006; Zeichner & Conklin, 2005). We need to find ways to ensure that these characteristics are present in all forms of pre-service teacher education, traditional or alternative. Doing so will require a greater investment of societal resources in teacher preparation and in research on teacher education (Zeichner, 2005a, 2005b).

The solution to the current problems in American public education, where the teaching force is about 3.6 million teachers who teach in about 90,000 schools or in other systems where these same forces are now operating, is not to continue to supply underfunded and overregulated public schools with teachers who meet minimum state standards and who are only positioned to raise standardized test scores by implementing external directives and teaching scripts. We must not give up on the idea of preparing teachers who are able to exercise their judgment in their classrooms in the best interests of their students, and with giving teachers access to meaningful professional development that recognizes the knowledge and expertise that teachers bring to these experiences, and treats them with respect. Underlying efforts to improve the quality of teacher education is the need to fight for the survival of public education and for the dignity of the work of teaching in public schools. To do this, we of course also need to address all of the "rotten outcomes" and injustices that exist beyond schools (providing access to housing, nutritious food, healthcare, jobs that pay a living wage (Berliner, 2006)).

Attempts to defend college and university teacher education in the US that are isolated from other struggles for social justice in public schooling and in the broader society will be seen as largely self-serving and will fail. In responding to these problems and to external critiques, we need to recognize and confront the underlying neo-liberal and neo-conservative forces that are connected to the current troubles of public education and teacher education and begin to challenge them rather than demonizing and blaming particular individuals. It has been very rare in US teacher education literature for there to be any discussion of the neo-liberal and neo-conservative thinking connected to current developments (see Hinchey & Cadiero-Kaplan, 2005; Sleeter, 2008; Weiner, 2007 for exceptions) and of the global nature of their existence. What I have described in this chapter with regard to teacher education in the US is clearly going on in many parts of the world, often aided by the efforts of organizations like the World Bank and OECD (Dahlstrom, 2007; Reimers, 1994; Zeichner & Ndimande, 2008).

Because of the growing influence of the neo-liberal agenda in both K–12 schooling and teacher education, the very idea of public education as we have known it in the US is in serious jeopardy right now. Hess's (2006) comments in an American Enterprise Institute's publication advocating an increased role for the market in public schooling and teacher education even question the need for public schools.

> There is growing recognition that it may be possible to serve public purposes and cultivate civic virtues in places other than state run schools. Consider that public schools may be those that serve public ends regardless of how they are funded, operated and monitored. Any school that helps children master reading, writing, and mathematics and other essential elements is advancing significant and public purposes.
>
> *(pp. 62–63)*

This neo-liberal logic transforms education from a public good into a private consumer item. Apple (2001) argues that this begins to transform the very idea of democracy (of the common good) making it an economic concept, not a political one, and that one of the effects of this thinking is the destruction of what might best be seen as "thick democracy" substituting a much thinner version of possessive individualism.

A strong and well-supported system of public education is essential to the realization of the democratic society that the US aspires to be. Barber, a prominent scholar on democracy, has argued in response to recent attacks on public education:

> In attacking public education critics are attacking the very foundation of our democratic civic culture. Public schools are not merely schools for the public, but schools of publicness: institutions where we learn what it means to be a public and start down the road toward common national and civic identity. They are the forges of our citizenship and the bedrock of our democracy. Vilifying public school teachers and administrators and cutting public school budgets even as we subsidize private educational opportunity puts us in double jeopardy: for as we put our children at risk, we undermine our common future, at the same moment, in constraining the conditions of liberty for some, we undermine the future of democracy for all.
>
> *(Barber, 1997, p. 22)*

It is essential that teacher educators stand up and be counted in collaboration with public school educators and parents and students in the struggle to protect and strengthen both public K–12 education and a strong role for college and universities in teacher education. The survival of our hopes to build a genuinely democratic society depend on it.

This new and more collaborative form of teacher education that is required in the US to support the development of more democratic forms of professionalism in teaching and teacher education must lead to a greater democratization of knowledge in teacher education programs and to the building of strong alliances across the boundaries of universities, schools, and communities that are less hierarchical and more inclusive of the expertise that exists in all three spheres. University teacher education in the US will need to become more closely linked with and more relevant to supporting progressive struggles in schools and communities than it is currently if it is to survive. Because of the knowledge histories that exist in universities that often undermine genuine collaboration with those outside of the academy (e.g., Duffy, 1994), there may be a need to develop new hybrid spaces where more egalitarian forms of interaction in teacher education are possible such as have begun to occur in some countries such as Israel (Gorodetsky & Barak, 2008).

This is both a very exciting and dangerous time for teacher education in the US. There is both a real opportunity to establish forms of democratic professionalism in teaching and teacher education where universities, schools, and communities come together in new ways to prepare teachers who will provide everyone's children with the same high quality of education. There is also a real danger, however, that teacher education in the US will be dismantled into a purely market economy divorced from universities and that the "good enough" teacher who can only faithfully implement teaching scripts (but no more) with "other people's children" will become the norm. In order to achieve the former of these worlds, university teacher educators in the US must look beyond a purely defensive reaction to the forces discussed in this paper and take a more offensive stance learning how to do things in ways that they have not been done before.

Notes

1   Based on a keynote address presented at the International Conference—Justice, Equality, and Efficiency: Educational Policy under the situation of Multiple Societies, East China Normal University, Shanghai, October, 2008.
2   According to Harvey (2005), "neoliberalism is in the first instance a theory of political economic practices that proposes that human well-being can be advanced by liberating individual entrepreneurial freedoms and skills within an institutional framework characterized by strong private property rights, free markets, and free trade. The role of the state is to create and preserve the institutional framework appropriate to such practices" (p. 2).
3   This marketization of teacher education is similar to the growth of for-profit higher education in general (Morey, 2001).
4   Paige (2002).
5   An example of state policies that encourage alternatives to college and university teacher education is the practice of placing a limit capping Education credits in a pre-service teacher education program. See Zeichner and Hutchinson (2008) for a discussion of the evolution of alternative certification policies in the US.

6 ABCTE.org. The states participating in this program are: Florida, Idaho, Mississippi, Missouri, New Hampshire, Pennsylvania, South Carolina, and Utah and Oklahoma.

7 Miner (2010) documents the link between Teach for America in the US and some of the major funders of efforts to privatize K–12 education such as the Walton Family Foundation (Wal-Mart) and the Doris and Donald Fisher Fund (The Gap).

8 Sachs (2003) correctly points out that this same kind of corporate managerialism has also become more common in other parts of the public sector in addition to education.

9 Many of these programs use standardized course syllabi and employ mostly adjunct faculty to teach courses. Baines (2006a, 2006b, 2010) has also shown how some colleges and universities are now designing "minimalist programs" to be able to compete with the non-college and non-university programs.

10 The term was used by a high ranking official in the US Department of Education at a meeting held at the Carnegie Foundation for the Advancement of Teaching in June 2002.

11 Two examples of this are the scandal over the Reading First program initiated by a government audit (Grunwald, 2006) and criticisms of the inappropriate use of money in three states to buy educational products from a company owned by the president's brother, Neil Bush (Thompson, 2007). There is strong evidence that the so called "Texas miracle" on which Bush Jr. administration policies emphasizing standardized testing were based did not produce the kinds of success for students that were claimed by the Bush administration (e.g., Haney, 2000; Valenzuela, 2005).

12 Feistritzer and Haar (2008) report that in 2006, approximately 50,000 individuals were teachers of record in schools across the country while they were still in the process of completing their pre-service teacher education programs.

13 In 2005, the number of individuals certified through alternative routes in just three states (California, New Jersey, Texas) accounted for nearly one-half of all teachers in the United States certified through alternative routes that year. In this same year, New Jersey reported that nearly 40 percent of new hires entered through alternative programs while the percentage in Texas and California was about one third (Feistritzer & Haar, 2008).

14 For example, between 2002 and 2006, Title I funding was underfunded by $31.5 billion dollars and IDEA was underfunded by $ 37.6 billion dollars. Retrieved from the National School Board Association website on September 8, 2006: www.nsba.org/site/docs/38600/38542.pdf

15 Alaska, North Dakota, and Wyoming.

16 By hyper-rationality, I mean extreme pressure on teacher education institutions to rationalize their programs and student assessment systems to a point where the demands for accountability and compliance begin to interfere with and undermine the accomplishment of the goal of educating teachers (See Wise, 1979 for a discussion of this term with regard to K–12 education).

17 See Bullough, Clark, and Patterson (2003) for a discussion of some of the problems in current accreditation methods based on the experience of teacher educators at one university.

18 It has been shown by research, however, that some forms of teacher testing have had a negative effect on efforts to develop a more ethnically and racially diverse teaching force (Darling-Hammond & Chung Wei, 2009).

19 A recent study by the National Research Council on teacher education in the US concluded that there is no empirical evidence supporting the effectiveness of any of these state and national teacher education program approval practices and has called for a major study of this area (National Research Council, 2010).

20 Currently, teacher education institutions are publicly ranked according to the standardized test scores of pupils taught by program graduates in Louisiana and Florida.

21 NCATE didn't actually have "a 'social justice' requirement": it had a requirement that all teacher education programs who listed "social justice" as a goal had to individually assess the disposition of each student to promote social justice. Since virtually all programs had such a goal, the guideline amounted to a *de facto* social justice requirement.

References

Aarons, D. (2008, August 27). Districts cut back bussing, seek ways to save energy. *Education Week*. Retrieved from www.edweek.org/ew/articles/2008/08/27/01econlocal.h28.html?qs=District+cut+back+bussing,+seek+ways+to+save+energy

Apple, M. (1996). *Cultural politics and education*. New York: Teachers College Press.

Apple, M. W. (2001). *Educating the "right way"*. New York: Routledge.

Baines, L. (2006a). Deconstructing teacher certification. *Phi Delta Kappan*, *88*(4), 326–329.

Baines, L. (2006b). The transmogrification of teacher education. *The Teacher Educator*, *42*(2), 140–156.

Baines, L. (2010). *The teachers we need vs. the teachers we have*. Lanham, MD: Rowman & Littlefield.

Ball, S. (June, 2004). Everything for sale: The commodification of everything. The annual education lecture. London Institute of Education.

Barber, B. (1997). Public schooling: Education for democracy. In J. Goodlad & T. McMannon (Eds), *The public purpose of education and schooling* (pp. 21–32). San Francisco, CA: Jossey Bass.

Bates, R. (2007). Regulation and autonomy in teacher education: system or democracy. In T. Townsend & R. Bates (Eds), *Handbook of teacher education: Globalization, standards and professionalism in times of change* (pp. 127–140). Dordrecht: Springer.

Berliner, D. (2006). Our impoverished view of educational reform. *Teachers College Record*. Retrieved from www.tcrecord.org

Bernstein, B. (1996). *Pedagogy, symbolic control and identity*. London: Routledge.

Beyer, L. (2007). Teacher education and the new professionalism: the case of the US. In J. Freeman-Moir & A. Scott (Eds), *Shaping the future: Critical essays on teacher education* (pp. 25–42). Rotterdam: Sense Publishers.

Blomeke, S. (2006). Globalization and educational reform in German teacher education. *International Journal of Educational Research*, *45*, 315–324.

Borsuk, A. J. (2008, September 25). MPS board backs away from ideas of dissolving the district. *Milwaukee Journal Sentinel*. Retrieved from www.jsonline.com

Boyd, D., Grossman, P., Hammerness, K., Loeb, S., McDonald, M., Ronfeldt, M., et al. (2008). Surveying the landscape of teacher education in New York City: Constrained variation and the challenge of innovation. *Educational Evaluation and Policy Analysis*, *30*(4), 319–343.

Bullough, R. (2008). *Counter narratives: Studies of teacher education and becoming and being a teacher*. Albany, NY: SUNY Press.

Bullough, R., Clark, C., & Patterson, R. (2003). Getting in step: Accountability, accreditation and the standardization of teacher education in the United States. *Journal of Education for Teaching, 29*(1), 35–51.

Carnoy, M. (1995). Structural adjustment and the changing face of education. *International Labor Review, 134*(6), 653–674.

Clark, K. (2007). *Declines in spending on public higher education in Wisconsin: An analysis of the University of Wisconsin system budget*. Madison: WISCAPE Policy Brief, University of Wisconsin-Madison.

Cochran-Smith, M., Feiman-Nemser, S., & McIntyre, D. J. (Eds). (2008). *Handbook of research on teacher education* (3rd ed.). New York: Routledge.

Cochran-Smith, M., & Zeichner, K. (Eds.). (2005). *Studying teacher education*. New York: Routledge.

Compton, M., & Weiner, L. (Eds). (2008). *The global assault on teaching, teachers and their unions*. New York: Palgrave Macmillan.

Dahlstrom, L. (2007). When eagles are allowed to fly: A global and contextual perspective on teacher education in Ethiopia. *International Journal of Progressive Education, 3*(3), 6–19.

Dahlstrom, L. (2009). Education in a post-neoliberal era: a promising future for the global south. *Power and Education, 1*(2), 167–177.

Dahlstrom, L., & Lemma, B. (2009). Critical perspectives on teacher education in neoliberal times: Experiences from Ethiopia and Namibia. *SARS, 14*(1–2), 29–42.

Darling-Hammond, L. (2004). Inequality and the right to learn: Access to qualified teachers in California's public schools. *Teachers College Record, 106*(10), 1936–1966.

Darling-Hammond, L. (2006). *Powerful teacher education*. San Francisco, CA: Jossey-Bass.

Darling-Hammond, L., & Bransford, J. (Eds.). (2005). *Preparing teachers for a changing world*. San Francisco, CA: Jossey-Bass.

Darling-Hammond, L., & Chung Wei, R. (2009). Teacher preparation and teacher learning: A changing policy landscape. In G. Sykes, B. Schneider, & D. Plank (Eds), *Handbook of education policy research* (pp. 613–636). New York: Routledge.

Duffy, G. (1994). Professional development schools and the disempowerment of teachers and professors. *Phi Delta Kappan, 75*(8), 596–600.

Duncan, A. (2009, October 22). *Teacher preparation: Reforming an uncertain profession* [Speech]. New York City: Teachers' College, Columbia University. Retrieved from www.ed.gov/news/speeches/teacher-preparation-reforming-uncertain-profession

Duthilleul, Y. (2005a). *Developing teachers' knowledge and skills: Policy trends in OECD countries*. Paris: UNESCO International Institute for Educational Planning.

Duthilleul, Y. (2005b). *Teacher education, professional development and certification policies in Latin America*. Paris: UNESCO International Institute for Educational Planning.

Emmeret, M. (2010). *Letter to the university community*. Seattle: University of Washington.

Evetts, J. (2009). The management of professionalism: a contemporary paradox. In S. Gewirtz, P. Mahony, I. Hextall, & A. Cribb (Eds), *Changing teacher professionalism: International challenges and ways forward*. London: Routledge.

Feistritzer, E., & Haar, C. (2008). *Alternative routes to teaching*. Upper Saddle River, NJ: Pearson Education Inc.

Foderaro, L. (2010, April 18). Alternative pathway for teachers gains ground. *New York Times*. Retrieved from www.nytimes.com/2010/04/19/education/19regents.html?pagewanted=all

Fraser, J. W. (2007). *Preparing America's teachers: A history.* New York: Teachers College Press.

Freeman-Moir, J., & Scott, A. (Eds). (2007). *Shaping the future: Critical essays on teacher education.* Rotterdam: Sense Publishers.

Furlong, J. (2005). New labour and teacher education: The end of an era. *Oxford Review of Education, 31,* 119–134.

Furlong, J., Barton, L., Miles, S., Whiting, C., & Whitty, G. (2000). *Teacher education in transition: Re-forming professionalism.* Buckingham, UK: Open University Press.

Furlong, J., Cochran-Smith, M., & Brennan, M. (2009). *Policy and politics in teacher education: International perspectives.* London: Routledge.

Goodnough, A. (2001, June 14). Strain of fourth-grade tests drives off veteran teachers. *New York Times.* P.A-1. Retrieved from www.nytimes.com/2001/06/14/nyregion/strain-of-fourth-grade-tests-drives-off-veteran-teachers.html?pagewanted=all

Gorodetsky, M., & Barak, J. (2008). The educational-cultural edge: A participative learning environment for co-emergence of personal and institutional growth. *Teaching and Teacher Education, 24,* 1907–1918.

Greene, J., & Shock, C. (2008). Adding up to failure: Ed schools put diversity before math. *City Journal, 18*(1). Retrieved from www.city-journal.org/html/adding-failure-13072.html

Grimmett, P., Fleming, R., & Trotter, L. (2009). Legitimacy and identity in teacher education: a micro-political struggle constrained by macro-political pressures. *Asia-Pacific Journal of Teacher Education, 37*(1), 5–26.

Grossman, P., & Loeb, S. (Eds). (2008). *Taking stock: An examination of alternative certification.* Cambridge, MA: Harvard Education Press.

Grunwald, M. (2006, October 1). Billions for an inside game on reading. *The Washington Post.* Retrieved from www.washingtonpost.com

Hamel, F., & Merz, C. (2005). Reforming accountability: A preservice program wrestles with mandated reform. *Journal of Teacher Education, 56*(2), 157–167.

Haney, W. (2000). The myth of the Texas miracle in education. *Educational Policy Analysis Archives, 41.*

Hartocolis, A. (2005). Who needs education schools? *New York Times Education Life,* 22–28.

Harvey, D. (2005). *A brief history of neo-liberalism.* New York: Oxford University Press.

Hess, F. (2009). The human capital challenge: Toward a 21st century teaching profession. In D. Goldhaber & J. Hannaway (Eds), *Creating a new teaching profession.* Washington, DC: Urban Institute Press.

Hess, F. M. (2006). *Tough love for schools: Essays on competition, accountability, and excellence.* Washington, DC: AEI Press.

Hinchey, P., & Cadiero-Kaplan, K. (2005). The future of teacher education and teaching: Another piece of the privatization puzzle. *Journal of Critical Educational Policy Studies, 3*(2). Retrieved from www.jceps.com/archives/502

Holland, R. G. (2004). *To build a better teacher: The emergence of a competitive education industry.* Westport, CT: Prager.

Honawar, V. (2007). Gains seen in retooled teacher education. *Education Week.* Retrieved from www.edweek.org/ew/articles/2007/10/31/10louisiana.h27.html

Howey, K. (2007). *A review of urban teacher residencies in the context of urban teacher preparation, alternative routes to teaching and a changing teacher workforce.* Washington, DC: National Council of Accreditation for Teacher Education.

Hypolito, A. M. (2004). Teachers' work and professionalization: The promised land or dream denied? *Journal for Critical Education Policy Studies, 2*(2). Retrieved from www.jceps.com

Ingersoll, R. (2003). *Who controls teachers' work: Power and accountability in America's schools.* Cambridge, MA: Harvard University Press.

Izumi, L. T., & Coburn, K. G. (2001). *Facing the challenge: Teacher training and teacher quality in California's schools of education.* San Francisco, CA: Pacific Research Institute.

Johnson, D., Johnson, B., Farenga, S., & Ness, D. (2005). *Trivializing teacher education: The accreditation squeeze.* Lanham, MD: Rowman & Littlefield.

Kornfeld, J., Grady, K., Marker, P., & Ruddell, M. (2007). Caught in the current: A self-study of state-mandated compliance in a teacher education program. *Teachers College Record, 109*(8), 1902–1930.

Kozol, J. (2005). *The shame of American education: The restoration of apartheid schooling in America.* New York: Crown.

Kumar, K., Priyam, M., & Saxena, S. (2001). The trouble with para-teachers. *Frontline, 18*(22). Retrieved from www.frontline.in/static/html/fl1822/18220930.htm

Kumashiro, K. (2010). Seeing the bigger picture: Troubling movements to end teacher education. *Journal of Teacher Education, 61*(1–2), 56–65.

Levine, A. (2006). Will universities maintain control of teacher education? *Change, 38*(4), 36–43.

Lyall, K., & Sell, K. (2006). *The true genius of America at risk: Are we losing our public universities to de facto privatization?* Westport, CT: Praeger.

McDonald, M., & Zeichner, K. (2009). Social justice teacher education. In W. Ayers, C. Quinn, & D. Stovall (Eds), *Handbook on social justice in education.* New York: Routledge.

McNeil, M. (2008). State fiscal woes start to put squeeze on K–12 budgets. *Education Week.* Retrieved from www.edweek.org/ew/articles/2008/05/07/36budget.h27.html

Miner, B. (2010). Looking past the spin: Teach for America. *Rethinking Schools, 24*(1). Retrieved from www.rethinkingschools.org/archive/24_03/24_03_tfa.shtml

Morey, A. (2001). The growth of for-profit higher education: Implications for teacher education. *Journal of Teacher Education, 52*(4), 300–311.

National Research Council. (2010). *Preparing teachers: Building evidence for sound policy.* Washington, DC: National Academies Press.

New York Times. (2009). Do teachers need education degrees? *Room for Debate.* Retrieved from www.newyorktimes.com

Newfeld, C. (2008). *Unmaking the public university.* Cambridge, MA: Harvard University Press.

Paige, R. (June, 2002). *Meeting the highly qualified teacher challenge: The second annual report on teacher quality.* Washington, DC: US Department of Education.

Payzant, T. (2004). Should teacher preparation take place at colleges and universities? Invited address at the annual meeting of the American Association of Colleges for Teacher Education.

Peske, H. G., & Haycock, K. (2006). *Teaching inequality: How poor and minority students are shortchanged on teacher quality.* Washington, DC: Education Trust.

Pitman, A. (2007). Ontario, Canada: The state asserts its voice or accountability supersedes responsibility. In M. Tatto (Ed.), *Reforming teaching globally* (pp. 97–118). Oxford: Symposium Books.

Randi, J., & Zeichner, K. (2004). New visions of teacher professional development. In M. Smylie & D. Miretszky (Eds), *Preparing the teacher workforce: Yearbook of the national society for the study of education* (pp. 180–227). Chicago, IL: University of Chicago Press.

Raphael, J., & Tobias, S. (1997). Profit-making or profiteering? Proprietaries target teacher education. *Change, 29*(6), 44–49.

Reimers, F. (1994). Education and structural adjustment in Latin America and sub-Saharan Africa. *International Journal of Educational Development, 14,* 119–129.

Rennert-Ariev, P. (2008). The hidden curriculum of performance-based teacher education. *Teachers College Record, 110*(1), 105–138.

Robertson, S. (2000). *A class act: Changing teachers' work, the state, and globalization.* New York: Falmer Press.

Robertson, S. (2008). Remaking the world: Neoliberalism and the transformation of education and teachers' labor. In M. Compton & L. Weiner (Eds), *The global assault on teaching, teachers and their unions* (pp. 11–36). New York: Palgrave Macmillan.

Rosen, A. (2003). For-profit teacher education [Transcript]. *The Chronicle of Higher Education,* Colloquy Live. Retrieved from http://chronicle.com/colloquylive

Sachs, J. (2003). *The activist teaching profession.* Buckingham: Open University Press.

Sleeter, C. (2008). Equity, democracy, and neo-liberal assaults on teacher education. *Teaching and Teacher Education, 24*(8), 1947–1957.

Smyth, J., Dow, A., Hattam, R., Reid, A., & Shacklock, G. (2000). *Teachers' work in a globalizing economy.* London: Routledge.

Steensen, J. (2006). Global trends on local grounds—the case of teacher education in Denmark and Sweden. Umeå University. In L. Dahlström & J. Mannberg (Eds), *Critical educational visions and practices in neo-liberal times* (pp. 91–102). Sweden: Global South Network Publisher.

Tamatea, L. (2010). The Dakar framework: Constructing and deconstructing the global neo-liberal matrix. *Globalisation, Societies and Education, 3*(3), 311–334.

Tatto, M. T. (2007a). International comparisons and the global reform of teaching. In M. T. Tatto (Ed.), *Reforming teaching globally* (pp. 7–18). Oxford: Symposium Books.

Tatto, T. T. (Ed.). (2007b). *Reforming teaching globally.* Oxford: Symposium Books.

Tatto, M. T., & Plank, D. (2007). The dynamics of global teaching reform. In T. Tatto (Ed.), *Reforming teaching globally* (pp. 267–278). Oxford: Symposium Books.

Thompson, M. W. (2007). Bush brother's firm faces inquiry over purchases. *New York Times.* Retrieved from www.nytimes.org

Valenzuela, A. (Ed.). (2005). *Leaving children behind: How Texas style accountability fails Latino youth.* Albany, NY: SUNY Press. Sector Improvement Program.

Walsh, K. (2004). A candidate-centered model for teacher preparation and licensure. In F. Hess, A. Rotherham, & K. Walsh (Eds), *A qualified teacher in every classroom* (pp. 119–148). Cambridge, MA: Harvard Education Press.

Wasley, P. (2006). Accreditor of education schools drops controversial "social justice" language. *The Chronicle of Higher Education.* Retrieved from http://chronicle.com/article/Accreditor-of-Education/14458

Weiner, L. (2007). A lethal threat to teacher education. *Journal of Teacher Education, 58*(4), 274–286.

Wilson, S., & Tamir, E. (2008). The evolving field of teacher education. In M. Cochran-Smith, S. Feiman-Nemser, & D. J. McIntyre (Eds), *Handbook of research on teacher education* (3rd ed.) (pp. 908–935). New York: Routledge.

Wise, A. (1979). *Legislated learning: The bureaucratization of the American classroom.* Berkeley, CA: University of California Press.

Young, M. (1998). Rethinking teacher education for a global future: lessons from the English. *Journal of Education for Teaching, 24*(1), 51–62.

Zeichner, K. (1991). Contradictions and tensions in the professionalization of teaching and the democratization of schooling. *Teachers College Record, 92*(3), 363–379.

Zeichner, K. (2005a). Learning from experience with performance-based teacher education. In F. Peterman (Ed.), *Designing performance assessment systems for urban teacher preparation* (pp. 3–20). New York: Erlbaum/Routledge.

Zeichner, K. (2005b). A research agenda for teacher education. In M. Cochran-Smith & K. Zeichner (Eds), *Studying teacher education* (pp. 737–759). New York: Routledge.

Zeichner, K. (2009). *Teacher education and the struggle for social justice.* New York: Routledge.

Zeichner, K., & Conklin, H. (2005). Teacher education programs. In M. Cochran-Smith & K. Zeichner (Eds), *Studying teacher education* (pp. 645–735). New York: Routledge.

Zeichner, K., & Hutchinson, E. (2008). The development of alternative certification policies and programs in the US. In P. Grossman & S. Loeb (Eds), *Alternative routes to teaching* (pp. 15–29). Cambridge, MA: Harvard Education Press.

Zeichner, K., & Ndimande, B. (2008). Contradictions and tensions in the place of teachers in educational reform: reflections on teacher preparation in the USA and Namibia. *Teachers & Teaching: Theory and Practice, 14*(4), 331–343.

3

VENTURE PHILANTHROPY AND TEACHER EDUCATION POLICY IN THE US

The Role of the New Schools Venture Fund

Kenneth M. Zeichner and César Peña-Sandoval

> In a democratic nation, it is altogether proper that private efforts to reshape public institutions even for the most beneficent purposes be accorded the same hard look that greets any policy proposal. ... Addressing the implications of these developments requires an informed public conversation that establishes the facts and in turn enables reformers, policymakers, donors, parents, and citizens to grapple with them. Unfortunately, the deliberations today are clouded by ambiguity surrounding even the most elemental facts.
>
> *(Hess, 2005, pp. 8–9)*

This chapter examines the increasing role of venture philanthropy (Reckhow, 2013; Saltman, 2010; Scott, 2006) and the ideas of educational entrepreneurship and disruptive innovation in influencing the course of federal and state policies and practices in teacher education in the US.

According to Saltman (2010),

> Venture Philanthropy is modeled on venture capital and the investments in the technology boom of the early 1990s. ... VP treats giving to public schooling as a social investment that, like venture capital, must begin with a business plan, involve quantitative measurement of efficacy, be replicable to be brought to scale and ideally leverage public spending in ways compatible with the strategic donor. ... One of the most significant aspects of this transformation in educational philanthropy involves the ways that the public and civic purposes of public schooling are re-described by VP in distinctly private ways.
>
> *(pp. 2–3)*

We focus in particular on one example of these under-scrutinized influences on public policy: the influence of the New Schools Venture Fund (NSVF) in supporting policy and programs intended to disrupt the current largely public teacher education system. According to Smith and Peterson (2006), "This view holds that the public education system must change so profoundly that only the disruptive force of entrepreneurs who think beyond the current constraints and resources can get us there" (p. 42). Smith and Peterson (2006) defined educational entrepreneurs as

> visionary thinkers who create new for-profit or nonprofit organizations from scratch that redefine our sense of what is possible. These organizations stand separate and independent from institutions like public school districts and teachers' colleges; as such the entrepreneurs who start them have the potential to spark more dramatic change than might otherwise be created by status quo organizations.
>
> *(pp. 21–22)*

We begin by presenting a framework that we believe describes the major positions that exist today regarding the future of US teacher education (defenders, reformers, transformers) and introduce the narratives of crisis and salvation that underlie reformers' critiques of university teacher education. We then discuss relatively recent changes in the nature and extent of educational philanthropy's role in influencing teacher education policies and practices. Following this analysis of the changing role of philanthropy in teacher education, we present the example of the role of the New Schools Venture Fund, one of most influential venture philanthropy groups in US education in promoting deregulation and competition in teacher education.

To assess the wisdom of these efforts to further deregulation and the development of a teacher education market economy, we then analyze the broader questions of whether university teacher education has failed in its role in educating the nation's teachers, as reformers have alleged, and whether the entrepreneurial programs that are rapidly being created with funds provided by venture philanthropists represent an improvement over our current situation. In doing so, we examine the ways in which the national study of teacher education conducted by Arthur Levine (2006) has been misrepresented by critics of university teacher education and used as "evidence" that university teacher education has supposedly failed. We also show how other reports on university teacher education that present a more positive view of teacher education by program graduates have been ignored by critics. We conclude with a call for more trenchant dialogue about the options before us and for greater transparency about the ways that private interests are influencing public policy and practice in teacher education.

Situating Educational Entrepreneurs: Stances toward the Status Quo in US Teacher Education

From our perspective, there are three major positions taken by those interested in improving the current situation in teacher education in the US. First, there is the position taken by some college and university teacher educators that the criticisms of teacher education from the outside are wrong and motivated by a selfish desire to make money and/or advance personal or professional standing at the expense of students living in poverty who are currently underserved by public schools. We call this the position of the defenders. The defenders call for greater investment in the current system of teacher education in order to build greater capacity in the existing institutions that currently prepare teachers (i.e., colleges and universities). The defenders do not see the need for significant changes in the way things are now done.

Second, there are groups of outsiders to the current system, and even some within, who have argued that education schools have failed and that the current system needs to be blown up or disrupted and replaced by an alternative one based on deregulation, competition, and markets. These critics refer to themselves as *reformers*.[1]

> If history is any guide, it is unlikely that today's colleges of education will substantially reform themselves without substantial competition from other providers. In other words, new entrants to teacher training hold the most promising prospects for redirecting the massive resources now sunk into ineffective teacher education programs.
>
> *(Rotherham, 2008, p. 112)*

Finally, there are those who see the need for substantive transformation in the current system of teacher education but do not support "blowing up" the current system and replacing it with a deregulated market economy. This position is that of the *transformers*.

Those within the transformation camp have sought to improve the quality of teacher education in many ways in recent years, including: (1) developing more shared responsibility for teacher education among schools, universities, and local communities; (2) more effectively connecting coursework in programs to the complexities of the schools for which teachers are being prepared; (3) focusing more intensely on helping teacher candidates learn how to enact teaching practices that will promote student learning; (4) strengthening meaningful accountability systems for teacher candidates and programs; and (5) improving the quality of school and community experiences in teachers' education and the quality of the mentoring that supports these experiences (e.g., Berry et al., 2008; Grossman, 2011; National Council of Accreditation for Teacher Education, 2010; Zeichner & Payne, 2013).

A system of categorization like this inevitably oversimplifies a much more complex situation. There is much variation within each of these three camps (e.g., in terms of the intensity and substance of positions) as well as multiple points of overlap between positions (e.g., transformers who, like defenders, support maintaining aspects of the current system). That said, the distinctions between groups offer a meaningful lens for considering differing views on how to move forward in teacher education.

Although the two of us are largely seen by many reformers as defenders of the current system because we are situated in an education school and have been critical of privileging market-based solutions to problems of teacher quality and teacher preparation, we have called for fundamental changes in pre-service teacher education and position ourselves within the transformer camp. Our location in this camp reflects our recognition that an "education debt" (Ladson-Billings, 2006) is owed to many students living in poverty who attend US public schools and that improving the quality of teaching and teacher preparation is part of the solution to paying it off. We believe, however, that the quality of teaching, although fundamentally important, is not the major cause of the education debt. We also recognize that there is a need to vastly improve working conditions for educators within public schools and their access to high-quality professional development, to restructure the teaching profession so that first-year teachers do not have the same responsibilities as a 20-year veteran, and to address the roots of poverty and their consequences for student learning.

We also locate ourselves in the transformer camp because we have not been persuaded by the evidence that the entrepreneurial solutions seen by funders and policy makers as the answers to our problems will address the injustices in public schooling. In fact, we believe that the deregulation and disruption of public education and teacher education that are being aggressively promoted by private interests with little public discussion and debate will serve to widen rather than eliminate the opportunity and achievement differences in the quality of education available to children from different backgrounds.

It is clear that there is potentially a lot of money to be made by those who want to replace education schools in teacher preparation; indeed, market advocates sometimes show unembarrassed excitement as public education is privatized. For example, Jain (2013) recently proclaimed in a *Forbes* magazine article, "I want all entrepreneurs to take notice that [public education] is a multi-hundred-billion-dollar opportunity that's ripe for disruption" (p. 1).

Despite the potential to make a lot of money through investment in the disruption and re-creation of the current public education and teacher education systems, and the high degree of confidence, and sometimes blatant arrogance, of some reformers about the superiority of their entrepreneurial ventures, we do not question the motives of those who seek to dismantle the current system of teacher education in the US and replace it with a deregulated market.[2] Self-serving behavior, greed, and lack of concern for the common good can be found in all the various camps on educational reform, including in education schools; so too can genuine concern for the common good be found in all camps of the education debates.

Our purpose in writing this article is not to throw stones or impugn the character of those with whom we disagree. Rather, our purpose is to bring a greater level of transparency to the forces influencing public policy in teacher education so that they can be more clearly seen, discussed, and debated. Discussion and debate of public policy issues is the cornerstone of a healthy democratic society, and we are greatly concerned that many educators and the general public seem to be largely unaware of the ways in which private money and interests are determining the future of teacher preparation in the US. We are also concerned about the lack of discussion and debate in the public arena of these issues and practices.

Katz (2013) recently noted that in the early part of the twentieth century, philanthropists such as Carnegie and Rockefeller encountered a severe backlash for what was perceived to be their efforts to subvert democratic policy making. This same concern now exists as major foundations such as The Walton Family Foundation, The Broad Foundation, and The Bill and Melinda Gates Foundation, and groups like the NSVF, employ an aggressive stance and actions in efforts to shape public policy with regard to education and teacher education (Tompkins-Stange, 2016). Hess (2012) has used the term *muscular philanthropy* to describe the way in which many current venture philanthropists are unapologetically tied to influencing education policies in particular ways to create an environment supportive of their preferred market-based solutions.

Bringing Teacher Education into the Story of Crisis and Salvation

Parker (2011) has discussed the dominant narrative that has framed discussion about public schooling for the last 30 years. In this narrative, public schooling is seen as the cause of all our economic, social, and political problems, and educational reform is seen as a panacea for solving them. According to Parker (2011), what we have seen for the last 30 years in the US is "a stream of disdainful talk and action about public schooling, animated by the belief that public schooling is miserably broken, but also that it is the one thing that can save our society" (p. 413).

As part of locating the blame for our problems and the potential for salvation in public schooling, a discourse of derision is needed to convince policy makers and the public about the failure of the current system. What we have experienced in recent years is the blaming of teachers and their unions, school administrators, and now education schools for the alleged failures of public schooling (Barkan, 2011a). Even though most of the variation in student achievement is related to out-of-school factors like poverty, and related factors such as the lack of access to high quality early childhood education, health care, nutritious food, and so on

(Berliner, 2014; Duncan & Murnane, 2012; Rothstein, 2004), reformers often imply that educational interventions alone can fix the inequities in opportunities to learn and in educational outcomes in public schools. Furthermore, they argue that deregulation and markets, and entrepreneur-led charter schools and teacher education programs are the particular changes that will solve these problems (Ball, 2012).

What Parker (2011) described in relation to public schooling in general can also be seen with regard to teacher education, which, despite all the changes that have taken place in the last 30 years, remains largely a public enterprise in the US. We hear the constant drumbeat that tells us that education schools, an "industry of mediocrity" (Keller, 2013; National Council on Teacher Quality, 2013), have failed to educate the nation's teachers well and that if we replace this system with deregulation and markets, better teachers will result, and all our problems will be solved. Meredith Liu, a fellow at the Innosight Institute, an organization devoted to promoting "disruptive innovation" in education and health care, recently asserted:

> From a societal perspective, such programs appear to be a questionable investment given the limited evidence that they at least in the aggregate are actually creating effective teachers. ... Education schools with their high costs and stranglehold on the teacher preparation market are ripe for disruption.
>
> *(Liu, 2013, pp. 1–2)*

This kind of dismissal of the value of teacher education offered by education schools has led to calls for the elimination of the state's role in monitoring the quality of new teachers in favor of a teacher education market to regulate quality. For example, John Chubb, who was a distinguished visiting fellow at the Hoover Institution, has argued that policy makers

> should end teacher licensure, as we know it. Given the lack of firm knowledge of how best to prepare teachers for the classroom, state policymakers should lift all public school teaching requirements other than a bachelor's degree and a background check for public school teachers. ... It makes no sense to require specific forms of training or testing when there is no evidence that those requirements improve teaching. The federal government should lift the highly qualified teacher provisions of the Elementary and Secondary School Act that mandate certification. Schools and school systems should be free to decide what training they want to require.
>
> *(Chubb, 2012, p. 126)*

That John Chubb would advocate for the deregulation of teacher education should be no surprise given his advocacy of choice for K–12 education in the past:

Without being too literal about it, we think reformers would do well to entertain the notion that choice is a panacea. ... It has the capacity all by itself to bring about the kind of transformation that for years, reformers have been seeking to engineer in a myriad of other ways.

(Chubb & Moe, 1990, p. 217; Reckhow, 2013, p. 22)

Many scholars believe, contrary to Chubb's (2012) assertions, that there is evidence that teacher certification does matter and that we have learned a number of things from research about the characteristics of effective teacher education programs, such as a clear and consistent vision of teaching that is shared across the program, and carefully supervised clinical experience. These scholars believe that the problem is that these characteristics do not exist in every teacher education program (e.g., Boyd, Grossman, Lankford, Loeb, & Wyckoff, 2008; Darling-Hammond, 2006; Humphrey, Wechsler, & Hough, 2008; Zeichner & Conklin, 2005).

Clearly, some programs run by universities and by others are weak and have not been improved or shut down under current accountability mechanisms. Rather than "profoundly disrupt" the current system of teacher education because of the uneven quality in programs, transformers seek to independently evaluate and then redesign program accountability systems as recommended in the National Research Council (2010) study of teacher education in the US and to strengthen the ways in which teacher candidates are assessed before licensure (e.g., Darling-Hammond, 2010; Zeichner, 2011).

The Growing Influence of Venture Philanthropy in US Education and Teacher Education

Public policy can create new opportunities for entrepreneurs by changing the structure of the market. It can also create opportunities by reallocating resources which usually means an increase or decrease in dollars available and who can access them.

(Smith & Peterson, 2006, p. 28)

Historically, private foundations and the federal government have invested heavily in improving the design, quality, and content of teaching and teacher education in the US (e.g., Lagemann, 1992; Suggs & deMarrais, 2011; Sykes & Dibner, 2009; Woodring, 1960). Examples of federal investment in strengthening the college and university system of teacher education include the National Teacher Corps (1965–1981), which focused on preparing teachers to teach in poverty-impacted urban and rural schools (Smith, 1980), and the current Teacher Quality Partnership grants, which fund school and university partnerships in teacher education, including a number of urban teacher residency programs across the country. The Ford Foundation, the Carnegie Corporation, and the Rockefeller Brothers Fund are examples of foundations that have invested for many years in stimulating various kinds of innovation in the public system of teacher education. The $100 million-plus Teachers for a New Era project (2001–2009), led by Carnegie, is the most visible recent example of the efforts of foundations to improve the quality of our current teacher education system (Kirby, McCombs, Naftel, & Barney, 2005). Over the years, private foundations have supported a number of the major reports on US teacher education (e.g., Carnegie, 1986; Charters & Waples, 1929; Conant, 1963; Darling-Hammond & Bransford, 2005; Holmes Group, 1986) and highly visible reform initiatives (e.g., Goodlad, 1994; National Commission on Teaching and America's Future (NCTAF), 1996; Stone, 1968).

Recently, it has become clear that the philanthropic community has turned away from building capacity in the current college and university system of teacher education and toward funding alternative teacher education providers and programs. Reckhow (2013) has described a similar shift in philanthropy in K-12 education since 2000 from funding school districts to directly funding nonprofits and charter schools that compete with school districts.

Major conferences and the national media have been flooded with speeches, papers, and opinion pieces that question the very idea of a college and university system of teacher education (e.g., Hartocollis, 2005; Keller, 2013; Payzant, 2004; Vedder, 2011).[3] Levine (2010) has claimed, "There is a growing sense among the critics that it would be more fruitful to replace university-based teacher education than to attempt to reform it" (pp. 21–22). "Frustrated by the apparent resistance of these institutions to change, many funders have turned their attention to alternative pathways to certification. These include support for new organizations focused on recruiting and training teacher candidates and for teacher residency programs" (Suggs & deMarrais, 2011, p. 14).

An example of this can be seen by examining funding for Teach for America (TFA). Between 2000 and 2008, TFA received about $213 million in foundation grants, which represents 31 percent of foundation grants during this period to matters related to teachers and teaching (Suggs & deMarrais, 2011). This review noted, "As interest in TFA and other non-traditional programs has increased, funder interest in schools of education as a mechanism for bolstering the supply and quality of teachers has lagged" (Suggs & deMarrais, 2011, p. 35).

Additionally, since 2000, TFA has received over $200 million in federal funding (usaspending.gov) and has set a goal of raising $350 million per year in state funding by 2015 (Simon, 2013). In 2011, the Walton Family Foundation gave TFA $49.5 million to help double its size (Schiller, 2012) and then gave it another $20 million in June 2013. Over the last 24 years, the Walton Family Foundation has given more than $100 million to TFA (Blume, 2013). The 8,200 TFA corps members in 2010–2011 represented less than 1 percent of the teaching force in the US that year (Suggs & deMarrais, 2011).

In 1999, a guide for funders interested in improving teacher education prepared for the Kellogg Foundation by the Educational Development Center (EDC) focused exclusively on strengthening university teacher education programs (EDC, 1999). By contrast, a more recent report commissioned by the Ford Foundation (Suggs & deMarrais, 2011), Rotherham's guide for investors who want to help improve teacher and principal quality (Rotherham, 2008), and the actual funding allocations to various kinds of teacher education programs all make clear that disrupting the current system of college and university teacher education to provide room for new entrants to a teacher education market has become today's philanthropists' preferred solution to the alleged ills of the field. For example, Democrats for Education Reform (DFER), an advocacy group that focuses on creating a political environment favorable to market-based solutions in education and critical of teacher unions (Sawchuck, 2012), has stated, "We must encourage and invest in new models and enlist a broader range of expertise to develop and nurture the next generation of educators" (Democrats for Educational Reform, 2011).

Unlike educational philanthropy of the past—*before* the entry into teacher education of individual venture capitalists and large funders like the Gates and Walton Foundations—current educational philanthropy in teacher education has taken a more hands-on approach and openly political role in pushing particular policies through their allocations of funds. This new wave of philanthropy supports policies that create conditions favorable to establishing a teacher education market and room for new entrants to the field (Ball, 2012; Barkan, 2011b; Reckhow, 2013; Saltman, 2010). This new brand of activism by philanthropists in promoting particular policies has managed to shape contemporary debates about teacher education policy and advance particular definitions of what it means to be an educated person, what good teaching is, and what should be involved in judging the quality of a teacher education program.

Specifically, the entrepreneurial community has been able to establish the goal of judging the quality of a teacher education program based on how many of its graduates are able to raise students' standardized test scores at a given moment in time. They have been successful in drawing attention away from questions about the potential costs incurred in doing so (e.g., narrowing the curriculum in both K-12 and teacher education), how long these graduates stay in teaching, and how well they are able to support student learning in a broader sense beyond test scores.

Quinn, Tompkins-Stange, and Meyerson (2013) argued that developing and enforcing evaluative frameworks to assess the alternative institutional forms their funding helps create is one of the social processes that have been used by philanthropists to elevate and scale up the new entrants to the education field that they fund.

Secretary of Education Duncan's "Blueprint for Teacher Education" (A. Duncan, 2011) also promotes the idea that the quality of teacher education programs should be judged primarily by the value-added test scores of the students taught by teacher education program graduates. This has been the case despite the substantial concerns raised by assessment experts about the appropriateness of using student test scores to evaluate teachers and teacher education programs (e.g., Economic Policy Institute, 2010; Plecki, Elfers, & Nakamura, 2012; Polikoff & Porter, 2014). The goal of establishing the value-added analysis of the test scores of pupils taught by program graduates as the norm for evaluating the quality of teacher education programs has been furthered by the massive amount of federal money allocated to building state data systems that would make this possible and by the requirements of the ongoing Race to the Top competitions sponsored by the US Department of Education (Crowe, 2011).

The history of the role of philanthropy and public policy reveals that foundations have always been key participants in the "politics of knowledge" (Lagemann, 1992) that is associated with the allocation of private funds.

> There is nothing especially novel in the subject of foundations and public policymaking, especially when we ask what tactics foundations have had at their disposal in the pursuit of new or changed public policies. They have worked to shape policies by using their influence on boards, by molding elite public opinion, by pursuing campaigns of public information and education, by creating demonstration projects, by using their financial resources strategically to leverage public funds, and by pursuing direct legislative lobbying, judicial strategies, and executive branch persuasion. They have worked at every level of government.
>
> *(Smith, 2009, p. 45)*

Despite this role of foundations in advocating particular policies, there has also been a focus over time in philanthropy in the US on what has been called "scientific philanthropy." Here, foundations have encouraged the study of problems and the exploration of various solutions, and there was an effort to base the advocacy of particular positions to some extent on sound scientific evidence (Smith, 2009; Zunz, 2012). There also has been an emphasis historically on institution building, strengthening the capacity of the public institutions to deliver various services such as education (Gassman, 2012). However, although philanthropy has played a role in education in the US for many years, the amount of money that is now provided to education is much larger than it has been in the past. Quinn et al. (2013) noted that "the combined asset size of approximately 76,000 grant making foundations in the United States increased from $272 billion in 1995 to $625 billion in 2012" (p. 1).

There is a growing concern that the new turn in educational philanthropy toward shifting control of public education institutions to private organizations will narrow the purpose of public education to its economic aspects and ignore the broader civic and political purposes that have historically been a part of our hopes for our public education system (Cuban, 2006; Labaree, 1997; Nelson & Joanes, 2007; Ravitch, 2010). As Saltman (2010) noted, "The commodification of the social world imperils collective public values and collective political agency as well as the public deliberation necessary for democratic governance" (p. 16).

In calling for more democratic deliberation about public policy in education and teacher education, we need to be careful, as Scott (2006) noted, not to romanticize a more traditional public policy-making process "because numerous examples abound of policy maker neglect of poor communities, wasteful public expenditures, and inefficient and ineffective use of educational resources" (p. 128).

The efforts of private foundations to shape public policy in education and teacher education are not new; what is new is the effort to disrupt and dismantle public institutions in favor of a preferred *a priori* solution of deregulation and markets in the absence of sound empirical evidence that has been subjected to a rigorous vetting process of peer review (Reckhow, 2013; Scott, 2006).

Although many of the new "ventures" in public education and teacher education are referred to as nonprofit, they receive generous tax advantages from the public and are able to outsource services to for-profit providers who are often associated with the venture organizations. Saltman (2010) discussed this "circle of privatization" in which public finances are giving control of public institutions to private interests, and public institutions for the poor are controlled more and more by private entities using public funds. Barkan (2013) estimated that "a substantial portion of the wealth—35% or more, depending on tax rates—has been diverted from the public treasury, where voters would have determined its use" (p. 48).

The New Schools Venture Fund and the Disruption of the Teacher Education Market

> "Well beyond its financial investment, New Schools has helped shape the ideas that brought RGSE [Relay Graduate School of Education] into being and continues to be supportive in creating the field in which we operate," said Norm Atkins, RGSE's Co-founder and President. "New Schools funded the charter school movement, and now it's playing a key role in teacher preparation."
>
> *(NSVF, n.d.-c)*

The NSVF was founded and developed in 1998 by social entrepreneur Kim Smith and venture capitalists John Doerr and Brook Byers (Horn & Libby, 2011).[4] According to its 2012 annual report, NSVF ventures have operated in 331 schools that enroll 130,500 students (83 percent of whom live in low-income situations). The report also states that 35,000 students have been taught by teachers trained by their ventures, the equivalent of the numbers of students in the largest school districts in the nation. Finally, the report states that it has raised $248 million since its founding (NSVF, 2012a).

The NSVF has been a major player in the K-12 charter school movement, investing mainly in established charter management organizations that have included ASPIRE, the Achievement Network, KIPP, Match Teacher Residency,

Rocketship, Uncommon Schools, and the Academy for Urban School Leadership (AUSL), which runs "turnaround schools" in Chicago. The NSVF's work in "disrupting" K–12 education brought it and its recently departed CEO, Ted Mitchell, acclaim from *Forbes* magazine.[5] In 2012, *Forbes* named the NSVF one of its top two choices for philanthropically minded donors and put Ted Mitchell on its list of the top 15 "education disruptors."

Although the NSVF's role in teacher preparation has been relatively minor to date, it has funded a number of the most visible "early-entry" programs in which much of teacher preparation is completed while they are teachers of record (Grossman & Loeb, 2008), including Teach for America, The New Teacher Project, and Relay Graduate School of Education, as well as a residency program for Match charter schools. The NSVF has also funded the Urban Teacher Center, which prepares teachers for charter and public schools in Baltimore and Washington, DC. The goal of the NSVF's investments has been to promote deregulation and privatization in K–12 teacher and leader education so that there will be room for the new programs it funds.

In teacher education, the NSVF has adopted the mantra that the college and university system needs to be profoundly disrupted. It has promoted the belief that current teacher education programs create unnecessary barriers to entering the teaching profession by focusing too much on what is viewed as unnecessary educational theory (e.g., Hess, 2009; Matthews, 2010). The teacher education ventures supported by the NSVF have focused on making teacher education more clinically based and preparing teachers for the "gritty realities" of teaching. These schools use an accountability model that requires candidates to demonstrate that they can raise their students' standardized test scores as a completion benchmark. According to former NSVF staffer Jonathan Schorr (2013),[6]

> The new generation of teacher education programs offers new solutions to an old problem and are committed not to fixing ed schools, but to reinventing them. Most emerge not from universities, but from autonomous, typically nonprofit organizations. They move the locus for much of their training to the school building, aiming to be more practical and clinical in approach than their traditional forbears.
>
> *(p. 5)*

The Role of New Schools Venture Fund in the GREAT Act

> New Schools aims to seed a market of autonomous, outcomes-oriented teacher preparation organizations, and set a new standard for teacher preparation with student learning at the center. ... Our policy advocacy work supports this effort by advancing public policy that helps to create demand and provide support and funding for performance-based teacher preparation.
>
> *(NSVF, n.d.-b)*

The move to create a vibrant market for high quality teacher training took an important step today.

(*NSVF, 2012b*)

To further the goal of creating a market in teacher education by reducing the role of university teacher education programs, two staff of the NSVF, together with two other reform leaders, helped develop and promote a particular piece of legislation that will potentially have a major impact on the nature of teacher education in the US. These efforts to disrupt the teacher education market and "create the space for innovation" (NSVF, 2012b) occurred in March 2011. These individuals came together with several sympathetic legislators and their staff in Washington, DC to discuss ways to further the deregulation of teacher education. These four people are: Norm Atkins, the founder of Teacher U/Relay Graduate School of Education; Tim Knowles, the director of the Urban Education Institute at the University of Chicago; Julie Mikuta, who led the Learning to Teach Fund for the NSVF until recently moving to the Schusterman Family Foundation[7]; and Ben Riley, a staffer at the NSVF.

The result of these conversations was a legislative initiative cosponsored by Colorado Senator Michael Bennett (D), Tennessee's Lamar Alexander (R), Maryland's Barbara Mikulski (D), and Mark Kirk (R) of Illinois. This bill, the Growing Excellent Achievement Training Academies for Teachers and Principals Act (GREAT Act), would establish state-based competitive grant programs to create charter teacher and principal preparation programs called *academies* that would be free of many of the state regulations that are used to monitor the quality of teacher education programs. This bill was included as a part of the federal education or No Child Left Behind (NCLB) reauthorization in both houses of Congress that was not acted on in the 112th Congress.

On May 23, 2013, the GREAT Act was reintroduced in both the Senate and House of Representatives in the 113th Congress by two bipartisan groups of representatives and senators. The charter teacher preparation programs that would result from the passage of these bills in Congress would be required to prepare teachers to serve in "high needs" areas and hard-to-staff subjects. Additionally, these programs would have the following characteristics: (1) rigorous selection based on the perceived potential to be an effective teacher; (2) hands-on clinical training that will prepare teachers to be effective from their very first day on the job; and (3) a program completion requirement standard that requires candidates to demonstrate their ability to improve student academic achievement.

A key element of the legislation is that states and state authorizers of the charter programs must agree to free these programs of "unnecessary input-based regulations" that currently exist to monitor the quality of teacher preparation programs, including the current requirement in some states that all programs be nationally accredited. Education schools can apply to be classified as charter programs or academies and receive the money that these programs would be granted by states.

The logic here is very similar to the strategy that has been used by the Obama administration in the over $4 billion Race to the Top (RTT) competition. States will be able to compete for federal funds to support charter teacher academies if they agree to policy conditions that are supportive of the market-driven reforms favored by the administration. According to Crowe (2011), this strategy was very successful in getting states to change their laws in ways that supported a market-based approach, such as allowing non-university programs to operate within their borders. It should be noted that Joanne Weiss, former chief operating officer of the NSVF and the former chief of staff for Secretary of Education Arne Duncan, directed the initial RTT competition.[8]

A letter dated June 21, 2011 was circulated to selected groups and individuals across the county to seek endorsements for the GREAT Act. Among its advocates are organizations that have been supportive of the NSVF's agenda and in some cases have received investment funds from the NSVF. These include a number of major charter management organizations, like Green Dot, KIPP, Aspire, and Match; teacher education programs like Teach for America, The New Teacher Project, the Urban Teacher Center, Boston Teacher Residency, Academy for Urban School Leadership, and Relay Graduate School of Education; educational advocacy organizations such as Democrats for Education Reform, Stand for Children, and the Education Trust; and various individuals and units, such as Karen Symms Gallagher, the dean of the Rossier School of Education at the University of Southern California; the Johns Hopkins School of Education; Jane Hannaway of the Urban Institute; and Jean Claude Brizard, the former CEO of Chicago Public Schools.[9] The NSVF spent $102,000 lobbying for charter schools, the GREAT Act, and teacher preparation in 2011 and 2012 (The Center for Responsive Politics, n.d.). It is not clear from the record how much of this money went to support the teacher and principal preparation bill.

It is very clear that the NSVF is seeking to position its current and future ventures in teacher education as the prototypes to be scaled up once the GREAT Act passes and to use these ventures to shut down and/or mold existing university teacher education programs. "The vision is to keep expanding so that in a decade from now, 10,000 teachers in cities around the country are enrolled in an umbrella of Relays" (Caperton & Whitmire, 2012, p. 80).

Jonathan Schorr (2013), a former NSVF staffer, published an article in the *Stanford Social Innovation Review* in which the Relay Graduate School of Education was featured as the future for the field. This and other articles, such as Kronholz's (2012) piece on Relay in the journal *Education Next*, identified the program as bold and innovative, and Schorr (2013) claimed that Relay "has become the leading symbol of a burgeoning revolution in how America is learning to teach" (p. 2). In a College Board publication, Caperton and Whitmire (2012) asserted that Relay is "a leader in the burgeoning movement to overhaul the way America trains its teachers for work in the highest-need schools" (p. 76). Kronholz (2012) quoted Arthur Levine, a member of the board of Relay, whose 2006 report on education schools in the US was quoted by every reformer who declared university teacher education to be a failure, stating, "Relay is the model. ... It is the future" (p. 2).

Articles proclaiming Relay as bold and innovative have also appeared in the *Wall Street Journal* (Lemov, 2012) and the *New York Times* (Otterman, 2011). These and other articles and a radio broadcast on American RadioWorks (Smith, 2013) have appeared, praising the innovativeness of Relay even though even Relay's admirers have conceded that "it's too soon to tell whether the model works" (Kronholz, 2012, p. 2).

Two reasons are given by most for calling Relay a bold, innovative program: (1) its requirement that teachers must demonstrate their ability to increase student achievement on standardized tests in order to complete the program,[10] and (2) its emphasis on what is referred to as "hands on clinical training." No data have been provided about the success of Relay graduates beyond personal testimonials such as:

> Many also told me that Relay's lessons have changed their classroom culture. "The culture went from being compliant to being invested," said Max Silverstein, a Penn State business major now teaching in an early childhood classroom at Newark Legacy charter school. I heard the same thing from Alonte Johnson, a Morehouse College English major who is teaching middle school English at Kings Collegiate Center School in Brooklyn. A few days earlier, his students designed a seating chart that paired the better and slower readers. "The environment is more interdependent instead of everyone working for me," he said.
>
> *(Kronholz, 2012, p. 6)[11]*

A video presentation of a seminar at the University of Michigan by Brent Maddin, the "provost" of Relay, on the program's development and content[12] does not indicate attention to any existing peer-reviewed research in teacher education in the development of the program and indicates a strong emphasis in the curriculum on ensuring that its teachers master the classroom management strategies compiled by Relay faculty member Doug Lemov (Lemov, 2010). Lemov is also the managing director of Uncommon Schools, one of the three charter school networks involved in the founding of Relay. Otterman (2011) noted that Lemov's work is the backbone of instruction at Teacher U, which evolved into Relay.

Lemov's (2010) strategies are based on his own observations and conversations with teachers and administrators in various charter schools that he claims are high performing. By any reasonable standard, these strategies do not possess the kind of rigorous scientific warrant that is being called for in teacher education curriculum (Pianta, 2011). In fact, there is substantial evidence demonstrating the negative effects on students living in poverty of an obsessive pursuit of higher test scores in "no excuses" environments, such as when the curriculum is stripped down to focus primarily on drill and practice for test taking (Lipman, 2004; McNeil, 2000; Nichols & Berliner, 2007; Valenzuela, 2005).

> You can prep students for a standardized test, get a bump in scores, yet not be providing a very good education. The end result is the replication of a troubling pattern in American schooling: poor kids get an education of skills and routine, a lower tier education, while students in more affluent districts get a robust course of study.
>
> *(Rose, 2013, p. 13)*

Beyond the media blitz promoting Relay, the most obvious effort of the NSVF to position its own ventures to expand and grow as soon as the GREAT Act becomes law has been its announcement of Learning to Teach Entrepreneur in Residence Program (NSVF, n.d.-a), developed in partnership with Teach for America. In this program, which began in the summer of 2013, the NSVF funds two TFA alumni or teams of TFA alumni to spend 6–10 months "laying the groundwork for a new organization that will prepare teachers for schools in low-income communities" (p. 1). The NSVF proudly proclaims that it

> is aiming to profoundly disrupt the current teacher preparation market by unleashing talent in growing bold, innovative solutions where the primary focus is on developing new teachers who are able to make student growth of at least one year from their first year as a classroom teacher.
>
> *(p. 1)*

The entrepreneurs will receive assistance from the NSVF and Teach for America in developing their ventures (program models) and will be able to learn

> "from other pioneers" (other founders and funders) in the field by spending time with New Schools existing portfolio organizations like the Relay Graduate School of Education, New Teacher Center, the Urban Teacher Center, Match Charter Sposato School of Education/Match Teacher Residency.
>
> *(p. 1)*

Another effort by the NSVF to legitimate its ventures in teacher education and position itself and its ventures to develop and grow in influence in the field is its formation in 2009—with support from the Carnegie Corporation and the Carnegie Foundation for the Advancement of Teaching and, later, from the Gates Foundation—of a Learning to Teach Community of Practice. This community of practice involves about 40 teacher education programs, including those situated in education schools at Stanford University, the University of Michigan, the

University of Southern California, and the University of Washington, and what are referred to as "entrepreneurial" programs such as Relay, the Boston Teacher Residency, the Academy for Urban School Leadership Residency, Match Teacher Residency, The New Teacher Project, and TFA (NSVF, 2011).

The NSVF has also partnered with the School of Education at the University of Michigan to form TeachingWorks, an organization that brings together entrepreneurial and university programs identified on the TeachingWorks website as "leading innovators across the country who are engaged in major redesign of teacher training and beginning teacher support" (TeachingWorks, n.d.). TeachingWorks holds regular seminars at the University of Michigan, where leaders of the various member programs present aspects of their works (NSVF, n.d.-d).

Although there is nothing wrong *per se* with bringing together teacher educators from a variety of different programs to share practices and learn from one another, many entrepreneurial programs are linked to a movement that aims to reduce or eliminate public oversight of teacher preparation and to create a market economy in teacher education in the US rather than investing in building greater quality and capacity in the now largely public teacher education system. Although both sets of programs share a concern with teaching teachers how to enact teaching practices that, according to alleged evidence, will support desired student learning outcomes, the university and entrepreneurial programs often have very different visions of the role of teacher for which individuals are being prepared and regarding the measures of teaching success. Entrepreneurial programs like Relay are designed in part to prepare teachers for "no excuses" charter and turnaround schools that emphasize increasing student test scores as the major goal.[13]

Conversely, some university programs that are under attack have attempted to link the preparation of teachers to supporting teacher candidates' abilities to enact "high-leverage" teaching practices to teach particular subject matter content and to a broader view of the teaching role. These programs focus on preparing teachers who are able to provide students with access to a rich curriculum that includes a focus on understanding, critical thinking, and the application of knowledge to real-life contexts (Zeichner, 2012). Market-based solutions and the no-excuses schools that are a central part of venture capital and big philanthropy's approach to educational reform are staffed mostly by those prepared in the entrepreneurial programs and exclusively serve children living in poverty. In these no-excuses, stripped-down versions of schools, there is substantial evidence of the narrowing of the curriculum (Berliner, 2011) and of limiting students' opportunities to interact with knowledge in meaningful and genuine ways (e.g., Cuban, 2012; Goodman, 2013; Orfield & Frankenberg, 2013) by engaging in a "pedagogy of poverty" (Haberman, 1991).

One argument put forth by some faculty in education schools involved with the NSVF is that getting involved with the group will create potential opportunities to influence members and educate them about the field they seek to transform but often know little about. We believe that this conviction is illusory and that, in the end, entrepreneurial programs will benefit from the status of research universities like Stanford, Michigan, and Washington, but that they will allow little influence on their policy agendas. This belief was confirmed by a session at the 2012 New Schools Annual Summit, which attracts funders and reformers from throughout the nation: "Building Better Teachers: How to Start a Teacher Education Program." This session included participants from several entrepreneurial programs (Aspire, Match, and AUSL teacher residencies and Relay) but not a single university teacher educator, although a number were in attendance.

One thing that the education schools can potentially gain from linking up with the NSVF and programs like the ones it funds is access to some of the enormous amount of money that has accumulated in the entrepreneurial sector. Given the deep cuts that states have made in public universities in recent years and the limited degrees of freedom that education schools have to raise tuition (e.g., Lyall & Sell, 2006; Newfield, 2008), many public education schools have been put in the position of having to find new revenues to replace the lost state support. TeachingWorks' partnership with the NSVF led to an NSVF investment of $100,000 in 2012 (NSVF, n.d.-d).

In an *Education Week* article titled "Teacher-Prep Programs Zero in on Effective Practice" (Sawchuck, 2013), several teacher education programs (Match & Boston Teacher Residencies, Relay, and the University of Washington elementary teacher education program) are lumped together because of their common focus on providing strong school-based clinical experiences for teacher candidates. In these programs, teacher candidates learn to enact a set of teaching and classroom management practices that allegedly will help them be successful in the settings for which they are being prepared to teach. These programs accomplish this by repeated practice of these teaching strategies in real classrooms with careful mentoring.

What is not addressed in this article or in the alliance within TeachingWorks of entrepreneurial and university programs are the very different visions of the role of teacher and what is required to teach well.[14] For example, programs like Relay place a strong emphasis on the mastery of Lemov's (2010, 2012) 49 techniques to become a champion teacher (e.g., "strong voice"). University programs typically situate the acquisition of the ability to enact high-leverage teaching practices within a vision of teachers who understand the communities in which they work and are culturally competent; who have acquired the ability to adapt their teaching to meet the constantly changing needs of their students; who have learned how to learn in and from their practice to become better at teaching over time; and who have developed an in-depth understanding of content knowledge and pedagogical practices that will promote understanding of this content and of research on learning and development, assessment, how second languages are acquired, and so on. The different ideological agendas with which these programs are associated are also ignored: One set of programs seeks to contribute to strengthening public education while the other aims to deregulate and create market competition in public education and teacher education. Underlying the push by the NSVF and others to deregulate and develop a teacher education market are the narratives that college and university teacher education has failed and that entrepreneur-designed programs are the remedy for this failure.

Has University Teacher Education Failed, and Is Educational Entrepreneurism the Answer?

> By almost any standard, many, if not most, of the nation's 1,450 schools, colleges, and departments of education are doing a mediocre job of preparing teachers for the realities of the 21st century classroom.
>
> *(A. Duncan, 2009)*

> America has a broken teacher preparation system. The majority of teachers attest to feeling ill-equipped for the classroom and leave the profession at astonishing rates.
>
> *(Knowles, 2013, p. 6)*

The mantra recited over and over by reformers in the academic literature and popular media that the university teacher education system is broken and needs to be replaced by deregulation and greater competition[15] is based on several major assertions, such as: (a) teacher education programs are not selective in whom they admit; (b) teacher educators spend too much time on theory *at the expense* of the acquisition of practical expertise; (c) teacher educators lack recent teaching experience and are not familiar with the schools for which teachers are being prepared; (d) about half of teachers leave teaching by the end of 5 years; and (e) universities do not adequately support their teacher education programs (e.g., Knowles, 2013; Kronholz, 2012; Levine, 2011).

The reform literature rarely cites any of the major peer-reviewed studies of the field sponsored by such groups as the National Research Council, the American Educational Research Association, and the National Academy of Education (Cochran-Smith & Zeichner, 2005; Darling-Hammond & Bransford, 2005; National Research Council, 2010).[16] In almost every indictment of the current system of teacher education, critics cite Arthur Levine's (2006) study of teacher education programs within education schools.

Arthur Levine's Study of Teacher Education in Education Schools

Several aspects of Levine's (2006) report should be noted in light of the extensive reference to it by critics of university teacher education who advocate for deregulation and a teacher education market. First is the lack of any evidence of the simplest test of rigor: independent peer review. Although there are elements of truth revealed in this report about weaknesses in some teacher education programs, there are a number of instances in which inadequately substantiated assertions are made that highlight the negative and, in some cases, either overstate a point or are clearly inaccurate. Take, for example, the inaccurate assertion in a statement about the alleged lack of attention to clinical experience in teacher education programs: "Students have limited clinical or fieldwork experience today in most teacher education programs; it consists only of the short time spent student teaching" (p. 39).[17]

Although this statement may have been true in the 1960s and 1970s, most states have formulated regulations over the last 30 years that require not only student teaching but also additional pre-student teaching clinical experiences. For example, according to the database compiled by the National Association of State Directors of Teacher Education and Certification (www.nasdec.net), 38 states require observation and clinical experiences prior to student teaching, and 36 states require at least 10 weeks of student teaching.

These data are confirmed by a recent report by the American Association of Colleges for Teacher Education (2013) that includes survey responses from 95 percent of its 800 institutional members. With regard to the issue of how pervasive clinical experiences are in university-sponsored teacher education programs, the report stated:

> Virtually all programs require supervised student teaching or an internship for graduation, although the required duration varies: The average bachelor's-level clinical requirement ranges from 500 to 562 total clock hours (mean = 14.50 weeks); the average master's-level clinical requirement ranges from 480 to 586 total clock hours (mean = 14.52 weeks). Preparation programs also require students to participate in early field experiences: The average bachelor's-level requirement ranges from 114 to 189 clock hours; the average master's-level requirement ranges from 111 to 164 clock hours.
>
> *(p. 9)*

A second aspect of Levine's (2006) report centers on his extreme and unsupported comments in various places that would never survive a rigorous peer-review process. For example, he asserted, "Most universities, after a barrage of reports over the past two decades on the need to strengthen teacher education did little or nothing" (p. 22).

Levine also attempted, without any grounds for doing so, to tie the alleged lack of clinical experience in programs to program graduates' dissatisfaction with their preparation programs. One element of this study was a series of surveys of university teacher education faculty, deans of education schools, graduates of university teacher education programs, and principals. Citing these surveys,[18] Levine noted,

Alumni who were critical of their teacher education programs often pointed to the price they paid later for their limited practical experience. As one of them put it, "I do not feel that I was prepared for the realities of life in a school or classroom as a teacher."

(p. 41)

Another graduate is cited in the following excerpt:

"I could talk about Carl Jung, scaffolding, cooperative learning groups (and) the advantages of constructivism," but [the graduate] had no idea about what to do when "Johnny goes nuts in the back of the class, or when Lisa comes in abused, or when Sue hasn't eaten in three days."

(p. x)

Reformers have frequently cited Levine's (2006) study as evidence that university teacher education graduates feel unprepared to teach. For example, Schorr (2013) noted, "In a seminal 2006 study by Arthur Levine, more than three in five teachers said their training left them unprepared for the classroom and principals agreed" (p. 3).

US Secretary of Education Arne Duncan (2009) also referred to Levine's (2006) surveys in his address at Teachers College, Columbia University:

As you know, the most recent comprehensive study of teacher education was carried out by Arthur Levine, President of Teachers College. ... More than 3 in 5 ed. school alums surveyed for the Levine report said that their training did not prepare them adequately for their work in the classroom.

(p. 3)

Finally, when the GREAT Act was reintroduced to the Senate and House of Representatives on May 23, 2013, both Michael Bennett (CO-D) in the Senate and Tom Petri (WI-R) in the House referred to the Levine (2006) study to help make their case for the bill. No other study or report was referred to in either presentation.

A leading study of 28 teacher training programs revealed that more than 60 percent of alumni said that they were not adequately prepared for the classroom.[19]

According to a leading study 61 percent of ed. school alumni reported that schools of education at four-year colleges did not adequately prepare their graduates for the classroom.[20]

Although the surveys in Levine's (2006) study identified some of the problems in teacher education that have been discussed in the literature for many years, it is not the only survey that has been conducted on teachers' assessments of their preparation programs. Although some of the more recent surveys also show that teachers have problems with aspects of their preparation, they also present a more positive picture than Levine's surveys. For example, a recent survey of 500 beginning teachers in the first 3 years of their careers commissioned by the American Federation of Teachers (2012), an organization that has been critical of the status quo in teacher education (American Federation of Teachers, 2012), found that "Two-thirds (66 percent) of new teachers felt completely (19 percent) or mostly (47 percent) prepared when they first started teaching while 34 percent said they felt just somewhat prepared or not prepared at all" (p. 21). This study also found that "Teachers who completed an alternative training or certification program recall feeling less prepared (only 42 percent felt completely or mostly prepared) than teachers who followed the traditional path" (p. 22).

Several other surveys of teachers that asked them to evaluate the quality of their preparation programs also show a more positive portrait of university teacher education programs than Levine's surveys, including: Eduventures' (2009) study of 1,504 teachers with 5 years or less in the field, which indicated that 78 percent of teachers felt well prepared when they entered the field; (b) the National Comprehensive Center for Teacher Quality and Public Agenda surveys of 641 first-year teachers conducted in the spring of 2007, which indicated that 80 percent of teachers felt very or somewhat prepared for teaching in their first year (Rochkind et al., 2007); and (c) a 2011 survey of 2,500 randomly selected K–12 public school teachers, which found that 65 percent of teachers rated their preparation program as excellent or very good, and another 24 percent rated it as good (Feistritzer, Griffin, & Linnajarvi, 2011).

All these surveys reveal some teacher dissatisfaction with the quality of their preparation for teaching, and none of them was independently peer reviewed. The question should be asked as to why critics of university education schools and advocates for deregulation and markets continue to cite only Levine's (2006) study and additionally only report the negative aspects of Levine's findings while ignoring the positive findings about university teacher preparation in his study and similar ones.

Despite the negative assertions made by Levine about the satisfaction of teacher education program graduates with the quality of their preparation programs, there are a number of places in the report where he noted excellence in university teacher education and noted the limited amount of responsibility that can reasonably be placed on education schools alone for the problems in public education. For example,

> It is critical to recognize that weaknesses in teacher education are not the primary reason we do not have more and better teaching. Schools and government bear a larger responsibility for low salaries ... for an absence of

teacher induction programs, low hiring standards, and poor working conditions which cause high teacher turnover.

(p. 21)

Despite these moments of more nuanced analysis, the overwhelming focus in public accounts of the report is on what are seen as negative aspects of teacher education. This negativity was picked up by the media reports of the study soon after its release, as evidenced in headlines such as, "Study Says Teacher Training is Chaotic" (Feller, 2006), "Prominent Teacher Educator Assails Field" (Honawar, 2006), "Report Critical of Training of Teachers" (Finder, 2006), and "No Teacher Left Behind" (2006).

Theory vs. Practice in Teacher Education

One major aspect of the critique of the role of universities in educating teachers is the construction of stereotypes about the nature of these programs, in which they are seen as emphasizing theory at the expense of preparation in effective teaching practices. Caperton and Whitmire's (2012) discussion of what they saw as the positive aspects of the Relay Graduate School of Education's teacher preparation program clearly reveals this caricature of university teacher education: "Gone are the courses on education theory and history with no practical bearing. ... Professors are not lofty academics, they are accomplished practitioners in the field" (p. 77).

Relay provost Brent Maddin said "The key is not to weed out theory, but rather to distill it down to essential points for the extremely busy teacher" (p. 83).

The image of university teacher preparation presented in the reform literature is of preparation programs with instructors who have not been teachers for many years and who are out of touch with the complexities of today's public schools. In contrast, the reform-oriented teacher education programs like Relay are portrayed as intensely focused on drilling teachers in the mastery of particular teaching and classroom management practices. For example, a class at Relay was described as follows:

> The classroom lessons are heavily scripted. During the first three minutes of the Engaging Everybody class, for example, the Relay students are to report on how often they're using the four techniques. The script then lists four paragraphs of narrative and questions for the Relay professor to pose over the next four minutes. For five minutes after that, there's a review, with 10 questions for the professor to ask, and then a suggested transition: "All right, our minds are fresh on today's content and we're ready to move." Then there's a guided 7-minute guided "table discussion," 5 minutes of classroom discussion, 11 minutes of partner feedback, and so on.
>
> *(Kronholz, 2012, p. 4)*

The caricature of university teacher education programs common in the reform literature ignores the growing presence of teachers and former teachers with recent experience who have assumed instructional and coaching roles in teacher education programs (Zeichner, 2010), the shift over the last two decades to conducting more teacher preparation in schools, and the shift over many years toward a competency and standards- or practice-based approach that focuses on the acquisition of particular teaching strategies (Zeichner, 2005, 2012).

What's Wrong with the Critique of Education Schools

The peer-reviewed literature on teacher education shows variable quality in the preparation of teachers. Although there is some truth to the criticisms of the reformers, their analyses greatly oversimplify a much more complex situation.

To hold teacher education up as solely responsible for the problem of teacher quality and retention in urban schools, as much of the reform literature and the introduction of the GREAT Act in the 113th Congress have done, ignores a substantial amount of evidence that ties, for example, teachers' learning and attrition to the conditions in their workplace (e.g., Ingersoll, 2003; Johnson, Kraft, & Papay, 2012). To only look at which teachers can raise standardized test scores at a given moment in time, and to ignore the in-service realities and problems with retaining teachers, as well as variation in different communities' access to experienced teachers, flies in the face of research that has documented the relevance of teachers' working conditions and teacher experience to student learning (Ronfeldt, Loeb, & Wyckoff, 2013) and the high cost of teacher turnover (NCTAF, 2007). Even advocates of deregulation like John Chubb acknowledge the benefits of research demonstrating the importance of teacher experience when they make statements like the following: "research is very clear that teachers become more effective in raising student achievement with classroom experience" (2012, p. 66).

Those who criticize the academic qualifications of the graduates of university teacher education programs ignore the evidence that shows the improvements made over time in the academic competence of teacher education students/teachers (Goldhaber & Walch, 2013), particularly at the secondary level (e.g., Gitomer, 2007). Such comparisons also ignore the challenges posed by the size of the teaching force in the US (about 3.6 million) versus other countries like Finland and Singapore, with small teaching forces that only admit individuals from among their top secondary school graduates to teacher education programs (Tucker, 2011). Although there are clearly problems in some programs with regard to the academic qualifications of teacher candidates (Zumwalt & Craig, 2005), a general indictment of university teacher education in this regard seems unwarranted. Finally, to indict teacher educators in university programs as being uniformly out of touch with current classroom conditions ignores the growing presence of hybrid roles in teacher education that have engaged more practicing teachers in instruction in university preparation programs (Zeichner, 2010; Zeichner & Bier, 2013).

Advocates of disrupting the teacher education system frequently call for only admitting individuals from the top tiers of secondary school performance to teacher education, and they point to the strong academic caliber of the TFA and other early-entry program recruits who mostly do not continue in teaching beyond the first few years (Donaldson & Johnson, 2011). They claim that it is possible for us to staff our nation's schools with academically stronger individuals if we increase our reliance on these programs that encourage individuals to teach only for a few years.

Although it may be less expensive in the short run to depend on a teaching force with a larger percentage of inexpensive and temporary teachers to be replaced when they leave with similar teachers, using this as a strategy for improving teacher quality is problematic given the research on the negative effects of teacher attrition on student learning (Ronfeldt et al., 2013). This strategy becomes even more problematic when we consider that these short-term teachers work almost exclusively in schools attended by urban and rural students in communities greatly impacted by poverty (Peske & Haycock, 2006).

It is clear that there is a need for much improvement in the college and university system of teacher education and that state program approval and national program accreditation have failed to improve or eliminate some weak programs (National Research Council, 2010). The need to improve the system does not mean that many improvements have not been and are not currently being made and that the solution is to turn the job of preparing teachers over to the private sector.

Are Entrepreneur-Designed Programs the Solution?

On the other side, the claims about the superiority of the programs like Relay that have been funded by venture philanthropy over university programs are based on an acceptance of the claim that these programs have proven success at producing graduates who have demonstrated the ability to raise the standardized test scores of their pupils at least a year. Advocates also sometimes point to some evidence that standardized test scores have gone up, and more students than before have gone to college in the charter schools where teachers prepared by the entrepreneurial programs have taught.

The educational entrepreneurs who are brought in by venture philanthropists to develop and run start-up teacher education programs are referred to in glowing terms in the literature on educational entrepreneurship. For example, Hess (2006) referred to them as "pioneers," "visionary thinkers," "the engines of progress," "imaginative, creative and talented," and these assertions are taken at face value in calls to deregulate and create a market economy in US teacher education.[21]

The dearth of research demonstrating the superiority of entrepreneurial programs supported by the NSVF like Relay, Match Teacher Residency, and the Urban Teaching Center in the preparation of teachers, even by their own standard of quality based in student standardized test scores, raises serious questions about the warrant for these claims. Saying over and over again that these programs are innovative, groundbreaking, and bold does not make it true in the absence of solid research evidence. It is ironic that college and university teacher education is criticized for not being able to put forth evidence demonstrating the efficacy of its programs, when those who engage in these criticisms are unable to do so themselves.

Even in some cases in which it can be shown that students in charter schools staffed by graduates of these entrepreneurial programs have improved test score results and graduation rates, it has not been demonstrated that the nature and quality of the teacher education programs have been responsible for these gains (see Zeichner & Conklin, 2005, for a discussion of this issue). Although the evidence shows that some charters have outperformed public schools in raising standardized test scores, most of them have not done so (CREDO, 2009, 2013).

Further concerns are raised about the ethics of this approach when we read statements like the following in the literature on educational entrepreneurship:

> The expectation is not that the typical venture will improve upon the status quo, only that some will do so. Some ideas won't pan out and many will fail.
>
> *(Hess, 2006, p. 3)*

> Both philanthropists and the broader public must accept that it is ok for investments to fail, so long as the failure is in pursuit of results-oriented solutions.
>
> *(Hess, 2006, p. 253)*

We must not forget that these entrepreneurial solutions for the ills of teacher education have direct consequences exclusively for children living in poverty and not for the children of the entrepreneurs and middle- and upper-middle-class children generally. This situation has negative consequences for the quality of the society as well, given the consequences of creating a stripped-down and inferior set of schools for many students living in poverty. We are comfortable in asserting that very few, if any, entrepreneurs and other advocates for teacher education programs like Relay send their own children and grandchildren to the schools that they refer to as tremendously innovative, schools that are staffed by teachers who enter teaching through these entrepreneurial programs. Henig, Hula, Orr, and Pedescleaux's (2001) study of school reform in Baltimore, Detroit, and Atlanta supports this assertion. We do not think it is acceptable to use the children who can least afford to experience diminished opportunities for access to a rich learning experience in schools as guinea pigs for the entrepreneurial revolution in teacher education.

The Uncritical Reproduction of the Narrative of Derision and Salvation through Entrepreneurism by the Media

In addition to the uncritical promotion of entrepreneurial teacher education programs like Relay, described earlier, the local and national media have taken up, largely in an uncritical way, the narrative about the failure of university teacher education that is being promoted by groups like the New Schools Venture Fund and Democrats for Education Reform—groups that are shaping teacher education policy in the Obama administration and in the current Congress. For example, on October 7, 2011, the *Seattle Times* lead editorial "Refocusing the Teacher Quality Debate"[22] praised the main element in Duncan's plan for teacher education accountability that requires the value-added evaluation of teacher education institutions, and then reprinted the following comment made by a teacher educator in a forum in Washington DC sponsored by the American Enterprise Institute. This quote was probably taken by the *Seattle Times* from the Democrats for Education Reform white paper *Ticket to Teach* or from the inclusion of the quote in articles in the *New York Times* and *US News and World Report*.[23]

> A growing chorus of critics, including prominent education professors, are amplifying concerns about weaknesses in teacher-prep programs. The director of teacher education at the Harvard Graduate School of Education was quoted on a New York Times online forum as saying that of the nation's 1,300 graduate teacher training programs only about 100 were doing a competent job. The rest could be shut down tomorrow, said Harvard's Kay Merseth.
>
> *(p. A13)*

This type of derogatory depiction of university teacher education programs has been repeated over and over again in local newspapers around the country. It does not seem to matter that there are not 1,300 graduate teacher education programs in the country or that Arne Duncan's (2011) assertion in his blueprint for teacher education that "only 50 percent of current teacher candidates received supervised clinical training" (p. 5) was inaccurate. It seems that people can say whatever they want or call things whatever they want, and their assertions are taken at face value. When the National Council on Teacher Quality issues a report on university-based teacher education, it is covered by the national media (e.g., Levin, 2011) as if it has been vetted through an independent peer review process. It does not seem to matter that these reports have not been reviewed independently.

Conclusion

The future of the public system of teacher education in the US is in doubt as the movement to deregulate and privatize the preparation of teachers gains resources, policy support, and momentum. Teaching and learning are clearly not at acceptable levels in all US public schools given the undeniable existence of the "education debt" that continues to affect many students living in poverty. In addition, even though some university teacher education programs have been long committed to self-improvement and have been engaged in high-quality preparation for many years (e.g., Darling-Hammond, 2006), overall, things are not okay in the world of business as usual in teacher education. Although there is no disagreement that both public schooling and teacher education need to be greatly improved, we disagree with advocates of deregulation and privatization in teacher education about the causes of our problems, whether university teacher education programs have been changing and improving, and how to address the problems.

There is no evidence in our view that the entrepreneurial teacher education programs that have been touted as the future of teacher education are the bold, innovative, and pioneering entities that they are claimed to be. Merely requiring teachers to demonstrate their ability to raise standardized test scores to complete a program is not the kind of measure of teaching performance that we should use to assess the readiness of teachers to be successful in the classroom. There are other, more meaningful ways to assess the performance of teachers, including attention to teacher performance and student learning (Darling-Hammond, 2010; Feuer, Floden, Chudowsky, & Ahn, 2013; Zeichner, 2011). Just because we hear endlessly that these entrepreneurial programs are revolutionary does not make them so. The programs themselves are too new to have long-term retention data or data about the quality of graduates' teaching over time.

Reducing the measure of success in schooling to how much standardized test scores can be raised at a given moment in time or even over the 3-year minimum period required for sound value-added analysis, only for students living in poverty, while we continue to seek a richer and broader education in the arts, humanities, critical thinking, and so on for middle-class children is ethically unacceptable.[24]

One of the biggest flaws in the arguments of advocates for deregulation and privatization in teacher education is their claim, implicit or otherwise, that educational interventions alone can address our education debt and the serious differences in opportunities to interact with knowledge in school in meaningful ways that exist for students of different backgrounds. Although improvements in teaching, schooling, and teacher education are a part of the solution, we must also address the numerous consequences of poverty for many students in our public education system. Without doing this, any solution to our educational problems will fall short of success (Carter & Welner, 2013; Noguera, 2011).

We are on a course to dismantle and replace the college and university system of teacher education in the US that continues to prepare most of the nation's teachers. This would be a serious mistake in our view. Among countries that have performed strongly on international comparisons of student achievement, none has a free-market system of teacher education, nor have any of these nations utilized the kind of deregulation and privatization that is being put into place in the US. On the contrary, a strong university system of teacher education is a prerequisite for a strong system of public schooling in most high-performing countries (Darling-Hammond & Liebermann, 2012).

Advocates of deregulation and markets frequently complain about the high cost of university teacher education and the waste of public resources. Most of the federal contributions to teacher education in public universities are in financial aid to students and not in funds to develop innovation in programs. For example, Arne Duncan (2009) has stated that "all told, the federal government provides $4 billion a year in Pell grants and federal loans to support students and our university teacher education programs." (p. 2) Over the last decade or more, there have been severe cuts in the state contributions to our public universities that have undermined efforts to innovate in teacher education programs and make them more connected and responsive to the needs of public schools (Newfield, 2008).

The Obama administration, which has largely been supportive of deregulation and developing a free market in teacher education, has taken an ironic stance by calling for lowering of standards in federal rules for the preparation of teachers while calling for raising standards for K-12 pupils through its advocacy of the new Common Core Curriculum.

We agree with Welner (2011), who has argued that

> educational opportunities should be one of our most precious public goods. While public education does provide important private benefits to children and their families, it also lies at the center of our societal well-being. Educational opportunities should therefore never be distributed by market forces because markets exist to create inequalities—they thrive by creating winner and losers.
>
> *(p. 40)*

As an alternative to the market-based solutions to problems of teacher education that we criticize in this article, we have suggested here and elaborated elsewhere elements of what we have referred to as a transformation agenda for teacher education. We believe, based both on empirical research (e.g., Darling-Hammond & Bransford, 2005) and a belief in a strong public sector, that these changes will better address the enduring the problems of the field and will be more likely than market-based approaches to provide a high-quality education and teachers for everyone's children (Zeichner, 2009, 2010; Zeichner & Payne, 2013; Zeichner, Payne, & Brayko, 2015).

These strategies build on the work of John Goodlad and many others who have worked for many years for significant transformation of teacher education in the US (Goodlad, 1991). They emphasize: (a) more shared responsibility for preparing teachers among universities or other program operators, schools, and local communities; (b) situating the process of learning to teach more strongly in relation to the kinds of settings for which individuals are being prepared to teach, while preparing teachers with content and professional knowledge as well as knowledge of and commitment to the communities in which they work; (c) focusing on preparing teachers to be able to enact teaching practices that evidence suggests will help provide opportunities for students to interact with knowledge in authentic ways and develop understanding; and (d) strengthening accountability systems for teacher education programs in ways that involve the assessment of teachers' abilities to promote student learning beyond their ability to raise standardized test scores.

Finally, and most important, it is crucial that the agendas and activities of venture philanthropists like those connected to the New Schools Venture Fund and their partnerships with those working in higher education be more visible to the public and scholarly communities in education so their assertions and claims can be given the same scrutiny and critique that all proposals deserve in a democratic society. This is particularly important when the proposals involve the shifting of the control of the largely public system of teacher education to private entities.

Since the beginnings of philanthropy in the US, there has always been public skepticism about its possible negative effects on democratic deliberation about public policy.

> ...at no time in American history—not even now, when private wealth and its creators are so effusively celebrated—have these nonprofit institutions been unshadowed by public skepticism and distrust. Inevitably, private initiatives in the public interest, whether promoted by wealthy individuals or by groups of citizens in support of causes that do not command majority support, are—and always have been—problematic among people with a foundational commitment to democratic governance and principles of equality.
>
> *(Hall, 2013, p. 139)*

Although he is a strong supporter of market-based approaches to education reform, Hess (2012) of the American Enterprise Institute has called for a new level of civic responsibility and willingness to embrace criticism and feedback with regard to philanthropic efforts to improve education. He criticizes the lack of openness to dialogue and criticism among the major foundations that have been steering education policy and reform and concluded,

> Hard-hitting public exchanges—not private confabs—are the most effective forums for surfacing overlooked challenges, informing courses of action, or reframing the context in which decisions are made. The groups convened by

foundations tend to include, naturally enough, friends, allies, and grantees. These aren't the folks likely to offer a fresh take on strategy or to challenge comfortable assumptions—especially given the sensible disinclination of grantees to offend benefactors or of reformers to offend the engine funding their cause.

(p. 5)

In addition to the invitation-only annual summits sponsored by the NSVF and similar gatherings sponsored by other entrepreneurial groups and by university teacher education organizations, we all should be seeking actively and with great humility to support a genuine public dialogue about the wisdom of applying market-based and other solutions to the problems of teacher education. Given the size of the US teaching force, at over 3.5 million, it is unlikely that any system of teacher education can be developed that does not include significant involvement of the nation's colleges and universities. The problems of public education and teacher education are too important to be permitted to operate without rigorous vetting of claims about innovative practices and a trenchant public dialogue.

Notes

1 The reformers often refer to teacher education as "teacher training." Teacher education is also referred to in this community as a component of "human capital development" (Corcoran, 2009) or "strategic talent management" (Odden, 2013).
2 According to Smith and Peterson (2006), "It is important to understand that entrepreneurs have a vision for a better way of doing things; thinking beyond the constraints of current rules and resources" (p. 22).
3 Also see this video clip from the 2013 meeting of Jeb Bush's Foundation for Excellence in Education on "revolutionizing America's teacher preparation programs": www. youtube.com/watch?v=Odt_I3RUVW0
4 Kim Smith, along with another key former NSVF staffer, Jonathan Schorr, was also part of the founding team of Teach for America.
5 Mitchell has recently been confirmed to become the Undersecretary of Education in the US Department of Education, a job that makes him the official in the US government responsible for overseeing higher education.
6 Schorr has joined the communications team in the US Department of Education.
7 Julie Mikuta is also a former TFA teacher, vice president for alumni affairs for TFA, and the former chair of the board of the education advocacy group Stand for Children.
8 James Shelton, a former NSVF and Gates Foundation staffer, directed the Office of Innovation and Improvement, the entity that runs the other major Education Department competition, the Innovation in Education Grants. Shelton is currently the Acting Deputy US Secretary of Education.
9 Julie Mikuta, formerly a key member of the NSVF and one of the key players in pushing the GREAT Act was a visiting Fellow at Johns Hopkins Education School in

2011. This School of Education, which did not publicly support the original bill, signed on in support of the bill after Mikuta's time at Hopkins.

10 All the teachers in Relay are teachers of record fully responsible for classrooms, and although they are classified by federal law as "highly qualified," they are uncertified; see www.washingtonpost.com/blogs/answer-sheet/wp/2013/08/27/how-the-public-is-deceived-about-highly-qualified-teachers/)

11 After our search of the literature for studies on the impact and effectiveness of the program did not turn up any studies, we confirmed on May 8, 2013 with Relay's research director Billie Gastic that there was no existing research on the impact of the program at that time.

12 See www.teachingworks.org/training/seminar-series/event/detail/relay-graduate-school-of-education.

13 See Goodman (2013) for an example of some negative consequences of an extreme emphasis on raising test scores rather than a broader focus on learning.

14 Also see this NSVF-produced video on "performance based" teacher education. http://vimeo.com/74750074

15 NSVF staffer Ben Riley referred to teacher education as "the most retrograde sector of education" in his remarks to the American Association of Colleges for Teacher Education in February 2013 (www.aacte.org).

16 One exception to this is in a July 24, 2012, hearing on alternative teacher certification in the House Education and Workforce Committee, in which reference was made twice to an AERA peer-reviewed synthesis of the research on alternative pathways to teaching (Zeichner & Conklin, 2005). In these references to this review by the chair of the committee and one of the witnesses who was asked to testify, the review was inaccurately portrayed as concluding that there is no difference in the competence of teachers prepared in traditional university programs and alternative programs. In fact, one of the main conclusions of the review was that the poor quality of much of the peer-reviewed research prevented definitive conclusions about the efficacy of pathways into teaching (Education and the Workforce Committee, 2012).

17 Duncan (2011) went further in misrepresenting the reality in university teacher education by asserting, "Only 50 percent of current teacher candidates receive supervised clinical training" (p. 5).

18 It is not clear from the information that Levine made publicly available whether those who actually responded to the surveys—53 percent of the deans, 40 percent of the faculty, and 34 percent of alumni—were representative of the population surveyed. No claims were made about the representativeness of the sample of principals. In addition, inadequate information was provided about how the specific data collected in the case studies were gathered and how the examples from the case studies cited in the report were warranted by these data.

19 www.bennet.senate.gov/newsroom/press/release/bennet-introduc-es-bipartisan-bill-to-create-academies-that-prepare-great-teachers-and-principals

20 See http://petri.house.gov/press-releasepetri-polis-introduce-bipartisan-bill-improve-teacher-and-principal-preparation

21 See this brief video of NSVF staffer Julie Mikuta talking about the transformation of teacher education by increasing entrepreneurial programs: http://vimeo.com/74750074

22 Retrieved from www.seattletimes.com/opinion/refocusing-the-teacher-quality-debate/ on October 7, 2011.
23 See http://roomfordebate.blogs.nytimes.com/2009/08/16/education-de-grees-and-teachers-pay/ and http://www.usnews.com/ education/blogs/on-education/2009/03/25/what-you-should-consider-before-education-graduate-school
24 This same ethical argument was made in the latter part of the nineteenth century with regard to philanthropic efforts to support the Hampton-Tuskegee program of industrial training for Blacks in the US (Anderson, 1988).

References

American Association of Colleges for Teacher Education. (2013). *The changing teacher preparation profession: A report from AACTE's professional education data system* (PEDS). Washington, DC: Author.
American Federation of Teachers. (2012). *Raising the bar: Aligning and elevating teacher preparation and the teaching profession.* Washington, DC: Author.
Anderson, J. D. (1988). *Education of Blacks in the South: 1860–1935.* Chapel Hill: University of North Carolina Press.
Ball, S. (2012). Voting with dollars: Philanthropy, money, and educational policy. *Pedagogy, Culture, and Society, 20*(3), 485–491.
Barkan, J. (2011a). Firing line: The grand coalition against teachers. *Dissent.* Retrieved from www.dissentmagazine.org/online_articles/firing-linethe-grand-coalition-against-teachers
Barkan, J, (2011b). Got dough? How billionaires rule our schools. *Dissent.* Retrieved from www.dissentmagazine.org/article/got-dough-how-billionaires-rule-our-schools
Barkan, J. (2013). Big philanthropy vs. democracy: The plutocrats go to school. *Dissent.* Retrieved from https://www.dissentmagazine.org/article/plutocrats-at-work-how-big-philanthropy-undermines-democracy
Berliner, D. (2011). Rational responses to high-stakes testing: The case of curriculum narrowing and the harm that follows. *Cambridge Journal of Education, 41*(3), 287–302.
Berliner, D. (2014). Effects of inequality and poverty vs. teachers and schooling on America's youth. *Teachers College Record, 116*(1). Retrieved from www.tcrecord.org/content.asp?contentid=16889
Berry, B., Montgomery, D., Curtis, R., Hernandez, M., Wurtzel, J., & Snyder, J. (2008). *Creating and sustaining urban teacher residencies: A new way to recruit, prepare and retain effective teachers in high needs districts.* Washington, DC: Center for Teacher Quality. The Aspen Institute.
Blume, H. (2013). $20 million Walton donation will boost Teach for America in L.A. *Los Angeles Times.* Retrieved from www.latimes.com/local/lanow/la-me-ln-20-million-walton-tfa-20130730-story.html
Boyd, D., Grossman, P., Lankford, H., Loeb, S., & Wyckoff, J. (2008). Surveying the landscape of teacher education in New York City: Constrained variation and the challenge of innovation. *Educational Evaluation and Policy Analysis, 30*(4), 319–343.
Caperton, G., & Whitmire, R. (2012). *The achievable dream.* New York, NY: The College Board.
Carnegie Corporation. (1986). *A nation prepared: Teaching for the 21st century: Report on the Taskforce on Teaching as a Profession.* Hyattsville, MD: Carnegie Forum on Education and the Economy.

Carter, P., & Welner, K. (Eds). (2013). *Closing the opportunity gap: What America must do to give every child an even chance*. Oxford: Oxford University Press.

The Center for Responsive Politics. (n.d.). New Schools Venture Fund. Retrieved from http://www.opensecrets.org/orgs/summary.php?id=D000054628

Charters, W. W., & Waples, D. (1929). *The Commonwealth Teacher-Training Study*. Chicago, IL: University of Chicago Press.

Chubb, J. (2012). *The best teachers in the world: Why we don't have them and how we could*. Palo Alto, CA: Hoover Institute Press.

Chubb, J., & Moe, T. (1990). *Politics and markets in America's schools*. Washington, DC: Brookings Institution Press.

Cochran-Smith, M., & Zeichner, K. (Eds). (2005). *Studying teacher education: The report of the American Educational Research Association Panel on Research in Teacher Education in the US* New York, NY: Routledge.

Conant, J. (1963). *The education of American teachers*. New York, NY: McGraw-Hill.

Corcoran, S. P. (2009). Human capital policy and the quality of the teacher workforce. In D. Goldhaber & J. Hannaway (Eds), *Creating a new teaching profession* (pp. 29–52). Washington, DC: Urban Institute Press.

CREDO. (2009). *Multiple choice: Charter school performance in 16 states*. Stanford, CA: Author. Retrieved from http://credo.stanford.edu/reports/MULTIPLE_CHOICE_CREDO.pdf

CREDO. (2013). *National charter school study of 2013*. Stanford, CA: Author. Retrieved from http://credo.stanford.edu/documents/NCSS%202013%20Final%20Draft.pdf

Crowe, E. (2011). *Race to the Top and teacher preparation*. Washington, DC: Center for American Progress.

Cuban, L. (2006). Educational entrepreneurs redux. In F. M. Hess (Ed.), *Educational entrepreneurship: Realities, challenges, possibilities* (pp. 243–260). Cambridge, MA: Harvard Education Press.

Cuban, L. (2012, February 19). Are Rocketship schools the future? Part 3. Larry Cuban on school reform and classroom practice [Blog post]. Retrieved from https://larrycuban.wordpress.com/2012/02/19/are-rocketship-schools-the-future-part-3/

Darling-Hammond, L. (2006). *Powerful teacher education*. San Francisco, CA: Jossey-Bass.

Darling-Hammond, L. (2010, October). *Evaluating teacher effectiveness: How teacher performance assessments can measure and improve teaching*. Washington, DC: Center for American Progress.

Darling-Hammond, L., & Bransford, J. (Eds). (2005). *Preparing teachers for a changing world*. San Francisco, CA: Jossey-Bass.

Darling-Hammond, L., & Lieberman, A. (Eds). (2012). *Teacher education around the world: Changing policies and practices*. New York, NY: Routledge.

Democrats for Education Reform. (2011). *Ticket to teach*. Retrieved from http://blogs.edweek.org/edweek/teacherbeat/TickettoTeach_1.3.11.pdf

Donaldson, M. L., & Johnson, S. M. (2011). Teach for America teachers: How long do they teach? Why do they leave? *Phi Delta Kappan, 93*(2), 47–52.

Duncan, A. (2009, October). *Teacher preparation: Reforming the uncertain profession*. Remarks of Secretary Arne Duncan at Teachers College, Columbia University. Retrieved from http://www2.ed.gov/news/speeches/2009/10/10222009.html

Duncan, A. (2011, September). *Our future, our teachers: The Obama administration's plan for teacher education reform and improvement*. Washington, DC: US Department of Education.

Duncan, G., & Murnane, R. (Eds). (2012). *Whither opportunity: Rising inequality, schools, and children's life chances.* New York, NY: Russell Sage Foundation, and Chicago, IL: Spencer Foundation.

Economic Policy Institute. (2010, August). *Problems with the use of student test scores to evaluate teachers.* Washington, DC: Author.

Education and the Workforce Committee. (2012). Discussing the value of alternative teacher certification [Video]. Retrieved from http://edworkforcehouse.granicus.com/MediaPlayer.php?view_id=2&clip_id=105

Educational Development Center. (EDC). (1999). *Improving teacher preparation programs: A briefing paper for funders* (Prepared for the W. K. Kellogg Foundation). Battle Creek, MI: W. K. Kellogg Foundation.

Eduventures. (2009). Educator preparation: Strengths and areas for improvement in preparation programs: Executive summary. Retrieved from http://oapcte.org/Eduventures_Report_on_Teach_Prep.pdf

Feistritzer, E., Griffin, S., & Linnajarvi, A. (2011). *Profile of teachers in the US Washington, DC: National Center for Education Information.* Retrieved from www.edweek.org/media/pot2011final-blog.pdf

Feller, B. (2006, September 19). Study says teacher training is chaotic. Associated Press. Retrieved from http://www.edschools.org/news/Associated_Press_091906.htm

Feuer, M., Floden, R., Chudowsky, N., & Ahn, J. (2013). *Evaluation of teacher preparation programs: Purposes, methods, and policy options.* Washington, DC: National Academy of Education. Retrieved from http://naeducation.org/NAED_080456.htm

Finder, A. (2006, September 19). Report critical of training of teachers. *The New York Times.* Retrieved from http://www.nytimes.com/2006/09/19/education/19report.html

Gassman, V. (2012). What's new is old? Philanthropic influences on education. *Phi Delta Kappan, 93*(8), 8–11.

Gitomer, D. (2007). *Teacher quality in a changing policy landscape.* Princeton, NJ: Educational Testing Service.

Goldhaber, D., & Walch, J. (2013). Gains in teacher quality. *Education Next.* Retrieved from http://educationnext.org/gains-in-teacher-quality

Goodlad, J. (1991). Why we need a complete redesign of teacher education. *Educational Leadership, 49*(3), 4–10.

Goodlad, J. (1994). *Educational renewal: Better teachers, better schools.* San Francisco, CA: Jossey-Bass.

Goodman, J. (2013). Charter management organizations and the regulated environment: Is it worth the price? *Educational Researcher, 42*(2), 89–96.

Grossman, P. (2011). A framework for teaching practice: A brief history of an idea. *Teachers College Record, 113*(12). Retrieved from www.tcrecord.org/content.asp?contentid=16495

Grossman, P., & Loeb, S. (2008). *Alternative routes to teaching: Mapping the new landscape of teacher education.* Cambridge, MA: Harvard Education Press.

Haberman, M. (1991). The pedagogy of poverty versus good teaching. *Phi Delta Kappan, 73,* 290–294.

Hall, P. D. (2013). Philanthropy, the nonprofit sector and the democratic dilemma. *Daedalus, 142*(2), 139–158.

Hartocollis, A. (July 31, 2005). Who needs education schools? *The New York Times,* pp. 24–28.

Henig, J. R., Hula, R. C., Orr, M., & Pedescleaux, D. S. (2001). *The color of school reform: Race, politics, and the challenge of urban education.* Princeton, NJ: Princeton University Press.

Hess, F. M. (2005). Introduction. In F. M. Hess (Ed.), *With the best of intentions: How philanthropy is reshaping K-12 education* (pp. 1–17). Cambridge, MA: Harvard Education Press.

Hess, F. M. (2006). Politics, policy, and the promise of entrepreneurship. In F. M. Hess (Ed.), *Educational entrepreneurship: Realities, challenges, possibilities* (pp. 243–260). Cambridge, MA: Harvard Education Press.

Hess, F. M. (2009). Revitalizing teacher education by revisiting our assumptions about teaching. *Journal of Teacher Education, 60*(5), 450–457.

Hess, F. M. (2012, May 16). Philanthropy gets into the ring: Edu funders get serious about education policy. *Education Week.* Retrieved from www.edweek.org/ew/articles/2012/05/16/kappan_hess.h31.html

Holmes Group. (1986). *Tomorrow's teachers.* East Lansing: Michigan State University College of Education.

Honawar, V. (2006, September 20). Prominent teacher educator assails field, suggests new accreditation body in report. *Education Week*, 26. Retrieved from www.edschools.org/pdf/Education_Week_092006.pdf

Horn, J., & Libby, K. (2011). The giving business: Venture philanthropy and the New Schools Venture Fund. In P. Kovacs (Ed.), *The Gates Foundation and the future of US public education* (pp. 168–185). New York, NY: Routledge.

Humphrey, D. C., Wechsler, M. E., & Hough, H. J. (2008). Characteristics of effective alternative certification programs. *Teachers College Record, 110*(1), 1–63.

Ingersoll, R. (2003). *Who controls teachers' work?* Cambridge, MA: Harvard University Press.

Jain, N. (2013, March 24). Rethinking education: Why our education system is ripe for disruption. *Forbes Magazine.* Retrieved from http://www.forbes.com/sites/naveenjain/2013/03/24/disrupting-education/#7fb610a37d06

Johnson, S. M., Kraft, M., & Papay, J. (2012). How context matters in high-need schools: The effects of teachers' working conditions on their professional satisfaction and their students' achievement. *Teachers College Record, 114*, 1–39.

Katz, S. N. (2013). Reshaping US public education policy. *Stanford Social Innovation Review.* Retrieved from http://ssir.org/articles/entry/reshaping_US_public_education_policy

Keller, B. (2013, October). An industry of mediocrity. *The New York Times.* Retrieved from www.nytimes.com/2013/10/21/opinion/keller-an-industry-of-mediocrity.html

Kirby, S. N., McCombs, J. S., Naftel, S., & Barney, H. (2005). *Teachers for a new era: Some promising indicators of change.* Santa Monica, CA: Rand Corporation.

Knowles, T. (2013). *New pathways for teachers, new promises for students: A vision for developing excellent teachers* (Special Report 3). Washington, DC: American Enterprise Institute.

Kronholz, J. (2012). A new type of Ed school: Linking candidate success to student success. *Education Next.* Retrieved from http://educationnext.org/a-new-type-of-ed-school/

Labaree, D. (1997). Public goods, private goods: The struggle over educational goals. *American Educational Research Journal, 34*(1), 39–81.

Ladson-Billings, G. (2006). From the achievement gap to the education debt: Understanding achievement in US schools. *Educational Researcher, 35*(7), 3–12.

Lagemann, E. C. (1992). *The politics of knowledge: The Carnegie Corporation, philanthropy, and public policy.* Chicago, IL: University of Chicago Press.

Lemov, D. (2010). *Teach like a champion.* San Francisco, CA: Jossey-Bass.

Lemov, D. (2012, October 26). Practice makes perfect and not just for jocks and musicians. *The Wall Street Journal.* Retrieved from www.wsj.com/articles/SB1000142405297020 4530504578078602307104168

Levin, T. (2011, July 21). Training of teachers is flawed study says. *The New York Times,* Retrieved from http://www.nytimes.com/2011/07/21/education/21teaching.html

Levine, A. (2006, September). Educating school teachers. *The Education Schools Project.* Retrieved from www.edschools.org/pdf/Educating_Teachers_Report.pdf

Levine, A. (2010). Teacher education must respond to change in America. *Phi Delta Kappan, 92*(2), 19–24.

Levine, A. (2011, May 8). The new normal of teacher education. *The Chronicle of Higher Education.* Retrieved from http://chronicle.com/article/The-New-Normal-of-Teacher/127430/

Lipman, P. (2004). *High-stakes education: Inequality, globalization, and urban school reform.* New York, NY: Routledge.

Liu, M. (2013). Disrupting teacher education. *Education Next, 13*(3). Retrieved from http:// educationnext.org/disrupting-teacher-education

Lyall, K., & Sell, K. (2006). *The true genius of America at risk: Are we losing our public universities to de facto privatization?* Westport, CT: Praeger.

Matthews, J. (2010, October 2). ED school professors resist teaching practical skills [Blog post]. Class Struggle. *The Washington Post.* Retrieved from http://voices. washingtonpost.com/class-struggle/2010/10/ed_school_professors_still_res.html

McNeil, L. (2000). *Contradictions of school reform: The costs of standardized testing.* New York, NY: Routledge.

National Commission for Teaching and America's Future. (NCTAF). (1996, September). *What matters most: Teaching for America's future.* New York, NY: Author.

National Commission on Teaching and America's Future. (NCTAF). (2007). *The high cost of teacher turnover.* Washington, DC: Author.

National Comprehensive Center for Teacher Quality & Public Agenda. (2008). *Teaching in changing times. Lessons learned: New teachers talk about their jobs, challenges, and long-range plans.* Washington, DC: Author. Retrieved from http://www.publicagenda.org/files/lessons_learned_3.pdf

National Council of Accreditation for Teacher Education. (2010). *Transforming teacher education through clinical practice: A national strategy to prepare effective teachers.* Washington, DC: Author.

National Council on Teacher Quality. (2013). *Teacher prep review: A review of the nation's teacher prep programs.* Washington, DC: Author.

National Research Council. (2010). *Preparing teachers: Building evidence for sound policy.* Washington, DC: National Academies Press.

Nelson, T., & Joanes, A. (2007). The end of the "public" in public education. *Teacher Education Quarterly, 34*(2), 5–10.

Newfield, C. (2008). *Unmaking the public university.* Cambridge, MA: Harvard University Press.

New Schools Venture Fund. (2011). *Learning to Teach Community of Practice.* Retrieved from www.newschools.org/event/learning-to-teach-community-of-practice

New Schools Venture Fund. (2012a). *Annual report*. Retrieved from www.newschools. org/annualreport

New Schools Venture Fund. (2012b). *GREAT Act update*. Retrieved from www. newschools.org/news/great-act-update/

New Schools Venture Fund. (n.d.-a). Learning to Teach Entrepreneur in Residence Program. Retrieved from www.newschools.org/wp/wp-content/uploads/ NewSchools-LTT-Entrepeneur-in-Residence.pdf

New Schools Venture Fund. (n.d.-b). *New Schools Venture Fund*. Retrieved from www. newschools.org

New Schools Venture Fund. (n.d.-c). *Relay Graduate School of Education*. Retrieved from www.newschools.org/venture/relay-school-of-education

New Schools Venture Fund. (n.d.-d). *Venture snapshot: TeachingWorks*. Retrieved from www.newschools.org/venture/teachingworks

Nichols, S., & Berliner, D. (2007). *Collateral damage: How high stakes testing corrupts America's schools*. Cambridge, MA: Harvard Education Press.

Noguera, P. (2011). A broader, bolder approach uses education to break the cycle of poverty. *Phi Delta Kappan, 93*(3), 8–14.

No teacher left behind. (2006, September 22). *The Wall Street Journal*. Dow Jones Web Report Service. Retrieved from www.edschools.org/news/Wall_Street_Journal_ 092206.Htm

Odden, A. (2013). *Getting the best people in the toughest jobs: Changes in talent management in education*. Washington, DC: Center for American Progress.

Orfield, G., & Frankenberg, E. (Eds). (2013). *Educational delusions? Why choice can deepen inequality and how to make schools fair*. Berkeley, CA: University of California Press.

Otterman, S. (2011, July 21). Ed schools' pedagogical puzzle. *The New York Times*. Retrieved from www.nytimes.com/2011/07/24/education/edlife/edl-24teacher-t. html?pagewanted=all

Parker, W. (2011). Constructing public schooling today: Derision, multiculturalism, and nationalism. *Educational Theory, 61*(4), 413–432.

Payzant, T. (2004, February). *Should teacher education take place at colleges and universities?* Invited address presented at the annual meeting of the American Association of Colleges for Teacher Education, Chicago, IL.

Peske, H., & Haycock, K. (2006). *Teaching inequality: How poor minority students are shortchanged on teacher quality*. Washington, DC: Education Trust.

Pianta, R. C. (2011) *Teaching children well: New evidence-based approaches to teacher professional development and training*. Washington, DC: Center for American Progress.

Plecki, M., Elfers, A., & Nakamura, Y. (2012). Using evidence for teacher education program improvement and accountability: An illustrative case of the role of value-added measures. *Journal of Teacher Education, 65*(5), 318–334.

Polikoff, M., & Porter, A. (2014). Instructional alignment as a measure of teacher quality. *Education Evaluation and Policy Analysis, 36*(4), 399–416.

Quinn, R., Tompkins-Stange, M., & Meyerson, D. (2013, April). *Beyond grant making: Philanthropic foundations as agents for change and institutional entrepreneurs*. Paper presented at the annual meeting of the American Educational Research Association, San Francisco, CA.

Ravitch, D. (2010). *The death and life of the great American school system*. New York, NY: Basic Books.

Reckhow, S. (2013). *Follow the money: How foundation dollars change public school politics*. New York, NY: Oxford University Press.

Rochkind, J., Ott, A., Immerwahr, J., Doble, J., & Johnson, J. (2007). *Lessons learned: New teachers talk about their jobs, challenges, and long-range plans.* Report form the National Comprehensive Center on Teacher Quality and the Public Agenda. Retrieved on January 12, 2010 from https://www.publicagenda.org/files/lessons_learned_3.pdf

Ronfeldt, M., Loeb, S., & Wyckoff, J. (2013). How teacher turnover harms student achievement. *American Educational Research Journal, 50,* 4–36.

Rose, M. (2013). The mismeasure of teaching and learning: How contemporary school reform fails the test. In M. B. Katz & M. Rose (Eds), *Public education under siege* (pp. 9–20). Philadelphia: University of Pennsylvania Press.

Rotherham, A. (2008). *Achieving teacher and principal excellence: A guidebook for donors.* Washington, DC: Philanthropy Roundtable.

Rothstein, R. (2004). *Class and schools: Using social, economic, and educational reform to close the Black and White achievement gap.* Washington, DC: Economic Policy Institute.

Saltman, K. (2010). *The gift of education: Public education and venture philanthropy.* New York, NY: Palgrave Macmillan.

Sandler, M. (2010). *Social entrepreneurship in education: Private ventures for the public good.* New York, NY: Rowman & Littlefield.

Sawchuck, S. (2012, March 14). New advocacy groups shaking up education field. *Education Week.* Retrieved from www.edweek.org/ew/articles/2012/05/16/31adv-overview_ep.h31.html

Sawchuck, S. (2013, March 25). Teacher-prep programs zero in on effective practice. *Education Week.* Retrieved from www.edweek.org/ew/articles/2013/03/27/26 practice_ep.h32.html

Schiller, J. (2012). Venture philanthropy's market strategies fail urban kids. *Phi Delta Kappan, 93*(8), 12–16.

Schorr, J. (2013). A revolution begins in teacher prep. *Stanford Social Innovation Review, 11*(1). Retrieved from http://ssir.org/articles/entry/a_revolution_begins_in_teacher_prep

Scott, J. (2006). The politics of venture philanthropy in charter school policy and advocacy. *Educational Policy, 23*(1), 106–136.

Simon, S. (2013, October 21). Teach for America rises as a political powerhouse. *Politico Education Pro.* Retrieved from www.politico.com/story/2013/10/teach-for-america-rises-as-political-powerhouse-098586

Smith, J. A. (2009). Private foundations and public policymaking: A historical perspective. In J. Ferris (Ed.), *Foundations and public policy* (pp. 41–78). New York, NY: The Foundation Center.

Smith, K., & Peterson, L. (2006). What is educational entrepreneurship? In F. M. Hess (Ed.), *Educational entrepreneurship: Realities, challenges, and possibilities* (pp. 21–44). Cambridge, MA: Harvard Education Press.

Smith, S. (Host). (2013, June 21). *New grad school for teachers* [Audio podcast]. American RadioWorks. Retrieved from https://soundcloud.com/americanradioworks/american-radio-works-new-grad.

Smith, W. (1980). The American Teacher Corps programme. In E. Hoyle & J. Megarry (Eds), *Professional development of teachers* (pp. 204–218) London: Nichols.

Stone, J. T. (1968). *Breakthrough in teacher education.* San Francisco, CA: Jossey-Bass.

Suggs, C., & deMarrais, K. (2011, July). *Critical contributions: Philanthropic investment in teachers and teaching.* Atlanta, GA: Kronley & Associates.

Sykes, G., & Dibner, K. (2009, March). *Fifty years of federal teacher policy: An appraisal.* Washington, DC: Center on Education Policy.

TeachingWorks. (n.d.). *Annual reports.* Retrieved from www.teachingworks.org/about/annualreport

Tompkins-Stange, M. E. (2016). *Policy patrons: Philanthropy, education reform, and the politics of influence.* Cambridge, MA: Harvard Education Press.

Tucker, M. (2011). *Surpassing Shanghai: An agenda for American education built on the world's leading systems.* Cambridge, MA: Harvard Education Press.

Valenzuela, A. (2005). *Leaving children behind: How "Texas-style" accountability fails Latino youth.* Albany, NY: SUNY Press.

Vedder, R. (2011, September). Who should educate the educators? *Chronicle of Higher Education.* Retrieved from http://chronicle.com/blogs/innovations/who-should-educate-the-educators/30362

Welner, K. (2011). Free-market think tanks and the marketing of educational policy. *Dissent,* 39–44.

Woodring, P. (1960). The Ford Foundation and teacher education. *Teachers College Record, 62*(3), 224–231.

Zeichner, K. (2005). Learning from experience with performance-based teacher education. In F. Peterman (Ed.), *Designing performance assessment systems for urban teacher education* (pp. 3–19). New York, NY: Routledge.

Zeichner, K. (2009). *Teacher education and the struggle for social justice.* New York, NY: Routledge.

Zeichner, K. (2010). Rethinking the connections between campus courses and field experiences in college and university-based teacher education. *Journal of Teacher Education, 89*(11), 89–99.

Zeichner, K. (2011). Assessing state and federal policies to evaluate the quality of Teacher preparation programs. In P. Earley, D. Imig, & N. Michelli (Eds), *Teacher education policy in the US: Issues and tensions in an era of evolving expectations* (pp. 75–105). New York, NY: Routledge.

Zeichner, K. (2012). The turn once again toward practice-based teacher education. *Journal of Teacher Education, 63*(5), 376–382.

Zeichner, K., & Bier, M. (2013). The turn toward practice and clinical experiences in US teacher education. *Beitrage Zur Lehrerbildung [Swiss Journal of Teacher Education], 30*(2), 153–170.

Zeichner, K., & Conklin, H. (2005). Teacher education programs. In M. Cochran-Smith & K. Zeichner (Eds), *Studying teacher education* (pp. 645–735). New York, NY: Routledge.

Zeichner, K., & Payne, K. (2013). Democratizing knowledge in urban teacher education. In J. Noel (Ed.), *Moving teacher education into urban schools and communities* (pp. 3–19). New York, NY: Routledge.

Zeichner, K., Payne, K., & Brayko, K. (2015). Democratizing teacher education. *Journal of Teacher Education, 66*(2), 122–135.

Zumwalt, K., & Craig, E. (2005). Teachers' characteristics: Research on the indicators of quality. In M. Cochran-Smith & K. Zeichner (Eds), *Studying teacher education* (pp. 157–260). New York, NY: Routledge.

Zunz, O. (2012). *Philanthropy in America: A history.* Princeton, NJ: Princeton University Press.

4

BEYOND KNOWLEDGE VENTRILOQUISM AND ECHO CHAMBERS

Raising the Quality of the Debate in Teacher Education

Kenneth M. Zeichner and Hilary G. Conklin

For over two decades, there has been a steady call for deregulating US teacher education, closing down allegedly poor-quality college and university programs, and creating greater market competition (Chubb, 2012; Kanstoroom & Finn, 1999; Hess, 2001; Knowles, 2013; Walsh, 2001). In response to this call to disrupt the dominance of colleges and universities in teacher education, and because of the policies and funding allocations of the US Education Department and private foundation funding,[1] non-university providers of teacher education have proliferated in certain areas of the country. Some of these providers, like the Relay Graduate School of Education (Schorr, 2013) and the Sposato Graduate School of Education—both independent education schools founded by charter school organizations—and the American Museum of Natural History, have been empowered by their states to award master's degrees with full teacher certification. Other for-profit teacher education programs, such as A+ Texas Teachers and iteachTEXAS, along with teacher education programs at online for-profit universities like the University of Phoenix, Grand Canyon University, and Kaplan University, have also emerged and are preparing many teachers across the nation. Currently, approximately 20 to 30 percent of teachers in the US enter the workforce through a non-university pathway (National Research Council, 2010), although in certain states like Texas, and in certain local labor markets like New Orleans, the percentage is much higher. The graduates of these non-university programs tend to be concentrated in low-income urban and rural areas (Darling-Hammond, 2004; Zeichner, 2014).

Although colleges and universities dominated teacher preparation in the United States from approximately 1960–1990, beginning in the mid-1980s, more alternative pathways into teaching beyond the traditional undergraduate and post-graduate models emerged (Zeichner & Hutchinson, 2008). As Fraser (2007) has pointed out, diversity in pathways into teaching has been the norm in the United States rather than the exception. What is new in the current push toward greater diversity in pathways into teaching in the US is (1) the active support of the US Department of Education in promoting non-college and university programs and (2) the investment of substantial amounts of corporate and government money into developing chains of non-college and university-sponsored programs like Relay, Match, The New Teacher Project (TNTP), Teach for America, and the Urban Teacher Center,[2] whose standardized models can be scaled up and spread across the country (Zeichner & Peña-Sandoval, 2015). Much of this new activity is linked to preparing teachers for the growing number of K–12 charter schools in certain areas of the country (Stitzlein & West, 2014).[3]

A critical aspect of the current call for greater deregulation and market competition in teacher education has been the declaration that university teacher education has failed and represents an "industry of mediocrity" (Keller, 2013). Kate Walsh, President of the National Council on Teacher Quality (NCTQ), has been quoted as declaring, "It is an accepted fact that the field is broken" (Kronholz, 2012). These assessments of teacher education have also been used to justify and promote greater federal accountability for teacher education programs (Crowe, 2010; Duncan, 2011; US Department of Education, 2014), including the highly controversial use of test scores of program graduates to evaluate the quality of teacher education programs—a practice that many experts in educational assessment and the American Statistical Association have criticized (American Statistical Association, 2014; Baker et al., 2010; Berliner, 2014; National Research Council, 2010).

There is no dispute about the need for improvements in the dominant college and university system of teacher education. The field itself has a history of self-critique that has called for substantive changes in how teachers are prepared (e.g., Goodlad, 1998; Holmes Partnership, 2007; National Council for Accreditation of Teacher Education, 2010). Yet, just as scholars within the field have raised important critiques about university-based teacher education practices (Fullan, Galluzzo, Morris, & Watson, 1998), it is also important to critically evaluate the warrants for the value of programs that critics claim should replace college and university programs.

One notable characteristic of current debates about the future of teacher education in the US is the distortion and misuse of research in order to justify efforts to deregulate and privatize teacher education. Our focus in this chapter is to illustrate how research has been misrepresented to support policies and programs that would simultaneously reduce the role of colleges and universities in preparing US teachers and support the expansion of the role of non-university providers, many of which are funded by philanthropists, and promoted by the US Department of Education (Zeichner & Peña-Sandoval, 2015).

We also contend that the print news media has given disproportional attention to allegedly innovative non-college and university programs developed by educational entrepreneurs, and to organizations like the National Council on Teacher Quality (NCTQ)—attention that has served to inflate the public perception of these organizations and programs beyond what is warranted by the available evidence. The media has also reproduced in an uncritical way some of the claims about the poor quality of college and university teacher preparation and about the research on alternative pathways into teaching—claims that have been made based on blatant misrepresentations of research. The media's role in uncritically reproducing a narrative of failure about university teacher education and promoting the success of new non-university programs is, in part, a result of: (1) the considerable effort that non-university programs and the advocacy organizations, funders, and think tanks that promote them devote to branding and marketing these programs; and (2) the reduction of budgets and staff in traditional media outlets and the need for them to compete for the attention of readers/viewers with new nontraditional forms of communication (Bowden, 2009; Lubienski, Scott, & DeBray, 2014; Malin & Lubienski, 2015; Yettick, 2015). The media's reproduction of this narrative of failure contributes to the limited or biased use of research in policymaking.

Contrary to the ideal of policymakers carefully weighing research evidence on complex issues as they seek to design education policies, scholars have argued for many years that policymakers often have used research politically, selectively drawing on evidence to support already held views (e.g., Henig, 2008; Weiss, 1979). Scholars have also argued that as a result of this selective use of research in the policymaking process, there has often been a tenuous link between research evidence and policymaking in education (e.g., Malin & Lubienski, 2015). In this chapter we focus on teacher education as a specific example of the tenuous link between research evidence and policy in education.

In particular, we focus on several cases of the misrepresentation of research to support political ends: (1) the misuse of Levine's (2006) study of teacher education as a means to denigrate schools of education; (2) the NCTQ's misrepresentation of research to position university teacher education as "an industry of mediocrity" and to elevate its role as a judge of the quality of teacher preparation programs; (3) the false assertion of a research warrant coupled with a media branding campaign to promote the Relay Graduate School of Education; and (4) the selective interpretation of research on the effects of different pathways into teaching generally, and particularly of an American Educational Research Association-commissioned research synthesis on US teacher education (Zeichner & Conklin, 2005).

To frame our discussion, we find the concepts of knowledge ventriloquism and echo chambers relevant. Robertson (2012) has coined the term "knowledge ventriloquism" to describe situations where a very narrow menu of studies, either those commissioned by a program or by its own small circle of like-minded supporters, are counted as evidence for policy. Robertson explains, "By limiting as what might count as evidence for policy, it in turn limits potential challenges to this evidence" (p. 201). An echo chamber, as defined in journalism and media studies, is the amplification and reinforcement of ideas by repetition inside an enclosed system where different or competing views are censored or disallowed. This term has also been used in the study of education policymaking to document how "a small or unrepresentative sample of studies is repeatedly cited to create momentum around a policy proposal" (Goldie, Linick, Jabbar, & Lubienski, 2014). With regard to teacher education, we argue that a network of publicly subsidized and interrelated think tanks, advocacy groups, and philanthropists (Katz, 2013; Sawchuck, 2012; Welner, 2013) have used the practices of knowledge ventriloquism and echo chambers to gain enormous influence in shaping teacher education policies. By using research in tactical and symbolic ways (Tseng, 2012), this network has shaped the current US teacher education policy environment in ways that have undermined equity in our public education system and democracy in the making of education policy.[4]

Following our discussion of how research has been misrepresented through knowledge ventriloquism and echo chambers to support a particular policy direction, we will offer suggestions on how to reframe the debates about the future of US teacher education.

Manufacturing a Narrative of Failure

> By almost any standard, many, if not most, of the nation's 1,450 schools, colleges, and departments of education are doing a mediocre job of preparing teachers.
>
> *(Duncan, 2009)*

In order to justify deregulating and supporting greater market competition in US teacher education, the US Department of Education, politicians, think tank pundits, and venture philanthropists have made consistent efforts to establish the belief among the public that the dominant system of college and university teacher education has failed and that we need to replace many existing programs with new, allegedly more innovative ones. The print news media, in turn, has circulated this same belief. In the section below, we examine the efforts to brand existing teacher education programs as failures. We also discuss some of the strategies that deregulation advocates have used to attempt to convince the public and policymakers that the new, largely early-entry[5] programs that philanthropists, venture capitalists, and the US Department of Education are promoting are innovative and desirable.

The Levine and American Federation of Teachers: Studies of Teacher Education in the United States

One of the most prevalent rhetorical moves in seeking to establish the failure of university teacher education is the citation of a report by Levine (2006) that included a survey of teacher education program graduates in which they reflected back on the value of the programs. This report was one of three issued by Levine and his privately funded "Education Schools Project."[6] In addition to case studies of several schools and departments of education, surveys of principals and deans, and case studies of several exemplary programs, Levine's teacher education report surveyed a sample of 15,468 education school alumni who received degrees ranging from the baccalaureate to the doctorate in 1995 and 2000 from a sample of 28 schools and departments of education chosen "to reflect the diversity of the nation's education schools by region, control, religion, racial composition, gender, and Carnegie Foundation institutional classifications" (pp. 5–6). Notably, only 34 percent of this sample responded to the survey. No information has been made available publicly, or to us personally when we requested it in December 2014, about the representativeness of those who responded to the survey. According to Levine (2006), 66 percent of those who responded agreed with the statement "schools of education do not prepare graduates to cope with classroom reality" (p. 32). The fact that some alumni in the sample received doctoral degrees in the two years sampled adds some confusion to the meaning of these findings since no program in the nation offers a doctoral degree with certification for teaching.

This lone finding in Levine's (2006) study has been cited repeatedly as "evidence" that university teacher education graduates feel unprepared to teach. For example, Schorr (2013)[7] noted, "In a seminal 2006 study by Arthur Levine, more than three in five teachers said their training left them unprepared for the classroom and principals agreed" (p. 3).

US Secretary of Education Arne Duncan (2009) also referred to Levine's (2006) surveys in his address on teacher education at Teachers College, Columbia University:

> As you know, the most recent comprehensive study of teacher education was carried out by Arthur Levine, the former president of Teachers College. … More than three out of five ed school alums surveyed for the Levine report said that their training did not prepare them adequately for their work in the classroom.
>
> *(p. 3)*

Finally, when the GREAT Act—a bill that has been incorporated into the 2014 and 2015 ESEA reauthorization process that would promote the development of "charter" teacher education programs that would be exempt from many of the regulations that other programs would need to meet—was reintroduced to the

Senate and House of Representatives on May 23, 2013, both Senator Michael Bennett (CO-D) in the Senate and Representative Tom Petri (WI-R) in the House referred to the Levine (2006) study to help make their case for the bill. Despite the extensive body of research literature on teacher education programs, no other study or report was referred to in either presentation. For example: "According to a leading study 61 percent of ed school alumni reported that schools of education at four-year colleges did not adequately prepare their graduates for the classroom."[8]

Although the surveys in Levine's (2006) study identified some of the persistent problems long noted in the teacher education research literature (Wilson, 2014), it is not the only survey that has been conducted on teachers' assessments of their preparation programs. While some more recent surveys also show that teachers have concerns with aspects of their preparation, these surveys also present a more positive and complicated picture than Levine's survey. For example, a survey commissioned by the American Federation of Teachers (2012)—an organization that has been critical of the status quo in teacher education (American Federation of Teachers, 2012)—of 500 of its US members in their first 3 years of teaching found that "two-thirds (66 percent) of new teachers felt completely (19 percent) or mostly (47 percent) prepared when they first started teaching while 34 percent said they felt just somewhat prepared or not prepared at all" (p. 21).[9]

In the proposed federal rules for teacher education accountability released in December 2014 by the US Department of Education, the text of the rules and the supporting materials once again cite the 66 percent figure from Levine's study,[10] as well as selected findings from the American Federation of Teachers study.

However, rather than reporting one of the major findings—namely, that two thirds of those surveyed in the AFT survey felt completely or mostly prepared when they started teaching—three pieces of data are selected and cited in the proposed teacher education accountability rules:

- 82 percent of the 500 beginning teachers surveyed suggest better coordination between teacher preparation programs and school districts.
- 77 percent of teachers suggest better aligning curricula with field experiences.[11]
- 50 percent of teachers "indicated that their teacher preparation program did not adequately prepare them for the challenges of teaching in the real world" (Teacher Preparation Issues: Proposed Rule, 2014).[12]

Although all of this information is accurate, these three findings are stated without including the main survey findings that 66 percent of teachers felt completely or mostly prepared when they began teaching and that, by their third year of teaching, teachers looked back on their first year and 74 percent felt completely or mostly prepared. This move to support a narrative of failure is deceptive, especially given the finding that third-year teachers "who completed an alternative training or certification program recalled feeling less prepared (only 42 percent felt completely or mostly prepared) than teachers who followed the traditional path (72 percent)" (p. 22).

The AFT report of the results of their teacher survey is filled with contradictory findings about how teachers viewed their preparation programs. To select a few statements that support a particular narrative while ignoring other significant data that do not is an ethically questionable practice. For the US Department of Education to reiterate these selective ideas in an official policy document is deeply troubling and undermines the integrity of the process.

Several other surveys completed after 2006 that asked teachers to evaluate the quality of their preparation programs show a more positive portrait of university teacher education programs than Levine's surveys, including: (a) Eduventures' (2009) study of 1,504 teachers with 5 years or less in the field, which indicated that 78 percent of teachers felt well prepared when they entered the field; (b) the National Comprehensive Center for Teacher Quality and Public Agenda surveys of 641 first-year teachers conducted in the spring of 2007, which indicated that 80 percent of teachers felt very or somewhat prepared for teaching in their first year (Rochkind, Ott, Immerwahr, Doble, & Johnson, 2007); and (c) a 2011 survey of 2,500 randomly selected K–12 public school teachers, which found that 65 percent of teachers rated their preparation program as excellent or very good, and another 24 percent rated it as good (Feistritzer, 2011).

All these surveys reveal some teacher dissatisfaction with the quality of their preparation for teaching, and none of them was independently peer reviewed. The question that should be asked, however, is why critics of university education schools and advocates for deregulation and market competition continue to cite only Levine's (2006) study, and additionally only report the negative aspects of Levine's findings while ignoring the positive findings about university teacher preparation in his study and similar ones.

Despite Levine's negative assertions about the satisfaction of teacher education program graduates with the quality of their preparation programs, there are a number of places in the report where he noted both excellence in university teacher education and the limited amount of responsibility that can reasonably be placed on education schools alone for the problems in public education. For example, he explained:

> It is critical to recognize that weaknesses in teacher education are not the primary reason we do not have more and better teaching. Schools and government bear a larger responsibility for low salaries … for an absence of teacher induction programs, low hiring standards, and poor working conditions which cause high teacher turnover.
>
> *(p. 21)*

Despite these instances of more nuanced analysis, the overwhelming focus in public accounts of the report is on what are seen as problematic aspects of teacher education. This negativity was picked up by the media reports of the study soon after its release, as evidenced in headlines such as "Study Says Teacher Training is Chaotic" (Feller, 2006), "Prominent Teacher Educator Assails Field" (Honawar, 2006), and "Report Critical of Training of Teachers" (Finder, 2006).

The National Council on Teacher Quality and the Equity Standard

> Advocacy groups put considerable effort into strategies that advance their agendas, often by assuming the mantle of expertise and projecting that assumed status into the media and policy debates.
>
> *(Malin & Lubienski, 2015, p. 3)*

Another case of questionable and unethical manipulation of research in teacher education is the rationale that the National Council on Teacher Quality (NCTQ) uses for its equity standard in its national rankings of teacher education programs. The NCTQ was founded in 2000 by the Thomas B. Fordham Foundation, one of the leading national advocates for deregulation in teacher education (Kanstoroom & Finn, 1999). Walsh, who had established herself nationally as a critic of the value of teacher education (Walsh, 2001), was appointed president of the organization. In 2001, then Secretary of Education Rod Paige gave NCTQ $5 million from his discretionary fund to start a new national certification organization, The American Board for the Certification of Teacher Excellence, which was conceived as a competitor to the National Board for Professional Teaching Standards. This organization offers online teacher certification programs in several states that do not require the completion of a teacher education program.[13]

Beginning in 2006, NCTQ began issuing a series of uniformly critical reports on the quality of teacher education programs across the nation. Unlike the widely vetted standards of the teacher education accrediting agencies, the Council for the Accreditation of Educator Preparation, and the Council of Chief State School Officers (CCSSO, 2012), the NCTQ reports are based on a set of standards developed by its own advisory group dominated by advocates of deregulation and market competition. Beginning with reports on the preparation of elementary teachers to teach reading (2006) and math (2008), NCTQ followed in 2009 and 2010 with reports on what it termed "the essentials of teacher preparation" in several states (IL, TX, CO, NM, UT, WY, IN), and then with reports on specific areas of teacher education in programs nationally: student teaching (2011), assessment (2012), classroom management (2013), and academic rigor (2014).

Additionally, NCTQ formed a partnership with *US News & World Report* and published two sets of evaluations of teacher education programs nationally based on its own revised set of standards. These reports (e.g., Greenberg et al., 2015) have been heavily criticized by both professional societies (Pearson & Goatley,

2013) and by education scholars (Darling-Hammond, 2013; Fuller, 2014) for their faulty methodology and partisan nature, and more than 50 percent of teacher education institutions boycotted the first national evaluation in 2013.

One of the NCTQ standards—a standard that focuses on equity—illustrates the problematic nature of the NCTQ evaluations and the way in which NCTQ misrepresents research. In this standard, the NCTQ dismisses the entire field of research on multicultural teacher education as anecdotal. Specifically, NCTQ's equity standard states:

> As there are no findings from solid, large-scale and non-anecdotal research that coursework dedicated to eliminating gender and racial biases has any impact … we concluded that the best way for teacher candidates to internalize appropriate values is to spend time in high-poverty schools that are at least relatively high-performing.
>
> *(NCTQ, 2014, p. 47)*

Dismissing more than 40 years of research on the development of cultural competence and culturally responsive teaching in teacher education as offering nothing of value illustrates a lack of understanding of the available research, or an unwillingness to examine it. Although most of the major independent peer-reviewed syntheses of this body of research have acknowledged the limitations of the studies, all of these research syntheses identify specific effects of particular teacher education strategies that have enhanced the cultural competence of teacher candidates. For example, in a review conducted under the sponsorship of the National Academy of Education, and in another review in the Fifth Edition of the *Handbook of Research on Teaching* (a publication of the American Educational Research Association [AERA]), community-based learning, under certain conditions, was found to enhance the cultural competence of teacher candidates (e.g., Cochran-Smith & Villegas, 2016; Darling-Hammond & Bransford, 2005). Additionally, in the report of the AERA-supported effort to synthesize research on teacher education in the US, Hollins and Guzman (2005) identify clear trends in the research with regard to a variety of teacher education practices that are associated with enhancing aspects of teachers' cultural competence, including prejudice reduction.

Rejecting the value of an entire field of teacher education research, NCTQ instead justifies its equity standard based on a study that Ronfeldt (2012) conducted in one labor market in New York City.[14] In this study, Ronfeldt found "that learning to teach in easier-to-staff field placement schools has positive effects on teacher retention and student achievement gains, even for those teachers who end up working in the hardest-to-staff schools" (p. 3). These findings are based on a measure for each field placement school's "stay-ratio"—a measure of teacher turnover. Ronfeldt (2012) finds evidence that a school's stay-ratio can be used as a proxy for school working conditions and climate; it is not used as a measure for a school poverty or performance as NCTQ seems to infer. In fact, Ronfeldt includes separate measures for school performance and poverty that are mostly unrelated to teachers' retention and achievement gains.

The NCTQ's reliance on one study as the sole basis for the equity standard is especially puzzling because Ronfeldt is quite clear in his analysis about the tentative nature of his findings:

> Although this study's results are suggestive of a causal relationship between field placement stay-ratio and teacher retention and effectiveness, the evidence is by no means definitive. More studies are needed to reproduce these findings. Given the very unique student demographics and teacher labor market of NYC, these should include studies in different kinds of districts and states to see if the effects of field placement stay-ratio still hold. Moreover, well designed experimental studies with random assignment of teachers to easy-to-staff and difficult-to-staff field placements would be useful in bolstering, or countering, the case for a causal relationship. ... This study has provided a blunt signal for identifying quality placements, and more research is needed to understand the specific features that give rise to these average effects.
>
> *(p. 22)*

An additional problem with the basis for NCTQ's equity standard is the assertion that merely spending time as a student teacher in a high-poverty school that is at least relatively high performing will result in teacher candidates learning what they need to learn to be successful. In addition to not directly addressing the "stay-ratio" that is the basis for Ronfeldt's findings, this learning-by-mere-immersion theory of teacher learning is at odds with research that indicates that immersion without carefully designed preparation, mediation, and ongoing support can undermine teacher learning (Grossman, Ronfeldt, & Cohen, 2012; Hammerness et al., 2005), and in some cases strengthen and reinforce deficit stereotypes about students (Banks et al., 2005).

The misuse of research in this equity standard is representative of the ways in which NCTQ has manipulated research findings in its teacher education studies in an effort to legitimate itself as an arbitrator of the quality of teacher education programs, and to support its claims that university teacher education is broken. Fuller (2014) examined the ways in which research was used in developing several other standards used in the NCTQ program ratings and reached similar conclusions about the misrepresentation of research.

Despite the shaky grounds on which this and many of the other NCTQ standards rest, the various reports that NCTQ has issued on the quality of particular teacher education programs in the US have received prominent coverage in the national and local media (e.g., Banchero, 2013; Berrett, 2013; Sanchez, 2013; Sawchuck, 2013). Although Walsh has gone on record in the US

Congress as advocating for the federal government to remove barriers to non-university teacher education programs,[15] the NCTQ reports do not explicitly advocate for further deregulation and privatization of teacher education. The sound bites in Walsh's speeches and in the NCTQ reports like "an industry of mediocrity" and "teacher education is broken" are repeated in major national media outlets (Berrett, 2013; Keller, 2013) and by those who advocate for promoting greater market competition in US teacher education, such as Norm Atkins and David Levin.[16] Further, while most of these news reports mention some of the critiques of the motivations and methods of NCTQ's evaluations,[17] the cumulative effect of the media reports has been to legitimize the credibility of NCTQ and its methods and standards. For example, in the text of the proposed teacher education accountability rules distributed by the US Department of Education as a part of the 2014 reauthorization of the Higher Education Act, NCTQ is referred to as one of two "major national organizations focused on teacher preparation" (US Department of Education, 2014). The other organization mentioned is CAEP, the major national accreditation body of teacher education.

To place NCTQ, with its highly partisan mission and history, on the same plane as the official national accreditation body of the field is not warranted given the questionable quality of its reports and a president, Walsh, makes statements about teacher education that create inaccurate caricatures of education schools. For example, at a 2013 session at the Foundation for Excellence in Education that she chaired, Walsh said the following about education schools when introducing the session: "Their faculty is answerable to no one, not even the Dean, when it comes to deciding what the content of a class ought to be."[18] Similarly, in the 2014 NCTQ rankings of teacher education programs, it is asserted:

> because there is now a widespread assumption that the general incompetence of first-year teachers is unavoidable, teacher educators are given license (particularly by state departments of education) to prepare teachers any way they please regardless of the effectiveness or lack thereof.
>
> *(p. 14)*

These statements do not reflect the reality of state regulations that require teacher education programs to constantly gather, analyze, and report on the alignment of their curriculum with state requirements, and the performance of their teacher candidates on state and/or national teaching standards. Neither do the statements reflect the influence of the voluntary national accreditation system, which results in detailed requirements related to program inputs and outcomes. While it is legitimate to argue whether these state and national regulations and standards have made a difference in the quality of teacher education programs, and while faculty members have some flexibility in how they address state regulations, it is not reasonable to assert that these constraints on teacher education programs do not exist.

Further, none of NCTQ's reports have been independently peer reviewed, as was required for most of the major evaluations of research and practice in teacher preparation in the US (Cochran-Smith & Zeichner, 2005; National Research Council, 2010; Wilson, Floden, & Ferini-Mundy, 2001). Additionally, no credible empirical research has been presented showing whether graduates from NCTQ-endorsed prep programs are, in fact, doing better than graduates from other programs. In fact, a recent study of the predictive validity of the NCTQ program ratings in relation to the test scores and principal evaluations of graduates from different programs in North Carolina (Henry & Bastian, 2015) has shown that "in our analysis there is not a strong relationship between NCTQ ratings and meeting their standards and the performance of TPP graduates" (p. 7).

In the 2014 NCTQ Report on teacher education programs, the authors compare their report to the influential Flexner Study of medical education over a hundred years ago (Flexner, 1910) that transformed the field of medical education, a fundamentally problematic comparison given the scholarly nature of Flexner's study. The NCTQ and its reports do not warrant the kind of media coverage that they have garnered, given (1) the absence of independent peer review in their reports, (2) the lack of attention to the realities of program approval and accreditation in the regular statements of the NCTQ president, and (3) the fatally flawed methodology of the NCTQ ranking exercise, which does not consider "the actual quality of instruction that programs offer, what students learn, and whether graduates can actually teach" (Darling-Hammond, 2013).

The Echo Chamber Surrounding Relay Graduate School of Education

In an effort to break the dominance of colleges and universities in teacher education, critics of education schools have made many claims about the superiority of programs funded by philanthropy and the US Department of Education. These claims are based on critics' assertions that these new programs have proven their success at producing graduates who have demonstrated the ability to raise the standardized test scores of their pupils. Advocates of these new programs also sometimes point to alleged evidence that more students than before have gone to college in the charter schools where teachers prepared by the entrepreneurial programs have taught. Similarly, in the literature on educational entrepreneurship, the educational entrepreneurs who are brought in by venture philanthropists to develop and run start-up teacher education programs are referred to in glowing terms. For example, Hess (2006) referred to them as "pioneers," "visionary thinkers," "the engines of progress," and "imaginative, creative and talented." Assertions like these are taken at face value in calls to deregulate and create a market economy in US teacher education.[19]

However, the dearth of research demonstrating the superiority of entrepreneurial programs like Relay Graduate School of Education, the Academy for Urban School Leadership (AUSL), Match Teacher Residency, and the Urban Teaching Center in the preparation of teachers—even by the entrepreneurs' own standard of quality based in student standardized test scores—raises serious questions about the warrant for these claims. Repeatedly declaring that these programs are innovative, groundbreaking, and bold does not make it true in the absence of solid research evidence. While in some cases it can be shown that students in charter schools staffed by graduates of these entrepreneurial programs have improved test score results and graduation rates, it has not been demonstrated that the nature and quality of the teacher education programs have been responsible for these gains (see Cochran-Smith & Villegas, 2016; Zeichner & Conklin, 2005, for a discussion of this issue). Although research evidence shows that *some* charters have outperformed public schools in raising standardized test scores, most of them have not done so (CREDO, 2009, 2013; Henig, 2008).

Examining the evidence regarding the effectiveness of one of these entrepreneurial programs, the Relay Graduate School of Education provides one informative case. Teacher U, the predecessor to Relay Graduate School of Education, was founded in 2007 by representatives of three charter school networks (Achievement First, KIPP, and Uncommon Schools), at first primarily to prepare teachers for the three founding charter networks. For 3 years, Teacher U operated within Hunter College, a campus in the City University of New York system. Norm Atkins was named president of Teacher U, and the program was funded initially by a $10 million gift from a hedge fund operator, Larry Robbins, followed by a $30 million gift from the Robin Hood Foundation, where Atkins had served as co-executive director from 1989–1994. Teacher U became an independent graduate school authorized to grant master's degrees in teaching in New York state, and changed its name to Relay in 2011. It has also attracted substantial funding from major philanthropists including the New Schools Venture Fund, and the Carnegie, Dell, Fisher, Gates, Schusterman, and Walton foundations.

The teacher education programs that Relay offers are 2-year, part-time programs available to full-time teachers teaching with provisional certification. About 40 percent of the program is delivered through online instruction. Relay currently operates teacher education programs in New York City, Newark, Chicago, New Orleans, Philadelphia, Camden, Memphis, and Houston. Caperton and Whitmire (2012) say, "The vision is to keep expanding so that in a decade from now, 10,000 teachers in cities around the country are enrolled in an umbrella of Relays" (p. 80).

Teacher U and Relay have been proclaimed as innovative, path breaking, and bold largely based on their requirement that teachers show that they can raise student achievement at least 1 year in the second year of the program in order to successfully graduate from the program. Arthur Levine, a member of the Relay board, stated, "Relay is the model. … It's the future" (cited in Kronholz, 2012), while Caperton and Whitmire (2012) in their College Board published report assert that "Relay is a leader in the burgeoning movement to overhaul the way America trains its teachers for work in the highest-need schools" (p. 76). Several articles have appeared praising Relay in the national press (e.g., Carey, 2009; Lemov, 2012; Otterman, 2011), in publications aimed at entrepreneurs and philanthropists (e.g., Barbic, 2013; Schorr, 2013), and in educational journals (Kronholz, 2012). Relay was also featured in an uncritical way in an episode on American RadioWorks[20] and in the University of Michigan's "Teaching Works" seminar series.[21]

Further, both the White House and US Department of Education featured Relay as one of a handful of innovative programs in press releases connected to the issuing of new federal rules regulating the quality of teacher education programs (US Department of Education, 2014, November; the White House, 2014). For example, in a press release, the US Department of Education noted that Relay

> holds itself accountable for both program and employer satisfaction as well as requiring that teachers meet high goals for students' learning growth before they can complete their degrees. Students of Relay's teachers grew 1.3 years in reading proficiency in 1 year.
>
> *(US Department of Education, 2014)*

Given all of this media attention and press for Relay, it is reasonable to ask what evidence exists to support the repeated assertion that this program is a model for the future of teacher education. There are several types of warrants that have been offered in support of the success of Relay. First, there are testimonials of individuals who have been enrolled in the program. For example, Kronholz (2012) reports the following statements that were made to him by Relay teachers:

> Many also told me that Relay's lessons have changed their classroom culture. "The culture went from being compliant to being invested," said Max Silverstein, a Penn State business major now teaching in an early childhood classroom at Newark Legacy charter school. I heard the same thing from Alonte Johnson, a Moorehouse College English major who is teaching middle school English at King's Collegiate Center school in Brooklyn. A few days earlier his students designed a seating chart that paired the better and slower readers. "The environment is more interdependent instead of everyone working for me," he said.
>
> *(p. 6)*

The second type of warrant that has been offered to support claims about the success of Relay are internal analyses of Relay teacher candidates' master's projects that present data on the ability of its teacher candidates to raise students' achievement, including standardized test scores. Until recently, there was nothing at all on Relay's website or in the literature attempting to document the claims about the effectiveness of its teacher candidates. In late fall 2014, Relay redesigned its website and now presents what it terms "key data that indicate graduate student success in our educator preparation programs." The website explains that as a part of the master's defense that is required for successfully completing the program, graduate students should "meet and exceed an achievement floor"—a baseline for their students' performance. Examples that the website provides include having teacher candidates' students: (1) achieve a year's worth of growth as measured by the STEP literacy assessment; (2) achieve 70 percent mastery of the fifth-grade state science standards; and (3) grow at least one level on average writing rubric scores as measured by a five-point, six-traits rubric.[22] The program also encourages its teacher candidates to achieve more ambitious goals in each of these areas.

Relay reports on its website that 94 percent of its class of 2013 met their achievement floor and approximately half of the class met their ambitious goals in at least one subject. The website also states "on average, the K-12 students taught by Relay GSE's class of 2013 grew 1.3 years in reading performance in one year's time." Additionally, the Relay website references "regular institutional surveys" of graduates and polls of graduates' employers that attest to the effectiveness of Relay-prepared teachers (Relay GSE, 2014).

Another type of evidence that is put forth about the success of Relay is the assertion that it is based on practices that have been proven effective by research. For example, Gastic (2014), the Research Director at Relay, asserted with regard to teacher prep 2.0 programs including Relay: "These programs are deliberately anchored in best practices and insights drawn from classroom and school experience and educational research" (p. 96).

Relay has proudly proclaimed that faculty member Doug Lemov's classroom management strategies are the central core of its curriculum (e.g., Otterman, 2011). Lemov's (2010) strategies are based on his own observations and conversations with teachers and administrators in various charter schools that he claims are high performing. By any reasonable standard, these strategies do not possess the kind of rigorous scientific warrant that is being called for in teacher education programs (Pianta, 2011).

Given the extensive media coverage of Relay and the US Department of Education's and White House's statements of support, it is surprising that there is not a single independently conducted study (peer reviewed or not) that shows the effectiveness of Relay graduates, even according to the very narrow criterion of raising test scores. Any teacher education program can produce internal evaluation results, testimonials from graduates, and surveys that show that employers like to hire the graduates. Given Relay's branding as an exemplar for US teacher education, it seems reasonable to require that the program be able to produce independently conducted and preferably peer-reviewed research to substantiate its claims about success in achieving its goals.

Further, Relay's singular focus on the raising of student achievement scores is a cause for concern. Researchers have argued for decades that in order to fairly evaluate the quality of a teacher education program, we need to examine a broad range of costs and benefits associated with particular programs (Levin, 1980) rather than only focus on a narrow set of alleged benefits. There is clear evidence of the negative effects of the narrowing of the curriculum that have been shown to be associated with an exclusive focus on raising test scores (e.g., Berliner, 2011). Researchers have also documented that control-oriented classroom management practices like those of Lemov (2010) that are the core of Relay's curriculum sometimes have negative psychological effects on students who are subjected to them (e.g., Gatti & Catalano, 2015; Goodman, 2013). Finally, as Rose (2013) has pointed out, a singular focus on raising test scores can reinforce persistent inequities in US public education. As Rose explains:

> You can prep kids for a standardized test, get a bump in test scores, yet not be providing a very good education. The end result is the replication of a troubling pattern in American schooling: poor kids get an education of skills and routine, a lower-tier education, while students in more affluent districts get a robust course of study.
>
> *(p. 13)*

Knowledge Ventriloquism and Research on the Impact of Different Pathways into Teaching

> The body of research leads one to expect students in the classrooms of corps members—recruited, trained, and supported by Teach for America—to learn as much or more than they would if assigned a more experienced teacher in the same school.
>
> *(Teach for America, 2014)*

There has been a great deal of controversy in recent years about the research on the effects of different pathways into teaching, and the impact of these pathways on teacher and student learning. Research on the differences across pathways has been misrepresented in a number of ways to support an anti-university teacher education policy agenda. Here we examine a single example: the take-up of a research synthesis we wrote that was published in the AERA-commissioned volume, *Studying teacher education: The report of the AERA panel on research and teacher education* (Cochran-Smith & Zeichner, 2005). In this review, we analyzed 37 peer-reviewed research studies that examined the effectiveness of different kinds of teacher education programs in the US conducted between 1985 and 2004 (Zeichner & Conklin, 2005). The research we reviewed used a variety of teacher and student outcome measures to assess the effectiveness of different kinds of teacher education programs on a variety of outcomes including teacher efficacy, evaluations of teachers' practices, teacher retention, and student learning.

Drawing on the categories of comparison made by researchers, we structured our analysis by examining research on 4-year programs versus 5-year programs, state-sponsored alternative programs versus traditional programs, university-sponsored alternative programs versus traditional programs, school district-sponsored alternative programs versus traditional programs, studies involving Teach for America, and comparisons of multiple alternative and traditional programs. Although there have been many differing definitions of an "alternative" program, in this review we defined an alternative program as any program other than a 4- or 5-year undergraduate program at a college or university.[23] We acknowledged the problematic nature of this definition, given the tremendous variation that exists within each of these categories.

In view of the fierce public policy debates about how to best prepare teachers, in the conclusion of our review, we were careful to be clear about what we could and could not conclude based on the set of research studies we analyzed. For example, after reviewing four studies that examined the relative effectiveness of the Teach for America (TFA) program, we concluded that the research:

> presented mixed evidence. TFA teachers in New York City felt less prepared and less successful than did other new teachers, although actual teacher performance and student learning were not assessed. The studies in Houston and Arizona and the national study presented conflicting results about how much students achieved in reading and mathematics when taught by TFA versus those taught by other new teachers. In the case of Arizona, TFA teachers were shown to be less effective. In Houston, the students of TFA teachers had better achievement test results in some instances. In the national study, the students taught by TFA teachers experienced greater growth in mathematics achievement, but not in reading. ... These four studies comparing TFA with other programs clearly do not settle the issue of the efficacy of the TFA program in comparison with that of other programs.
>
> *(Zeichner & Conklin, 2005, p. 684)*

Throughout our analysis, we pointed out various limitations in the design of much of this research, as well as the need for future research to examine the character and quality of the actual preparation received by teachers in these comparisons in order to illuminate the impact of different program characteristics.

At the conclusion of our review, we cautioned:

> there is a danger that in the currently highly charged ideological debates about teacher quality in the current political context of the US that supporters of specific positions will go into this review and pull out selected

findings that support their particular point of view, ignoring other findings. For example, those who want to argue that there is no difference in terms of teacher quality between an alternative program sponsored by a school district or other non-university agency and traditional university-based programs can find examples in this review that taken out of context could wind up being used as "evidence" that non-university-sponsored alternative certification is justified.

This selective use of evidence from particular studies to support a particular policy direction without regard to the complexities of the analysis of the studies would be a distortion of what the research as a whole shows. This review does not support an uncritical adoption of either alternative or traditional programs or resolve the issue of whether particular programs like TFA are more effective than particular alternatives. The weight of the evidence of peer-reviewed research on teacher education programs in the US suggests certain characteristics of programs that may be important in terms of teacher quality and student learning. It remains for future research, however, to establish an evidentiary warrant for the validity of these claims about program excellence.

(Zeichner & Conklin, 2005, p. 704)

The Misuse of this Review

Despite our efforts to guard against the misuse of our research review, recent policy events have illustrated that politically motivated groups have done exactly what we warned about: pulling out findings to support their own views and, in some cases, blatantly misrepresenting the conclusions in our review. For example, in a letter to Congress dated July 16, 2012, a group of organizations—including 45 branches of Teach for America, the New Schools Venture Fund, the National Council for Teacher Quality, the Thomas B. Fordham Institute, the National Alliance for Public Charter Schools, the Relay Graduate School of Education, and Students First—requested that a definition of highly qualified teacher be incorporated into upcoming legislation that allowed less than fully certified teachers to be called "highly qualified" under NCLB (TFA et al., 2012).[24] The second paragraph of the letter states:

> Rigorous studies have consistently shown that alternatively certified teachers, as a whole, are as effective, if not more effective, than traditionally certified teachers. For example, a 2009 national randomized study commissioned by the US Department of Education found that there is no statistically significant difference in performance between students taught by teachers certified through alternative as opposed to traditional routes. Similarly, a comprehensive study of teacher education research published by the American Educational Research Association found *there were no*

> *differences in teacher efficacy or teaching competence, as measured by classroom*
> *observations, between alternatively and traditionally certified teachers.*
>
> *(TFA et al., 2012, emphasis added)*

The next paragraph goes on to state, "The most rigorous independent studies have demonstrated that Teach for America corps members outperform non-Teach for America teachers (including veteran teachers) in multiple subjects and grade levels." The authors of this letter use "these facts" to argue that "participating in an alternative route to certification does not preclude a teacher from being highly effective, and thus should never prevent that teacher from being considered 'highly qualified'" (TFA et al., 2012). While this letter does not name (or cite) it specifically, the statement italicized above comes from our review.

This statement comes from page 663 of our study, a section in which we reviewed four studies that compared graduates from state-sponsored alternative programs and university-based programs, and is followed by:

> Principal and supervisor ratings of teacher competence were mixed, favoring alternative certification in one case and traditional certification in the other. The value of these observations and ratings are extremely limited, however, due to the lack of specificity with regard to the evaluation criteria and the schools in which the graduates taught. In all four cases, although some details were provided about the alternative programs, traditional programs from an unknown number of different institutions were lumped together into a single category ignoring any differences in the programs. Because of the lack of information about the preparation received by the comparison group and the characteristics that they brought to this preparation, it was not possible to disentangle the influence of teacher characteristics from those of their preparation programs. Even if we assume the preparation made the difference in the reported outcomes, it was impossible to determine which characteristics of the teacher education programs might have accounted for these differences.
>
> *(Zeichner & Conklin, 2005, p. 663)*

To cite the sentence that is used for these highly political purposes without explaining its full context and complexity is a gross misrepresentation of what we actually said in our review.

Records of a Congressional hearing on July 24, 2012, before the House Subcommittee on Early Childhood, Elementary and Secondary Education's Committee on Education and the Workforce, entitled "Education Reforms: Discussing the value of alternative teacher certification programs," make similar reference to our study. Chairman Duncan Hunter went on to echo the same claim written in the letter noted above, including the statement that "an American Educational Research Association report determined there were no differences in teacher efficacy or teaching competence, between alternatively and traditionally certified teachers" (Hunter statement, 2012). Further, he noted that:

> While Republicans know there is no one-size-fits-all federal solution to help put more effective teachers in the classroom, supporting the availability and acceptance of alternative certification programs is one way the public and private sectors can join together to ensure more students have access to a quality education from an extraordinary educator.
>
> *(Hunter statement, 2012)*

Part of the same Congressional hearing included testimony from Cynthia Brown, Vice President for Education Policy at the Center for American Progress.[25] In her statement, she noted that "Research shows that graduates of alternative certification programs, on average, perform at the same level as traditionally prepared teachers who work in similar schools" and included a footnote to the AERA volume of which our review is part (Cochran-Smith & Zeichner, 2005).

As a follow up to the hearing,[26] Chairman Hunter wrote on August 14, 2012, to one of the people who testified, Jennifer Mulhern, Vice President of The New Teacher Project, asking whether there is "any evidence that teachers who have gone through traditional certification routes are more effective educators?" As part of her response, Mulhern again cited our study as follows:

> A 2005 comprehensive study on teacher education research published by the American Educational Research Association found that, "there were no differences between alternatively and traditionally certified teachers in terms of teacher efficacy or in teaching competence as measured by classroom observations."
>
> *(Cochran-Smith & Zeichner, 2005)*

These examples illustrate how research like ours has been repeatedly misused for high-stakes political gain while simultaneously perpetuating the problematic framing of the debate. Although we and others (cf. Cochran-Smith et al., 2012; Grossman & Loeb, 2008) have recommended a more productive path forward that involves focusing on the impact of specific teacher education program features, opponents of university-based teacher education like those cited above have continued to reinforce the notion in the public and political spheres of a dichotomy between "alternative" and "traditional" pathways into teaching. By cherry-picking evidence that supports the arguments they want to make, supporters of these so-called "alternative" routes are misleading politicians and the public—people who may not have access to this research or know how to use and interpret it.

Research Since Our 2005 Review

It is important for the educational research community, policymakers, and the public alike to have an understanding not only of the ways in which previous research is being misused, but also of more recent research that provides further insight into these ongoing debates. Although research published since our 2005 study has continued to paint a complex and inconclusive portrait of the teacher education program terrain, it has begun to identify more productive ways to focus research and policy on teacher preparation. For example, a group of researchers who studied pathways into teaching in New York City provided a more focused distinction between the types of teacher preparation pathways and how distinctions among pathways shape outcomes. In their analysis of 31 elementary teacher preparation pathways in New York City—including university-based teacher education programs, Teach for America, and the New York City Teaching Fellows program—these researchers found that preparation coursework across pathways is more similar than different, that many so-called "alternative" programs usually include coursework at a university, and that the more important distinguishing feature among programs is in the timing of coursework: whether teachers complete the majority of their coursework prior to becoming full-time teachers of record, or whether most of this coursework occurs once they have become classroom teachers (Boyd et al., 2008). Thus, they adopt the distinguishing terminology of "early entry" and "college recommending" programs to highlight the nature of teachers' preparation before they begin full-time teaching.

Two other analyses from the same New York City teaching pathways research further illustrate that understanding the effectiveness of differing preparation pathways requires both nuanced research designs and precise interpretation of results. In an early analysis, this research team compared the third- through eighth-grade student achievement of teachers who completed university-based teacher education programs with those teachers who had reduced coursework prior to becoming first-year teachers (Boyd et al., 2006). Based on this comparison, the researchers found that the "early entry" teachers often produced smaller initial gains as measured by standardized test scores in math and reading, yet these differences mostly disappeared as the cohorts gained teaching experience. Further, based on this particular analysis, the variation in teacher effectiveness was far greater within pathways than between. Yet in a more recent analysis, the researchers examined the distinctions among pathways in far greater detail, analyzing data on the specific features of 31 elementary teacher education programs in New York City—26 of which involved teachers completing coursework prior to becoming a teacher of record, and five of which involved teachers completing coursework while teaching full time (Boyd et al., 2008). The researchers examined the relationship between these features of teacher preparation and elementary students' math and reading achievement. Through this more fine-grained analysis, Boyd et al. (2008) found that some programs produced teachers with a significantly greater effect on student achievement than others. And, while the researchers were very careful to note that their research was a first step in discerning these complex relationships, they also found that features of teacher preparation that are focused on the practice of teaching relate to student achievement gains in teachers' first year of teaching.

These analyses from the New York City pathways study, as well as other recent analyses, point to the importance of focusing on particular features of teacher education programs. Another more recent study, which examined numerous preparation pathways to teaching in North Carolina using a value-added analysis of teacher entry portals on student achievement, further illuminated the complexity of examining teacher effectiveness from these different pathways (Henry et al., 2014). Like other studies comparing different preparation pathways, this research highlighted how teacher effectiveness within common entry portals varies depending on subject matter and grade level, revealing, for example, that TFA corps members were more effective than in-state public undergraduates in seven different grade level/subject comparisons (e.g., elementary grades math), but were no different in three other grade-level comparisons (Henry et al., 2014).

Finally, the most recent comprehensive vetted review of the peer-reviewed studies on the effects of different pathways into teaching, published in the American Educational Research Association's *Handbook of Research on Teaching*, concludes:

> Not surprisingly, studies in this line of research, which compared the impact on students' achievement of teachers with alternative certification and/or from "alternative" pathways or compared the impact of teachers from a particular "alternative" program with those from other sources of new teachers, are inconsistent and ultimately inconclusive at a broad level in terms of what they tell us about the effects of particular programs. ... Some studies found small or no differences in the achievement of students taught by teachers from different pathways, some found university-recommended teachers were more effective in some areas and some levels, and some found that teachers from alternative routes or from a particular alternative pathway, such as TFA or the Boston Teacher Residency program, were more or less effective in some areas and at some levels than non-alternative pathway teachers.
>
> *(Cochran-Smith & Villegas, 2016, p. 453)*

Similarly, the most recent National Research Council study of teacher education (2010) concluded:

> Though there is ample room for debate on how much and what kind of education is best for preparing effective teachers, inferring that one type of

preparation does or does not yield better outcomes for students is not warranted by the evidence.

(pp. 41–42)

The National Research Council report (2010) further adds that this conclusion about the lack of clear findings "does not mean that the characteristics of pathways do not matter. Rather it suggests research on the sources of variation in preparation such as selectivity, timing, and specific components and characteristics is needed" (p. 2).

Look to the Future

We have argued in this chapter that advocates of teacher prep 2.0 programs and the deregulation of teacher education have not presented persuasive evidence for their claims, either of the failures of university teacher education or the successes of non-university programs. We have asserted that a combination of entrepreneurial branding and marketing, along with distortion of the findings of education research, have been used to make a case for "disruptive innovation" (Liu, 2013) in teacher education. We have illustrated several specific cases of this misrepresentation in this chapter.

Through the examples that we have presented of the misrepresentation of research to support a political agenda of deregulation in teacher education, we have not intended to suggest that status-quo university-sponsored teacher education is acceptable. On the contrary, we believe that university-sponsored teacher education programs need to change in significant ways and that philanthropists, states, and the federal government need to make investments in supporting high-quality teacher education for the teachers of everyone's children.

In fact, there is clear evidence of a number of shifts that are now underway within traditional models of college and university programs—those programs that continue to prepare the majority of US teachers. These efforts include: a greater focus on connecting coursework (e.g., methods and foundations courses) to the complexities of schools for which teachers are being prepared; a greater emphasis on teaching teachers to enact rather than just learn about research-based teaching practices; new efforts to prepare teachers to work in respectful and responsive ways with students' families and communities and to build in positive ways on the cultural resources that students bring to school with them; and the development of new ways to share responsibility for teacher education across institutional boundaries, such as in urban teacher residencies (Cochran-Smith & Villegas, 2016; Zeichner & Bier, 2015; Zeichner, Payne, & Brayko, 2015).

We are also not opposed to providers of teacher education other than universities and to the idea of multiple pathways into teaching, as long as all of the different programs are held to the same high standards of quality and the research and evidence that support all programs' practices are represented accurately and fairly.

In order to hold all programs to common standards of quality and evidence, there are several things we believe need to be done to minimize the kind of misuse of educational research that we have attempted to illustrate in this chapter. First, all researchers who conduct studies that purport to offer information on the efficacy of different program models, and those who produce syntheses of studies done by others, should reveal their sources of funding, their direct and indirect links to the programs, and subject their work to independent and blind peer review. Although independent peer review does not guarantee the lack of a conflict of interest or high quality, it is widely considered to be a critical part of the functioning of scientific communities and of quality control (American Educational Research Association, 2008; Shavelson & Towne, 2002).

Second, given that much academic research on education is inaccessible to policymakers, practitioners, and the general public (Lubienski, Scott, & DeBray, 2014), researchers should take more responsibility for communicating their findings in clear ways to various stakeholders and participate in discussions about the meaning of their research in different contexts (Zeichner, 1995). They should also speak out publicly when they know that their research is being misrepresented in efforts to reform policies and practices. Such work may require institutions to invest in training and supporting educational researchers in learning how to convey research findings to both academic and more general audiences.

Third, the media should cover claims about issues in teacher education in proportion to the strength of the evidence that stands behind them. In this chapter, we have illustrated how both claims that education schools have failed and that new teacher prep 2.0 programs are superior are based on either the absence of credible research or misrepresentations of research. Specifically, we have shown that the media's attention to Levine's (2006) study of education schools, to the Relay Graduate School of Education, and to the reports of the National Council on Teacher Quality are out of proportion to the attention that these groups deserve given the lack of scientifically vetted evidence supporting their claims. While many of the media reports of these groups have included some mention of the critiques of their work, the amount of attention the media has given to groups like the NCTQ has served to legitimize their work. While we recognize the cuts in resources that media outlets have experienced and their need to compete with new nontraditional forms of media communication, we believe they have a responsibility in a democratic society to critically scrutinize the reports and studies that are brought to them by advocates of all kinds of alleged innovations in teacher education.

Fourth, we should assess the quality of programs based on an analysis of a variety of costs and benefits associated with particular programs, and not just look at whose graduates can raise test scores the most. In the 1970s, when arguments for competency-based teacher education were focused almost exclusively on which teacher behaviors could most effectively raise students' standardized test scores, Kliebard (1973) called for reformulating the questions that were asked to assess the quality of teaching and teacher education programs. Specifically, he called for an abandonment of exclusive attention to one-dimensional questions of effectiveness based on test scores (what he referred to as "raw empiricism") and for an approach that looked more broadly and deeply at teaching. Kliebard said:

> The typical research on teaching is essentially a horse race. Sometimes one horse wins, sometimes the other; often it is a tie. In any case the outcome of the question adds nothing to our understanding of the complex processes that are involved in teaching.
>
> *(1973, p. 21)*

Several years later Levin (1980) argued for a cost-utility approach that evaluates the perceived costs and benefits of various alternatives in evaluating particular policy choices about teacher education. While we support the shift to attention to the outcomes of teacher education, we believe that in evaluating the quality of teacher education programs, we need to heed both Kliebard's (1973) and Levin's (1980) advice to assess a broader range of program outcomes. This includes examining program graduates' abilities to promote students' socio-emotional development, civic development, creativity, problem solving and critical thinking abilities, and so on. We also need to examine the retention data on graduates from different programs, and whether there has been a narrowing of the curriculum in schools in which the graduates from different programs teach. As we noted earlier, there is substantial evidence that in many schools serving students living in poverty, students are denied access to a rich and broad curriculum and opportunities to interact with knowledge in authentic ways. Further, there is significant inequity in the distribution of fully prepared and experienced teachers to schools serving students from different social class backgrounds (Peske & Haycock, 2006). We know from research that teacher turnover is costly to districts and that it interferes with student learning (Ronfeldt, Loeb, & Wycoff, 2013). Thus, as part of the array of outcomes we should examine when making judgments about the quality of teacher education programs, we should consider the impact of hiring teachers from different programs on communities' access to fully prepared and experienced teachers.

Assessing a broader range of program outcomes would mean that even if proponents of new non-university sponsored programs like Relay are able to consistently produce peer-reviewed research that shows that graduates of their programs increase students' test scores more than the graduates from other programs, this would not be sufficient evidence to support the claim that these programs are superior. In fact, the research literature suggests that a stronger emphasis only on raising test scores will deepen and increase the extent of education inequities and continue to create a second-class system of schooling for students living in poverty.

The selective and biased use of findings from studies, the consultation of limited and select research (knowledge ventriloquism), and the repeated assertion that teacher prep 2.0 programs are superior and that university teacher education is broken (echo chambers)—assertions spread by mostly uncritical media coverage—have set us on a course to destroy the university-based teacher education system that has dominated the preparation of teachers in the US since the 1960s. Gastic's (2014) forecast for the future of teacher education capitalizes on these strategies, warning teacher education programs:

> The next decade will see the proliferation of teacher prep 2.0 models as the benefits of their collective approach to teacher education become better known and more widely recognized.
>
> *(p. 105)*

> Those programs that fail to join this learning community will soon reveal their obsolescence and find themselves struggling to justify their existence. Demand will shift to more relevant, affordable and flexible programs where teachers are held to high professional standards of knowledge and skill under advisement of strong instructors and coaches who are committed to improving a teacher's effectiveness.
>
> *(p. 109)*

The stripping of substantial state resources from the public universities that continue to prepare most of the nation's teachers, together with the massive amounts of federal and philanthropic funds that continue to pour into expanding the proliferation of teacher prep 2.0 programs, have significantly hindered the ability of education schools to transform their programs. We believe that it is a mistake to continue to dismantle the college and university system of teacher education and to attempt to remake it in the image of 2.0 programs like Relay.

Further, given the clear evidence that exists showing that poverty and inequality are strong correlates of variations in student achievement (Duncan & Murnane, 2011), the implication by some teacher prep 2.0 advocates that university-based teacher preparation programs have failed in their efforts to address inequities in education, and that teacher prep 2.0 programs alone will address the problems, is not warranted. In fact, there is very little discussion in the literature on teacher prep 2.0 programs about the close connection between poverty and its associated "rotten outcomes" (Schorr & Schorr, 1988) and student learning in school. A recent study of federal data by the Southern Education Foundation (2015) has reported that the majority (51 percent) of students in US public schools qualify for free and reduced lunches (up from 38 percent in 2000), and that a majority of these children live in poverty in 21 states. It seems clear that, while what happens in classrooms and schools can help make a difference in addressing inequities in opportunities and outcomes, we must deal nonetheless with poverty if we expect to achieve our goals (Berliner, 2013). Additionally, there are no examples of education systems that have consistently performed well on international comparisons of achievement, including equity in achievement, by using the market-based approach that has been promoted by advocates of deregulation and greater market-based competition (e.g., Darling-Hammond & Lieberman, 2012).

To move forward more productively to improve teacher education will require transparent dialogue about the outcomes that all children deserve. Further, the improvement of teacher education will require a willingness from all those engaged in the enterprise to examine the strengths and limitations of all current and proposed approaches, and to learn from the available research and evidence about the specific types of knowledge, preparation, and experiences needed for teachers to be able to successfully educate all students to the same high standard of quality.

The recommendations that we have offered in this chapter for raising the quality of the debate about the future of teacher education in the US are not aimed at the unattainable and undesirable goal of removing politics from research production and utilization related to teacher education. Politics and vigorous debate are fundamental to the functioning of a genuinely democratic society. Rather, we are calling for greater transparency in this process, for a vetting of the research evidence that informs the debate, and for a genuine examination of different policy options.

As we write this chapter, the GREAT Act, a bill that would greatly accelerate the disruptive process we describe, sits in Congress as a part of the reauthorization of the Elementary and Secondary Education Act.[27] Passage of the GREAT Act without a rigorous and honest examination of the full range of available research and evidence supporting the claims that have been made about both university and 2.0 programs subverts the process of democracy in policymaking and will, in our view, significantly weaken the value of resulting policies and the practices and structures that result from them. We need to carefully evaluate the multiple policy options available for improving the quality of teacher education in the US, and all of us need to be willing to recognize that the status quo is not acceptable. In our view, continuing down the current path of destroying and replacing the college and university system of teacher education in the US will serve to widen, not narrow, the inequities in opportunities and outcomes that currently exist.

Notes

1 For example, since 2000, the US Education Department has given over $200 million to support Teach for America (https://www.usaspending.gov/Pages/AdvancedSearch. aspx?k=Teach%20for%20America). The US Department of Education's Race to the Top competitions for funds have encouraged and in some cases required states to allow non-university providers of teacher education to operate and have resulted in many

states changing their policies to do so (Crowe, 2011). Also, private foundations have invested increasing amounts of their resources in promoting alternatives to college and university sponsored teacher education programs (Zeichner & Peña-Sandoval, 2015).

2 The term "2.0" has been used by Gastic (2014) and by Teach for America's former Co-CEO Matt Kramer (Rich, 2015) in connection with these non-university teacher education programs and university programs that try to emulate them.

3 In addition to the Relay and Sposato schools of education mentioned above, other teacher education programs like the Aspire, Capital, Chicago, and the High Tech High teacher residencies have been initiated to prepare teachers for particular charter schools.

4 Tseng (2012) describes the tactical or symbolic use of research as when "research is used to justify a position already taken. In this case policymakers or practitioners know whether they support or oppose a particular piece of legislation or reform effort and they marshal research to back their position" (p. 7).

5 In early-entry programs like Teach for America and The New Teacher Project, individuals enter schools as teachers of record after a brief summer pre-service program and complete most of their requirements for a teaching license while they are legally responsible for a classroom.

6 See http://edschools.org/. The other two reports focused on the preparation of educational leaders and on education research.

7 Schorr was the Acting Assistant Secretary for the Office of Communications and Outreach of the US Department of Education.

8 See www.congress.gov/crec/2013/05/23/CREC-2013-05-23-pt1-PgE750-2.pdf

9 No information is provided in the report about how this sample of 500 teachers was selected beyond the criteria noted above.

10 A White House press release dated April 24, 2014, previewing the release of the rules, also cited the Levine education school alumni survey, finding that "almost two-thirds report that their teacher preparation program left them unprepared for the realities of the classroom" (www.whitehouse.gov/the-press-office/2014/04/25/fact-sheet-taking-action-improve-teacher-preparation).

11 See slide No. 14 in the presentation slide deck on "Improving Teacher Preparation" (www.ed.gov/teacherprep).

12 This data was a result of teachers responding to a question about what the top problem they experienced in their teacher preparation programs was.

13 At the time of this writing, 11 states allowed ABCTE to operate within their borders. NCTQ no longer has ties to ABCTE.

14 It should be noted that NCTQ has recently compiled research inventories of studies that allegedly support each standard. There are 62 studies listed in support of the equity standard. (http://nctq.org/dmsView/Standard_Book_13). Since we were not able to find any discussion of how NCTQ thinks these studies support the equity standard, we maintain our position about the lack of empirical support for the standard. Merely listing a string of studies does not constitute empirical evidence in our view.

15 See http://edworkforce.house.gov/uploadedfiles/07.27.11_walsh.pdf

16 See comments by Norm Atkins and Dave Levin at https://www.youtube.com/watch?v=uSQNIUj_EJY and http://www.relay.edu/blog-entry/freakonomics-features-relay-latest-podcast

17 For example, see http://aacte.org/resources/nctq-usnwr-review

18 See https://www.youtube.com/watch?v=_w5VPahqy70

19 For example, Arnett (2016); Liu (2013).

20 See https://soundcloud.com/americanradioworks/american-radioworks-new-grad

21 Seehttp://www.teachingworks.org/training/seminar-series/event/detail/relay-graduate-school-of-education

22 See www.relay.edu/about/results

23 Not all of the researchers used the same definitions of alternative and traditional programs, and this definition, which was originally proposed by Adelman (1986) and has been more recently used by others, enabled us to make the most use of the data in the 37 studies.

24 See https://www.washingtonpost.com/news/answer-sheet/wp/2013/08/27/how-the-public-is-deceived-about-highly-qualified-teachers/ for background information on the controversy about the definition of highly qualified teachers.

25 No scholars who conducted any of the major syntheses of this body of research were invited to be on this "expert" panel.

26 See http://edworkforce.house.gov/calendar/eventsingle.aspx?EventID=303327

27 See Zeichner and Peña-Sandoval (2015) for a discussion of the role of the New School Venture Fund (a major investor in teacher prep 2.0 programs) in developing and promoting the GREAT Act.

28 This was the title of the article at its original publication. Since then, the title has been altered on the online version. "Corps of temporary teachers" has been removed and "Teach for America" has been inserted in its place.

References

Adelman, N. (1986). *An exploratory study of teacher alternative certification and retraining programs.* Washington, DC: U.S. Department of Education.

American Educational Research Association (2008). Alternative definition of scientifically-based research. Accessed May 10, 2014. Retrieved from www.aera.net/Portals/38/docs/About_AERA/KeyPrograms/DefinitionofScientificallyBasedResearch.pdf

American Federation of Teachers Teacher Preparation Task Force. (2012). *Raising the bar: Aligning and elevating teacher preparation and the teaching profession.* Washington, DC.

American Statistical Association. (2014). ASA statement on using value-added models for educational assessment. Retrieved from www.scribd.com/doc/217916454/ASA-VAM-Statement-1

Arnett, T. (2016, January 28). ESSA unlocks teacher prep innovation. Brookings Center Chalkboard. Retrieved on February 10, 2016 from https://www.brookings.edu/blog/brown-center-chalkboard/2016/01/28/essa-unlocks-teacher-prep-innovation/

Banchero, S. (2013, June 18). Teacher training's low grade. *The Wall Street Journal.* Retrieved from www.wsj.com/articles/SB10001424127887323836504578551904167354358

Baker, E. L., Barton, P. E., Darling-Hammond, L., Haertel, E., Ladd, H. F., Linn, R. L., Ravitch, D., Rothstein, R., Shavelson, R. J., & Shepard, L. A. (2010, August). *Problems with the use of student test scores to evaluate teachers.* (EPI Briefing Paper #278). Washington, DC: Economic Policy Institute.

Banks, J., Cochran-Smith, M., Moll, L., Richert, A., Zeichner, K., LePage, P., Darling-Hammond, L., & Duffy, H. (2005). Teaching diverse learners. In L. Darling-Hammond & J. Bransford (Eds), *Preparing teachers for a changing world* (pp. 232–274). San Francisco, CA: Jossey-Bass.

Barbic, K. (2013). Mediocrity be gone. *The Philanthropy Roundtable*. Retrieved from www.philanthropyroundtable.org/topic/excellence_in_philanthropy/mediocrity_be_gone

Berliner, D. (2011). Rational responses to high-stakes testing: The case of curriculum narrowing and the harm that follows. *Cambridge Journal of Education*, *41*(3), 287–302.

Berliner, D. (2013). Effects of inequality and poverty vs. teachers and schooling on America's youth. *Teachers College Record*, *115*(12), 1–26.

Berliner, D. (2014). Exogenous variables and value-added assumptions: A fatal flaw. *Teachers College Record*, *116*(1), 1–31.

Berrett, D. (2013, June 18). "An industry of mediocrity": Study criticizes teacher-education programs. *The Chronicle of Higher Education*. Retrieved from http://chronicle.com/article/An-Industry-of-Mediocrity-/139887/

Bowden, M. (2009, October). The story behind the story. *The Atlantic*. Retrieved from www.theatlantic.com/magazine/print/2009/10/the-story-behind-the-story/307667

Boyd, D., Grossman, P. L., Hammerness, K., Lankford, R. H., Loeb, S., McDonald, M., et al. (2008). Surveying the landscape of teacher education in New York City: Constrained variation and the challenge of innovation. *Educational Evaluation and Policy Analysis*, *30*(4), 319–343.

Boyd, D., Grossman, P., Lankford, H., Loeb, S., & Wyckoff, J. (2006). How changes in entry requirements alter the teacher workforce and affect student achievement. *Education Finance and Policy*, *1*(2), 439–454.

Boyd, D. J., Grossman, P. L., Lankford, H., Loeb, S., & Wyckoff, J. (2009). Teacher preparation and student achievement. *Educational Evaluation and Policy Analysis*, *31*(4), 416–440.

Caperton, G., & Whitmire, R. R. (2012). *The achievable dream.* New York, NY: The College Board.

Carey, K. (2009, December 13). "Teacher U": A new model in employer-led higher education. *The Chronicle of Higher Education*. Retrieved from http://chronicle.com/article/Teacher-U-A-NewModel-in/49442

Chubb, J. E. (2012). *The best teachers in the world: Why we don't have them and how we could.* Stanford, CA: Hoover Institution Press.

Cochran-Smith, M., Cannady, M., McEachern, K., Mitchell, K., Piazza, P., Power, C., & Ryan, A. (2012). Teachers' education and outcomes: Mapping the research terrain. *Teachers College Record*, *114*(10), 1–49.

Cochran-Smith, M. & Villegas, A. M. (2016). Research on teacher preparation: Charting the landscape of a sprawling field. In D. Gitomer & C. Bell (Eds), *Handbook of Research on Teaching (5th ed.)* (pp. 439–548). Washington, DC: American Educational Research Association.

Cochran-Smith, M., & Zeichner, K. (Eds). (2005). *Studying teacher education.* New York, NY: Routledge.

Council of Chief State School Officers (2012). *Our responsibility, our promise: Transforming educator preparation and entry into the profession.* Washington, DC.

Center for Research on Education Outcomes (CREDO). (2009). *Multiple choice: Charter school performance in sixteen states.* Retrieved from http://credo.stanford.edu/reports/ MULTIPLE_CHOICE_CREDO.pdf

Center for Research on Education Outcomes (CREDO). (2013). *National charter school study.* Retrieved from http://credo.stanford.edu/documents/NCSS%202013%20 Final%20Draft.pdf

Crowe, E. (2010). *Measuring what matters: A stronger accountability model for teacher education.* Washington, DC: Center for American Progress.

Crowe, E. (2011). *Race to the Top and teacher preparation: Analyzing state strategies for ensuring real accountability and fostering program innovation.* Washington, DC: Center for American Progress.

Darling-Hammond, L. (2004). Inequality and the right to learn: Access to qualified teachers in California's public schools. *Teachers College Record, 106*(10), 1936–1966.

Darling-Hammond, L. (2013, June 13). Why the NCTQ teacher prep ratings are nonsense. *The Washington Post.* Retrieved from www.washingtonpost.com/blogs/ answer-sheet/wp/2013/06/18/why-the-nctq-teacher-prep-ratings-are-nonsense/

Darling-Hammond, L. & Bransford, J. (Eds). (2005). *Preparing teachers for a changing world: What teachers should learn and be able to do.* San Francisco, CA: Jossey-Bass.

Darling-Hammond, L., & Lieberman, A. (Eds). (2012). *Teacher education around the world: Changing policies and practices.* New York, NY: Routledge.

Duncan, A. (2009, October 22). Teacher preparation: Reforming the uncertain profession. Speech presented at Teachers College, Columbia University. Retrieved from www. ed.gov/news/speeches/teacher-preparation-reforming-uncertain-profession

Duncan, A. (2011). *Our future, our teachers: The Obama administration's plan for teacher education reform and improvement.* Washington, DC: United States Department of Education.

Duncan, G. J., & Murnane, R. J. (Eds). (2011). *Whither opportunity?: Rising inequality, schools, and children's life chances.* New York, NY: Russell Sage and Spencer Foundations.

Eduventures. (2009). Executive Summary: Educator preparation—Strengths and areas for improvement in preparation programs. *Recruiting and Preparing Teachers Series.* Retrieved from http://oapcte.org/Eduventures_Report_on_Teach_Prep.pdf

Feistritzer, C. E. (2011). *Profile of teachers in the U.S, 2011.* Washington, DC: National Center for Education Information. Retrieved from www.edweek.org/media/ pot2011final-blog.pdf

Feller, B. (2006, September 19). Study says teacher training is chaotic. *The Education Schools Project, Associated Press.* Retrieved from www.edschools.org/news/Associated_ Press_091906.htm

Finder, A. (2006, September 19). Report critical of training of teachers. *The New York Times.* Retrieved from www.nytimes.com/2006/09/19/education/19report. html?_r=0

Flexner, A. (1910). *Medical education in the US and Canada: A report to the Carnegie Foundation for the Advancement for Teaching.* Bulletin No. 4. New York, NY: Carnegie Foundation for the Advancement of Teaching.

Fraser, J. (2007). *Preparing America's teachers: A history.* New York, NY: Teachers College Press.

Fullan, M., Galluzzo, G., Morris, P., & Watson, N. (1998). *The rise and stall of teacher education reform.* Washington, DC: American Association of Colleges for Teacher Education.

Fuller, E. J. (2014). Shaky methods, shaky motives: A critique of the National Council for Teacher Quality's review of teacher preparation programs. *Journal of Teacher Education, 65*(1) 63–77.

Gastic, B. (2014). Closing the opportunity gap: Preparing the next generation of effective teachers. In R. Hess & M. McShane (Eds), *Teacher quality 2.0: Toward a new era in education reform.* Cambridge, MA: Harvard Education Press.

Gatti, L., & Catalano, T. (2015). The business of learning to teach: A critical metaphor analysis of one teacher's journey. *Teaching and Teacher Education, 45,* 149–160.

Goldie, D., Linick, M., Jabbar, H., & Lubienski, C. (2014). Using bibliometric and social media analysis to explore the "echo chamber" hypothesis. *Educational Policy, 28*(2), 281–305.

Goodlad, J. (1998). *Educational renewal: Better teachers, better schools.* San Francisco, CA: Jossey-Bass.

Goodman, J. (2013). Charter management organizations and the regulated environment: Is it worth the price? *Educational Researcher, 42*(2), 89–96.

Greenberg, J., Walsh, K., & McKee, A. (2015). 2014 Teacher prep review. Washington, DC: National Council on Teacher Quality.

Grossman, P., & Loeb, S. (2008). *Alternative routes to teaching: Mapping the new landscape of teacher education.* Cambridge, MA: Harvard Education Press.

Grossman, P., Ronfeldt, M., & Cohen, J. (2012). The power of setting: The role of field experience in learning to teach. In K. Harris, S. Graham, T. Urdin, et al. (Eds), *APA educational psychology handbook Vol 3: Application to learning and teaching* (pp. 311–334). Washington, DC: American Psychological Association.

Hammerness, K., Darling-Hammond, L., Bransford, J., Berliner, D., Cochran-Smith, M., McDonald, M., & Zeichner, K. (2005). How teachers learn and develop. In L. Darling-Hammond & J. Bransford (Eds), *Preparing teachers for a changing world* (pp. 358–389). San Francisco, CA: Jossey-Bass.

Henig, J. (2008). *Spin cycle: How research is used in policy debates—The case of charter schools.* New York, NY: Russell Sage Foundation.

Henry, G. T., & Bastian, K. C. (2015, May). *Measuring up: The National Council on Teacher Quality's ratings of teacher preparation programs and measures of teacher performance.* Chapel Hill, NC: The Education Policy Initiative at Carolina.

Henry, G., Purtell, K., Fortner, C. K., Thompson, C., Campbell, S., & Patterson, K. M. (2014). The effects of teacher entry portals on student achievement. *Journal of Teacher Education, 64*(5), 439–453.

Hess, F. (2001). *Tear down this wall: The case for a radical overall of teacher certification.* Washington, DC: Progressive Policy Institute.

Hess, F. M. (2006). Politics, policy, and the promise of entrepreneurship. In F.M. Hess (Ed.), *Educational entrepreneurship: Realities, challenges, possibilities* (pp. 243–260). Cambridge, MA: Harvard Education Press.

Hollins, E. R., & Guzman, M. T. (2005). Preparing teachers for diverse populations. In M. Cochran-Smith & K. Zeichner (Eds), *Studying teacher education: The report of the AERA panel on research and teacher education* (pp. 477–548). Washington, DC: American Educational Research Association.

Holmes Partnership. (2007). *The Holmes Partnership trilogy: Tomorrow's teachers, tomorrow's schools, tomorrow's schools of education.* New York, NY: Peter Lang.

Honawar, V. (2006, September 20). Prominent teacher-educator assails field, suggests new accreditation body in report. *Education Week, 26*(4). Retrieved from www.edschools. org/pdf/Education_Week_092006.pdf

Hunter statement (2012, July, 24). Hearing on 'Education reforms: Discussing the value of alternative teacher certification programs' [Committee Statement]. Retrieved from http://edworkforce.house.gov/news/documentsingle.aspx?DocumentID=304099

Kanstoroom, M., & Finn, C. (1999, July). *Better teachers, better schools.* Washington, DC: Thomas B. Fordham Foundation.

Katz, S. (2013). Reshaping US public education policy. *Stanford Social Innovation Review.* Retrieved from http://ssir.org/articles/entry/reshaping_US_public_education_policy

Keller, B. (2013, October 20). "An industry of mediocrity." *The New York Times.* Retrieved from www.nytimes.com/2013/10/21/opinion/keller-an-industry-of-mediocrity.html?_r=0

Kliebard, H. (1973). The question in teacher education. In D. McCarty (Ed.), *New perspectives on teacher education* (pp. 8–24). San Francisco, CA: Jossey-Bass.

Knowles, T. (2013, January). New pathways for teachers, new promises for students: A vision for developing excellent teachers. *Teacher Quality 2.0 (Special Report 3).* Washington, DC: American Enterprise Institute.

Kronholz, J. (2012). A new type of Ed school: Linking candidate success to student success. *Education Next, 12*(4). Retrieved from http://educationnext.org/a-new-type-of-ed-school/

Lemov, D. (2010). *Teach like a champion: 49 techniques that put students on the path to college (K–12).* San Francisco, CA: Jossey-Bass.

Lemov, D. (2012, October 26). Practice makes perfect and not just for jocks and musicians. *The Wall Street Journal.* Retrieved from www.wsj.com/articles/SB1000142405297020 4530504578078602307104168

Levin, H. M. (1980). Teacher certification and the economics of information. *Educational Evaluation and Policy Analysis, 2*(4), 5–18.

Levine, A. (2006). *Educating school teachers.* The Education Schools Project. Retrieved from www.edschools.org/pdf/Educating_Teachers_Report.pdf

Liu, M. (2013). Disrupting teacher education. *Education Next, 13*(3). Retrieved from http://educationnext.org/disrupting-teacher-education/

Lubienski, C., Scott, J., & DeBray, E. (2014). The politics of research production, promotion, and utilization in educational policy. *Educational Policy, 28*(2), 131–144.

Malin, J. R., & Lubienski, C. (2015). Educational expertise, advocacy, and media influence. *Education Policy Analysis Archives, 23*(6). Retrieved from http://dx.doi. org/10.14507/epaa.v23.1706

National Council for Accreditation of Teacher Education. (2010). *Transforming teacher education through clinical practice: A national strategy to prepare effective teachers.* Washington, DC.

National Research Council. (2002) *Scientific research in education,* Committee on Scientific Principles for Education Research (R. J. Shavelson & L. Towne, Eds.). Washington, DC: The National Academies Press.

National Research Council. (2010). *Preparing teachers: Building evidence for sound policy.* Committee on the Study of Teacher Preparation Programs in the United States, Center for Education. Division of Behavioral and Social Sciences and Education Washington, DC: The National Academies Press.

NCTQ (2014). III: Findings by standard. *NCTQ teacher prep review* (pp. 33–57). Retrieved from www.nctq.org/dmsView/Chapter3_FindingsByStandard

Otterman, S. (2011, July 21). Ed schools' pedagogical puzzle. *The New York Times.* Retrieved from www.nytimes.com/2011/07/24/education/edlife/edl-24teacher-t. html?pagewanted=all&_r=0

Pearson, P. D., & Goatley, V. (2013, July 2). Response to the NCTQ teacher education report. On the *International Literacy Association's Literacy Daily Blog* [Blog post]. Retrieved from www.literacyworldwide.org/blog/literacy-daily/2013/07/02/ response-to-the-nctq-teacher-education-report

Peske, H., & Haycock, K. (2006). Teaching inequality: How poor minority students are shortchanged on teacher quality. Washington, DC: Education Trust.

Pianta, R. C. (2011). *Teaching children well: New evidence-based approaches to teacher professional development and training.* Washington, DC: Center for American Progress.

Public Agenda (2008). *Lessons learned: New teachers talk about their jobs, challenges, long-range plans.* Public Agenda & the National Comprehensive Center for Teacher Quality. Retrieved from www.publicagenda.org/files/lessons_learned_3.pdf

Relay Graduate School of Education. (2014). *About: Our Institution.* Retrieved from www.relay.edu/about/institution

Rich, M. (2015, February). Fewer top graduates want to join corps of temporary teachers.[28] *The New York Times.* Retrieved from: www.nytimes.com/2015/02/06/education/ fewer-top-graduates-want-to-join-teach-for-america.html

Robertson, S. L. (2012). The strange non-death of neoliberal privatization in the World Bank's Educational Strategy 2020. In S. Klees, J. Samoff, & N. Stromquist (Eds), *The World Bank and education: Critiques and alternatives* (pp. 190–205). Rotterdam: Sense Publishers.

Rochkind, J., Ott, A., Immerwahr, J., Doble, J., & Johnson, J. (2007). *Lessons learned: New teachers talk about their jobs, challenges, and long-range plans.* Report form the National Comprehensive Center on Teacher Quality and the Public Agenda. Retrieved on January 12, 2010 from https://www.publicagenda.org/files/lessons_learned_3.pdf

Ronfeldt, M. (2012). Where should student teachers learn to teach? Effects of field placement school characteristics on teacher retention and effectiveness. *Educational Evaluation and Policy Analysis, 34*(1), 3–26.

Ronfeldt, M., Loeb, S., & Wycoff, J. (2013). How teacher turnover harms student achievement. *American Educational Research Journal, 50*(1), 4–36.

Rose, M. (2013). The mismeasure of teaching and learning: How contemporary school reform fails the test. In M. B. Katz & M. Rose (Eds.), *Public education under siege* (pp. 9–20). Philadelphia, PA: University of Pennsylvania Press.

Sanchez, C. (2013, June 18). Study: Teacher prep programs get failing marks. *National Public Radio Morning Edition.* Retrieved from www.npr.org/2013/06/18/192765776/ study-teacher-prep-programs-get-failing-marks

Sawchuck, S. (2012, May 14). New advocacy groups shaking up education field. *Education Week, 31*(31), 1, 16–17, 20. Retrieved from www.edweek.org/ew/articles/2012/05/ 16/31advoverview_ep.h31.html?tkn=RNRFbJeTs%2F4P9tN7iON7zi8tDCFVXFB TooQT&intc=es

Sawchuck, S. (2013, July 9). Disputed review finds disparities in teacher prep. *Education Week.* Retrieved from www.edweek.org/ew/articles/2013/07/10/36nctq-2.h32. html

Schorr, J. (2013). A revolution begins in teacher education. *Stanford Social Innovation Review.* Retrieved from www.ssireview.org/articles/entry/a_revolution_begins_in_ teacher_prep

Schorr, L. B., & Schorr, D. (1988). *Within our reach: Breaking the cycle of disadvantage.* New York: Anchor Press/Doubleday.

Shavelson, R., & Towne, L. (2002) (Eds.). *Scientific research in education.* Committee on scientific principles for education research. Washington, DC: National Academies Press.

Southern Education Foundation. (2015, January). A new majority: Low income students now a majority in the nation's public schools [Research Bulletin]. Retrieved from www.southerneducation.org/Our-Strategies/Research-and-Publications/New-Majority-Diverse-Majority-Report-Series/A-New-Majority-2015-Update-Low-Income-Students-Now

Stitzlein, S. M., & West, C. K. (2014). New forms of teacher education: Connections to charter schools and their approaches. *Democracy and Education, 22*(2), Article 2. Retrieved from http://democracyeducationjournal.org/home/vol22/iss2/2

Teach for America. (2014). What the research says. Retrieved from https://www. teachforamerica.org/sites/default/files/what_the_research_says_1.pdf

TFA et al. (2012, July 16). Letter to the House and Senate [Letter]. Retrieved from https://www.scribd.com/doc/100453326/TFA-Letter-to-House-and-Senate

Tseng, V. (2012). The uses of research in policy and practice. *Social Policy Report, 26*(2), 2–16.

US Department of Education (2014, November 25). US Department of Education proposes plan to strengthen teacher education [Press release]. Retrieved from www.ed.gov/news/ press-releases/us-department-education-proposes-plan-strengthen-teacher-preparation

US Department of Education. (2014). Teacher education issues: Proposed rules. *Federal Register, 79*(232). Retrieved from https://www.federalregister.gov/articles/2014/ 12/03/2014-28218/teacher-preparation-issues

Walsh, K. (2001). *Teacher certification reconsidered: Stumbling for quality.* Baltimore, MD: Abell Foundation.

Walsh, K. (2013). 21st century teacher education: Ed schools don't give teachers the tools they need. *Education Next, 13*(3), 19–24.

Weiss, C. (1979). The many meanings of research utilization. *Public Administration Review, 39*(5), 426–431.

Welner, K. (2013). Free-market think tanks and the marketing of educational policy. In M. Katz & M. Rose (Eds), *Public education under siege* (pp. 67–74). Philadelphia, PA: University of Pennsylvania Press.

The White House (2014, April 25). FACT SHEET: Taking action to improve teacher preparation [Press Release]. Retrieved from www.whitehouse.gov/the-press-office/2014/04/25/fact-sheet-taking-action-improve-teacher-preparation

Wilson, S. (2014, July). Innovation and the evolving system of US teacher preparation. *Theory into practice, 53*(3), 183–195.

Wilson, S., Floden, R., & Ferrini-Mundy, J. (2001). *Teacher preparation research: Current knowledge, gaps, and recommendations (R-01-3).* Center for the Study of Teaching and Policy, University of Washington. Retrieved from http://depts.washington.edu/ ctpmail/PDFs/TeacherPrep-WFFM-02-2001.pdf

Yettick, H. (2015). One small droplet: News media coverage of peer-reviewed and university-based education research. *Educational Researcher, 44*(3), 173–184.

Zeichner, K. (1995). Beyond the divide of teacher research and academic research. *Teachers & Teaching, 1*(2), 153–172.

Zeichner, K. (2014). The struggle for the soul of teaching and teacher education in the USA. *Journal of Education for Teaching: International Research and Pedagogy, 40*(5), 551–568.

Zeichner, K., & Bier, M. (2015). Opportunities and pitfalls in the turn toward clinical experiences in US teacher education. In E. Hollins (Ed.), *Rethinking clinical experiences in preservice teacher education* (pp. 20–46). New York, NY: Routledge.

Zeichner, K., & Conklin, H. (2005). Teacher education programs. In M. Cochran-Smith & K. Zeichner (Eds), *Studying teacher education: The report of the AERA Panel on Research and Teacher Education* (pp. 645–735). Mahwah, NJ: Lawrence Erlbaum.

Zeichner, K., & Hutchinson, E. (2008). The development of alternative certification policies and programs in the United States. In P. Grossman & S. Loeb (Eds), *Alternative routes to teaching: Mapping the new landscape of teacher education* (pp. 15–29). Cambridge, MA: Harvard Education Press.

Zeichner, K., Payne, K., & Brayko, K. (2015). Democratizing teacher education. *Journal of Teacher Education, 66*(2), 122–135.

Zeichner, K., & Peña-Sandoval, C. (2015). Venture philanthropy and teacher education policy in the U.S.: The role of the New Schools Venture Fund. *Teachers College Record, 117*(5), 1–44.

5

INDEPENDENT TEACHER EDUCATION PROGRAMS

Apocryphal Claims, Illusory Evidence

Kenneth M. Zeichner

Executive Summary

Teacher education provided in US colleges and universities has been routinely criticized since its inception in the early nineteenth century, sometimes deservedly. These programs are uneven in quality and can be improved. What makes today's situation different is an aggressive effort by advocacy groups and self-proclaimed social entrepreneurs to deregulate the preparation of teachers and to expand independent, alternative routes into teaching. This effort has gained considerable momentum and legitimacy, with venture capitalists, philanthropy, and the US Department of Education all providing sponsorship and substantial funding. The strength of this effort is such that the US may quickly proceed to dismantle its university system of teacher education and replace much of it with independent, private programs. The resulting system of teacher preparation may differ dramatically in its governance, structure, content, and processes, moving away from its current location alongside legal, medical, and other professional preparation that pairs academic degrees with professional training.

Given the enormity of this prospective shift, policymakers should consider carefully the extant evidence about the nature and impact of different pathways into teaching, including the entrepreneurial, stand-alone programs that advocates proclaim to be the future of teacher preparation. This consideration is particularly critical because, to date, these new alternatives focus almost exclusively on preparing teachers to teach "other people's children" in schools within high-poverty communities—not on public school teachers in advantaged communities. Therefore, their entry into the field raises important questions not only about effectiveness, but also about equity.

After surveying historical and contemporary trends in teacher preparation, this policy brief reviews what is known about the quality of five of the most prominent independent teacher education programs in the US, including their impact on teacher quality and student learning. Independent teacher education programs should be understood to be a subset of alternative routes to teaching, and the five examined in this brief were included because they: (a) are not university-based, and (b) themselves provide most or all of the candidates' preparation. These five independent programs are: The Relay Graduate School of Education (Relay), Match Teacher Residency (MTR), High Tech High's Internship (HTH), iTeach, and TEACH-NOW. Excluded from this review are other alternative programs such as Teach for America (TFA) and TNTP (The New Teachers Project), because they differ significantly in that they have substantive partnerships either with universities or with other independent entities (such as the five listed above) that provide much of the candidates' preparation.

Two bodies of work are included in the analyses of what is known: 1) findings from syntheses of peer-reviewed research on alternative pathways into teaching, and 2) research and other sources of information about the five specific programs reviewed, including claims that enthusiasts make about program quality and internal evaluations of program impact. While many advocates assert that independent programs are bold, innovative, and successful in accomplishing their goals, the analysis here demonstrates that such claims are not substantiated by independent, vetted research and program evaluations. This analysis indicates that the promotion and expansion of independent teacher preparation programs rests not on evidence, but largely on ideology. The lack of credible evidence supporting claims of success is particularly problematic given the current emphasis on evidence-based policy and practice in federal policy and professional standards.

The analysis also concludes that two of the programs, MTR and Relay, contribute to the inequitable distribution of professionally prepared teachers and to the stratification of schools according to the social class and racial composition of the student body. These two programs prepare teachers to use highly controlling pedagogical and classroom management techniques that are primarily used in schools serving students of color whose communities are severely impacted by poverty. Meanwhile, students in more economically advantaged areas have greater access to professionally trained teachers, less punitive and controlling management practices, and broader and richer curricula and teaching practices. The teaching and management practices learned by the teachers in these two independent programs are based on a restricted definition of teaching and learning and would not be acceptable in more economically advantaged communities.

Findings from the analysis of research on alternative pathways into teaching and from the analysis of available evidence on the nature and impact of independent teacher education programs have several implications for teacher education policymaking. The following four specific recommendations are based on those findings:

- State and federal policymakers should not implement policies and provide funding streams that promote the development and expansion of independent teacher education programs unless and until substantive credible evidence accrues to support them. There currently is minimal evidence.
- State policymakers should be very cautious in authorizing "teacher preparation academies" under a provision in the new federal education law (Every Student Succeeds Act, or ESSA). Such authorization would exempt those programs from the higher standards for teacher preparation that states typically seek to enforce for other teacher education programs. Policies should hold all teacher preparation programs to clear, consistent, and high standards.
- Teacher education program quality should be determined by an analysis of the costs and benefits of multiple outcomes associated with the programs. Policymakers should thus reject the argument made by two of these five programs (MTR and Relay) that the sole or overriding indicator of teacher and program quality should be students' standardized test scores.
- State and federal policies that are designed to support the development of independent teacher education programs should include monitoring provisions to ensure that they do not contribute to a stratified system, where teachers serving more economically advantaged communities complete programs in colleges and universities to become professional educators, while teachers serving low-income communities receive only more technical, narrow training on how to implement a defined set of curricular, instructional, and managerial guidelines.

Introduction

Over the last 25 years, a variety of people and organizations have been increasingly critical of teacher education programs in colleges and universities, which some in the media have branded "an industry of mediocrity."[1] Such criticisms typically focus on issues regarding programs' intellectual rigor, practical relevance, and ability to meet schools' staffing needs. This is not a new development, however. Teacher education programs in colleges and universities have been criticized from their inception.[2] What is new about the current critiques is that these criticisms have—with the help of philanthropists, think tanks and advocacy groups, the US Department of Education, and policymakers—been coupled with aggressive promotion of new programs outside of higher education intended to "disrupt" the teacher education field and stimulate innovation.[3]

These new programs, developed by so-called social entrepreneurs—people who apply business approaches to social services and needs—have been referred to as 2.0 programs. Advocates of these programs have declared college and university programs obsolete and warned that if they are not realigned with the newer programs, they will disappear.

> The next decade will see the proliferation of teacher prep 2.0 models as the benefits of their collective approach to teacher education become better known and more widely recognized. ... Those programs that fail to join this learning community will soon reveal their obsolescence and find themselves struggling to justify their existence. Demand will shift to more relevant, affordable and flexible programs where teachers are held to high professional standards of knowledge and skill under advisement of strong instructors and coaches who are committed to improving a teacher's effectiveness.[4]

To determine whether such claims and predictions are grounded in credible evidence, this chapter analyzes what is known about the quality of independent teacher education programs in the US, including their impact on teacher quality and student learning.[5]

Independent teacher education programs should be understood to be a subset of alternative routes to teaching, and they are included in this chapter if they (a) are not university-based, and (b) themselves provide most or all of the candidates' preparation. Included in the analysis are five independent teacher education programs initiated within the last 15 years: The Relay Graduate School of Education (Relay), Match Teacher Residency (MTR), High Tech High Internship (HTH), iTeach, and TEACH-NOW. While these five programs differ from each other in some ways, they also share some similarities, as detailed below. Excluded from the review are alternative programs not based at universities that outsource much of their teacher preparation to universities or other independent providers. These excluded programs include, for example, TFA (Teach for America), TNTP (The New Teacher Project), Urban Teachers, Aspire Teacher Residency, and the Chicago Teacher Residency.

Given recent state and federal policies and incentives that have supported the rapid growth of independent programs, and given the declining enrollments in many college and university programs,[6] it is important to examine the quality of the evidence available to support this significant shift in US teacher preparation. Close examination is also important because the countries that lead in international comparisons of educational equity and quality rely on consistent and substantial government investment in strong university systems of teacher preparation—in contrast to current US trends.[7] There are no examples of high-performing education systems that have relied heavily on the kind of deregulation and market competition, grounded in test-based accountability that many supporters of independent teacher education programs promote.[8]

The need to critically consider current trends is also important because teacher quality is interwoven with equity issues. The teachers prepared by these programs overwhelmingly teach in schools located in lower-income communities of color. At a time when inequities among US schools have been documented over and over again, and when schools are steadily becoming increasingly segregated,[9] it is especially important to understand the impact of new programs intended to supply teachers most likely to teach "other people's children"[10] in schools within communities suffering high levels of poverty. It is, after all, the perceived lack of highly qualified teachers in such schools that is often used to justify the push for new forms of teacher education.

Alternative Pathways into Teaching in the US: Past, Present, and Future

The Past

Historically the US has had many different pathways to teaching, including school district sponsored programs, academies, seminaries, teacher institutes, normal schools, teachers' colleges, community colleges, and 4-year colleges and universities. In fact, for much of the nation's history, most teachers entered teaching through what would be referred to today as "alternative routes,"[11] including a substantial number of teachers who were prepared in school district programs and in programs developed to prepare African Americans, Native Americans, and Latinos to teach in segregated schools in their communities.[12] For only a very brief period (approximately 1960–1990) did colleges and universities hold a virtual monopoly in teacher education.[13]

Since the mid-1980s, there has been steady growth in the number of alternatives to the traditional undergraduate and post-graduate college and university models of teacher education. Some of the earliest of these included programs run by states (such as the New Jersey Provisional Teacher Program begun in 1985) and school districts (such as the LA Unified School District Teacher Trainee Program launched in 1984, and the Houston Independent School District Teacher Trainee Program initiated in 1985).[14] During this early period, the state of Florida required all districts to offer competence-based alternative certification programs, developed either by the state for a district or developed by a district and approved by the state.[15]

Additionally, many colleges and universities sponsored alternative programs. These typically offered either the standard institutional program at more convenient times and locations, to attract people with commitments that precluded their participation in a traditional program, or were alternative academic programs with reduced requirements.[16] The majority of the alternative routes to teaching have been sponsored by colleges and universities.[17]

There are several reasons for the growth of alternatives to the campus-based teacher education programs that had dominated the field for three decades. Perhaps the most often cited rationale for alternative programs has been the need to address real or projected shortages in particular disciplines and in hard-to-staff schools in urban and remote rural areas, where high teacher attrition rates are common. The specialty areas often said to have shortages include special education, bilingual/English-learner education, mathematics, and science. To meet perceived needs, alternative routes can potentially draw people into teaching who might not otherwise consider becoming teachers and can potentially attract people seeking career changes—retired military personnel and engineers, for example. Other efforts tried to attract more people of color into teaching, so that the nation's teaching force would better reflect the diversity of American society and of the pupils in public schools.[18]

In addition, the financial costs and time commitment of university teacher education might be a barrier keeping potentially good teachers out of teaching, thus making lower cost and less lengthy alternatives desirable.[19] Also, new pathways to teaching were seen by some policymakers as better alternatives to the large number of "emergency" credentialed teachers that existed in some areas of the country.[20]

Persistent criticism of schools and colleges of education also fueled the reemergence of alternative pathways. Critics charged that traditional programs did not prepare teachers willing to teach in the hard-to-staff schools that needed them, and they also charged that even those who were willing to try were not adequately prepared to be successful over time.[21] Pointing out (correctly) that students who most need high-quality teachers instead typically are given the nation's least prepared and least experienced teachers,[22] critics of schools and colleges of education have attributed this problem to inadequate preparation of teachers willing and able to teach in urban and remote rural schools in high-poverty areas.[23]

Finally, some support for alternative certification programs came from within the college and university teacher education community, based on the supposition that new programs would stimulate innovation in the field.[24]

The Present

The founding of Teach for America (TFA) in 1990 marked the beginning of a shift in the nature of the alternatives provided for students and schools in high-poverty areas. Rather than academic institutions, states, and districts, private entities began assuming a significant role in developing alternative programs. Initially, because of the "highly qualified" teacher provisions in No Child Left Behind (NCLB) and in state certification policies, TFA and other programs like it (such as The New Teacher Project, or TNTP)[25] partnered with accredited college and university programs. However, changes in federal and state regulations[26]—incentivized in part by the US Department of Education[27]—later made it possible for independent teacher education providers to offer their own programs independent of colleges and universities.[28]

Generally, then, since the time of early authorization of internship and teacher trainee programs in California as well as similar programs in Texas and New Jersey during the 1980s, there has been a steady increase in alternative certification programs. And, during the last decade, there has also been a steady increase in independent programs that provide all of the preparation themselves, with no partnering college or university.

The expansion of such independent programs seems partially linked to the shortages of teachers nationwide that are a result of three factors: declining enrollments in college and university preparation programs, the lack of alignment between the teachers who are prepared to teach and the hiring needs of districts, and the salaries and working conditions for teachers.[29] For example, in the fall of 2015, there were still approximately 300 unfilled teaching positions on the opening day of school in the Denver Public Schools, and then in May 2016, Relay announced that it would soon be setting up a new campus of its teacher certification program there. College and university teacher education program enrollments are declining in many parts of the country,[30] and some states that are facing teaching shortages are actively seeking the entry of new program providers. This is true even in states like Washington that historically have resisted expanding teacher preparation beyond colleges and universities. For example, in June 2016, as a result of teacher shortages in Washington in certain subjects and in particular geographical areas, the Washington Professional Educator Standards Board issued a call for new providers to offer alternative programs:

Seeking New Alternative Route Program Providers

Our Alternative Route program provider interest is growing in the community college, non-profit, and university systems. We are excited to see new providers interested in becoming approved programs and offering Alternative Route programs. If you are interested in becoming an approved Alternative Route provider, please contact … We will be hosting provider information sessions for interested parties in the Summer and Fall.[31]

The growth of independent alternative route providers has also been driven by the steady growth of national charter school networks, such as Rocketship and the Knowledge is Power Program (KIPP). These networks can and do run their own programs specifically designed to prepare teachers for their schools.[32] For example, Relay was founded by the leaders of three charter school networks (Achievement First, KIPP, and Uncommon Schools), and both Match and High Tech High charter schools founded their own independent teacher certification programs (MTR and HTH). Philanthropic and government resources have supported such growth by promoting the deregulation of teacher education, which has allowed independent teacher education programs and networks to compete with college and university teacher education programs.[33]

A concurrent decline in philanthropic support for college and university-based teacher education has been coupled with substantial reductions in state funding for the public universities that prepare most of the nation's teachers, sparking tuition increases and exacerbating the disincentive of cost.[34] The attractiveness of a shorter and cheaper alternative route increases if the price tag goes up for the higher-education option. Such declining support for the public universities where most US teachers are still prepared is, not surprisingly, creating a two-tiered system of teacher preparation. Increasingly, non-university programs are preparing teachers who will serve students in high-poverty communities ("other people's children"), while colleges and universities continue to prepare teachers who will predominantly serve students in more economically advantaged middle-class communities. Unless the alternative routes taken by teachers heading to less advantaged communities are of high quality, this extension of the bifurcation of the public school system in the US is likely to widen the opportunity gaps for learning that currently exist.[35]

The twin trends noted earlier—deregulation and the fostering of competitive environments— are associated with the ascendency of a market ideology of education reform. Placing their confidence in private sector solutions to social problems, advocates of greater deregulation and market competition consistently work to foster greater and greater choice and competition in the education "marketplace."[36] Philanthropic and government entities have adopted this perspective and supported the growth of privately run charter schools to compete with public schools overseen by local school districts.[37] Similarly, philanthropists, venture capitalists, and the US federal government have all promoted policies and provided substantial funding to enable expanded development of independent teacher education programs,[38] asserting that the new independent programs will pressure college and university programs to innovate and thus raise the overall quality of teacher preparation. For example, Rick Hess of the American Enterprise Institute has argued:

> weaker teacher preparation programs would likely fall by the wayside. The fact that Schools of Education could no longer rely on a captive body of aspiring teachers would expose them to the cleansing winds of competition. Schools would have to contribute value by providing teacher training, services, or research that created demand and attracted support—or face significant cutbacks.[39]

Implicitly endorsing this perspective, the federal government has recently enacted legislation—the "teacher preparation academy" provision in the 2015 Every Student Succeeds Act (ESSA)—that provides a potentially significant push toward an even more competitive environment for teacher education, with fewer safeguards on teacher quality.

Going Forward

The teacher preparation academy provision is part of ESSA's Title II. The concept was first promoted in 2011 under the title of the "Great Teachers and Principals Act" (or GREAT Act) and failed to pass Congress in two different sessions. It was originally developed by leaders of the New Schools Venture Fund, the Relay Graduate School of Education, and several members of Congress as a way to provide additional financial support for the growth of programs like Relay.[40] Importantly, states are not required by this ESSA provision to authorize the academies; if they do, they will open the door to lower standards for teacher preparation programs in several specific ways.

For example, states that authorize academies and use their Title II funds to support them will be required to allow the teacher-education students to serve as teachers of record while enrolled in the academies—essentially allowing individuals with little or no preparation to serve as professional teaching staff. States will also be required to exempt academies from "unnecessary restrictions" on their operational methods. Specifically, states will not be able to do any of the following: require academy faculty to have advanced degrees; require academies to seek accreditation; or impose regulations on undergraduate or professional coursework. For example, states will not be able to require teacher candidates in academies to have an academic major in the subjects they teach. These sorts of requirements are generally mandated by states for traditional college and university teacher education programs.

About the Rationale for Current Trends

Two primary narratives underlie the desire by philanthropists, venture capitalists, and federal policymakers to disrupt the field of teacher education and bring in new programs developed by social entrepreneurs. First is a derisive narrative about university teacher education that insists schools of education have failed and therefore their role in preparing teachers should be reduced.[41] Second is the contention that deregulation and market competition will raise the quality of teacher preparation.

The first contention does find some support among researchers and leaders; there are indeed problems in university teacher education programs that have been documented for many years.[42] Attempts to address these problems have focused on raising the standards for entry to and exit from teacher education programs, strengthening the connections between the coursework and clinical components of programs, and a stronger focus on teaching teachers how to enact research-based teaching practices.[43] Today's charge that university programs have totally failed (and should therefore be replaced) is overstated. This overstatement is grounded in part on instances of advocates manipulating or misrepresenting research and then using the distorted pictures of research evidence to discredit university programs and to promote non-university programs.[44]

For example, in a 2012 Congressional hearing on Alternative Certification, both the committee chair and members of the "expert panel" stated that a 2005 report[45] sponsored by the American Educational Research Association, synthesizing research on the effects of alternative pathways into teaching, concluded that "there were no differences in teacher efficacy or teaching competence, as measured by classroom observations, between alternatively and traditionally certified teachers."[46] This and similar statements made during the hearing contradict the actual conclusions of the research review. In fact, the review itself explicitly warned against selective use of research evidence to support specific positions on pathways to teaching, and it found extant credible research insufficient to provide a definitive answer to the exceedingly complex question of comparative program quality.[47] Additional discussion of this point appears below, in a review of existing peer-reviewed literature.

Characteristics of the Five Independent Programs

The five post-baccalaureate independent programs reviewed in this chapter vary along several dimensions (see Table 5.1). One dimension is how much, if any, preparation students receive before assuming responsibility for a classroom. In the iTeach Internship option, TEACH-NOW, and High Tech High Internship (HTH) program, many of the students are teachers of record while they complete most or all program requirements. This is also true for all of those enrolled in the original Relay model.[48] In contrast, both MTR, and Relay's new Teacher Residency option provide students with a year of preparation under the guidance of a mentor teacher before they become teachers of record. In the iTeach clinical option (which is a very small part of the iTeach enrollment), iTeach students are not teachers of record until they first complete coursework and a 12-week supervised clinical experience under the supervision of a mentor teacher.[49]

Programs also vary in length and accreditation status. The length of four of the programs ranges from nine months (TEACH-NOW) to two years (HTH, MTR, and Relay). In iTeach, students complete their program in six months to two years depending on the program option selected. And, while all the programs are authorized by the states in which they are located, two are also nationally and/or regionally accredited: iTeach, and Relay by the Council for the Accreditation of Educator Preparation. Relay is also regionally accredited by the Middle States Commission on Higher Education Accreditation.

iTeach offers a teacher education program and a principal certification program in Texas and Louisiana, and the other four (MTR, Relay, TEACH-NOW, and HTH) have formed graduate schools of education that offer a range of programs in addition to their initial teacher certification programs, including programs for principals, already certified teachers, and in one case (MTR), for tutors.[50]

TABLE 5.1 Independent certification programs

Name of Program and Date of Establishment	Who Runs the Program	2015–2016 Enrollment	Length of Program(s)	Type of Program Early Entry[1] or Residency[2]	Location(s)	Regional and National Accreditation	Online Learning Components
Relay GSE[3] 2011	Relay Graduate School of Education	Certification – 120 Degree & certification – 836	Residency Program – 2 years Master of Arts in Teaching certification program – 2 years	Residency Program – Master of Arts in Teaching Program – Early Entry	Baton Rouge[4] Chicago Connecticut[5] Delaware Denver[6] Houston Memphis Nashville[7] New Orleans New York City Newark Philadelphia & Camden	Council for the Accreditation of Educator Preparation & Middle States Commission on Higher Education Accreditation	Residency Program – around 40% of content is delivered online[8] Master of Arts in Teaching – around 40% of content is delivered online[9]
Match Teacher Residency[10] 2012	The Charles Sposato Graduate School of Education	First-year students – 41 Second-year students – 38	2 years	Residency	Boston	Has applied for regional accreditation from the New England Association of Schools and Colleges	None

(continued overleaf)

TABLE 5.1 (continued)

Name of Program and Date of Establishment	Who Runs the Program	2015–2016 Enrollment	Length of Program(s)	Type of Program Early Entry[1] or Residency[2]	Location(s)	Regional and National Accreditation	Online Learning Components
High Tech High Intern Program[11] 2004	High Tech High Credentialing Program	Intern Program Year 1 – 38 students. Intern Program Year 2 – 45 students[12]	2 years	Early Entry	San Diego county, California	None	1–2 preservice courses are delivered online
iTeachUS[13] 2003	iTeachUS	2,049	Internship option – 2 semesters of internship as the teacher of record (Students have up to 2 years to finish the program) Clinical teaching – one semester of clinical teaching under the supervision of a mentor teacher along with self paced coursework that can be completed in 6 months to 1 year	Internship Program – Early Entry[14] Clinical Teaching program option – Residency	Texas-Internship and Clinical option Louisiana and Hawaii Internship option only	Council for the Accreditation of Educator Preparation	All coursework is completed online
TEACH-NOW[15] 2012	TeachNow/ Educatore School of Education	800	Teacher Preparation Certificate Program – 9 months Master's degree programs – 12 months	Teacher Preparation Certificate Program – both options are available	Online International program	Has applied for accreditation by the Council for the Accreditation of Educator	Coursework is completed online with virtual class sessions

Preparation and the Distance Education Accrediting Commission

Master's degree in Education with Teacher Preparation program – both options available
Master's degree in Education with Globalization and Research Emphasis – both options available

1 Early entry means the candidate receives some summer training courses and is the teacher of record during the rest of the teacher preparation program.
2 Residency here means the candidate receives training and works under the supervision of a practicing teacher for at least a school year before becoming the teacher of record.
3 Relay was piloted as Teacher U within Hunter College 2008–2011. www.relay.edu/
4 The Relay Baton Rouge campus plans to open and offer two programs in 2016, www.relay.edu/campuses/baton-rouge
5 The Relay Connecticut campus hopes to open and offer two programs in 2016 by obtaining institutional and licensure approval. www.relay.edu/campuses/connecticut
6 The Relay Denver campus only offers the Teaching Residency Program. www.relay.edu/programs/relay-teaching-residency-denver/admissions
7 The Relay Nashville campus plans to open and offer two programs in 2016. www.relay.edu/campuses/nashville
8 www.relay.edu/programs/relay-teaching-residency-philadelphia-camden/details
9 www.relay.edu/programs/chicago-teaching-residency/details
10 www.matcheducation.org/sposato/overview/
11 http://gse.hightechhigh.org/teacherInternProgram.php
12 Experienced teachers in the program can apply to take an exam that changes the program completion time from 2 years into 1 year. There are some of these students included within the year two enrollment numbers.
13 http://www.iteach.net/
14 The iTeach internship is a different type of early entry program because teachers are not required to complete coursework before they enter the classroom.
15 http://teach-now.com/

Additionally, all three of the charter-affiliated programs have formed partnerships with other charter schools that share their philosophies. For example, Relay has formed partnerships with additional charter organizations in different cities, such as the Noble charter network in Chicago, which offers the Noble-Relay Teaching Residency. The Boston-based MTR has formed partnerships with charter schools in Dallas, Chicago, Denver, and New Orleans.

One similarity within the group of charter-affiliated programs is that all claim to minimize the division between teacher education coursework and clinical practice that is common in university teacher education programs. For example, it is asserted that in the HTH Intern program, "There is a direct connection between what students learn and do in courses and what's happening in their classrooms."[51]

Another similarity within this group is that the MTR, Relay, and HTH programs all use the particular philosophies and preferred teaching methods in their associated charter schools as a base for teacher preparation and certification. Each program is, in fact, highly prescriptive about teaching methods. For example, the MTR website states that "The program is direct and prescriptive in its teaching of specific pedagogical moves and habits."[52] And, not surprisingly, these programs seek and admit candidates who appear philosophically aligned with their respective missions.

Philosophically and practically, however, the charter-affiliated programs overall reflect a variety of visions and goals. Relay and MTR pursue the narrow goal of preparing teachers who can raise students' standardized test scores; therefore, their programs offer instruction in classroom management and teaching strategies focused on raising those scores. Both require graduates to demonstrate a certain level of proficiency in raising student test scores, and both promote their alleged effectiveness to potential applicants and districts and charter schools by claiming that their graduates have proven records of classroom success based on raising test scores. Although it is also affiliated with charter schools, HTH's much broader mission is to prepare reflective teachers who can develop democratic classrooms in socioeconomically diverse schools; it promotes project-based learning as a methodological means to that end.

None of the five independent programs appears to employ more than a few traditional doctorally prepared university teacher educators as instructors.

The two programs not affiliated with charters also take a different approach, basing their programs on common sets of national teaching standards. The iTeach program and TEACH-NOW use the INTASC Model Core Teaching Standards, developed by the Council of Chief State School Officers (CSSO)[53] and used as the basis for many state standards. Additionally, a central focus in TEACH-NOW's cohort and activity-based program is on preparing teachers to use technology and digital tools in their teaching.

The five programs utilize online instruction to varying degrees. While HTH and MTR provide little or no online instruction, Relay, iTeach, and TEACH-NOW use extensive online instruction, ranging from Relays' approximately 40 percent of the curriculum housed online to iTeach and TEACH-NOW's online placement of all curriculum except for the clinical component. Some advocates promote online instruction as one way of lowering operational costs and helping to develop a "sustainable business model."[54]

Another common characteristic among the charter-affiliated programs is that instruction and mentoring are typically provided by teachers who have mastered the methods taught in the program (and used in the charter schools). In the two non-charter-affiliated programs (TEACH-NOW and iTeach), experienced K-12 teachers not affiliated with any particular set of teaching practices provide most of the instruction. This approach stands in contrast to conventional teacher education programs, where clinical instructors of this type are also used but only as an addition to professors and doctoral students. As is the case with other professional schools (law, business, medicine, etc.), these scholar-instructors are also generally former practitioners, but they supplement that practitioner knowledge with research knowledge.

None of the five independent programs appears to employ more than a few traditional doctorally prepared university teacher educators as instructors. In addition, all five programs—but particularly those associated with charter schools—claim to provide significantly more feedback and coaching to their teachers than university programs provide (often with video playing a role). HTH also employs student feedback: "student consultants" in the charter schools provide regular observations of and feedback on interns' teaching.

Ongoing expansion is yet another common characteristic. Some programs discuss plans relevant to "going to scale" and increasing the number of teachers they prepare in different sites across the US, and in one case—TEACH-NOW— even around the world. In 2015, TEACH-NOW leaders stated that globally, they hoped to prepare 10,000 teachers in the next 5 years.[55] Relay began as Teacher-U in 2007 in New York City and soon thereafter expanded to Newark; in 2016 it will operate in 12 sites around the country and has plans to continue growing.[56] Both MTR and HTH began by preparing teachers for their own charter schools, but now both have developed additional partnerships to prepare teachers for other charter schools with philosophies and methods similar to their own. iTeach, which began in Texas, has expanded to Louisiana and Hawaii.

With the exception of iTeach, which receives no external funding, all of the programs have received external funding from groups such as the Gates Foundation and the New Schools Venture Fund that, along with many private funders, promote the "scaling up" of programs.[57] Julie Mikuta, who was with the New Schools Venture Fund when it first supported MTR and Relay, has been quoted as saying that two motivations for funding such programs were to drive change in the larger field of teacher education and to lower the cost of preparing teachers—so that what individuals pay for a program is appropriate for the salaries they will receive.[58]

Peer-Reviewed Syntheses of Research on Teacher Education Pathways

Four peer-reviewed syntheses of credible research on various approaches to teacher education spanning more than a decade have reached the same conclusions: credible research has not yet demonstrated one specific approach to teacher education as superior to others.[59]

This conclusion regarding insufficient evidence is not the same as a finding that there is no difference. As noted above, despite the frequent assertion by programs themselves (and in the media and the halls of Congress) that research has shown a particular program or programs to consistently produce better teacher and/or student outcomes than others, or that research has shown various types of teacher education to make no practical difference, credible research in fact supports neither of those claims. Instead, these four peer-reviewed syntheses of the existing research on alternative pathways find that key questions about teacher preparation still lack definitive answers.

For example, in 2010 a National Research Council panel of experts reviewed the existing body of research and concluded: "There is currently little definitive evidence that particular approaches to teacher preparation yield teachers whose students are more successful than others."[60] In the studies that were reviewed by the panel, success in teaching was measured almost entirely by growth in pupil test scores for teachers who were prepared in different programs. Occasionally, other factors such as classroom management problems were considered. Importantly, the panel report also emphasized that this conclusion about the lack of clear findings does not mean that the characteristics of pathways do not matter. Rather it suggests research on the sources of variation in preparation such as selectivity, timing, and specific components and characteristics is needed.[61]

The most recent peer-reviewed synthesis of this research, in the American Educational Research Association's 2016 *Handbook of Teaching*, reaches similar conclusions:

> Not surprisingly, studies in this line of research, which compared the impact on students' achievement of teachers with alternative certification and/or from "alternative" pathways or compared the impact of teachers from a particular "alternative" program with those from other sources of new teachers, are inconsistent and ultimately inconclusive at a broad level in terms of what they tell us about the effects of particular programs.[62]

The findings of these two peer-reviewed research syntheses aligned with the conclusions of two earlier syntheses, one sponsored by the American Educational Research Association, and one sponsored by the US Department of Education—that not enough is yet known to gauge comparable merit of programs and approaches.[63]

The fact that all four research syntheses have reached the same conclusions indicates that claims boasting research support for any one approach or program are overstated and inaccurate—as are claims that the type of preparation a teacher candidate receives makes no difference in teacher performance. While much or most of the descriptive material available on independent program websites and in promotional articles in the media proclaim independent pathways to teacher education to be bold, innovative efforts that represent the future of teacher education,[64] credible evidence to support such judgments simply does not appear in existing research.

Other Evidence on the Impact of Independent Teacher Education Programs

There is in fact very little peer-reviewed research that has been conducted on the impact of specific independent teacher education programs. Although some efforts in this vein are in progress,[65] only one study was identified in research for this brief. It examined the effects of communicating with families using strategies[66] that are a part of the MTR Curriculum. This study[67] found several positive effects of using MTR methods of teacher-family communication. Specifically, 6th and 9th grade students received a daily phone call and written text message at home during a mandatory summer school program. Such MTR techniques for frequent teacher-family communication increased student engagement as measured by homework completion rates, on-task behavior, and class participation. However, only a single element of a summer school program was examined—shedding little or no light on the impact of the full MTR approach. Beyond this one study, other evidence on the five programs' effectiveness is found only in various claims the programs make about their effectiveness, supported primarily by testimonials from those involved and by non-rigorous claims regarding standardized test scores—the former neither an unbiased nor random sample, the latter an inadequate single measure backed by no solid studies, as discussed below. Additional sources of documentation include other internal measures unique to particular programs.

Programs often cite the graduates' opinions as offering evidence of a program's effectiveness, as in this example from TEACH-NOW:

> The TEACH-NOW program provided me a better understanding of effective instructional strategies, collaboration skills, and classroom management. Their 21st century platform shapes the minds of educators by pairing a multilayered curriculum with innovative tools and strategies. I walked away with a new view of what differentiation looks like in a classroom and fresh knowledge on how to more effectively reach all of my students. Additionally, I was introduced to several websites, graphic

> organizers and tools that I was able to use in my classroom. In short, the experience was amazing.[68]

Testimonials have also been reported secondhand by the journalists and advocates of the deregulation of teacher education, who promote the expansion of independent programs and who are often connected to think tanks, advocacy groups, or to the funders. The following example was published in *Education Next*, a journal that is sponsored by the Hoover Institution, Thomas Fordham Institute, and the Harvard Kennedy School Program on Education Policy and Governance.

> Many also told me that Relay's lessons have changed their classroom culture. "The culture went from being compliant to being invested," said Max Silverstein, a Penn State business major now teaching in an early childhood classroom at Newark Legacy charter school. I heard the same thing from Alonte Johnson, a Moorehouse College English major who is teaching middle school English at King's Collegiate Center School in Brooklyn. A few days earlier his students designed a seating chart that paired the better and slower readers. "The environment is more interdependent instead of everyone working for me," he said.[69]

Another claim about the effectiveness of independent programs associated with some charter school networks is that student test scores increase in the charter schools where the program graduates teach. While the links between the allegedly successful charter schools and the preparation programs they run are not explicitly made, it is strongly implied that their teacher education programs are high quality because of the record of the charter schools in raising test scores. For example, a Pioneer Institute report on MTR asserted that:

> In the 2012–13 school year Match 10th graders placed first state-wide among high schools where more than 70 percent of students are low-income: they placed 22nd among all 305 high schools in the Commonwealth. … Match High School has been cited by the US Department of Education (USDOE) as one of the nation's best charter high schools, and Match Middle School, and High School have both received the prestigious EPIC award, which recognizes value-added proficiency gains by students, for each five years between 2008 and 2012.[70]

Given the emphasis on raising test scores in MTR's teacher preparation program, information on student test performance can be offered by advocates as indirectly demonstrating that program's effectiveness. But studies such as this, whatever their strengths and weaknesses, were not even designed to evaluate the effectiveness of the underlying teacher preparation programs. No credible causal inferences could possibly be made about the teacher education programs merely from the charter school evaluations.

Two of the programs (Relay and MTR) also present data from their own internal analyses of their graduates' teaching effectiveness. Relay sets student learning goals for teachers and then asks the teachers to set their own goals within those parameters. At the program's end, teachers discuss results at their master's defenses. Several examples of goals set by Relay teachers in the 2014 cohort are presented on the program website:

> (1) On average, my students will achieve a year's worth of growth as measured by the STEP Literacy Assessment; (2) On average, my fifth grade students will achieve 70% mastery of the fifth-grade state science standards; and (3) On average, my students' average writing rubric scores will improve 1.5 levels as measured by a five-point, 6 Traits rubric.[71]

Teachers must achieve both minimum goals in two content areas, and they are encouraged to set ambitious goals in each area. Several examples of teachers' ambitious goals are provided on Relay's website, such as, "At least 80% of my students will meet their student-specific goals in reading as measured by the STEP Literacy Assessment."[72]

Relay also presents a list of what are termed "notable achievements" of their 2014 cohort in relation to the teachers' goals.[73] For example: "94% of graduate students in our New York M.A.T. program met or exceeded their minimum learning goals for students and 54% of them met their ambitious goal in at least one content area related to their teaching placement." The implication is that Relay's teacher preparation is effective because a large percentage of teachers meet minimum achievement goals and many meet ambitious achievement goals.

There is nothing in the design of these internal evaluations, though, that would support causal inferences attributing the meeting of student achievement targets to the teacher education program. Even in many of the well-funded studies of the impact of alternative pathways into teaching, researchers have been unable to distinguish the effects of the programs studied from those of the individual characteristics candidates bring to the programs and of the contexts in which they teach.[74]

The Relay website also presents summary data on their graduates' and employers' perspectives about the program. For example, with regard to their graduates' perspectives, it is stated, "Across a variety of indicators, 92% of the graduates in the class of 2014 reported their agreement with the effectiveness of Relay faculty and instruction." With regard to the perceptions of employers (who, keep in mind, are not independent of the Relay program), it is stated, "Across a variety of indicators, 92% of employing school leaders affirmed their satisfaction with the performance of their teachers who were enrolled at Relay."[75]

MTR also presents vague internal data about its teachers' effectiveness, in its 2014 annual letter from Sposato GSE, the institution in which MTR is situated. The letter claims that "students taught by first-year teachers trained by Sposato grow more than 64% of students with comparable academic histories (many of whom are taught by veteran teachers)."[76] A footnote associated with this claim states that evaluation data from three sources during 2010–2014 were averaged to generate the data supporting this conclusion. These evaluations included: (1) principal evaluations that rate MTR teachers and other teachers in their schools at the end of the school year; (2) students' anonymous evaluations of their teachers; and (3) outside expert evaluations—blind evaluations of MTR graduates and graduates from other programs in the same school after they have been teaching from 4 to 7 months.

The evaluators, described as "school leaders and master teachers," observed and scored a lesson based on an internally developed rubric and did not know which were the MTR graduates. MTR did not specify what types of evidence principals, students, and outside evaluators offered to document their opinions.

Collecting such internal data is good practice, potentially helping with program improvement. But there are real problems with policymakers using such data to make evaluative judgments. As noted, the validity of internal analyses like those just discussed is open to question and less reliable than evidence based on independent and vetted research efforts. Many questions arise because websites for both Relay and MTR provide minimal information about the specifics of the evaluations and no information about how to obtain more detailed information on the internal assessments.

Beyond internal assessments, Relay seems to intend to bolster its case for effectiveness with yet one other claim: it asserts that its training approach is based on practices that research has proven effective. The former research director at Relay claimed in an American Enterprise Institute publication that Relay and programs like it (referred to as 2.0 programs) "are deliberately anchored in best practices and insights drawn from classroom and school experience and educational research."[77]

Relay, for example, has proudly proclaimed that faculty member Doug Lemov's classroom management strategies for "Teaching like a Champion"[78] are the core of its curriculum.[79] However, Lemov's strategies are based solely on his own observations and conversations with teachers and administrators in various charter schools that he claims are high performing. By any reasonable standard, the assertion that Lemov's strategies represent "best practices" does not possess the kind of rigorous scientific evidence-based validity that is being called for in teacher education programs.[80]

Thus, internal claims and analyses add little or no evidence of these programs' effectiveness. Given that neither program-specific reports nor syntheses of credible research demonstrate the effectiveness of the five programs analyzed (or of others like them), there is no case to be made in support of the current huge investment of resources into such independent programs or their expansion.

Rather, as noted earlier, program branding and marketing have co-opted the term "research" and offered misleading summaries of legitimate research findings, all to make a case for "disruptive innovation"[81] in teacher education based on ideology rather than evidence.[82]

What Is Meant by Effective, and What are the Costs and Benefits of Various Approaches?

Studies of the impact of two of the independent programs examined here (MTR and Relay) are currently being conducted by Mathematica and the Center for Education Policy Research at Harvard University. Even if these studies show that graduates of MTR and Relay are able to raise student tests scores to a greater extent than graduates from comparison programs, this would not be sufficient evidence that they are successful programs.[83] Partly, this is because of a lesson from the NCLB era: test scores are a limited measure of success. And partly this is because MTR and Relay have narrowed their focus toward preparing future teachers to succeed on test-score outcomes and, in doing so, have likely sacrificed other areas of teacher preparation.

Scholars have argued for many years that the quality of teacher education programs should not be gauged by any single measure. Instead, quality should be determined by examining the costs and benefits associated with a variety of outcomes.[84] These would include, for example, considering to what extent graduates of different programs are able to promote higher achievement test scores but also increased socio-emotional learning, aesthetic learning, civic development, creativity, problem solving and critical thinking abilities.[85]

Another critical factor is retention: how much do graduates of different programs contribute either to teacher stability in schools or to disruptive "teacher churn"—especially in the high-poverty schools where graduates from the charter-affiliated independent programs primarily teach?[86] Little is known in this area, in part because independent teacher education programs are so new that retention data on graduates is lacking. Research on teacher retention in alternative pathways generally is mixed, and it suggests that a complex set of factors affects retention outcomes, including the relationships between the characteristics and abilities of the people being prepared, the quality of their preparation, and the conditions in the schools where they teach.[87]

Although claims are made that teacher retention is higher for alternatively certified than traditionally certified teachers, these analyses have not taken into account selection effects and the effects of school contexts. The most recent vetted analysis of teacher retention data nationally using Schools and Staffing Study (SASS) data shows, controlling for school contexts, that alternatively certified teachers are more likely to leave the profession than traditionally certified teachers.[88] In the end, though, claims about teacher retention that are not designed to distinguish program effects from both selection and school context effects, and that present only unadjusted turnover rates, are not very useful to policymakers.[89] Broad statements about alternative certification programs are also not nearly as useful as analyses of specific programs or types of programs.

In addition, assessment should take into account not only benefits of particular programs but also their costs and unintended consequences. For example, there is clear evidence that one unintended consequence of the recent singular focus on improved test scores has been the narrowing of the curriculum, which has produced a range of negative effects.[90] The same prioritizing of test scores has led to the "no excuses" classroom management practices emphasized in independent programs like MTR and Relay, and research has also demonstrated negative effects of such practices on students.[91] Based on studies like these, a singular or overarching focus on raising student test scores often reinforces persistent inequities in public schools.[92]

Raising student test scores cannot be considered an obvious good that is intrinsically more valuable or desirable than all other goals, especially given that it is already known that such narrow focus demonstrably comes at the cost of other legitimate goals—including the goal of reducing existing opportunity gaps for student learning in high-poverty areas.[93] The evidence supports a more nuanced analysis of the costs and benefits associated with a variety of desired outcomes for teachers, students, and schools.

Discussion and Recommendations

Advocates of deregulating teacher education and expanding 2.0 programs argue that university teacher education is a questionable investment, given limited evidence that those university programs are actually are creating effective teachers.[94] As noted above, however, the same is true of newer, independent alternatives: there is essentially no evidence of their effectiveness.[95] That point applies to the five programs discussed here. That is, not enough is known to reach definitive judgments.

What does exist in the literature, however, is credible evidence about the characteristics of programs that are linked to desired outcomes for teachers and their students, including alternative certification programs.[96] One example of a program characteristic that appears to be associated with high-quality programs is program coherence, which includes a shared understanding across the program of the specific goals of the preparation.[97] Other examples of the characteristics of exemplary programs include extended clinical experiences that are carefully developed "to support the ideas and practices presented in simultaneous, closely interwoven coursework," and "curriculum that is grounded in knowledge of child and adolescent development, learning, social contexts, and subject matter pedagogy, taught in the context of practice."[98]

In reality, there is as much or more variation in quality within program types as there is across types (although it does seem reasonable to assume that "quality" and "effectiveness" are likely to be defined very differently by programs focused on "market share" and "going to scale" than by a traditional, university-based program).[99] As more is learned about which program features link to which desired outcomes, assessment of programs will be better informed and much more nuanced. Informed judgments about program quality—contemporary apocryphal claims notwithstanding—will have to wait until then. Funding for research that further illuminates the characteristics of high-quality university and non-university programs is an important investment that would help narrow the range of quality in these programs as state and national accreditation accountability systems incorporate what is learned from the research.

The call for more research to identify the characteristics of high-quality teacher education programs should not be interpreted as support for the continued expansion of independent teacher education programs until research somehow settles the issue of their quality. Fundamentally, the question of how high-quality programs should be defined is a question of values informed by, but not determined by, research.

It has been argued that raising students' standardized test scores, in and of itself, should not be taken as the sole measure of success for teachers and teacher education programs. This chapter has called for examination of the costs and benefits associated with multiple outcomes.

Given the undisputed evidence of the negative consequences associated with an exclusive focus on raising student test scores such as the narrowing of the curriculum, and negative consequences for students' psychological well-being of some of the controlling and punitive management systems taught to teachers in programs like MTR and Relay, policymakers should be very careful in lending support to non-university programs. The kind of teaching and management techniques that are taught in programs like Relay and MTR have been described as part of a "pedagogy of poverty" that reinforces the gap between those students who have opportunities to interact with knowledge in authentic and meaningful ways and those who do not.[100]

Based on the above analysis, then, it is recommended that:

- State and federal policymakers should not implement policies and provide funding streams that privilege the development and expansion of independent teacher education programs unless and until substantive credible evidence accrues to support them. There currently is minimal evidence.
- State policymakers should be very cautious in authorizing "teacher preparation academies" under a provision in the new federal education law (Every Student Succeeds Act, or ESSA). Such authorization would exempt those programs from the higher standards for teacher preparation that states typically seek to enforce for other teacher education programs. Policies should hold all programs to clear, consistent, and high standards.

- Teacher education program quality should be determined by an analysis of the costs and benefits of multiple outcomes associated with the programs. Policymakers should thus reject the argument made by two of these five programs (MTR and Relay) that the sole or overriding indicator of teacher and program quality should be students' standardized test scores.
- State and federal policies that are designed to support the development of independent teacher education programs should include monitoring provisions to ensure that they do not contribute to a stratified system, where teachers serving more economically advantaged communities complete programs in colleges and universities to become professional educators, while teachers serving low-income communities receive only more technical, narrow training on how to implement a defined set of curricular, instructional and managerial guidelines.

Notes and References

1 Keller, B. (2013). An industry of mediocrity. *New York Times*. Retrieved October 20, 2013, from www.nytimes.com/2013/10/21/opinion/keller-an-industry-of-mediocrity.html?_r=0

2 Fraser, J. (2007). *Preparing America's teachers: A history*. New York, NY: Teachers College Press.

3 Wilson, S. (2014). Innovation and the evolving system of US teacher preparation. *Theory into Practice, 53*, 183–195.

4 Gastic, B. (2014). Closing the opportunity gap: Preparing the next generation of effective teachers. In R. Hess & M. McShane (Eds), *Teacher quality 2.0.* (pp. 91–108). Cambridge, MA: Harvard Education Press.

5 Information about each program was obtained by reading everything on the program websites including following links and reading reports and articles about the programs. Interviews with a representative of each program were also requested in January 2016. During the winter and spring of 2016, interviews were conducted with a representative from Teach-Now, iTeach, and HTH. Relay and MTR did not respond to repeated requests for an interview, but in July 2016 they verified that there is currently no research available about their programs beyond what is discussed in this brief.

6 Currently alternative programs, including those not based at universities, prepare about one third of teachers in the US despite the decline in university program enrollments. https://title2.ed.gov/Public/42653_Title_II_Infographic_Booklet.pdf

7 Darling-Hammond, L., Burns, D., Campbell, C., Goodwin, A. L., Hammerness, K., Low, E. L., McIntyre, A., Sato, M., & Zeichner, K. (2017). *Empowered educators: How leading nations design systems for teaching quality*. San Francisco, CA: Jossey-Bass.

8 Tucker, M. S. (2016). The view from abroad: Does American education suffer from a deficit of innovation. In F. M. Hess & M. Q. McShane (Eds), *Educational entrepreneurship today* (pp. 95–104). Cambridge, MA: Harvard Education Press.

9 US Government Accountability Office (April, 2016). K12 education: Better use of information could help agencies identify disparities and address racial discrimination.

Washington, DC: Author. Retrieved July 2, 2016 from http://gao.gov/products/GAO-16-345

10 Delpit, L. (2012). *Multiplication is for white people: Raising expectations for other people's children*. New York, NY: New Press.

11 Different definitions of "alternative certification" programs have been used by policymakers and scholars. Some have defined alternative programs as those other than 4- or 5-year undergraduate programs at colleges and universities while others have included university postbaccalaurate programs within the definition of "traditional programs." Zeichner, K., & Conklin, H. (2005). Teacher education programs. In M. Cochran-Smith & K. Zeichner (Eds), *Studying teacher education: The report of the AERA Panel on Research and Teacher Education* (pp. 645–735). New York, NY: Routledge. The term "alternative program" is used here in a broad way to include the different definitions that exist in different states. Many scholars have moved away from the use of the term alternative and focus more on the specific characteristics of programs rather than on general labels. Grossman, P. & Loeb, S. (2008) (Eds), *Alternative routes to teaching: Mapping the new landscape of teacher education*. Cambridge MA: Harvard Education Press.

12 Anderson, J. (1988). *The education of Blacks in the south: 1860–1935*. Chapel Hill, NC: University of North Carolina Press; Fraser, J. (2007). *Preparing America's teachers: A history*. New York, NY: Teachers College Press; Maestas, S. (2011). *Children of the Normal School, 60 years in El Rito, 1909–1969*. Santa Fe, NM: Sunstone Press.

13 Fraser. J. (2007). *Preparing America's teachers: A history*. New York, NY: Teachers College Press.

14 Stoddard, T., & Floden, R. (1996). Traditional and alternative routes to teacher certification: Issues, assumptions, and misconceptions. In K. Zeichner, S. Melnick, & M. L. Gomez (Eds), *Currents of reform in preservice teacher education* (pp. 80–106). New York, NY: Teachers College Press; Feistritzer, E. & Haar, C. (2008). *Alternative routes to teaching*. Upper Saddle River, NJ: Pearson; Cooperman, S., & Klagholz, L. (1985). New Jersey's alternative route to certification. *Phi Delta Kappan, 66*, 691–695.

15 Feistritzer, E., & Haar, C. (2008). *Alternative routes to teaching*. Upper Saddle River, NJ: Pearson.

16 Darling-Hammond, L. (1990). Teaching and knowledge: Policy issues posed by alternative certification for teachers. *Peabody Journal of Education, 67*(3), 123–154.

17 Feistritzer, E., & Haar, C. (2008). *Alternative routes to teaching*. Upper Saddle River, NJ: Pearson.

18 Villegas, A. M., & Irvine, J. J. (2010). Diversifying the teaching force: An examination of major arguments. *Urban Review, 42*, 175–192.

19 Corcoran, T. (2009). Human capital policy and the quality of the teacher workforce. In D. Goldhaber and J. Hannaway (Eds), *Creating a new teaching profession* (pp. 29–52). Washington DC: The Urban Institute.

20 Oliver, B., & McKibbin, M. (1985). Teacher trainees: Alternative credentialing in California. *California Journal of Teacher Education, 36*(3), 20–23.

21 Haberman, M. (1971). Twenty-three reasons universities can't educate teachers. *Journal of Teacher Education, 22*(2), 133–40.

22 Peske, H., & Haycock, K. (2006, June 1). *Teaching inequality: How poor minority students are shortchanged on teacher quality*. Washington, DC: Education Trust.

23 Eubanks, E., & Parish, R. (1990). Why does the status quo persist? *Phi Delta Kappan*, 72(3), 196–197; Peske, H., & Haycock, K. (2006, June). *Teaching inequality: How poor and minority children are shortchanged*. Washington, D.C: Education Trust.

24 Wisniewski, R. (1986). Alternative programs in the reform of teacher education. *Action in Teacher Education*, 8(2), 37–44.

25 Now referred to as TNTP. Both TFA and TNTP continue to partner with universities, but TNTP now also does some of its own preparation and TFA partners with non-university programs like Relay in some locations.

26 The repeated approval of a waiver from the highly qualified teacher provision of No Child Left Behind enabled non-university programs to prepare teachers on their own without outsourcing some of the preparation to a college or university. https://www.washingtonpost.com/news/answer-sheet/wp/2013/08/27/how-the-public- is-deceived-about-highly-qualified-teachers/

27 For example, the Race to the Top Competition led to changes in the certification laws in many states that broadened the definition of who could be authorized to offer teacher education programs. Crowe, E. (2011, March). *Race to the Top and teacher preparation: Analyzing state strategies for ensuring real accountability and fostering program innovation*. Washington, DC: Center for American Progress.

28 Alternative certification programs based at IHEs are referred to by the US Department of Education as "Alternative route programs not IHE-based." US Department of Education (2013, April). *Preparing and credentialing the nation's teachers: The secretary's ninth report on teacher quality*. Washington, DC: Author. Because some of these programs partner with universities, the term "independent" programs will be used here to indicate those alternative programs that do their own preparation of teachers.

29 It is frequently argued that teacher shortages are a result of poor or not enough teacher preparation. This assumption has been challenged and it has been argued that the shortages are more a result of teacher attrition caused mostly by poor working conditions and other factors other than teacher preparation. Ingersoll, R. (2003, September). *Is there really a teacher shortage?* Seattle, WA: Center for Teaching and Policy, University of Washington.

30 Retrieved April 12, 2016 from http://blogs.edweek.org/edweek/teacherbeat/2016/03/teacher_preparation_enrollment_declines.html

31 Washington Professional Educator Standards Board Newsletter, June 16, 2016.

32 Stitzlein, S. M., & West, C. K. (2014). New forms of teacher education: Connections to charter schools and their approaches. *Democracy and Education*, 22(2). Retrieved December 1, 2014, from democracyeducationjournal.org/home

33 Zeichner, K., & Conklin, H. G. (2017). Beyond knowledge ventriloquism and echo chambers: Raising the quality of the debate in teacher education. *Teachers College Record*, 119(4). Retrieved January 5, 2016, from www.tcrecord.org/content.asp?contentid=18148

34 Zeichner, K. (2016). The changing role of universities in US teacher education. In R. Moon (Ed), *Do universities have a role in the education and training of teachers: An international analysis of policy and practice* (pp. 107–126). Cambridge: Cambridge University Press.

35 Carter, P., & Welner, K. (Eds), (2013). *Closing the opportunity gap: What America must do to give every child an even chance*. New York, NY: Oxford University Press.

36 Carey, K. (2009, December 13). "Teacher U": A new model in employer-led higher education. *The Chronicle of Higher Education*. Retrieved June 24, 2010, from http://chronicle.com/article/Teacher-U-A-NewModel-in/49442; Chubb, J. E. (2012). *The best teachers in the world: Why we don't have them and how we could*. Stanford, CA: Hoover Institution Press.

37 Reckhow, S. (2013). *Follow the money: How foundation dollars change public school politics*. New York, NY: Oxford University Press.

38 Zeichner, K., & Peña-Sandoval, C. (2015). Venture philanthropy and teacher education policy in the US: The role of the New Schools Venture Fund. *Teachers College Record*, *117*(5), 1–44.

39 Hess, F. M. (2002). Break the link. *Education Next*, *2*(1). Retrieved July 25, 2008, from educationnext.org/break-the-link/break-the-link/

40 Zeichner, K., & Peña-Sandoval, C. (2015). Venture philanthropy and teacher education policy in the US: The role of the New Schools Venture Fund. *Teachers College Record*, *117*(5), 1–44.

41 Keller, B. (October, 2013). An industry of mediocrity. *New York Times*. Retrieved October 20, 2013, from www.nytimes.com/2013/10/21/opinion/keller-an-industry-of-mediocrity.html?_r=0

42 Goodlad, J. (1990). *Teachers for our nation's schools*. San Francisco, CA: Jossey-Bass; Holmes Partnership (2007). *The Holmes Partnership trilogy: Tomorrow's teachers, tomorrow's schools, and tomorrow's schools of education*. New York, NY: Peter Lang; Labaree, D. (2004). *The trouble with ed schools*. New Haven, CT: Yale University Press.

43 Darling-Hammond, L. (2006). *Powerful teacher education*. San Francisco, CA: Jossey-Bass; Hollins, E. (2016) (Ed). *Rethinking field experiences in preservice teacher education: Meeting new challenges for accountability*. New York, NY: Routledge; Grossman, P. (2011). Framework for teaching practice: Brief history of an idea. *Teachers College Record*, *113*(12), 2836–2843.

44 See additional examples of the misrepresentation of research in Zeichner, K., & Conklin, H. (2017). Beyond knowledge ventriloquism and echo chambers: Raising the quality the debate on teacher education. *Teachers College Record*, *119*(4). Retrieved January 5, 2016, from www.tcrecord.org/content.asp?contentid=18148

45 Zeichner, K., & Conklin, H. (2005). Teacher education programs. In M. Cochran-Smith & K. Zeichner (Eds), *Studying teacher education: The report of the AERA Panel on Research and Teacher Education* (pp. 645–735). Mahwah, NJ: Lawrence Erlbaum.

46 Retrieved August 24, 2016, from https://www.gpo.gov/fdsys/pkg/CHRG-112hhrg75109/html/CHRG-112hhrg75109.htm

47 Zeichner, K., & Conklin, H. (2017). Beyond knowledge ventriloquism and echo chambers: Raising the quality the debate on teacher education. *Teachers College Record*, *119*(4). Retrieved January 5, 2016, from www.tcrecord.org/content.asp?contentid=18148

48 The Relay residency option is a 2-year program where teacher candidates work under the supervision of a mentor teacher for a full academic year. In the traditional Relay model, teachers complete the program while they are serving as teachers of record fully responsible for classrooms.

49 Currently, only about 1 percent of candidates opt for the iTeach clinical option, choosing instead to become a teacher of record without prior training. Personal Communication, June 1, 2016 with Diann Huber, program founder.

50 The Relay Graduate School of Education (founded in 2011), Sposato Graduate School of Education (MTR) (founded in 2012), and the HTH Graduate School of Education (founded in 2007) are all authorized to award master's degrees by their respective states although only MTR and Relay offer master's degrees to teacher credential candidates. Teach-Now has also formed an independent School of Education to house its certification programs (Educatore), but it is not affiliated with any particular charter schools.

51 Griswold, J., & Riordan, R. (2016). Another innovation from High Tech High – Embedded teacher training. *Phi Delta Kappan, 97*(7), 25–29.

52 Retrieved July 10, 2016 from www.sposatogse.org/about/overview/

53 Retrieved August 15, 2016 from www.ccsso.org/resources/publications/InTasc_model_core_teaching_standards_and_learning_progressions_for_teachers_10.html; www.ccsso.org/resources/publications/InTasc_model_core_teaching_standards_and_learning_progressions_for_teachers_10.html

54 Arnett, T. (2015, June). *Startup teacher education.* Redwood City, CA: Clayton Christensen Institute for Disruptive Innovation (p. 2). Retrieved June 29, 2016, from www.christenseninstitute.org/wp-content/uploads/2015/06/Startup-Teacher-Education.pdf

55 Brenneman, R. (2015, September 2). New online teacher-certification program plans for rapid expansion. *Education Week.* Retrieved September 8, 2015, from http://blogs.edweek.org/edweek/teacherbeat/2015/09/teach-now-online-certification-scaling-up.html?r=59094252

56 The growth of the Relay and MTR models includes expansion internationally to countries like UK and South Africa. www.instill.education/ and http://www.ippr.org/files/publications/pdf/beyond-the-plateau_July2016.pdf?noredirect=1

57 Zeichner, K., & Peña-Sandoval, C. (2015). Venture philanthropy and teacher education policy in the U.S: The role of the New Schools Venture Fund. *Teachers College Record, 117*(5), 1–44.

58 Candal, C. (2014, February). *Matching excellent students to excellent teachers: How a Massachusetts charter school organization innovates with teacher preparation.* Boston, MA: Pioneer Institute.

59 Cochran-Smith, M., & Villegas, A.M. (2016). Research on teacher preparation: Charting the landscape of a sprawling field. In D. Gitomer & C. Bell (Eds), *Handbook of research on teaching* (5th ed.) (pp. 439–538). Washington, DC: American Educational Research Association; National Research Council. (2010). *Preparing teachers: Building evidence for sound policy.* Committee on the Study of Teacher Preparation Programs in the United States, Center for Education. Division of Behavioral and Social Sciences and Education. Washington, DC: The National Academies Press; Wilson, S., Floden, R., & Ferrini-Mundy, J. (2001). *Teacher preparation research: Content knowledge, gaps, and recommendations.* Washington, DC: US Department of Education; Zeichner, K., & Conklin, H. (2005). Teacher education programs. In M. Cochran-Smith & K. Zeichner (Eds), *Studying teacher education: The report of the AERA Panel on Research and Teacher Education* (pp. 645–735). Mahwah, NJ: Lawrence Erlbaum.

60 National Research Council. (2010). *Preparing teachers: Building evidence for sound policy.* Committee on the Study of Teacher Preparation Programs in the United States, Center for Education. Division of Behavioral and Social Sciences and Education. Washington, DC: The National Academies Press, 41–42.

61 National Research Council. (2010). *Preparing teachers: Building evidence for sound policy.* Committee on the Study of Teacher Preparation Programs in the United States, Center for Education. Division of Behavioral and Social Sciences and Education. Washington, DC: The National Academies Press, 2.

62 Cochran-Smith, M., & Villegas, A. M. (2016). Research on teacher preparation: Charting the landscape of a sprawling field. In D. Gitomer & C. Bell (Eds), *Handbook of research on teaching* (5th ed.) (p. 453). Washington, DC: American Educational Research Association.

63 Zeichner, K., & Conklin, H. (2005). Teacher education programs. In M. Cochran-Smith & K. Zeichner (Eds), *Studying teacher education: The report of the AERA Panel on Research and Teacher Education* (pp. 645–735). Mahwah, NJ: Lawrence Erlbaum; Wilson, S., Floden, R., & Ferrini-Mundy, J. (2001). *Teacher preparation research: Content knowledge, gaps, and recommendations.* Washington, DC: US Department of Education.

64 Gastic, B. (2014). Closing the opportunity gap: Preparing the next generation of effective teachers. In R. Hess & M. McShane (Eds), *Teacher quality 2.0.* Cambridge, MA: Harvard Education Press; Kronholz, J. (2012). A new type of Ed school: Linking candidate success to student success. *Education Next, 12*(4). Retrieved March 15, 2013, from http://educationnext.org/a-new-type-of-ed-school/; Schorr, J. (2012). A revolution begins in teacher education. *Stanford Social Innovation Review.* Retrieved August 9, 2014 from www.ssireview.org/articles/entry/a_revolution_begins_in_teacher_prep; *The Economist* (June, 2016). Teaching the teachers. *Economist.* Retrieved August 1, 2016 from www.economist.com/news/briefing/21700385-great-teaching-has-long-been-seen-innate-skill- reformers-are-showing-best

65 Mathematica is currently conducting a study of the effectiveness of graduates of Relay teaching in New York City on student test scores in reading and language arts. Also, the Center for Education Policy Research at Harvard Graduate School of Education is conducting a study of the graduates of the Match Teacher Residency in comparison with the graduates of other teacher education programs. At this time, no findings have been shared publicly from either study.

66 Goldstein, M. (2013). *Phoning parents.* Boston, MA: Match Education.

67 Kraft, M., & Dougherty, S. (2013). The effect of teacher-family communication on student engagement: Evidence from a randomized field experiment. *Journal of Research on Educational Effectiveness, 6*(3), 199–222.

68 Statement from program graduate Samantha Koonce, District of Columbia, US Retrieved July 20, 2016, from http://teach-now.com/case-studies/

69 Kronholz, J. (2012). A new type of Ed school: Linking candidate success to student success. *Education Next, 12*(4). Retrieved June 1, 2013 from http://educationnext.org/a-new-type-of-ed-school/

70 Candal, C. (2014, February). *Matching students to excellent teachers: How a Massachusetts charter school innovates with teacher preparation.* Boston, MA: Pioneer Institute.

71 Retrieved July 18, 2016, from www.relay.edu/about/results

72 Retrieved July 18, 2016, from www.relay.edu/about/results

73 Retrieved May 25, 2016, from www.relay.edu/research/impact/institutional-assessment; www.cloud.relay.edu/research/Public%20Information_SGA_Final_2016.pdf

74 National Research Council. (2010). *Preparing teachers: Building evidence for sound policy.* Committee on the Study of Teacher Preparation Programs in the United States, Center for Education. Division of Behavioral and Social Sciences and Education. Washington, DC: The National Academies Press.

75 Retrieved July 18, 2016, from www.relay.edu/research/impact/publicinformation

76 Retrieved June 1, 2016, from www.sposatogse.org/annual-letter/

77 Gastic, B. (2014). Closing the opportunity gap: Preparing the next generation of effective teachers. In R. Hess & M. McShane (Eds), *Teacher quality 2.0* (p. 96). Cambridge, MA: Harvard Education Press.

78 Lemov, D. (2010). *Teach like a champion: 49 techniques that put students on the path to college (K–12).* San Francisco, CA: Jossey-Bass.

79 Otterman, S. (2011, July 21). Ed schools' pedagogical puzzle. *The New York Times.* Retrieved July 24, 2011 from www.nytimes.com/2011/07/24/education/edlife/edl-24teacher-t.html?pagewanted=all&_r=0

80 Pianta, R. C. (2011, November). *Teaching children well: New evidence-based approaches to teacher professional development and training.* Washington, DC: Center for American Progress.

81 Schorr, J. (2012). A revolution begins in teacher education. *Stanford Social Innovation Review.* Retrieved August 19, 2013 from www.ssireview.org/articles/entry/a_revolution_begins_in_teacher_prep; Liu, M. (2013). Disrupting teacher education. *Education Next, 13*(3). Retrieved August 24, 2016 from http://educationnext.org/disrupting-teacher-education

82 Zeichner, K., & Conklin, H. (2017). Beyond knowledge ventriloquism and echo chambers: Raising the quality of the debate on teacher education. *Teachers College Record, 119*(4). Retrieved January 5, 2016, from www.tcrecord.org/content.asp?contentid=18148

83 Zeichner, K., & Conklin, H.G. (2017). Beyond knowledge ventriloquism and echo chambers: Raising the quality of the debate in teacher education. *Teachers College Record, 119*(4). Retrieved January 5, 2016, from www.tcrecord.org/content.asp?contentid=18148

84 Levin, H. M. (1980). Teacher certification and the economics of information. *Educational Evaluation and Policy Analysis, 2*(4), 5–18; Feuer, M., Floden, R., Chudowsky, N., & Ahn, J. (2013). *Evaluation of teacher education programs: Purposes, methods, and policy options.* Washington, DC: National Academy of Education.

85 Goodlad, J. (2004). *A place called school* (2nd edition). New York, NY: McGraw Hill.

86 Ronfeldt, M., Loeb, S., & Wycoff, J. (2013, February). How teacher turnover harms student achievement. *American Educational Research Journal, 50*(1), 4–36.

87 Grossman, P., & Loeb, S. (2008) (Eds). *Alternative routes to teaching: Mapping the new landscape of teacher education.* Cambridge MA: Harvard Education Press.

88 Redding, C., & Smith, T. M. (in press). Easy in, easy out: Are alternatively certified teachers turning over at increased rates? *American Educational Research Journal.*

Retrieved August 9, 2016, from http://aer.sagepub.com.offcampus.lib.washington. edu/content/early/2016/06/17/0002831216653206.full.pdf+html

89 Grissom, J. (2008). But do they stay? Addressing issues of teacher retention through alternative certification. In P. Grossman & S. Loeb (Eds), *Alternative routes to teaching: Mapping the new landscape of teacher education* (pp. 129–156). Cambridge, MA: Harvard Education Press.

90 Berliner, D. (2011). Rational responses to high-stakes testing: The case of curriculum narrowing and the harm that follows. *Cambridge Journal of Education, 41*(3), 287–302.

91 Goodman, J. (2013). Charter management organizations and the regulated environment: Is it worth the price? *Educational Researcher, 42*(2), 8.

92 Rose, M. (2013). The mismeasure of teaching and learning: How contemporary school reform fails the test. In M. B. Katz & M. Rose (Eds), *Public education under siege* (pp. 9–20). Philadelphia, PA: University of Pennsylvania Press; Kozol, J. (2005). *The shame of American education: The restoration of apartheid schooling in America.* New York, NY: Crown Publishers; American Psychological Association (2012, August). *Ethnic and racial disparities in education: Psychology's contributions to understanding and reducing disparities.* Washington, DC: American Psychological Association. Retrieved August 5, 2016, from https://www.apa.org/ed/resources/racial-disparities.pdf

93 Berliner, D. (2011). Rational responses to high-stakes testing: The case of curriculum narrowing and the harm that follows. *Cambridge Journal of Education, 41*(3), 287–302; Tienken, C., & Zhao, Y. (2013). How common standards and standardized testing widen the opportunity gap. In P.L. Carter & K. G. Welner (Eds), *Closing the opportunity gap: What America must do to give every child a chance* (pp. 111–122). New York, NY: Oxford University Press; Pacheco, M. (2010). English language learners' reading achievement: Dialectical relationships between policies and practices in meaning-making opportunities. *Reading Research Quarterly, 45*(3), 292–317; Lafer, G. (April, 2014) *Do poor kids deserve lower quality education than rich kids? Evaluating school privatization proposals in Milwaukee, Wisconsin.* Washington, DC: Economic Policy Institute. Retrieved July 10, 2014, from www.epi.org/publication/ school-privatization-milwaukee/

94 Liu, M. (2013). Disrupting teacher education. *Education Next, 13*(3). Retrieved January 10, 2014, from http://educationnext.org/disrupting-teacher-education/

95 Zeichner, K., & Conklin, H. (2017). Beyond knowledge ventriloquism and echo chambers: Raising the quality of the debate on teacher education. *Teachers College Record, 119*(4). Retrieved January 5, 2016, from www.tcrecord.org/content. asp?contentid=18148

96 Grossman, P., & Loeb, S. (Eds), (2008). *Alternative routes to teaching: Mapping the new landscape of teacher education.* Cambridge, MA: Harvard Education Press.

97 Zeichner, K., & Conklin, H. (2005). Teacher education programs. In M. Cochran-Smith & K. Zeichner (Eds), *Studying teacher education: The report of the AERA Panel on Research and Teacher Education* (pp. 645–735). Mahwah, NJ: Lawrence Erlbaum.

98 Darling-Hammond, L. (2006). *Powerful teacher education.* San Francisco, CA: Jossey-Bass, p. 41.

99 National Research Council. (2010). *Preparing teachers: Building evidence for sound policy.* Committee on the Study of Teacher Preparation Programs in the United States,

Center for Education. Division of Behavioral and Social Sciences and Education Washington, DC: The National Academies Press.

100 Haberman, M. (1991). The pedagogy of poverty vs. good teaching. *Phi Delta Kappan*, 73(4), 90–294.

6

DEMOCRATIZING TEACHER EDUCATION

Kenneth M. Zeichner, Katherina A. Payne, and Kate Brayko

Teacher Education in Turmoil

> By almost any standard, many, if not most, of the nation's 1,450 schools, colleges, and departments of education are doing a mediocre job of preparing teachers.
>
> *(Duncan, 2009)*

> America has a broken teacher preparation system.
>
> *(Knowles, 2013, p. 6)*

This is a critical time for teacher education in the US. The college and university system of teacher preparation that has prepared most US teachers for over the last 50 years (Fraser, 2007) has been declared to be a failure by many policymakers and the mainstream media. The federal government and most of the philanthropic community are pouring resources into supporting greater market competition and the entry of new non-university providers into the field (Zeichner & Peña-Sandoval, 2015). Colleges and universities now face jurisdictional challenges to their authority to offer teacher education programs (Grossman, 2008); we are on a course to dismantle the college and university system of teacher education and replace it with a host of entrepreneurial programs that we believe will worsen rather than ameliorate the opportunity, and learning gaps that continue to plague our public schools.

There are three major positions on the current system of college and university teacher education. First, there is the position taken by some college and university teacher educators that the criticisms of teacher education from the outside are wrong and that what we need is greater investment by government and philanthropy in strengthening the current system. We call this position that of the *defenders*. The defenders do not see the need for significant changes in the ways in which things are done now and want more resources to do these things better.

Second, there are outsiders to the current system, and even some within, who have argued that education schools have failed and that the current system needs to be "blown up" or disrupted and replaced by an alternative based on deregulation, competition, and markets (Chubb, 2012; Schorr, 2013). These critics often refer to themselves as the *reformers*.

Finally, there are those inside and outside the system who see the need for substantive transformation in the current system of teacher education, but who do not support disrupting the current system by replacing it with a deregulated market economy. This position is that of the *transformers*.

A system of categorization such as this inevitably oversimplifies a much more complex situation. There is in reality much variation within these three "camps" (e.g., in terms of the intensity and substance of positions), as well as multiple points of overlap between positions (e.g., some transformers and reformers who support maintaining aspects of the current system). That said, the distinctions between groups offer a meaningful lens for considering different views on how to move forward in teacher education.

Currently, there are a variety of efforts underway to significantly transform aspects of college and university teacher education, including shifting teacher education more to schools and community-based settings and strengthening the clinical components of programs, as well as focusing preparation more on helping teacher candidates acquire the ability to enact specific teaching practices that are related to successful student learning (Grossman, 2011; Zeichner & Bier, 2013).

In this chapter, we discuss one aspect of the current efforts to transform college and university teacher education by addressing the issue of *whose knowledge counts* in the education of teachers. In this article, we call for a rethinking of the epistemology of teacher preparation in the US and for the development of new forms of shared responsibility for preparing teachers among colleges and universities, schools, and local communities.

The Epistemology of Teacher Education

One of the central issues underlying current debates about teacher education and teacher quality is concerned with the knowledge and skills that teachers need to be successful in teaching all students to high academic standards. There has been extensive writing over the years about what beginning teachers need to know and be able to do (e.g., Darling-Hammond & Bransford, 2005), including the particular teaching practices that novices need to learn how to enact (Ball & Forzani, 2009), and this work has focused on analyzing *what* teachers need to know and be able to do to be well-started beginners. Similarly, over the years, a substantial literature has emerged in the US and elsewhere on the question of *who* should be prepared as teachers to teach in democratic societies (e.g., Villegas & Irvine, 2010; Villegas & Lucas, 2004) and *how* this preparation should occur (e.g., Cochran-Smith, Davis, & Fries, 2004; Hollins & Guzman, 2005). Very little attention has been given, however, to the issue of *whose knowledge* should count in teacher education.

Currently, there are basically two general approaches to the pre-service education of teachers in the US despite all of the specific program variations: "early-entry" and "college recommending" (Grossman & Loeb, 2008). Even with the advent of "early-entry" programs in the 1980s, where much of pre-service preparation is completed by individuals while they serve as teachers of record, college- and university-based teacher education programs that include significant coursework and fieldwork prior to a candidate becoming a teacher of record continue to be the major source of teachers for our public schools (National Research Council, 2010).

College-Recommending Programs

The traditional model of college-recommending teacher education emphasizes the translation of academic knowledge into practice.[1] Candidates are supposed to learn what and how to teach in their courses and then go out and apply what is learned in schools during their field experiences. Historically, very little success has been achieved in coordinating what is done in the course and field components of teacher education programs (Anderson & Stillman, 2011; Zeichner, 2010a). Even in the current era of school-university partnerships, partner and professional development schools, colleges, and universities continue to maintain hegemony over the construction and dissemination of knowledge for teaching in teacher education (Duffy, 1994; Zeichner, 2009) and schools remain in the position of "practice fields" where candidates are to try out the practices provided to them by the university (Barab & Duffy, 2000).

Although the reality of how and from whom teacher candidates learn to teach is much more complex than portrayed here (e.g., Valencia, Martin, Place, & Grossman, 2009), the way in which college- and university-based teacher education is usually structured is fundamentally undemocratic and largely fails to strategically access knowledge and expertise, which exists in schools and communities, that could inform the preparation of teachers. Most prospective teachers spend a substantial amount of time in schools during their preparation; however, there is typically very little planning that is done (e.g., a practicum curriculum) as to how they can access practitioner and community-based knowledge to inform their preparation as teachers (Turney, Eltis, Towler, & Wright, 1985). We are neither suggesting that power differentials can be completely equalized nor that the goal should be to try to reach consensus on all issues. We are suggesting, though, that power hierarchies be lessened in teacher preparation programs, that more participants and more perspectives be brought into the decision-making process, and that different views be seriously considered despite important differences that will continue to exist about what constitutes good teaching and how teachers should learn (Apple, 2008).

Early-Entry Programs

The rapidly expanding "early-entry" programs place teacher candidates in schools with very little pre-service preparation, and emphasize, even sometimes uncritically glorify, practice and practitioner knowledge while minimizing the importance of professional education coursework that is not seen as directly connected to daily teaching practice. They have often falsely framed the issue as one of choosing between theory and practice in a teacher education program and sometimes proudly proclaim that they have minimized or eliminated theory from teacher preparation. They also often uncritically glorify practice:

> Gone are the courses on education theory and history with no practical bearing. ... Professors are not lofty academics, they are accomplished practitioners in the field ... Relay provost Brent Maddin said "the key is not to weed out theory, but rather than to distill it down to essential points for the busy teacher."
>
> *(Caperton & Whitmire, 2012, pp. 77, 83)*

This kind of thinking, represented in such programs as Relay Graduate School of Education and The New Teacher Project (TNTP, 2014; Schorr, 2013; Stitzlein & West, 2014; Zeichner & Peña-Sandoval, 2015), leads to such things as the definition of social foundations content as "non-essential" (Walsh & Jacobs, 2007) and to the preparation of teachers who can implement teaching scripts but who have not developed the professional vision, cultural competence, and adaptive expertise they need to meet the changing learning needs of their students or to continue to learn in and from their practice (Hammerness et al., 2005; Sherin, 2001; Zeichner, 2014b). Importantly, neither college-recommending nor early-entry programs often give much attention to the role of community-based knowledge in teacher preparation (e.g., Murrell, 2001).

Toward a More Democratic Epistemology for Teacher Education

Neither of these two stances toward the substance of teacher education (an emphasis on academic or practitioner knowledge alone) is sufficient for preparing teachers to be successful in the public schools today in the US. Despite the social justice rhetoric and multicultural content that is common in college and university teacher education programs across the nation, the hidden curriculum of existing models of teacher education (Ginsburg & Clift, 1990) often sends a very clear message about the lack of respect for the knowledge of P–12 practitioners and non-professional educators in communities.

In our view, the preparation of teachers for a democratic society should be based on an epistemology that in itself is democratic and includes a respect for and interaction among practitioner, academic, and community-based knowledge. This vision reflects the concept of "leveling" that can occur in "third spaces" or contexts in which individuals surrender outward status and come together to engage more as equals (Oldenburg, 1999). Whether this can take place in newly created spaces within universities such as "Centers of Pedagogy" (Patterson, Michelli, & Pacheco, 1999) or whether new institutional spaces need to be created for teacher education with different knowledge histories (Gorodetsky & Barak, 2008; Friedrich, 2014) remains to be seen. What is involved in what we are proposing is the creation of new hybrid spaces where academic, practitioner, and community-based knowledge come together in new ways to support the development of innovative and hybrid solutions to the problem of preparing teachers. Although the current wave of interest in teacher residencies (Duncan, 2009) offers the potential for developing genuinely hybrid contexts for teacher education, thus far they have not realized this potential and have experienced some of the same problems (e.g., connecting coursework with clinical work) that have plagued traditional college and university recommending programs and early-entry programs (Gatti & Catalano, 2015; Zeichner, 2014a).

Conceptualizing Hybrid Spaces in Teacher Education

We advocate for the creation of new hybrid spaces in university teacher education where academic, school-based, and community-based knowledge come together in less hierarchical and haphazard ways to support teacher learning. To further theorize collaborations and "spaces" between university-, school-, and community-based sources of knowledge, we use some of the conceptual tools afforded by cultural historical activity theory (CHAT). We believe that these tools not only help us interrogate the democratic nature of current efforts of collaboration but also provide a framework for teacher education programs as they rethink their relationships with, and the roles that schools and communities ought to have, in educating novice teachers. CHAT provides a way to think about bringing together sources of expertise that are valuable for learning to teach—particularly expertise that abounds in schools, colleges and universities, and communities. Two of the key ideas in cultural-historical theories are that expertise is distributed across systems and that individuals develop into the ways of thinking and acting that are afforded by the cultural practices and tools made available to them in the settings of their development (Ellis, Edwards, & Smagorinsky, 2010). From a CHAT perspective, teacher candidate learning takes place in "a changing mosaic of interconnected activity systems" (Engeström, 2001, p. 147).

Engeström (2001), who expanded Leont'ev's work on activity systems and Vygotsky's (1978) zone of proximal development (ZPD),[2] emphasizes that human activity is simultaneously constrained by macro-structures and socio-political contexts as well as transformed by individuals' actions, proclivities, and tendencies within their everyday activities. Specifically, activity theory acknowledges the community, distribution of work, and rules that affect both individual and collective activities. Thus, Engeström elaborated the ZPD from an individualistic account of learning and development toward a more expansive view of learning through participation with others within activity systems that are simultaneously enabling and constraining. In the case of educating teacher candidates, the novice teacher is participating in activity systems at the university, in their school field placement, and possibly within the community in which the school is situated. Each of these systems has varying constraints and affordances to support novice teacher learning; however, too often these systems are not in dialogue and leave the novice teacher as the sole mediator of multiple knowledge sources.

Engeström (1987, 2001) emphasizes the expansive aspects of learning that occur through engaging in the activity, particularly through the contradictions and tensions that are the "engines" of change and transformation in practices, tools, and activities. By centering the activity of teacher learning in the contradictory, conflictual spaces among the university, school, and community's knowledge and practice, the possibility for collaborative efforts around these contradictions can lead to remediation of novice teachers' learning. Furthermore, through these tensions in learning how to work with diverse learners, and toward the goal of accessing both school and community knowledge, activity theory allows us to look at novice teachers' learning in and across multiple spaces to recognize how those spaces expand and constrain learning opportunities.

Our view of democratizing teacher education through the fostering of such spaces rests on tenets of deliberative democracy (e.g., Gutmann & Thompson, 2004). Deliberative democracy assumes the value of mutual respect among participants. Gutmann and Thompson (2004) summarize their view of deliberative democracy as

> A form of government in which free and equal citizens (and their representatives), justify decisions in a process in which they give one another reasons that are mutually acceptable and generally accessible, with the aim of reaching conclusions that are binding in the present on all citizens but open to challenge in the future.
>
> *(p. 7)*

Like governments, teacher education has a number of people with varying stakes in the structures, implementation, and outcomes (i.e., the novice teachers) of its programs. Similar to CHAT, deliberative democracy accounts for these varying systems that are bound by different rules, accountable to different communities, and operating under different distributions and means of work. Our approach to democratizing teacher education rests on a belief that deliberative democracy, with its basic principle of reciprocity, allows for the conflictual spaces necessary to promote change when working and learning across the university, school, and community. Together, CHAT and deliberative democratic theory allow us to examine current collaborative efforts among universities, schools, and communities, and have the potential to point us toward greater democratic possibilities in teacher education.

Assuming that the knowledge and expertise needed by teacher candidates is located in schools, colleges, and universities, and in and among communities, and that the key problem of teacher education is to figure out how to provide teacher candidates with access to and mediation of this needed expertise from these different systems, the concepts of "horizontal expertise," "boundary-crossing/ boundary-zones," and "knotworking" have proved particularly useful in theorizing these hybrid relationships. For the sake of clarity, we present each conceptual tool separately here; however, we argue that these conceptual tools are bound together as an overarching approach toward democratizing teacher education.

Horizontal Expertise

In their examination of health care organizations, Kerosuo and Engeström (2003) developed useful concepts that can be applied to efforts that involve overlapping activity systems in teacher education. The impetus for the collaborative efforts among these health care providers was the tensions and contradictions that emerged for patients who navigated multiple types of health care providers (e.g., clinics, hospitals). Disruption in the communications within and across providers resulted in significant ruptures in the continuity of patient care. Moreover, multiple and different rules, tools, reporting systems, and patterns of interaction that guide these organizations made the establishment of common goals difficult to pursue concurrently.

To work collaboratively to articulate new goals, practices, and tools, participants had to cross the boundaries of their own organizations and work with others to create new solutions to their common problems. Through this process, horizontal expertise emerged as "professionals from different domains enriched and expanded their practices through working together to reorganize relations and coordinate their work" (Anagnostopoulos, Smith, & Basmadjian, 2007, p. 139). Horizontal expertise, in contrast to vertical notions of learning and expertise (i.e., "lower" and "higher" forms), recognizes the unique knowledge and understanding that each participant brought to the collective activity and treats the knowledge as equally valuable, relevant, and important. Each participant develops a range of expertise across work and organizational spaces. But working collaboratively, these forms of expertise serve as resources in joint problem-solving activity and help individuals and groups find innovative solutions to the compelling dilemmas that characterize their everyday work life. In this way, horizontal expertise relies on the same give-and-take as deliberative democracy. Creating these innovative tools, practices, and solutions not only addresses the joint activity and dilemma but also expands individuals' learning as they appropriate new tools and work in languages that they could not have created on their own with access only to their particular languages, rules, and systems.

Although originally developed in studies of workplace learning in Finland, these conceptual tools are useful for thinking about the more democratic political economy of knowledge that we believe is necessary to educate teachers to be successful in the complex and underfunded public schools where many of them will teach (e.g., Edwards, 2010; Edwards, Daniels, Gallagher, Leadbetter, & Warmington, 2009; Ellis et al., 2010; Engeström, 2001, 2008). The task of bringing together expertise from the different activity systems of university, school, and community for the benefit of teacher candidate learning can be considered analogous to the problem of coordinating the work of health care professionals who work in different systems, but who all serve the same patients (Engeström, 2008; see also, Edwards, 2010; Edwards et al., 2009).

Knotworking

Engeström (2008) defines knotworking as follows:

> The notion of a knot refers to a rapidly pulsating, distributed, and partially improvised orchestration of collaborative performance between otherwise loosely connected actors and activity systems. Knotworking is characterized by a movement of tying, untying, and retying together seemingly separate threads of activity.
>
> *(p. 194)*

The concept of "knotworking" offers a way to understand the learning of teacher candidates that occurs when there is collaboration across activity systems (university, school, and community). The different interests, values, and practices that exist in these different systems are mediated in the knots (Engeström, 2008; Engeström, Engeström, & Vahaaho, 1999). Knotworking emphasizes that there is no single locus of control, rather the locus changes time and again.

Boundary Zones

Max's (2010) use of "boundary zone" as "space where elements from two activity systems enter into contact" (p. 216) lessens the possibility of participants merely visiting a space; instead, the boundary zone creates the kind of fluctuating and flexible space in which continuing joint work can occur. We envision collaborative work among universities, schools, and communities toward novice teacher learning that has the flexibility to shift with time as each organization draws upon their knowledge of teaching and learning. Insights from international research on the pooling of expertise in these knots, or boundary settings between organizations (e.g., Edwards, 2010; Engeström, 2007), can benefit efforts in teacher education to build new hybrid or "inter-spaces" (Hartley, 2007) between schools, universities, and communities in ways that support teacher learning.

Third Space

Norton-Meier and Drake (2010) argue that a hybrid or "third space" in teacher education is more than moving university courses to schools or bringing P-12 teachers to the university campus. Merely bringing people together in the same physical space to plan, deliver, and renew teacher education programs will not necessarily alter the ways in which knowledge is utilized in the preparation of teachers and create the kind of leveling and greater social equality that is needed (Noel & Nelson, 2010; Popkewitz, 1975). There is substantial evidence that traditional knowledge hierarchies are maintained among universities, schools, and communities even in situations that have been characterized as genuinely collaborative (e.g., Zeichner, 1995).

As we indicated earlier, we are not suggesting that it is possible to create a situation of democratic deliberation free of power differentials, the kind of "ideal speech situation" that has been suggested by Habermas (1984) and Rawls (1971). There are real dangers involved in rhetorically romanticizing a model of teacher education based on deliberative democracy (Apple, 2008; see also, Sanders, 1997). There is no question that the negotiations that will need to take place in the hybrid spaces that we are suggesting (e.g., over different visions of what makes high-quality teachers and how to prepare them) will be difficult to navigate (e.g., Bartholomew & Sandholtz, 2009; Zeichner, 1991). There is some evidence in recent studies of collaborative efforts in inter-organizational spaces that achieving this inclusivity and reaching a situation where participants achieve "reasonable agreements" about certain elements of the situation at hand is generative of productive boundary work that results in new and creative solutions (e.g., Edwards, 2010). Furthermore, as Klein, Taylor, Onore, Strom, and Abrams (2013) have pointed out, a third space is a continual construction, a utopian prospect that is never fully achievable.

In the following sections, we examine how teacher education, and in particular pre-service teacher education, can attempt to use some of the conceptual tools of CHAT and deliberative democracy to create more expansive learning opportunities for pre-service teachers by creating spaces for the kind of horizontal expertise, knotworking, and boundary zones and boundary-crossing that will lead to more democratic teacher education. The examples below are intended to illustrate work in teacher education programs that is moving in the direction that we are advocating, and in some cases, they represent works in-progress.

Engaging Schools and Teachers in Teacher Education

There have been a number of inter-institutional teacher education efforts that have drawn upon horizontal expertise between teacher education programs and schools; this work exemplifies a range in recognition of horizontal expertise and creation of boundary zones for joint work. In the following section, we present a few examples that illustrate this range.

An example in which university- and school-based knowledge came together is the Cognitively Guided Instruction in Mathematics Project that was initiated in Madison, Wisconsin. Academic researchers at the University of Wisconsin-Madison collaborated with local teachers to figure out how to develop strategies for teaching elementary mathematics (Carpenter, Fennema, Franke, Levi, & Empson, 2000). The utilization of expertise of both academics and teachers about how children learn about addition and subtraction produced new and creative solutions to problems that could not be solved by either alone.[3]

School-based methods instruction (e.g., Jeffery & Polleck, 2013; Klein et al., 2013; Zeichner & McDonald, 2011; Morgan-Fleming, Simpson, Curtis, & Hull, 2010; Shirley et al., 2006) represents another space with potential for the exchange of university- and school-based expertise. At the University of Washington (UW) in Seattle,[4] some elementary methods courses are taught in local public schools where instructors strategically attempt to connect academic and school-based expertise. For example, in addition to the usual practice of professors providing teacher candidates with the theoretical basis for particular teaching strategies and showing them video examples of teachers using these practices, teacher candidates also have opportunities in these courses to observe a classroom teacher using a teaching strategy with students, to plan and rehearse lessons using these strategies that they then go and teach with students, and to debrief their teaching with their peers, and with the professor and teachers in the school (Lampert et al., 2013).

As we have suggested before, simply moving a methods course to a school and involving K–12 teachers in the instruction of teacher candidates does not necessarily mean that the teachers' expertise is valued and utilized in the ways that we advocate; attention to the democratic qualities of collaboration is necessary. In particular, we emphasize deliberative democracy's emphasis on finding solutions that are mutually acceptable and generally accessible. In the examples that best denote horizontal expertise, classroom teachers are active participants in the planning, instruction, and evaluation activities related to a course, thereby creating more authentic, acceptable, and accessible possibilities for inclusion of teachers' expertise.

Other examples of democratizing pre-service teacher education involve sustained efforts to include expert teachers in all aspects of university-based teacher education, including program planning, instruction, and ongoing evaluation and renewal. Two examples are the Teachers in Residence Program at the University of Wisconsin-Milwaukee and the Faculty Associate positions at Simon Fraser University in Canada (Beynon, Grout, & Wideen, 2004; Post, Pugach, Harris, & Hughes, 2006). In both of these cases, K–12 teachers' voices and expertise were an important part of all aspects of program planning, instruction, and evaluation. Horizontal expertise was essential to the program's structures and processes.

In the previous examples, most of the partnering teachers were handpicked by teacher education programs because of their notable strengths and expertise and/or because their philosophies and practices reflected those advocated by teacher education faculty. Alternatively, Anagnostopoulos and colleagues (2007) at the Michigan State University (MSU) have shared an important case in which there was substantial contradiction between school teachers' and university faculty's ideas about quality teaching, thus making horizontal expertise a more complicated effort.

As the authors explain, during the student teaching term of the secondary-English teaching program at Michigan State, many teacher mentors felt that the university assignments disrupted their curricula and endorsed practices counter to their own, while the university professors felt that the mentors were promoting ineffective practices and limiting student teachers' "learning-to-teach opportunities" (Anagnostopoulos et al., 2007, p. 140). In response to this contradiction and tension, university faculty and teacher mentors began a series of meetings to discuss English language arts pedagogy and research, with a particular focus on facilitating class discussion. Throughout the deliberative process, argumentation among participants allowed for competing views about purposes and practices related to classroom discussion practice to emerge and interact (Anagnostopoulos et al., 2007). By creating a space for multiple stakeholders to cross institutional boundaries and to engage in knotworking, the two groups eventually created a hybrid solution for their common problem of helping novice teachers effectively lead discussion in secondary English classrooms. Bringing together diverse forms of expertise, they created a rubric, which was identified as a "boundary-crossing object" (Anagnostopoulos et al., 2007; Max, 2010) that served as a tool for all stakeholders to better communicate via shared language and to navigate multiple activity systems. The knotworking in this example required notable commitment from both groups and represents what is needed to support the type of innovation in teacher education programs that can lead to expansive learning for candidates as well as those preparing candidates. The authors explain that

> Achieving common goals requires professionals to cross organizational boundaries and combine the resources, norms and values from their respective settings into new hybrid solutions. Horizontal expertise emerges from these boundary crossings as professionals from different domains

enrich and expand their practices through working together to reorganize relations and coordinate their work.

(Anagnostopoulos et al., 2007, p. 139)

Interestingly, the researchers found that the horizontal expertise that served as a resource in the co-creation of the rubric could not be easily appropriated by others who were not involved in the initial problem-solving practice (Anagnostopoulos et al., 2007); this indicates the importance of fostering spaces for continual knotworking opportunities among stakeholders if increasingly democratic models are to be sustained.

Anagnostopoulos and colleagues demonstrated how utilizing horizontal expertise as a conceptual tool can help university teacher educators actively analyze partnerships and joint work with school-based partners and ultimately work to overcome the notorious "two-worlds pitfall" (Feiman-Nemser & Buchmann, 1985) that has characterized the loose and sometimes conflicting relationship between traditional university-based teacher education and schools. The MSU example is particularly educative for teacher education faculty who have struggled to create meaningful school partnerships because of what they see as troubling curriculum and instruction policies and trends in schools (i.e., the narrowing of curricular opportunities as a way to raise test scores). Realistically, just as there is a wide range in quality in teacher education courses, not all K–12 classrooms and schools are the richest of contexts for candidates to learn about engaging instruction. This case and the recommended conceptual tools encourage teacher educators to not quickly "opt out" of collaboration solely because of differing visions or approaches. If we in teacher education regularly and readily use these tools to identify phenomena and processes such as contradiction, pooling expertise, boundary-crossing, and knotworking, while concurrently approaching situations from a deliberative democratic stance based in mutual respect, we will arguably be more likely to recognize these phenomena when they are present, consider them in program evaluation and systemic planning, and, ultimately, we are more likely to come to think of them as part of our work—that is, part of the practice of teacher education.

Engaging Community-based Educators and Contexts in Teacher Preparation

While the role of schools is essential in the enterprise of preparing effective teachers, the role of communities and the knowledge that exists among various groups and in various neighborhoods is also critical in teacher education (see Philip, Way, Garcia, Schuler-Brown, & Navarro, 2013, for an astute caution against the essentialization of "communities"). Engaging voices and eliciting involvement from historically non-dominant communities in teacher education efforts has not been a mainstream practice in either college-recommending or early-entry programs; this includes programs that specifically aim to prepare educators to work with students and families from these very communities. This trend persists despite the fact that our education system has had limited success in effectively and justly educating youth from non-dominant racial, linguistic, and economic groups (e.g., National Assessment of Educational Progress [NAEP], 2013). Its implications are particularly troublesome given rapid growth in numbers of students from these groups in the US public school population.

When teacher candidates had opportunities to participate in boundary zones outside of schools, they could encounter and engage with different perspectives and forms of knowledge from those they typically accessed in school- and university-based spaces (e.g., Gonzales, Moll, & Amanti, 2005). These opportunities potentially increase the likelihood that each teacher candidate can eventually become a "community teacher" (Murrell, 2001), which Murrell defines as "one who possesses contextualized knowledge of the culture, community, and identity of the children and families he or she serves and draws on this knowledge to create the core teaching practices necessary for effectiveness in diverse settings" (p. 52). Key to Murrell's definition and the argument we make here is that the knowledge is contextualized, and thus cannot be learned in a university classroom away from the communities with which and in which teachers will work. Furthermore, community-based collaborations should aim to grow teacher candidates' efficacy in leveraging such contextual knowledge and understandings in their teaching practice.

Multicultural Apprenticeships at the Ohio State University

Cross-cultural community-based field experiences represent one way in which teacher candidates can interact with social and geographical communities that were previously unfamiliar to them (Onore & Gildin, 2013; Sleeter, 2001, 2008; Sleeter & Boyle-Baise, 2000; Zeichner & Melnick, 1996). These experiences span a broad range, and often differ in their purpose and how they are situated in teacher preparation programs. They can be short-term visiting experiences in a single out-of-school setting, or they can be longer and more intensive immersion experiences. Some opportunities are elective and others are required.

One of the best-known examples of this type of community-based field experience is the Ohio State University's (OSU) partnership with Mt. Olivet, an African American church community located in Columbus (Seidl & Friend, 2002a, 2002b). Conceptualized as a multicultural apprenticeship, university- and community-based partners adamantly framed the placement as an equal-status, cross-cultural experience. The adults at Mt. Olivet were positioned as experts holding knowledge that was critical for learning to teach. Seidl and Friend, an OSU professor and Mt. Olivet community leader, jointly mediated candidates' fieldwork (e.g., they co-designed and co-evaluated candidates' narrative self-study assignments). They found in their collaborative research that the experience afforded valuable opportunities for candidates to practice relationship building with youth as well as adult community members and to question hegemonic beliefs (Seidl & Friend, 2002a). This partnership illustrates how cultivating horizontal expertise and mediated opportunities for knotworking across multiple spaces can create more robust learning opportunities for novice teachers. This example also makes clear the level of commitment and intentionality that is required. Without a doubt, sustaining this hybrid space in a way that systemically reaches beyond the individuals who initially established the relationship (Seidl and Friend) is difficult and complex work, but is essential for such spaces to survive.

Institutional Learning: Iterations of Engaging Community Expertise at UW

In recent years, UW's Elementary Teacher Education Program (ELTEP) has made a concerted effort to design opportunities for candidates to learn in and from communities as a way to better prepare them to work with youth and families in diverse, urban schools. This had led to changes in the elementary (ELTEP) and secondary (STEP) program activity systems, including developments in several of the CHAT system components such as the "community" (who is part of the system), the "rules" (i.e., norms in teacher education), the "division of labor" (who does what), and "tools" that are used to mediate candidate learning. We describe these developments here in the ELTEP, including the contradictions that prompted them, to provide an example of one program's continuing effort to be more horizontal, and thus, more democratic.

Field Placements in Community-based Organizations

McDonald and colleagues' work at UW examined the implementation and integration of community-based field experiences across the ELTEP. For one quarter early in a graduate certification program, pre-service teachers were placed in community-based organizations (CBOs). These organizations ranged from neighborhood community centers to culturally focused programs (e.g., one program specifically served Vietnamese Americans, another served Latino families). The community-based field experience was connected to and mediated by concurrent ELTEP coursework and projects throughout the quarter.

Analyses of a 3-year longitudinal data set showed that the expansion of ELTEP's activity system to include CBOs led to expanded learning opportunities for teacher candidates. The placements facilitated opportunities to learn key principles and practices related to *seeing children*—which McDonald and colleagues view as core to one's capacity to teach students (McDonald, Bowman, & Brayko, 2013; McDonald et al., 2011). Specifically, they found that CBO placements afforded candidates opportunities to develop deeper understandings of students and communities; develop more nuanced understandings of diversity, including intragroup diversity;

examine schools from an out-of-school perspective; attend to the role of context in learning; and learn and enact important relational aspects of teaching (McDonald et al., 2013). Brayko (2013) found that the CBO placements also facilitated opportunities for candidates to learn about literacy practices and literacy pedagogy, and to enact critical teaching practices that fostered engagement, oral language development, and reading comprehension for language-minority youth.

A close look at factors that contributed to the quality and salience of the learning opportunities revealed that CBO educators' expertise was a crucial component. They were particularly skilled at building and sustaining relationships with children and families, and crossing boundaries to mediate and advocate for students within and across multiple contexts (i.e., home, schools, CBOs; McDonald et al., 2013). Notably, this skill set was distinct from those of other teacher educators to which candidates had access in ELTEP. CBO educators' deep and contextualized knowledge of children and families, and nuanced ecological perspectives of the children in their care, reflect key aspects of Murrell's vision of community teachers. The recognition of how influential CBO educators' role was for pre-service teacher learning prompted ELTEP's increased interest in understanding and engaging the expertise that thrives in community-based contexts, particularly among adults in those contexts.

As can be expected with work that involves the expansion of activity systems, there were several dilemmas that surfaced with the CBO placements and partnerships. One dilemma involved the "uneven" experiences teacher candidates had at different CBOs, which mirrored the well-documented issue of uneven opportunities in school-based placements (National Council for Accreditation of Teacher Education [NCATE], 2010). Also, new hybrid spaces require new forms of activity, and some CBO educators were more skilled than others in their new roles as teacher educators (McDonald et al., 2013). For example, there was a range in their ability to articulate their knowledge and relational practices, invite teacher candidates into these practices, and support and guide candidates as they "tried out" the practices (McDonald et al., 2013). ELTEP leaders struggled to know how to best support the CBO educators in their new role.

Another tension involved the question of how horizontal and "level" the partnership and joint-work actually was. While there were instances of democratic activity around the CBO work, such as meetings that brought faculty and CBO educators together to discuss goals and assignments, and an increased focus in UW coursework on positioning CBO educators as experts in key practices, these were sometimes incidental and isolated; candidates bore much of the boundary-crossing burden. One institutional response to improve "knotworking" was a heightened effort to strengthen mediation by sending university supervisors to CBO placements to observe and coach. With more faculty and staff boundary-crossing and engaging more regularly in these new teacher education spaces, there were more opportunities for deliberation with CBO personnel about ELTEP expectations and assignments.

After four years, a number of programmatic changes and competing demands for candidates led ELTEP faculty and leadership to rethink the CBO placements and the overall strategy of engaging with and learning from and with community-based partners.

Renewed Emphasis on Engaging Community Members as Teacher Educators

Reflecting on four years of research findings and teaching experiences related to the CBO placements, leaders in UW's ELTEP moved to leverage the emphasis on the expertise of highly knowledgeable and skilled community-based educators. Subsequently, there was a shift from CBO placements *per se* to a focus on engaging people, particularly parents, community leaders and organizers, and CBO educators as mentors of teacher candidates. A community-family-politics (CFP) strand was born. Preparing "community teachers" continues to be the organizing concept of the strand. The CFP strand facilitates more opportunities for candidates to engage directly with community expertise across all four quarters of the program.

During 2013–2014, two community-based educators served as co-planners of field seminars with university instructors, and shared knowledge and insights about working with, in their words, "our kids" and their families. These two community-based teacher educators also worked directly with teacher candidates in the seminars and involved many parents, community educators, and leaders in various types of planned instructional encounters with teacher candidates in schools, community settings, and in university classes where community members served as mentors of teacher candidates. The family and community members who were involved in these seminar sessions are multicultural and multigenerational. Class sessions included topical conversations about race and privilege, positive communication and working relationships with families, the school-to-prison pipeline, contemporary civil rights movements and organizations, and teaching against the grain. Teacher candidates also learned about classroom management tools and practices in their university courses, in their school placements, and they also got to hear from parents and family members whose black and brown children had been targeted in management and discipline policies and practices in local schools.

Thus, many opportunities existed for candidates to encounter and engage in deliberative democratic activity in contexts where CBO educators, parents, and university faculty were all present. This structure allowed space for a range of knowledge sets to interact, which facilitates the potential for expansive learning. For example, candidates have the opportunity to learn about institutionalized racism from expert professors of multicultural education as well as from expert parents of current public school students who share experiences and contextualized knowledge of their own children in local schools.

As part of the CFP strand and the field seminar, teams of candidates who were placed in the same school were required in 2013–2014 to complete at least five activities from an "Action Menu." The 25 suggested actions were organized by focus on community, family, and politics[5] respectively, and include activities such as creating lists of organizations where their students (from their school practicum) spent time before and after school, participating in family visits, introducing themselves to parents at pick-up time, and attending school board meetings. To guide candidates to relate their CFP activities to teaching practice, these actions were explicitly linked to the Interstate Teacher Assessment and Support Consortium (INTASC) and state teaching standards as well as the performances, essential knowledge, and critical dispositions of community teachers. Research was conducted to examine the connections between what teacher candidates learn through the CFP work and how it impacts their teaching practice with a particular focus on the impact of the community mentors on teacher learning and practice (see Chapter 8).

The CFP strand is in its infancy, but already a number of tensions have surfaced as part of this work. Inviting educators with very different sets of perspectives, experiences, and communication and pedagogical styles than university faculty can contribute to the richness of the learning experience for candidates; yet, in some cases, these differences caused notable disruption and tension among students and faculty, making collaboration a fragile, contentious, and difficult endeavor (Zeichner, 1991).

Fostering Sustainability: From "Isolated Project" to "The Way We Do Things"

The examples of OSU and UW's networking with community-based educators and parents highlight powerful learning opportunities, but also indicate the complexities of creating and maintaining authentic models of engaging communities in the enterprise of teacher education. As we argue for increased attention to incorporating hybrid spaces and the inclusion of often excluded voices and expertise, we also call on the field to examine issues of sustainability, and to explore and share ideas around utilizing resources in ways that ensure a long-term commitment to this difficult but essential work. At a time of budget constraints, heavy demands, and accountability pressures on teacher education programs, many of the existing examples of community partnerships are fragile.

The OSU–Mt. Olivet collaboration has relied heavily on the investment and participation of two individuals; now that both individuals are not able to direct the work, it is unlikely that the partnership will survive (Seidl, personal communication, October, 2011). Similarly, UW's community-focused work in its elementary, secondary, and teacher residency programs currently runs primarily on the energy, interest, and funding of a small number of individuals in the teacher education programs. Unless there is a broader investment of will, and resources, the work could easily discontinue with the depletion of temporary funding sources and retirements or role changes of key faculty. Using CHAT as a framework for constructing, analyzing, and reforming our teacher education partnerships with schools and communities carries the possibility of supporting this work at a systemic level. A CHAT perspective helps us recognize that the "who" (community) in these teacher education activity systems is too limited for systemic change; without a larger number of key participants, democratic activity is compromised. CHAT can also highlight the ways in which—and the extent to which—the norms or "rules" of engagement for various participants allow for authentic exchange, as well as the extent to which particular tools (from co-planning protocols to fiscal resources) facilitate authentic and lasting exchange. Furthermore, CHAT can challenge us to view contradictions and disruptions that surface as potential opportunities for expansive learning rather than reasons to stop engaging. In this way, we recommend the use of CHAT and related conceptual tools to build and evaluate quality as well as *sustainability* in teacher education models that aim to engage expertise from communities and schools.

Implications: The Future of Teacher Education

In our view, teacher education needs a fundamental shift in whose expertise counts in the education of new teachers and in the work of college and university teacher educators. It is no longer enough to implement special projects here and there that are funded on temporary money. It is no longer enough to have university academics alone framing the discourse and inviting school-based educators and people from the broader community to "participate" in a university- owned teacher education program. It should no longer be acceptable for teacher educators in both schools and universities to marginalize or shut out the perspectives of those who send their children to public schools and live in the communities that schools are supposed to serve.

Given the labor-intensive nature of building inter-institutional collaborations in teacher education, the habits of those from schools and universities, and the low status of teacher education in many research universities, it is going to be difficult to achieve this cultural shift in teacher education. Figuring out how to achieve this shift is also complicated by the defunding of public schools and the continual decline of the percentage of state support for public universities, which continue to prepare most teachers (Newfield, 2008).

The analysis that we have offered in this chapter suggests a number of implications for policy and practice. First, we propose that policy incentives be provided to encourage both early-entry and college-recommending programs to create the kind of genuinely shared responsibility for teacher education that we advocate. This can be done either within existing teacher education institutions as in our examples or in newly created hybrid settings like some of the urban teacher residencies and community-based programs. The important factors are the quality of the knowledge and power relationships that exist, not the structure of the program. The National Teacher Corps, which existed from 1965–1981 (Eckert, 2011), is an example of a national-scale effort to more centrally engage schools and local communities in teacher preparation. Although this program achieved mixed success, there are lessons that can be learned from it to inform current efforts to democratize teacher education (e.g., Weiner, 1993).

At the program level, teacher educators and administrators in both early-entry and college-recommending programs should make efforts to establish more opportunities for members of local communities, schools, or universities to be more centrally engaged in conceptualizing, planning, implementing, and evaluating all aspects of the program on an ongoing basis. There is a big difference between bringing "others" from different institutional cultures into a setting for a guest contribution now and then within already established frameworks, and working together to create a more inclusive setting where the expertise of everyone is fully valued and accessed. We are proposing the latter form of inclusion that will change the nature of the culture into which the "others" come and lead to more shared responsibility and joint ownership of the program. In this article, we have presented a few examples of efforts of others and ourselves to move in this direction. Doing the kind of work that we are calling for is not easy, but we think that it is necessary for the survival of the role of universities in teacher education.

Conclusion

Almost every week, a new report is released in the US criticizing the quality of the contribution of colleges and universities to initial teacher education or praising one of the newly emerging alternative providers of teacher education programs (e.g., Chubb, 2012; Duncan, 2011; Keller, 2013; National Council on Teacher Quality, 2013). In 2010, the Obama administration's education department distributed $263 million on a competitive basis to promote innovation in various sectors of education. The only teacher education projects that were funded in this competition were those from two of the major alternative certification providers, "Teach for America," which received $50 million and "The New Teacher Project" (now TNTP), which received $20 million. None of the proposals for innovation in teacher education submitted by college and university teacher educators were funded.[6]

Although there continues to be some federal investment in recruiting talented individuals to teaching through various scholarship and loan programs, university teacher education is generally not seen today as worthy of investment by the federal government or many foundations even though it still prepares most of the nation's teachers (see, for example, Suggs & deMarrais, 2011). A situation has been framed in the US where colleges and universities are seen as obstacles to reform, and efforts are being made at the highest levels of government to figure out how to shut down university programs and to support the spread of non-university teacher education providers (Zeichner, 2010b; Zeichner & Peña-Sandoval, 2015).

This is both a very exciting and dangerous time for university-based teacher education. There is a real opportunity to establish forms of democratic professionalism in teaching and teacher education (Apple, 1996; Sachs, 2003) where colleges, universities, schools, and communities come together in new ways to prepare professional teachers who provide everyone's children with the same high quality of education. There is also a real danger, however, that teacher education will be transformed into a pure market economy divorced from universities where a constant supply of underprepared and temporary teachers will be sent into schools to teach students living in poverty. In the US, Hess (2009) has articulated a view shared by many others when he proposed decoupling the preparation of teachers from institutions of higher education rather than calling for an investment in the improvement of college and university programs. Hess and others want to create a system where teacher preparation is controlled by local school districts and where university faculty and staff are brought into the picture when the schools want to do so and on their terms. University teacher educators must pay attention to what is happening around them in the larger policy context, to take it seriously and not to act defensively to only try to protect their own position. Attempts to defend college- and university-based teacher education that is isolated from the struggles for greater social justice in other sectors of societies will be seen as largely self-serving and will fail.

In this chapter, we have suggested that what is required for university teacher education is a political response and a paradigm shift[7] in how we think about whose expertise should contribute to and who should be responsible for the education of professional teachers for public schools. We believe that without the shift in power relationships and the formation of the kind of political alliances that we have suggested, the future of teaching as a profession and the university's role in teacher education are in serious danger and the future for teacher preparation that is outlined by Hess (2009) above will become the norm.

We have argued in this article that neither schools nor universities can educate our nation's teachers alone and that even together, schools and universities cannot educate teachers well without accessing the expertise that exists in the communities that are supposed to be served by schools. Unless a college or university education school is willing to make a serious commitment to offering high-quality teacher education programs in which faculty invest their intellectual talent, then it should get out of the business of preparing teachers. Making a commitment to high-quality teacher education programs in research universities does not mean an abandonment of the responsibility for conducting research, including research on teacher education. On the contrary, a serious commitment to teacher education in research universities would involve utilizing their teacher education programs as laboratories for the study of teacher learning and development and effective practices in preparing teachers. We argue that by recasting who is an expert and rethinking how universities can cross institutional boundaries to collaborate with communities and schools, teacher education programs can more thoroughly interrogate their challenges and can collaboratively innovate and create new solutions to prepare the teachers our students need.

Notes

1   Clandinin (1995) has referred to this as the "sacred theory into practice story."
2   Vygotsky (1978) defined the zone of proximal development (ZPD) as "the distance between the actual development level as determined by independent problem solving and the level of potential development as determined through problem solving under adult guidance or in collaboration with more capable peers" (p. 86).
3   While in this example, the university educators and researchers played the dominant role in framing how the work would proceed, it represents clear movement toward the kind of the kind of democratic spaces that we are advocating.
4   Two of the authors, Brayko and Zeichner, have worked in this program.
5   The social foundations course aspects of the community–family–politics (CFP) strand involve a "place-based" approach to the teaching. See Gottesman and Bowman (2013) for a discussion of this work.
6   The Boston Teacher Residency Program, which is a joint effort of the Boston Public Schools and the University of Massachusetts Boston, also received US$4.9 million in a project submitted by a local foundation.
7   A 2010 national report on teacher education in the United States has referred to the kind of paradigm shift that we are calling for as "turning the education of teachers upside down" (National Council for Accreditation of Teacher Education, 2010, p. ii).

References

Anagnostopoulos, D., Smith, E. R., & Basmadjian, K. (2007). Bridging the university-school divide. *Journal of Teacher Education, 58*(2), 138–152.

Anderson, L., & Stillman, J. (2011). Student teaching for a specialized view of professional practice? Opportunities to learn in and for urban, high-needs schools. *Journal of Teacher Education, 62*(5), 446–464.

Apple, M. (1996). *Cultural politics and education*. New York, NY: Teachers College Press.

Apple, M. (2008). Is deliberative democracy enough in teacher education? In M. Cochran-Smith, S. Feiman-Nemser, & D. J. McIntyre (Eds), *Handbook of research on teacher education: Third edition* (pp. 105–110). New York, NY: Routledge.

Ball, D., & Forzani, F. (2009). The work of teaching and the challenge for teacher education. *Journal of Teacher Education, 60*, 497–510.

Barab, S., & Duffy, T. (2000). From practice fields to communities of practice. In D. Jonassen & S. Land (Eds), *Theoretical foundations of learning environments* (pp. 25–56). New York, NY: Routledge.

Bartholomew, S. S., & Sandholtz, J. H. (2009). Competing views of teaching in a school university partnership. *Teaching and Teacher Education, 25*(1), 155–165.

Beynon, J., Grout, J., & Wideen, M. (2004). *From teacher to teacher educator.* Vancouver, British Columbia, Canada: Pacific Education Press.

Brayko, K. (2013). Community-based placements as contexts for disciplinary learning: A study of literacy teacher education outside of school. *Journal of Teacher Education, 64*(1), 47–59.

Caperton, G., & Whitmire, R. R. (2012). *The achievable dream.* New York, NY: The College Board.

Carpenter, T., Fennema, E., Franke, M. L., Levi, L., & Empson, S. (2000). *Cognitively guided instruction: A research-based teacher professional development program for elementary school mathematics* (Research Report No. 003). Madison: Wisconsin Center for Education Research.

Chubb, J. (2012). *The best teachers in the world: Why we don't have them and how we could.* Palo Alto, CA: Hoover Institute Press.

Clandinin, J. (1995). Still learning to teach. In T. Russell & F. Korthagen (Eds), *Teachers who teach teachers* (pp. 25–31). London: Falmer Press.

Cochran-Smith, M., Davis, D., & Fries, K. (2004). Multicultural teacher education: Research, practice, and policy. In J. Banks & C. Banks (Eds), *Handbook of research on multicultural education* (2nd ed., pp. 931–975). San Francisco, CA: Jossey-Bass.

Darling-Hammond, L., & Bransford, J. (Eds). (2005). *Preparing teachers for a changing world.* San Francisco, CA: Jossey- Bass.

Duffy, G. (1994). Professional development schools and the dis-empowerment of teachers and professors. *Phi Delta Kappan, 75*(8), 596–600.

Duncan, A. (2009, October). *Teacher preparation: Reforming the uncertain profession.* Address given by Secretary of Education Arne Duncan at Teachers College, Columbia University, New York, NY.

Duncan, A. (2011, September). *Our future, our teachers: The Obama administration's plan for teacher education reform and improvement.* Washington, DC: U.S. Department of Education.

Eckert, S. A. (2011). The National Teacher Corps: A study of shifting goals and changing assumptions. *Urban Education, 46*(5), 932–952.

Edwards, A. (2010). *Being an expert professional practitioner: The relational turn in expertise.* Dordrecht, The Netherlands: Springer.

Edwards, A., Daniels, H., Gallagher, T., Leadbetter, J., & Warmington, P. (2009). *Improving professional collaboration: Multi-agency work for children's well-being.* London, England: Routledge.

Ellis, V., Edwards, A., & Smagorinsky, P. (Eds). (2010). *Cultural-historical perspectives on teacher education and development.* London: Routledge.

Engeström, Y. (1987). *Learning by expanding: An activity theoretical approach to developmental research.* Helsinki, Finland: Orienta-Konsultit.

Engeström, Y. (2001). Expansive learning at work: Toward an activity theoretical reconceptualization. *Journal of Education and Work, 14*(1), 133–156.

Engeström, Y. (2007). Enriching the theory of expansive learning: Lessons from journeys toward co-configuration. *Mind, Culture, and Activity, 14*(1-2), 23–39.

Engeström, Y. (2008). *From teams to knots: Activity-theoretical studies of collaboration and learning at work.* Cambridge: Cambridge University Press.

Engeström, Y., Engeström, R., & Vahaaho, T. (1999). When the center does not hold: The importance of knotworking. In S. Chaiklin, M. Hedegaard, & O. J. Jensen (Eds), *Activity theory and social practice: Cultural historical approaches* (pp. 345–374). Aarhus, Denmark: Aarhus University Press.

Feiman-Nemser, S., & Buchmann, M. (1985). Pitfalls of experience in teacher preparation. *Teachers College Record*, *87*(1), 53–65.

Fraser, J. (2007). *Preparing America's teachers: A history*. New York, NY: Teachers College Press.

Friedrich, D. (2014). We brought it upon ourselves: University-based teacher education and the emergence of boot-camp-style routes to teacher certification. *Education Policy Analysis Archives*, *22*(2). Retrieved from http://epaa.asu.edu/ojs/article/viewFile/1193/1189

Gatti, L., & Catalano, T. (2015). The business of learning to teach. *Teaching and Teacher Education*, *45*, 149–160.

Ginsburg, M., & Clift, R. (1990). The hidden curriculum of pre-service teacher education. In W. R. Houston (Ed.), *Handbook of research on teacher education* (pp. 450–468). New York, NY: Macmillan.

Gonzales, N., Moll, L., & Amanti, C. (Eds.). (2005). *Funds of knowledge: Theorizing practices in households, communities, and classrooms*. New York, NY: Routledge.

Gorodetsky, M., & Barak, J. (2008). The educational-cultural edge: A participative learning environment for co-emergence of personal and institutional growth. *Teaching and Teacher Education*, *24*, 1907–1918.

Gottesman, I., & Bowman, M. (2013). Why practice-centered teacher education programs need social foundations. *Teachers College Record*. Retrieved from www.tcrecord.org/content.asp?contentid=17066

Grossman, P. (2008). Responding to our critics: From crisis to opportunity in research on teacher education. *Journal of Teacher Education*, *59*(1), 10–23.

Grossman, P. (2011). A framework for teaching practice: A brief history of an idea. *Teachers College Record*, *113*(12), 2836–2843.

Grossman, P., & Loeb, S. (Eds). (2008). *Alternative routes to teaching*. Cambridge, MA: Harvard Education Press.

Gutmann, A., & Thompson, D. (2004). *Why deliberative democracy?* Princeton, NJ: Princeton University Press.

Habermas, J. (1984). *The theory of communicative action*. Boston, MA: Beacon Press.

Hammerness, K., Darling-Hammond, L., Bransford, J., Berliner, D., Cochran-Smith, M., McDonald, M., & Zeichner, K. (2005). How teachers learn and develop. In L. Darling-Hammond & J. Bransford (Eds), *Preparing teachers for a changing world* (pp. 358–389). San Francisco, CA: Jossey-Bass.

Hartley, D. (2007). Education policy and the "inter-regnum." *Journal of Education Policy*, *22*(6), 695–708.

Hess, F. (2009). Revitalizing teacher education by revisiting our assumptions about teaching. *Journal of Teacher Education*, *60*(5), 450–457.

Hollins, E., & Guzman, M. T. (2005). Research on preparing teachers for diverse populations. In M. Cochran-Smith & K. Zeichner (Eds), *Studying teacher education* (pp. 477–588). New York, NY: Routledge.

Jeffery, J. V., & Polleck, J. (2013). Transformations in site-based teacher preparation courses: The benefits and challenges. In J. Noel (Ed.), *Moving teacher education into urban schools and communities* (pp. 105–119). New York, NY: Routledge.

Keller, B. (2013, October 20). An industry of mediocrity. *The New York Times*. Retrieved from www.nytimes.com/2013/10/21/opinion/keller-an-industry-of-mediocrity.html?pagewanted=all&;_r=0

Kerosuo, H., & Engeström, Y. (2003). Boundary crossing and learning in creation of new work practice. *Journal of Workplace Learning, 15*(8), 345–351.

Klein, E., Taylor, M., Onore, C., Strom, K., & Abrams, L. (2013). Finding a third space in teacher education: Creating an urban teacher residency. *Teaching Education, 24*(1), 27–57.

Knowles, T. (2013). *New pathways for teachers, new promises for students: A vision for developing excellent teachers* (Special Report 3). Washington, DC: American Enterprise Institute.

Lampert, M., Franke, M., Kazemi, E., Ghousseini, H., Turrou, A., Beasley, H., & Crowe, K. (2013). Keeping it complex: Using rehearsals to support novice teacher learning of ambitious teaching. *Journal of Teacher Education, 64*, 226–243.

Max, C. (2010). Learning for teaching across knowledge boundaries: An activity theoretical analysis of collaborative internship projects in initial teacher education. In V. Ellis, A. Edwards, & P. Smagorinsky (Eds), *Cultural-historical perspectives on teacher education and development* (pp. 212–240). London: Routledge.

McDonald, M., Bowman, M., & Brayko, K. (2013). Learning to see students: Opportunities to develop relational practices of teaching through community-based placements in teacher education. *Teachers College Record, 115*(4). Retrieved from www.tcrecord.org

McDonald, M., Kazemi, E., & Kavanagh, S. (2013). Core practices and pedagogies of teacher education: A call for common language and collective activity. *Journal of Teacher Education, 64*(5), 378–386.

McDonald, M., Tyson, K., Brayko, K., Bowman, M., Delport, J., & Shimomura, F. (2011). Innovation and impact in teacher education: Community based organizations as field placements for pre-service teachers. *Teachers College Record, 113*(8), 1668–1700.

Morgan-Fleming, B., Simpson, D., Curtis, K., & Hull, W. (2010). Learning through partnership. *Teacher Education Quarterly, 37*(3), 63–80.

Murrell, P. (2001). *The community teacher.* New York, NY: Teachers College Press.

National Assessment of Educational Progress (2013). Retrieved from www.nationsreportcard.gov/reading_math_2013/#/achievement-gaps

National Council for Accreditation of Teacher Education. (2010). *Transforming teacher education through clinical practice: A national strategy to prepare effective teachers.* Washington, DC: Author.

National Council on Teacher Quality. (2013). *Teacher prep review: A review of the nation's teacher prep programs.* Washington, DC: Author.

National Research Council. (2010). *Preparing teachers: Building evidence for sound policy.* Washington, DC: National Academies Press.

Newfield, C. (2008). *Unmaking the public university.* Cambridge, MA: Harvard University Press.

The New Teacher Project. (2014). *Fast start: Training better teachers faster, with focus, practice and feedback.* New York, NY: Author. Retrieved from http://tntp.org/assets/documents/TNTP_FastStart_2014.pdf

Noel, J., & Nelson, T. (2010). Moving teacher education into schools and communities. *Teacher Education Quarterly, 37*(3), 3–8.

Norton-Meier, L., & Drake, C. (2010). When third space is more than the library: The complexities of theorizing and learning to use family and community resources to teach elementary literacy and mathematics. In V. Ellis, A. Edwards, & P. Smagorinsky (Eds), *Cultural-historical perspectives on teacher education and development* (pp. 196–211). London: Routledge.

Oldenburg, R. (1999). *The great good place: Cafes, coffee shops, bookstores, bars, hair salons, and other hangouts in the heart of a community* (2nd ed.). Cambridge, MA: Da Capo Press.

Onore, C., & Gildin, B. (2013). A community-university partnership to develop urban teachers as public professionals. In J. Noel (Ed.), *Moving teacher education into urban schools and communities* (pp. 152–168). New York, NY: Routledge.

Patterson, R., Michelli, N., & Pacheco, A. (1999). *Centers of pedagogy: New structures for educational renewal*. San Francisco, CA: Jossey-Bass.

Philip, T., Way, W., Garcia, A., Schuler-Brown, S., & Navarro, O. (2013). When educators attempt to make "community" a part of classroom learning: The dangers of (mis)appropriating students' communities into schools. *Teaching and Teacher Education, 34*, 174–183.

Popkewitz, T. (1975). Reform as a political discourse: A case study. *School Review, 84*, 311–336.

Post, L., Pugach, M., Harris, S., & Hughes, M. (2006). The teachers-in-residence program: Veteran urban teachers as teacher leaders in boundary-spanning roles. In K. Howey & N. Zimpher (Eds), *Boundary spanners: A key to success in urban P-16 university-school partnerships* (pp. 211–236). Washington, DC: American Association of State Colleges and Universities and Land Grant Colleges.

Rawls, J. (1971). *A theory of justice*. Cambridge, MA: Harvard University Press.

Sachs, J. (2003). *The activist teaching profession*. Buckingham, UK: Open University Press.

Sanders, L. (1997). Against deliberation. *Political Theory, 25*(2), 347–376.

Schorr, J. (2013). A revolution begins in teacher prep. *Stanford Social Innovation Review, 11*(1). Retrieved from http://ssir.org/articles/entry/a_revolution_begins_in_teacher_prep

Seidl, B., & Friend, G. (2002a). The unification of church and state: Working together to prepare teachers for diverse classrooms. *Journal of Teacher Education, 53*(3), 142–152.

Seidl, B., & Friend, G. (2002b). Leaving authority at the door: Equal-status community-based experiences and the preparation of teachers for diverse classrooms. *Teaching and Teacher Education, 18*, 421–433.

Sherin, M. (2001). Developing a professional vision of classroom events. In T. Wood, B. S. Nelson, & J. Warfield (Eds), *Beyond classical pedagogy: Teaching elementary school mathematics* (pp. 75–93). New York, NY: Routledge.

Shirley, D., Hersi, A., MacDonald, E., Sanchez, M. T., Scandone, C., Skidmore, C., & Tutwiler, P. (2006). Bringing the community back in: Change, accommodation, and contestation in a school and university partnership. *Equity & Excellence in Education, 39*, 27–36.

Sleeter, C. (2001). Preparing teachers for culturally diverse schools: Research and the overwhelming presence of whiteness. *Journal of Teacher Education, 52*(2), 94–106.

Sleeter, C. (2008). Preparing white teachers for diverse students. In M. Cochran-Smith, S. Feiman-Nemser, & D. J. McIntyre (Eds), *Handbook of research on teacher education* (3rd ed., pp. 559–582). New York, NY: Routledge.

Sleeter, C., & Boyle-Baise, M. (2000). Community service learning for multicultural teacher education. *Educational Foundations, 14*(2), 33–50.

Stitzlein, S., & West, C. (2014). New forms of teacher education: Connections to charter schools and their approaches. *Democracy & Education, 22*(2), 1–10.

Suggs, C., & deMarrais, K. (2011). *Critical contributions: Philanthropic investment in teachers and teaching*. Atlanta, GA: Kronley.

Turney, C., Eltis, K., Towler, J., & Wright, R. (1985). *A new basis for teacher education: The practicum curriculum*. Sydney, Australia: University of Sydney Press.

Valencia, S., Martin, S., Place, N., & Grossman, P. (2009). Complex interactions in student teaching: Lost opportunities for learning. *Journal of Teacher Education, 60*(3), 304–322.

Villegas, A. M., & Irvine, J. J. (2010). Diversifying the teaching force: An examination of major arguments. *The Urban Review, 42*(3), 175–192.

Villegas, A. M., & Lucas, T. (2004). Diversifying the teacher workforce: A retrospective and prospective analysis. In M. Smylie & D. Miretzky (Eds), *Developing the teacher workforce* (pp. 70–104). Chicago, IL: University of Chicago Press.

Vygotsky, L.S. (1978). *Mind in society*. Cambridge, MA: Harvard University Press.

Walsh, K., & Jacobs, S. (2007, September). *Alternative certification isn't alternative*. Washington, DC: National Council on Teacher Quality.

Weiner, L. (1993). *Preparing teachers for urban schools: Lessons from thirty years of school reform*. New York, NY: Teachers College Press.

Zeichner, K. (1991). Contradictions and tensions in the professionalization of teaching and the democratization of schooling. *Teachers College Record, 92*(3), 363–379.

Zeichner, K. (1995). Beyond the divide of teacher research and academic research. *Teachers and Teaching, 1*(2), 153–172.

Zeichner, K. (2009). *Teacher education and the struggle for social justice*. New York, NY: Routledge.

Zeichner, K. (2010a). Rethinking the connections between campus courses and field experiences in college and university-based teacher education. *Journal of Teacher Education, 89*(11), 89–99.

Zeichner, K. (2010b). Competition, increased surveillance and attacks on multiculturalism: Neo-liberalism and the transformation of teacher education in the U.S. *Teaching and Teacher Education, 26*, 1544–1552.

Zeichner, K. (2014a). Political dimensions of learning to reach from experience. In V. Ellis & J. Orchard (Eds), *Learning to teach from experience: Multiple perspectives* (pp. 257–268). London: Bloomsbury.

Zeichner, K. (2014b). The struggle for the soul of teaching and teacher education. *Journal of Education for Teaching*. Retrieved from www.tandfonline.com/doi/full/10.1080/02607476.2014.956544

Zeichner, K., & Bier, M. (2013). The turn toward practice and clinical experiences in U.S. teacher education. *Beitrage Zur Lehrerbildung/Swiss Journal of Teacher Education, 30*(2), 153–170.

Zeichner, K., & McDonald, M. (2011). Practice-based teaching and community field experiences for prospective teachers. In A. Cohan & A. Honigsfeld (Eds), *Breaking the mold of pre-service and inservice teacher education: Innovative and successful practices for the 21st century*. Lanham, MD: Rowman & Littlefield.

Zeichner, K., & Melnick, S. (1996). The role of community field experiences in preparing teachers for cultural diversity. In K. Zeichner, S. Melnick, & M. L. Gomez (Eds), *Currents of reform in pre-service teacher education* (pp. 176–198). New York, NY: Teachers College Press.

Zeichner, K., & Peña-Sandoval, C. (2015). Venture philanthropy and teacher education policy in the US: The role of the New Schools Venture Fund. *Teachers College Record, 117*(6). Retrieved from www.tcrecord.org/content.asp?contentid=17539

7

OPPORTUNITIES AND PITFALLS IN THE TURN TOWARD CLINICAL EXPERIENCE IN US TEACHER EDUCATION[1]

Kenneth M. Zeichner and Marisa Bier

The Current Landscape of Teacher Education in the US

A teaching force of around 3.6 million teachers works in about 90,000 public schools in the US. Throughout the formal history of teacher education in the US, there have been a variety of pathways into teaching both inside and outside colleges and universities (Fraser, 2007). Approximately 1,400 colleges and universities are authorized to offer teacher education programs and, despite the tremendous growth in non-college and university programs since the 1980s, about two-thirds of teachers in the US continue to be prepared by colleges and universities (National Research Council, 2010). Increasingly, a variety of other nonprofit and for-profit programs, including school district programs, currently prepare about one-third of the new teachers in the nation each year (Chubb, 2012; Schorr, 2013; Zeichner, 2014). In some parts of the country, however, nearly as many teachers enter the field through non-college and university pathways as through college and university programs (Feistritzer & Haar, 2008), and in at least one state (Florida) school districts are required to have their own teacher education programs (Emihovich, Dana, Vernetson, & Colon, 2011).

Today, despite a growing variety of specific program structures for teacher education (Zeichner & Conklin, 2008), there are three basic ways to become a public school teacher in the US. First, between 1960 and 1990, colleges and universities had a virtual monopoly on the preparation of teachers. With the exception of emergency credentialed teachers in subjects or geographical areas where enough qualified teachers could not be found (e.g., special education, remote rural schools), almost all teachers entering US public schools entered the teaching force through college-recommending programs sponsored by a college or university after completing an undergraduate program or post-graduate teacher education program of at least a year in length (Grossman & Loeb, 2008). In these programs, candidates complete the requirements for initial certification prior to becoming teachers of record. Beginning in the 1980s, an increasing number of teachers began to enter the teaching force through early entry programs and completed most of their teacher education programs after becoming the teacher of record in a public school classroom fully responsible for students (Grossman & Loeb, 2008).[2] Recently, a third and hybrid form of teacher education has re-emerged that is more school-based than the traditional university model, but where there is still a significant amount of preparation and mentoring support before candidates enter the teaching force as teachers of record. The urban teacher residency (UTR)[3] that involves shared responsibility for teacher preparation by different institutions and may or may not involve a substantive role for colleges and universities (Berry et al., 2008) is an example of a hybrid program model (also see Zeichner & Payne, 2013; Zeichner, Payne, & Brayko, 2015). In urban teacher residencies, residents work under the supervision of a mentor teacher and become teachers of record after they complete their residency year.

All of the early entry, hybrid, and some of the college-recommending programs occur at the post-graduate level and are 1 or 2 years in length. Most of the preparation of teachers in college-recommending programs takes place at the undergraduate level in 4- or 5-year programs. Education and teacher education in the US is controlled at the state level, and despite the existence of voluntary national program accreditation requirements and some degree of cooperation among the states, there is significant variation among the states in their requirements for teacher education programs (Levine, 2006; Zeichner, 2011). For example, although most states require some amount of clinical experience before individuals become teachers of record legally responsible for classrooms, the amount of clinical experiences varies greatly (American Association of Colleges for Teacher Education [AACTE], 2013).

In this chapter, we discuss examples of the various kinds of practice-centered models for pre-service teacher education that exist in the US today in the three basic forms of teacher education (early entry, hybrid, and college-recommending) and identify some of the central issues that teacher educators are working on in the US in relation to clinical experiences for prospective teachers. In doing so, we draw on work in which we have been involved at the University of Washington in Seattle (UW) and discuss the practice of moving college and university courses into schools and communities in order to more strategically access the expertise of teachers, community-based educators, and local community members in the preparation of urban teachers. Although it is clear that some of what teacher candidates need to learn to begin teaching can be acquired outside the elementary and secondary classrooms for which they are being prepared, it is also clear from several decades of research on teacher learning that a number of critical elements of professional practice can only be learned in the context of real or simulated classrooms under the guidance of strong mentoring (Ball & Cohen, 1999; Feiman-Nemser, 2010).

In 2010, the National Council for Accreditation of Teacher Education (NCATE) Blue Ribbon Panel on Clinical Preparation and Partnerships issued a widely discussed report calling for teacher education to be turned upside down and for making clinical practice the central focus of preparation (NCATE, 2010). This was followed by similar calls from the national organization of the Council of Chief State School Officers (CCSSO, 2012) and the two national teacher associations (American Federation of Teachers, 2012; National Education Association, 2011). In response, there have been a number of efforts involving programs throughout the country to improve the quality of clinical teacher education and its connections to the rest of the preparation programs. Before examining some of these efforts, we will provide a brief overview of some of the major issues that teacher educators have tried to address in this work.[4]

Issues and Problems in US Clinical Teacher Education

The clinical education for teachers that exists today in the US is highly varied in its characteristics and quality (Clift & Brady, 2005; NCATE, 2010; National Research Council, 2010). It consists of experiences for varying lengths of time in schools, in designed settings such as virtual classrooms and in community settings (Grossman, 2010). The quality of school placements, the frequency and quality of mentoring, supervision and coaching, the degree of connection between the clinical experiences and the other parts of the preparation program, and the overall degree of monitoring of the quality of the experiences vary greatly within and across programs (Grossman, 2010; Zeichner, 2010a).[5]

The Lack of Coordination of Coursework and Clinical Experiences

Historically, one of the major problems in teacher education within the dominant college-recommending model has been the lack of coordination between coursework and clinical experiences. Although most college-recommending programs include multiple clinical experiences over the length of their programs and often situate these experiences within some type of school and university (and sometimes community) partnership, the disconnect between what teacher candidates are taught in their courses and their opportunities to learn to enact these practices in their clinical placements is often very great, even within professional development and partner schools (Bullough, Hobbs, Kauchak, Crow, & Stokes, 1997; Zeichner, 2010b).[6]

For example, it is very common for the cooperating/mentor teachers with whom teacher candidates are placed to know very little about the specifics of the courses that teacher candidates take in their program, and the instructors of the courses often know very little about the classrooms where teacher candidates are placed for their clinical work (Zeichner, 1996). Even when school and university teacher educators are aware of each other's worlds, they do not necessarily share a vision of quality teaching and teacher preparation. As a result of this lack of a shared vision and common goals, the usual ways in which placements are determined and the structure of the cooperating/mentor teachers' roles, teacher candidates frequently do not have opportunities to observe, try out, and receive detailed feedback on their teaching of the methods they learn about in their coursework.[7] Even if the teaching practices that are taught in the courses exist in the classrooms where candidates are placed, candidates do not necessarily gain access to the thinking and adaptive decision-making processes of their experienced mentors (Hammerness et al., 2005; Zeichner, 1996), who are usually greatly undercompensated and underprepared and supported for the complex and important work they are expected to do in mentoring prospective teachers (Zeichner, 2010b).

The frequent lack of opportunities to practice and receive feedback on teaching methods that are addressed in courses is, in part, a reflection of the power and knowledge relations that exist in many programs that devalue the role of teachers and other K–12 educators in defining the meaning of good teaching practice (Cochran-Smith, 1991). In some of the newly re-emerged hybrid forms of teacher education, where responsibility for teacher preparation is shared to varying degrees by schools and universities, there is sometimes more of a joint construction of the meaning of good teaching practice, and the "gap" is smaller (Zeichner & Payne, 2013).

The hybrid models such as teacher residencies that focus on preparing teachers for specific school districts and claim to "wrap coursework around practice" do not necessarily lead to the kind of shared vision and cohesiveness that is an important element of good teacher education programs (Gatti & Catalano, 2015).[8] There are dangers associated with too much congruency between coursework and clinical work that should be kept in mind, including limiting the ability of teacher candidates to envision alternatives to current practices (Buchmann & Floden, 1990).

Uneven Mentoring and the Under-Resourcing of Clinical Experiences

In addition, the quality of mentoring and assessment of the work of teacher candidates in school and community placements is highly variable, and it is more common than not that very little preparation and continuing support are provided to cooperating/mentor teachers and program supervisors (Grossman, 2010; Hamel & Jaasko-Fisher, 2011; Valencia, Martin, Place, & Grossman, 2009). Even when this professional development is provided, the underfunding of clinical teacher education often undermines the capacity of supervisors and mentors to support teacher candidates. This under-resourcing of clinical teacher education leads to higher numbers of candidates being supervised by mentors/supervisors and has become a greater problem in recent years, as the public universities where most teachers in the US are still educated have lost significant amounts of financial support from their states (Newfield, 2008).

Although there have been some opportunities over the years for teacher educators to obtain external funding from state and federal governments and private foundations to support innovation in clinical teacher education (e.g., Sykes & Dibner, 2009), the long-term investment in carefully planned clinical teacher education prior to the assumption of responsibility for a classroom is disappearing. With the exception of the teacher residency model, the federal government and foundations have increased support to fast-track programs, where there is often little or no pre-service clinical experience (Levine, 2012; Rotherham, 2008; Suggs & deMarrais, 2011).

Over time, and especially in recent times with the disinvestment of states in public universities[9] where most teachers in the US are prepared, there is little evidence of programs being able to sustain the innovations that were initially supported by external funding. Because the federal government has seriously considered phasing out the Teacher Quality Partnership grant program that has supported many innovative efforts in clinical teacher education, including urban teacher residencies (AACTE, 2010; Rennie Center for Education Research & Policy, 2009), the extent to which these efforts will be sustained is not clear.

There are clearly links between efforts to shorten initial teacher education through early entry and UTR programs and efforts to reduce the role of colleges and universities in teacher preparation and to open the preparation of teachers up to other providers. These efforts to deregulate teacher education and to create a market economy (Chubb, 2012; Gatlin, 2009) are closely linked with efforts by the federal government and venture philanthropists to deregulate and privatize K–12 education (Saltman, 2010; Zeichner, 2014; Zeichner & Peña-Sandoval, 2015). A number of new non-university teacher education programs like the Relay Graduate School of Education and MATCH Teacher Residency (Burris, 2012; Schorr, 2013) have recently emerged to prepare teachers specifically for charter schools.[10]

One prominent feature of a number of these new non-university teacher education programs like Relay that have been funded by venture philanthropists to "disrupt the teacher education market"[11] and to provide space for new programs is that they focus on a narrowly defined vision of teaching as management that is primarily aimed at raising student standardized test scores. In fact, in some of these programs like Relay and the Urban Teacher Center, candidates cannot complete the program until they are able to raise student test scores by at least 1 year. Absent from these programs that focus heavily on classroom management moves (e.g., from Lemov, 2010) is attention to a more professional vision of teaching that involves preparation to help students achieve a broader range of outcomes beyond good scores on standardized tests in literacy and mathematics. The preparation of teachers to know the communities in which they teach, to develop their relational and cultural competence and how to thoughtfully adapt their teaching to meet the constantly changing needs of their students are not discussed in the literature on these "new-generation" teacher education programs (e.g., Kronholz, 2012; Schorr, 2013).

The Marginal Status of Clinical Teacher Educators

In university programs, the educators who currently provide the mentoring and assessment of teacher candidates' work in the field are often adjunct faculty or doctoral students with low status and little decision-making authority in the institution. There is frequent turnover among these supervisors, and they often feel that they are accorded second-class status in the program in comparison with research faculty (Bullough, Draper, Smith, & Burrell, 2004). When permanent tenure-line faculty are involved in field supervision, this work often does not count in their teaching load and is not valued highly in the reward system that exists in most universities (Labaree, 2004).

Additionally, the elementary and secondary teachers who serve as school-based mentors for teacher candidates in many clinical experiences are expected to do the important work of mentoring in addition to their full-time teaching loads, and this work is not usually highly valued in the reward systems in many school districts.

Building the capacity of schools to host teacher candidates for their clinical experiences and developing the capacity of teachers to be high-quality mentors must be priorities if we are serious about making clinical experiences the central aspect of teacher education. In 1963, James Conant, in his widely influential study of teacher education in the US, identified clinical experiences as the "one indisputably essential element in professional education" (p. 142). In outlining what he felt was needed to achieve high quality in these experiences, Conant emphasized the need to carefully select, prepare, and develop the mentoring abilities of the K–12 teachers in whose classrooms teacher candidates are placed for their clinical work. He also advocated that these teachers be adequately compensated and that their workloads reflect the additional responsibilities they have assumed as teacher educators.

> Public school systems that enter into contracts with a college or university for practice teaching should designate, as classroom teachers working with practice teaching, only those persons in whose competence as teachers, leaders, and evaluators they have the highest confidence, and should give such persons encouragement by reducing their work loads and raising their salaries.
>
> *(Conant, 1963, p. 212)*

As Conant (1963) suggested, careful attention must be paid to both the selection of mentor teachers and the ways in which they are compensated in order to elevate their professional status and the rigor of their work. A number of countries, such as Australia, Finland, and the Netherlands, provide additional resources and supports to the schools and teachers that work with teacher candidates during their clinical experiences and provide models for what can be done in the US to enhance the capacity of both schools and mentors to support high-quality clinical teacher education (Darling-Hammond & Lieberman, 2012). None of the reform initiatives in teacher education in the US since Conant's 1963 analysis (e.g., professional development schools, urban teacher residencies) has yet addressed these structural and resource issues in clinical teacher education in ways that can be sustained beyond temporary grant funding. The UTR literature discusses the potential of program sustainability beyond initial grant funding through the reallocation of school district funds that will allegedly become available as a result of greater alignment between the initial preparation and district frameworks and initiatives and greater teacher retention (e.g., Berry et al., 2008), but residencies have not been around long enough to determine if these predictions will be realized.

A further issue involved in undermining the opportunities for teacher candidates learning during clinical experiences is the frequent lack of a curriculum (similar to the curriculum that exists for all courses) that lays out a well-thought-out plan for how opportunities to learn for teacher candidates will be created over the course of the clinical experience and how the needs of teacher candidates for learning to teach can be addressed over the course of a clinical experience and coordinated with the primary classroom mission of promoting pupil learning (Feiman-Nemser & Buchmann, 1985; Turney, Eltis, Towler, & Wright, 1985).

There is also widespread consensus that the selection of classrooms as sites for clinical experiences has not been very effectively carried out in many programs (Greenberg, Pomerance, & Walsh, 2011; NCATE, 2010) and that the increased accountability pressures on schools around pupil test scores, together with the meager compensation provided for mentoring, have complicated the task of locating high-quality placements for many teacher candidates (Anderson & Stillman, 2011). For example, Ronfeldt (2012) refers to the growing movement to use student standardized test scores as a part of teacher evaluation and compensation that has resulted in a growing reluctance among teachers and principals in schools affected by these policies to turn over responsibility of their classrooms to teacher candidates.

Despite all of these problems, there is evidence of a great deal of activity across the country to focus attention on improving the quality of clinical teacher education in all three pathways into teaching. We now provide an overview of some of the major aspects of the current turn toward teaching practice and clinical experience and reflect upon the future for clinical teacher education in the US.

Examples of Efforts to Raise the Quality of Clinical Teacher Education in the US

The 2010 NCATE report asserts that the preparation of teachers must "move to programs that are fully grounded in clinical practice and interwoven with academic content and professional courses" (p. ii). A variety of models for practice-based teacher education exist in which attempts are made to more closely link coursework with school-based experiences. They include programs that: (a) create designed settings to provide "a sheltered opportunity for prospective teachers to engage in targeted practice of clinical skills" (Grossman, 2010, p. 2),[12] (b) provide early entry into the classroom in an effort to prepare teachers largely on the job, (c) include hybrid university-based teacher education programs like urban teacher residencies that focus on preparation for specific contexts and that are largely situated in schools, and (d) shift college-recommending programs into schools and communities.

One of the major aspects of the current turn toward clinical teacher education in the US is a return to a focus in all of the various pathways into teaching on more strategically teaching prospective teachers how to enact particular teaching practices that are thought to enhance student learning (Zeichner, 2012). One strand of these efforts in the US is to identify and teach core teaching practices associated with particular conceptions of *ambitious teaching* as the central focus of a teacher education program. The teaching of these practices is often embedded in relation to the teaching of specific school subjects (e.g., Ball & Forzani, 2009; Windschitl, Thompson, & Braaten, 2011) and claims to draw on research that has identified certain teaching practices that enhance student learning. Other strands of this work focus on teaching particular instructional and classroom management strategies that are not tied to particular subject matter areas or grade levels (e.g., Danielson, 2007; Lemov, 2010). In reality, there is a great deal of variability in the empirical warrant for these various models of effective teaching (Pianta, 2011).

There is also a big difference in the conceptions of teaching that are associated with these different efforts to teach core teaching practices. Some of this work is focused solely on equipping teachers with classroom management skills to foster better student performance on standardized tests (e.g., Gatti & Catalano, 2015), while other aspects of this work are focused more broadly on supporting richer and more successful student learning in a broader way. Anderson and Stillman (2013) contrast three alternative views of teaching in relation to clinical teacher education: teaching as management, teaching as the performance of particular pedagogies and strategies, and teaching as the facilitation of student learning. All of these varieties are found within the current movement to teach teacher candidates how to enact core teaching practices in teacher education programs.

Periodically, throughout the history of formal teacher education in the US, there has been a renewed focus on the enactment of particular teaching practices in American teacher education programs. Although the current incarnation of this trend differs in a number of significant ways from efforts of the past, it shares the intent to make teaching practice the center of teacher education (Zeichner, 2013).

Clinical Experience in Designed and Virtual Settings

In addition to placing teacher candidates in school and community settings for clinical experiences, teacher educators have also been involved in creating simulations of classroom practice within courses or connecting their courses to the practices of good teachers through technology. Grossman (2005, 2010, 2011) discusses various aspects of this work to create "laboratories" for clinical teacher education (Berliner, 1985), including the "microteaching" movement in the 1970s (Grossman, 2005) and current efforts to make the thinking and practices of teachers who are using particular teaching practices more visible to teacher candidates through technology. The Carnegie Foundation-funded Quest Project, where teacher educators used the web pages created by K–12 teachers in their teacher education methods courses, (insideteaching.org) is an example of this work.

In the Quest Project, Pam Grossman, a teacher educator at Stanford University, created a website where she documented how she incorporated the website of an experienced Los Angeles high school English teacher (Yvonne Divans Hutchinson) in her English methods course. One aspect of this work focused on the task of engaging students in text-based discussions of literature. In addition to reading academic literature on this topic, teacher candidates utilized Hutchinson's website, which includes images of her leading discussions around text in which students were very engaged, interviews with Hutchinson, and statements by her students, as well as examples of student work and methods and materials that Hutchinson used to prepare her students for discussions. This utilization of the work of a master Los Angeles teacher is an example of how Grossman made explicit connections between what teacher candidates were learning in theory and how it was enacted in practice in an actual classroom. The experience allowed teacher candidates to understand student learning related to the effective use of particular teaching practices.

The Rise of Early Entry Programs

Over the last two decades, there has been tremendous growth in *early entry* programs that place novices in classrooms as teachers of record with very little preparation beforehand. Most teacher learning in these programs takes place while teachers are fully responsible for classrooms and relies heavily on the quality of mentoring that is provided by the program and the school district. Examples of early entry programs that have received substantial support from foundations and the federal government include Teach for America (TFA)[13] and the New Teacher Project (now TNTP) founded by Michele Rhee, a graduate of TFA and a former superintendent of the Washington, DC, schools. This project sponsors teaching *fellows programs* in over 25 major US cities. Early entry teachers typically receive full beginning teacher salaries while they complete their preparation program.

These and other early entry programs typically include a brief summer institute for a few weeks prior to the beginning of the academic school year and then the assumption of full responsibility as a teacher for 1 or 2 years. During the 1 or 2 years in the program, the novice teachers who usually do not have any background in education continue to complete coursework that will qualify them for a state teaching license, and an experienced teacher mentor provides onsite support and guidance.[14] Early entry teachers complete their certification requirements in college and university or school district programs or in those sponsored by other nonprofit or for-profit entities. In New York State, New Orleans, Houston, Chicago and Newark, NJ, for example, many TFA teachers currently complete their certification requirements through the Relay Graduate School of Education, an independent, normal, school-like program that prepares teachers. The Relay Graduate School of Education (Kronholz, 2012) is part of a growing trend throughout the nation for charter school networks to prepare their own teachers in new, largely school-based programs that operate outside of the dominant university teacher education system.[15]

In early entry programs, individuals are usually required to make a commitment to teach in an urban or rural school in a high-poverty community for 1 or 2 years. For most of the teachers who enter the teaching force through one of the *fast-track* or early entry programs, most of the preparation occurs while these novice teachers are teachers of record fully responsible for a classroom in poor urban and rural communities (Darling-Hammond, 2004; Peske & Haycock, 2006). They are not found in public schools teaching students from the middle and upper-middle classes—the children of many of the advocates of the deregulation of teacher education.

Although the research on the effects of different pathways to teaching is not conclusive and has shown greater variability within types of pathways than across pathways (e.g., Constantine et al., 2009; Decker, Mayer, & Glazerman, 2006; Heilig & Jez, 2010; National Research Council, 2010; Zeichner & Conklin, 2005), there is some evidence of a "learning loss" by pupils as underprepared beginning teachers of record are catching up with teachers who completed all of their preparation for an initial teaching license prior to becoming responsible for classrooms (Zeichner & Conklin, 2005). Although there is a diversity of perspectives about the meaning of the research on different pathways into teaching, it is clear, given the high turnover of teachers in the most poverty-impacted schools (e.g., American Federation of Teachers, 2007; Lankford, Loeb, & Wyckoff, 2002), that the communities in which the schools staffed by many early entry teachers are located have become dependent on a constant supply of early entry teachers who stay for a few years and then leave.

The current teacher education system does not help these communities to develop the capacity to have access to a more experienced teaching staff in its schools and to lessen their dependence on inexperienced and underprepared teachers. Given the documented importance of teacher experience in teaching quality (e.g., Ronfeldt, Loeb, & Wyckoff, 2013), this is a serious problem of injustice for many poor communities. There is evidence that there are alternative approaches to preparing teachers for high-needs schools that are effective in bringing more fully prepared teachers into these schools and keeping them there over longer time than is typical (e.g., Berry et al., 2008; Skinner, Garreton, & Schultz, 2011). Any effort to assess the efficacy of different teacher education programs needs to take into account a full range of learning outcomes, including, but not limited to, standardized test scores and the retention records of teachers from different programs.

Urban Teacher Residency Programs

In 2004, Tom Payzant, then-superintendent of public schools in Boston, gave an invited plenary address at the national meeting of the major teacher education organization in the US: The American Association of Colleges for Teacher Education. The title of his talk was "Should teacher education take place at colleges and universities?" In this talk, Payzant complained about the quality of the teachers his district was getting from the many colleges and universities in the Boston area and threatened that if college and university teacher education did not improve the quality of their programs, he would start his own program within the Boston schools. Soon after, the largely school-based Boston Teacher Residency Program was opened as one of the first UTR programs in the US (Berry et al., 2008). As pointed out previously, however, the UTR is a new name for a type of program rather than a new program model. Largely school-based programs that prepare teachers to teach in specific school districts with a supervised year-long clinical experience have been around for many years and have re-emerged rather than emerged in urban teacher residencies.

Currently, the US Education Department is promoting the UTR model, and many teacher residencies are starting up across the country with federal and private financial support. In 2009–2010, the US Education Department allocated $143 million to support the start-up of 40 new teacher residencies. Additional teacher residency programs were funded in the 2014 Teacher Quality partnership awards of $35 million. In addition, a new organization has emerged with significant funding from private sources to support the development of residencies: Urban Teacher Residencies United.[16]

Although the specific designs of UTR programs across the country differ, they all provide a structure that falls between the fast-track program that places novices in classrooms as teachers of record with little preparation and traditional college and university programs where candidates complete all of their initial preparation before assuming responsibility for classrooms. Aspiring teachers—known as residents—are selected according to rigorous criteria aligned with the needs of particular school districts to participate in a 1- or 2-year program. During the program, the goal is to integrate coursework with an intensive, full-year classroom residency alongside an experienced mentor. According to an Aspen Institute report (Berry et al., 2008, p. 4), UTRs seek to:

- Tightly weave together education theory and classroom practice
- Focus on residents learning alongside an experienced, trained mentor
- Group candidates in cohorts to cultivate professional learning communities and foster collaboration
- Build effective partnerships among school districts, higher education institutions and nonprofit organizations
- Serve school districts by recruiting and training teachers to meet specific district needs
- Support residents once they are hired as teachers of record
- Establish and support differentiated career goals for experienced teachers

The UTR model can potentially contribute to urban schools where teacher attrition is high and student learning and teacher experience are low by providing teachers who are well prepared to work in those communities and committed to staying in them for a longer duration than is typically reported for graduates of early entry and college-recommending programs. Berry et al. (2008) propose that residencies are an important approach that policymakers, practitioners, and the public should consider in their efforts to ensure that they have a teaching workforce that is ethnically and racially diverse and prepared to succeed. They suggest that districts need to consider the full array of options and make informed decisions about how they invest in teachers and teaching.

UTRs are currently based in many cities across the nation (e.g., New York, Los Angeles, Chicago, Denver) and look different in different places in terms of how they are designed and implemented. Yet they are guided by a common set of principles that define the components of a high-quality residency program, inform the design of new residencies, and distinguish teacher residencies from other kinds of preparation programs. These principles include tightly woven clinical experiences as the central program element, with a focus on wrapping coursework around this practice, learning alongside an experienced mentor, and alignment between the curriculum of the residency program and the frameworks and practices used in particular districts. In addition, support is provided to residents in the first few years following the completion of their residency. Guided by these principles, programs such as those in Newark, New York, and Chicago offer different applications of the UTR model, but all pair master's-level pedagogical training and education content with a rigorous full-year classroom practicum under the supervision of expert teachers who have been trained to mentor novices and are compensated at a much higher level than is common in college-recommending programs.

Thus far, there is some research that has demonstrated that urban teacher residences help create a more ethnically and racially diverse teaching force and increase teacher retention in urban schools impacted by poverty. There is very limited evidence to date, however, about the ability of UTR-prepared teachers to raise student achievement (e.g., Papay, West, Fullerton, & Kane, 2011).

Moving College-Recommending Teacher Education into Schools and Communities

Following about a decade of activity to develop school–university partnerships in teacher education through the development of "professional development schools" (Boyle-Baise & Mcintyre, 2008)[17] and in response to recent national calls to place more emphasis on school-based teacher learning (e.g., National Commission on Teaching and America's Future, 2010), there are currently a number of university-based programs that are adopting a more situated approach to teacher education and moving instruction more into schools and communities where university instructors work side by side with practicing teachers in preparing teacher candidates (e.g., Noel, 2013). With a focus on context, courses are situated in schools, are planned around existing school curriculum, and draw on the expertise that exists within the schools. This structure is not common in typical university-based courses, which are often disconnected from schools and from practices candidates may encounter in their individual field experiences.

At UW, where we both have worked for the past 8 years, some of the methods and foundations courses in the elementary and secondary teacher education programs (both post-baccalaureate certification programs) are taught in local public schools where instructors strategically attempt to connect academic and school-based practices. For example, in addition to the usual practice of professors providing teacher candidates with the theoretical basis for particular teaching strategies, teacher candidates also have opportunities in these courses to observe a classroom in which particular teaching strategies teacher candidates are learning are used with students. They may also have time to plan and rehearse[18] lessons using these strategies that they then go and teach to students. In some cases, there is an opportunity to debrief their teaching with their teaching peers, as well as with the professor and teachers in the school (Lampert et al., 2013).

For example, each section of the fall quarter elementary mathematics methods class at UW is taught by a faculty member and an experienced teacher in an elementary school classroom in a public school that is partnered with the university. In this course, teacher candidates regularly use small video cameras to record their attempts to try out the teaching strategies they are learning about with individual and small groups of pupils, and they review these tapes as part of the debriefing process. They also submit the tapes to their university instructor, who provides each candidate with feedback several times during the quarter. This enables the instructor, who usually is not able to get around to see all of the candidates trying out the teaching strategies each week, to gain an understanding of how each candidate is using the strategies and what they need to work on. When the instructor, her teaching assistants, or the classroom teacher are in a small group directly observing candidates practicing specific teaching strategies, they also strategically intervene at times to model particular ways of asking pupils questions to accomplish such goals as eliciting students' reasoning in solving problems.

In this math methods course, the focus is on instructional practices that enable teachers to learn how to teach toward instructional goals as they learn to elicit and respond to students' mathematical ideas, treating students as sense-makers. The goal is to prepare teachers to create classroom learning environments where students are oriented toward each other's ideas and to produce disciplinary practices such as mathematical modeling, reasoning, and justification. Teacher educators also want to disrupt longstanding ideas embedded in urban schools about who can and cannot do mathematics and that mathematical success is an exception rather than a rule (Cornbleth, 2010).

The entry point for novice teachers to learn these instructional practices involves supporting them to lead instructional activities that embody the principles, practices, and disciplinary knowledge that are important in elementary mathematics teaching. Examples of instructional activities that foster the development of principled practice are: (a) counting and number tasks that engage K–5 students in reasoning about the base-10 structure of the number system and the meaning of the four operations, and (b) posing cognitively demanding word problems so that K–5 students have entry into the task, monitoring student work, and orchestrating discussions to meet a specified mathematical goal.

The fall quarter elementary literacy class at UW is also taught by a faculty member and a teacher in the teacher's partner school classroom. During each session, teacher candidates work with individual children and groups of children, many of whom are English learners. Teacher educators in this course focus on instructional practices that support children's learning in the areas of comprehension, word work, and vocabulary. The overarching approach is to help teacher candidates learn to assess children's reading needs, design lessons to meet those needs, and then engage in adaptive instruction. Through modeling, simulations, videotapes, and classroom observations, teacher educators help teacher candidates build deep conceptual understandings of reading processes and reading instruction and develop a variety of teaching strategies to promote children's learning.

Two teaching practices that are particularly useful in promoting teacher candidate learning in school-based courses are: (a) small-group guided reading, and (b) explicit instruction in word work and comprehension. Both practices require teacher candidates to simultaneously consider students' abilities to decode words and make sense of text. Candidates must also teach in a way that helps students learn to become strategic readers who are able to apply their skills and strategies to new text; at the same time, candidates must develop their own abilities to become teachers who can adapt their practices to meet students' evolving needs.

To learn about children's literacy abilities and development, teacher candidates support classroom teachers by administering high-leverage literacy assessments and closely observing students as they engage with reading and writing. In collaborative peer groups and with the support of the course instructor, students analyze children's literacy abilities and then plan and implement appropriate instruction. Debriefing with instructors and colleagues, teacher candidates continually analyze their own teaching and students' learning, using those insights to plan follow-up lessons. They provide feedback to the children's classroom teachers to support the instruction they are designing for children in their classrooms.

The secondary math methods course at UW meets at least six times over a 10-week quarter at a local high-needs partner high school, where teacher candidates, in groups, observe teachers as they instruct their ninth-grade algebra classes. These teachers implement many of the same equity-oriented teaching practices as those taught in the methods course and are often graduates of the UW program. Following the observations, the teacher candidates, university course instructor, and classroom teachers meet to debrief the lesson, during which time they examine the relationship between students, mathematics, and particular teaching practices. Further, during these debriefing meetings, the teacher candidates have opportunities to ask questions of the teachers about the students they observed and about particular teaching decisions that may have been made. In this particular version of a practice-based methods course that comes in the first quarter of a four-quarter master's program, teacher candidates do not have opportunities to try out the practices themselves. This comes during the second methods course, when teacher candidates enact the strategies with students in their practicum classroom and then carefully analyze them with their mentors and supervisors and in their campus-based methods course (Campbell, 2008, 2012).

For several years, secondary language arts methods at UW were taught entirely in a partner middle school. The class is completely immersed in the culture of the school and exposed to the typical occurrences that randomly happen during a school day (fire drills, people walking in and out of their classroom), as well as being privy to frequent discussions with expert educators within the school. The course also provides multiple structured opportunities for teacher candidates to learn about particular teaching practices. Typically, teacher candidates are instructed in particular reading and writing strategies and then work with small groups and individual students in a language arts classroom in the school, making use of those strategies to support students. The candidates then come back together as a group to debrief the experience of implementation.

In looking specifically at understanding text, teacher educators engage candidates in a diverse set of activities that they can use in their own classrooms to provide all students with access to text. One practice that is focused on is eliciting and responding to student ideas. Teacher educators engage candidates in this core practice through think-aloud/read-aloud activities. They show candidates representations, model, collaboratively plan with them, and engage candidates in rehearsals before enactment in their placement classrooms. After the enactment, teacher educators support teacher candidates in reflecting about their practice and student learning.

Teacher candidates also learn multiple ways to support student meaning-making through text discussions. In discussions, teacher educators model for candidates how to ask questions that probe student understanding and support student participation. Candidates learn how to create a discourse community where students feel comfortable disagreeing, agreeing, and furthering others' ideas by using the text and their lived experiences. The teacher candidates prepare for whole-class discussions by using a mentor text. Each candidate develops questions that support the deeper understanding of a particular chapter, and each candidate presses his or her peers to develop further questions.

Thus far, there is limited evidence about the value of these school-based courses and collaborative teaching by university and K–12 educators. There is some evidence that the learning and ability to enact the teaching practices by candidates is greater in this model than when coursework is offered in university classrooms. There is also some evidence of the power of situating instruction in the context of a classroom to disrupt teacher candidates' low expectations for the learning of students in high-needs urban schools (e.g., Campbell, 2012).

Clinical Experiences in Communities

In addition to teacher candidate learning in school-based clinical experiences, for many years some teacher educators in the US have advocated for placing teacher candidates for periods of time in the broader communities in which schools are situated (e.g., Flowers, Patterson, Stratemeyer, & Lindsey, 1948). These experiences have varied greatly in their purposes and in the activities in which teacher candidates are engaged. For example, some experiences have focused on service learning or on learning about how students learn in settings outside of school, while others have emphasized learning about the resources and practices in the community and learning from adults in the community (e.g., Boyle-Baise & Mcintyre, 2008; Mahan, 1982; Zeichner & Melnick, 1996) so that candidates can learn to teach in more culturally responsive ways (Lucas & Villegas, 2011).

These experiences can be short-term in a single course and/or community that may be characterized as visiting a community, or they can be longer and more intensive, which may be thought of as immersing pre-service teachers in local communities. Some programs are elective, such as Indiana University's cultural immersion programs, which provide opportunities for student teachers to work in local schools in other countries and within diverse communities in the

US (Longview Foundation, 2008). Other community experiences are required portions of teacher education programs in addition to or linked to school-based experiences (e.g., Zeichner et al., 2015). Despite repeated calls over many years for clinical teacher education to be broadened into local communities, very few early entry, college-recommending, and now hybrid programs like urban teacher residencies have done so. Some empirical evidence exists about the transformative power of community-based learning for prospective teachers in helping teacher candidates become more interculturally competent and teach in culturally responsive ways (Boyle-Baise & Mcintyre, 2008; Sleeter, 2008).

At UW, we are developing community strands in our elementary, secondary, and teacher residency programs that include a variety of clinical experiences in the communities in which teacher candidates are teaching in their year-long program. In each quarter of both our elementary and secondary programs, the community work is linked to particular courses and school-based clinical experiences, and although the specific purposes of the community work vary each quarter, the goal underlying the work across the programs is to develop "community teachers" who are knowledgeable of the communities in which they teach and are aware of the resources and funds of knowledge in those communities that can be accessed in their teaching (Murrell, 2001). In partnering with community-based organizations (CBOs), we are deepening relationships with CBO leaders and building an understanding of their work as educators in out-of-school settings. We are also working with local community members, leaders, and civil rights activists as teacher educators and asking them to share their diverse perspectives on the schools where they send their kids and grandchildren and the kind of teachers they hope they experience. These and other community experiences (e.g., training and experience in home visits) for teacher candidates have provided them with insights that can support the enactment of more culturally relevant teaching practices and support the development of the kind of teacher commitment to the urban neighborhoods in which they work that is important to school success for urban students (Ladson-Billings, 1994).

Conclusion

There is widespread agreement in the US that providing high-quality clinical experiences to teacher candidates is the key element in providing effective teacher preparation and that many individuals entering the teaching force in the US do not have access to it now (NCATE, 2010; National Research Council, 2010). While current efforts to build new, more clinically based models for teacher preparation in the US are needed, there are cautions that should be heeded as this widespread effort moves forward. First, one of us warned in 1980 that the then-national effort to add additional field experiences to largely campus-based university programs needed to give careful attention to the nature and quality of this additional time in schools and its relation to the rest of the preparation program (Zeichner, 1980). What was seen at that time—uncritical glorification of school-based experience and a lack of attention to illuminating the particular design features of these experiences that make them educative—is also characteristic of the current movement. This concern is similar to the concern raised by Ellis (2010), referred to previously, that the push to move teacher education more into schools in the UK has often been characterized by impoverished views of the role of experience in learning to teach.

The current literature is filled with discussions of programs that involve more school-based experience in university programs, the development of new school-based programs like urban teacher residencies, hundreds of early entry programs and discussions of the movement of teacher education coursework to school and community settings that imply that merely moving teacher education to schools and communities is necessarily beneficial (Zeichner, 2010b). This literature often does not clearly illuminate the specific ways in which these school- and community-based experiences operate (e.g., what co-teaching between university and school-based teacher educators looks like) and the ways in which particular features of these experiences are connected to various desired outcomes for teacher candidates and the schools. One hopeful sign in this regard is some recent research that seeks to identify the features of clinical placement sites and clinical experience design characteristics that support teacher candidate learning and pupil learning in schools (e.g., Anderson & Stillman, 2011; Cornbleth, 2010; Ronfeldt, 2012).[19]

A second caution has to do with what is eliminated from teacher education programs as they move more to the field. There is some historical evidence that as programs have become more school-based, the focus of the preparation narrows to a more technical focus on the mastery of teaching skills and that important elements of a teacher's education such as multicultural education and the social foundations of education are reduced or eliminated (Greene, 1979; Zeichner, 2014). While the mastery of teaching and classroom management skills and practices is among the most important aspects of teacher preparation, teachers also need to have a clear sense of the social, political, community, and cultural contexts in which they work to be able to build and sustain strong relationships with their students, adapt their practice in response to the changing needs of their students, and accomplish a host of other things that go beyond the mastery of specific teaching and classroom management practices (Bartolome, 1994; Bransford & Darling-Hammond, 2005). There is a danger that the current wave of emphasizing school-based experience in teacher education in the US will contribute to further deprofessionalizing teaching rather than strengthening teachers' abilities to teach in culturally responsive ways and to acquire the adaptive expertise that is needed to successfully teach in today's US public schools (Banks et al., 2005; Hammerness et al., 2005).

Finally, as briefly mentioned earlier, one of the major problems in US teacher education in the last 50 years has been the inability to institutionalize and sustain innovations that have initially been funded by private foundations, states, or the federal government. There is a whole litany of major efforts to transform teacher education throughout the country, ranging from the National Teacher Corps of the 1960s and 1970s, the Professional Development School movement of the 1980s and 1990s, and the over-$100 million effort led by the Carnegie Corporation Teachers for a New Era that have failed to achieve this transformation to any significant degree (Fraser, 2007). As the public universities and public schools where the majority of teacher education in the US still takes place have continued to lose their state and federal funding, private foundations have shifted toward funding alternatives to college and university teacher education and promoting charter schools (Levine, 2012; Suggs & deMarrais, 2011)[20] and new resources are needed to implement new and intrusive accountability requirements for teacher education programs (Zeichner, 2011). It is becoming harder to imagine how college and university teacher education programs will be able to transform and sustain clinical teacher education in the ways imagined by the recent national panel (NCATE, 2010).

Currently, there are strong efforts being led by the US education department[21] to require an accountability system for teacher education programs in the US that will involve the use of an enormous amount of resources in creating and implementing a system that rates teacher education programs according to the value analysis of the standardized test scores of the pupils taught by graduates of different teacher education programs (Duncan, 2011). Given the questionable value of this kind of data for evaluating teachers—let alone teacher education programs (Baker et al., 2010; Zeichner, 2011)—it would make more sense in our view to focus these resources on things that will enhance the quality of teacher preparation, such as building the capacity of schools and mentors to support high-quality clinical experiences.

There is a clear and growing evidence of private money in steering the course of teacher education policies away from colleges and universities playing a central role and toward the deregulation and privatization of teacher education in early entry programs (Saltman, 2010; Zeichner, 2010c; Zeichner & Peña-Sandoval, 2015). The success of this growing dominance of venture philanthropy, educational advocacy organizations, and education think tanks in making early entry and non-university programs the norm and the disappearance of genuine public dialogue about the future of US teacher education—more than anything else—will determine the ability of the nation to achieve the lofty vision to offer a high-quality clinical education to all individuals entering the US teaching force.

Notes

1   We would like to acknowledge the contributions of Elham Kazemi, Karen Mikolasy, and Sheila Valencia in providing information about their school-based methods courses at the University of Washington.

2 These "early entry" teachers teach almost exclusively in urban or rural schools serving students living in poverty (Peske & Haycock, 2006).

3 The UTR is not a new model; it is a new term for a form of mostly school-based teacher education for specific school districts that has been around for many years (e.g., Fraser, 2007; Weiner, 1993). It includes working under the supervision of a mentor teacher for a year together with some coursework.

4 This increased focus on school experience in teacher education is taking place in other countries as well (e.g., Mattsson, Eilertsen, & Rorrison, 2011; Reid, 2011).

5 Although our focus here is on the enduring problems of teacher education within a US context, there is a great deal of similarity to the international literature on this issue (e.g., Vick, 2006).

6 Despite repeated assertions that teachers prepared in professional development schools teach at a higher level and stay longer than those prepared in traditional clinical placements (e.g., Council of Chief State School Officers, 2012, p. 12), the great variation in the nature and quality of professional development schools (Zeichner, 2009) makes this kind of generalization problematic.

7 The point here is not that teacher candidates should learn to passively replicate teaching practices advocated either by university- or school-based teacher educators that represent an "impoverished view" of the role of experience in teacher learning (Ellis, 2010). Teacher candidates need to learn how to critically analyze and selectively utilize and adapt that which is offered to them by their programs.

8 See Darling-Hammond (2006) and Zeichner and Conklin (2008) for a discussion of the characteristics of exemplary teacher education programs.

9 This disinvestment in public higher education is part of a broader disinvestment in the public sphere that exists in some form or another in many countries (Zeichner, 2010c).

10 Both the MATCH Teacher Residency and the Relay Graduate School of Education have been authorized by their respective states (Massachusetts and New York) to offer master's degrees.

11 See www.newschools.org/venture/relay-school-of-education

12 The Institute for Simulation and Training at the University of Central Florida, with the support of a grant from the Gates Foundation, provides virtual classrooms to about a dozen other teacher education institutions. These virtual classrooms use artificial intelligence, child avatars and a behind-the-scenes actor (Cuban, 2012). Also see http://today.ucf.edu/ucfs-virtual-classroom-software-receives-grant-for-innovative-teacher-preparation-program/

13 Teach for America, which is the largest of the US early entry programs, received a federal grant of $50 million in 2010 to expand its capacity by 80 percent (Zeichner & Peña-Sandoval, 2015) and over the last decade has received funding of over $300 million from private foundations and the federal government (Suggs & deMarrais, 2011). There is currently a great deal of controversy about this program because of its placement of underprepared teachers with only 5 weeks of training in schools to exclusively teach students living in poverty, the ambiguity of the research about the effectiveness of these teachers (Heilig & Jez, 2010), their high turnover rate after their 2-year commitment (Donaldson & Johnson, 2011), and the ties between the program

and efforts to privatize public schools in the US (Sondel, Kretchmar, & Ferrare, 2014) and to avoid state certification requirements (Heilig, 2013).

14   Current federal legislation allows these teachers still in training to be considered "highly qualified" and therefore eligible to be responsible for classrooms.

15   The Aspire, MATCH, and Academy for Educational Leadership teacher residencies are examples of these emerging networks to prepare teachers for particular charter school networks.

16   See www.utrunited.org/. This organization is now called the National Center for Teacher Residencies. http://nctresidencies.org/

17   Despite evidence that professional development schools in some cases addressed some of the enduring problems of clinical teacher education enumerated previously (e.g., the disconnect between coursework and fieldwork), there is widespread agreement that the professional development school movement has not consistently addressed these problems, and that even when it did so, the improvements were not able to be sustained (Zeichner, 2009).

18   See Lampert et al. (2013) for a detailed discussion of the pedagogy of rehearsal that is being used in the methods courses at several research universities.

19   Like most other things in teacher education, there is a long history of efforts to identify the features of good clinical sites in teacher education that should be studied by current researchers. McIntosh (1968) made one of the earliest and most interesting efforts.

20   The US Department of Education has proposed phasing out one of the major recent sources of support for innovation in college and university programs: The Teacher Quality Partnership program.

21   The proposed standards of the new national teacher accreditation body, the Council for the Accreditation of Educator Preparation (CAEP), endorse the federal vision of an accountability system for teacher education.

References

American Association of Colleges for Teacher Education (AACTE) (2010). *The clinical preparation of teachers: A policy brief.* Washington, DC: Author.

American Association of Colleges for Teacher Education (AACTE) (2013). *The changing teacher preparation profession: A report from AACTE professional education data system* (PEDS). Washington, DC: Author.

American Federation of Teachers (AFT) (2007). *Meeting the challenge: Recruiting and retaining teachers in hard-to-staff schools.* Retrieved from www.aft.org/sites/default/files/hardtostaff_2007.pdf

American Federation of Teachers (AFT) (2012). *Raising the bar: Aligning and elevating teacher preparation and the teaching profession.* Washington, DC: Author.

Anderson, L., & Stillman, J. (2011). Student teaching for a specialized view of professional practice? Opportunities to learn in and for urban, high-needs schools. *Journal of Teacher Education, 62*(5), 446–464.

Anderson, L., & Stillman, J. (2013). Student teaching's contribution to preservice teacher development: A review of research focused on the preparation of teachers for urban and high-needs contexts. *Review of Education Research, 83*(1), 3–69.

Baker, E., Barton, P., Darling-Hammond, L., Haertel, E., Ladd, H., Linn, R., Ravitch, D., Rothstein, R., Shavelson, R., & Shepard, L. (2010). *Problems with the use of student test scores to evaluate teachers.* Washington, DC: Economic Policy Institute (EPI).

Ball, D., & Cohen, D. (1999). Developing practice, developing practitioners: Toward a practice-based theory of professional education. In L. Darling-Hammond & G. Sykes (Eds), *Teaching as a learning profession* (pp. 3–32). San Francisco, CA: Jossey-Bass.

Ball, D., & Forzani, E. (2009). The work of teaching and the challenge for teacher education. *Journal of Teacher Education, 60,* 497–510.

Banks, J., Cochran-Smith, M., Moll, L., Richert, A., Zeichner, K., LePage, P., Darling-Hammond, L., & Duffy, H. (2005). Teaching diverse learners. In L. Darling-Hammond & J. Bransford (Eds), *Preparing teachers for a changing world* (pp. 232–274). San Francisco, CA: Jossey-Bass.

Bartolome, L. (1994). Beyond the methods fetish: Toward a humanizing pedagogy. *Harvard Educational Review, 64*(2), 173–194.

Berliner, D. (1985). Laboratory settings and the study of teacher education. *Journal of Teacher Education, 36,* 2–8.

Berry, B., Montgomery, D., Curtis, R., Hernandez, M., Wurtzel, J., & Snyder, J. (2008). *Creating and sustaining urban teacher residencies.* Hillsborough, NC: Center for Teaching Quality and the Aspen Institute.

Boyle-Baise, M., & McIntyre, D.J. (2008). What kind of experience? Preparing teachers in PDS or community settings. In M. Cochran-Smith, S. Feiman-Nemser, & D. J. McIntyre (Eds), *Handbook of research on teacher education* (3rd ed., pp. 307–330). New York, NY: Routledge.

Bransford, J., & Darling-Hammond, L. (2005). *Preparing teachers for a changing world: Report of the National Academy of Education Committee on Teacher Education.* San Francisco, CA: Jossey-Bass.

Buchmann, M., & Floden, R. (1990). *Program coherence in the US: A view from the US.* East Lansing, MI: National Center for Research on Teacher Learning. Issue Paper, *90*(6).

Bullough, R., Draper, M. J., Smith, L., & Burrell, J. (2004). Moving beyond collusion: Clinical faculty and university public school partnership. *Teaching and Teacher Education, 20,* 505–521.

Bullough, R., Hobbs, S., Kauchak, D., Crow, N., & Stokes, D. (1997). Long-term PDS development in research universities and the clinicalization of teacher education. *Journal of Teacher Education, 48,* 85–93.

Burris, C. C. (2012, July 26). Some scary training for future teachers. *Washington Post.* Retrieved from www.washingtonpost.com

Campbell, S. S. (2008). Mediated field experiences in learning progressive teaching: A design experiment in teacher education. Paper presented at the annual meeting of the American Educational Research Association, New York, NY.

Campbell, S. S. (2012). Taking it to the field: Teacher candidate learning about equity oriented mathematics teaching in a mediated field experience. Unpublished doctoral dissertation, University of Washington-Seattle, College of Education, Seattle, WA.

Chubb, J. (2012). *The best teachers in the world: Why we don't have them and how we could.* Stanford, CA: Hoover Institution Press.

Clift, R., & Brady, P. (2005). Research on methods courses and field experiences. In M. Cochran-Smith & K. Zeichner (Eds), *Studying teacher education: The report of the American Educational Research Association panel on research on teacher education* (pp. 309–424). New York, NY: Routledge.

Cochran-Smith, M. (1991). Reinventing student teaching. *Journal of Teacher Education*, *42*(2), 104–118.

Conant, J. (1963). *The education of American teachers*. New York, NY: McGraw-Hill.

Constantine, J., Player, D., Silva, T., Hallgren, K., Grider, M., & Drake, J. (2009). *An evaluation of teachers trained through different routes to certification*. Washington, DC: US Department of Education.

Cornbleth, C. (2010). Institutional habitus as the de facto diversity curriculum of teacher education. *Anthropology and Education Quarterly*, *41*(3), 280–297.

Council of Chief State School Officers (CCSSO) (2012). *Our responsibility, our promise: Transforming educator preparation and entry into the profession*. Washington, DC: Author.

Cuban, L. (2012). *How much and what kind of teacher education do novices need?* Retrieved from http://larrycuban.wordpress.com

Danielson, C. (2007). *Enhancing professional practice*. Alexandria, VA: Association of Supervision and Curriculum Development.

Darling-Hammond, L. (2004). Inequality and the right to learn: Access to qualified teachers in California's public schools. *Teachers College Record*, *106*(10), 1936–1966.

Darling-Hammond, L. (2006). *Powerful teacher education*. San Francisco, CA: Jossey-Bass.

Darling-Hammond, L., & Lieberman, A. (Eds) (2012). *Teacher education around the world: Changing policies and practices*. London: Routledge.

Decker, P. T., Mayer, D. P., & Glazerman, S. (2006). Alternative routes to teaching: The impact of Teach for America on student achievement and other outcomes. *Journal of Policy Analysis and Management*, *25*(1), 75–96.

Donaldson, M. L., & Johnson, S. M. (2011). Teach for America teachers: How long do they teach? Why do they leave? *Phi Delta Kappan*, *93*(2), 47–52.

Duncan, A. (2011). *Our future, our teachers: The Obama administration plan for teacher education reform and improvement*. Washington, DC: US Department of Education.

Ellis, V. (2010). Impoverishing experience: The problem of teacher education in England. *Journal of Education for Teaching*, *36*(1), 105–120.

Emihovich, C., Dana, T., Vernetson, T., & Colon, E. (2011). Changing standards, changing needs: The gauntlet of teacher education reform. In P. Earley, D. Imig, & N. Michelli (Eds), *Teacher education policy in the US* (pp. 47–69). New York, NY: Routledge.

Feiman-Nemser, S. (2010, March 11). The case for strong clinical teacher education. Remarks made at a press conference at the National Press Club. "Strong clinical teacher preparation: A must for long-term school improvement efforts." Press briefing sponsored by the American Association of Colleges for Teacher Education.

Feiman-Nemser, S., & Buchmann, M. (1985). Pitfalls of experience in teacher education. *Teachers College Record*, *87*, 49–65.

Feistritzer, E., & Haar, C. (2008). *Alternative routes to teaching*. Upper Saddle River, NJ: Pearson.

Flowers, J. G., Patterson, A., Stratemeyer, F., & Lindsey, M. (1948). *School and community laboratory experiences in teacher education*. Oneata, NY: American Association of Colleges for Teacher Education (AACTE).

Fraser, J. (2007). *Preparing America's teachers: A history*. New York, NY: Teachers College Press.

Gatlin, D. (2009). A pluralistic approach to the revitalization of teacher education. *Journal of Teacher Education*, *60*(5), 469–477.

Gatti, L., & Catalano, T. (2015). The business of learning to teach: A critical metaphor analysis of one teacher's journey. *Teaching and Teacher Education, 45*, 149–160.

Greenberg, J., Pomerance, L., & Walsh, K. (2011). *Student teaching in the US.* Washington, DC: National Council on Teacher Quality.

Greene, M. (1979). The matter of mystification: Teacher education in unquiet times. In M. Greene (Ed.), *Landscapes of learning* (pp. 53–73). New York, NY: Teachers College Press.

Grossman, P. (2005). Pedagogical approaches to teacher education. In M. Cochran Smith & K. Zeichner (Eds), *Studying teacher education* (pp. 425–476). New York, NY: Routledge.

Grossman, P. (2010). *Learning to practice: The design of clinical experience in teacher preparation.* Policy Brief of the Partnership for Teacher Quality. Washington, DC: American Association of Colleges for Teacher Education (AACTE).

Grossman, P. (2011). A framework for teaching practice: A brief history of an idea. *Teachers College Record, 113*(12), 2836–2843.

Grossman, P., & Loeb, S. (Eds) (2008). *Alternative routes to teaching.* Cambridge, MA: Harvard Education Press.

Hamel, F., & Jaasko-Fisher, H. (2011). Hidden labor in the mentoring of pre-service teachers: Notes from a mentor teacher advisory council. *Teaching and Teacher Education, 27*, 434–442.

Hammerness, K., Darling-Hammond, L., Bransford, J., Cochran-Smith, M., McDonald, M., & Zeichner, K. (2005). How teachers learn and develop. In L. Darling-Hammond & J. Bransford (Eds), *Preparing teachers for a changing world* (pp. 358–389). San Francisco, CA: Jossey-Bass.

Heilig, J. V. (2013). Battle for California: TFA civil war, ELLs, and teacher quality. *Cloaking Inequity.* Retrieved from http://cloakinginequity.com/2013/03/05/battle-for-california-tfa-civil-war-ells-and-teacher-quality/

Heilig, J. V., & Jez, S. J. (2010). *Teach for America: A review of the evidence.* Boulder, CO: University of Colorado: Education and the Public Interest Center.

Kronholz, J. (2012). A new type of ed school. *Education Next, 12*(4). Retrieved from http://educationnext.org/a-new-type-of-ed-school/

Labaree, D. (2004). *The trouble with ed schools.* New Haven, CT: Yale University Press.

Ladson-Billings, G. (1994). *The dreamkeepers: Successful teachers of African American children.* San Francisco, CA: Jossey-Bass.

Lampert, M., Franke, M., Kazemi, E., Ghousseini, H., Turrou, A. C., Beasley, H., Cunard, A., & Crowe, K. (2013). Keeping it complex: Using rehearsals to support novice teacher learning of ambitious teaching in elementary mathematics. *Journal of Teacher Education, 64*(3), 226–243.

Lankford, H., Loeb, S., & Wyckoff, J. (2002). Teacher sorting and the plight of urban schools. *Educational Evaluation and Policy Analysis, 20*, 37–62.

Lemov, D. (2010). *Teaching like a champion.* San Francisco, CA: Jossey-Bass.

Levine, A. (2006). *Educating school teachers.* The Education Schools Project. Retrieved from www.edschools.org/ pdf/Educating_Teachers_Report.pdf

Levine, A. (2012). The new normal of teacher education. *The Chronicle of Higher Education.* Retrieved from http://chronicle.com/article/The-New-Normal-of-Teacher/127430/

Longview Foundation (2008). *Teacher preparation for the global age: The imperative for change.* Silver Spring, MD: Author.

Lucas, T., & Villegas, A. M. (2011). A framework for preparing linguistically responsive teachers. In T. Lucas (Ed.), *Teacher preparation for linguistically diverse classrooms* (pp. 55–72). New York, NY: Routledge.

Mahan, J. (1982). Native Americans as teacher trainers: Anatomy and outcomes of a cultural immersion project. *Journal of Equity and Leadership*, *2*, 100–109.

Mattsson, M., Eilertsen, T.V., & Rorrison, D. (Eds) (2011). *A practicum turn in teacher education*. Rotterdam, Netherlands: Sense Publishers.

McIntosh, R. G. (1968). *An approach to the analysis of clinical settings for teacher education*. The Third Florence Stratemeyer Lecture, Annual meeting of the Association for Student Teaching, Chicago, IL.

Murrell, P. (2001). *The community teacher*. New York, NY: Teachers College Press.

National Commission on Teaching and America's Future (NCTAF) (2010). *Who Will teach: Experience matters*. Retrieved from http://nctaf.org/wp-content/uploads/2012/01/NCTAF-Who-Will-Teach-Experience-Matters-2010-Report.pdf

National Council of Accreditation for Teacher Education (NCATE) (2010). *Transforming teacher education through clinical practice: A national strategy to prepare effective teachers*. Washington, DC: Author.

National Education Association (NEA) (2011). *Transforming teaching: Connecting professional responsibility with student learning*. Washington, DC: Author.

National Research Council (NRC) (2010). *Preparing teachers: Building evidence for sound policy*. Washington, DC: National Academies Press.

Newfield, C. (2008). *Unmaking the public university*. Cambridge, MA: Harvard University Press.

Noel, J. (2013) (Ed.). *Moving teacher education into urban schools and communities*. New York, NY: Routledge.

Papay, J., West, M., Fullerton, J., & Kane, T. (2011). *Can practice-based teacher preparation increase student achievement? Evidence from the Boston Teacher Residency*. New York, NY: National Bureau of Economic Research Working Paper #17646.

Payzant, T. (February 2004). Should teacher education take place at colleges and universities? Invited address presented at the annual meeting of the American Association of Colleges for Teacher Education, Chicago, IL.

Peske, H., & Haycock, K. (2006). *Teaching inequality: How poor minority students are short changed on teacher quality*. Washington, DC: Education Trust.

Pianta, R. C. (2011). *Teaching children well: New evidence-based approaches to teacher professional development and training*. Washington, DC: Center for American Progress.

Reid, J. (2011). A practice-turn for teacher education? *South Pacific Journal of Teacher Education*, *39*(4), 293–310.

Rennie Center for Education Research & Policy (2009). *Preparing tomorrow's teachers: The role of practice-based teacher preparation programs in Massachusetts*. Cambridge, MA: Author.

Ronfeldt, M., Loeb, J., & Wyckoff, J. (2013). How teacher turnover harms student achievement. *American Educational Research Journal*, *50*(1), 4–36.

Ronfeldt, R. (2012). Where should student teachers learn to teach: Effects of placement school characteristics on teacher retention and effectiveness. *Education Evaluation and Policy Analysis*, 34, 3–26.

Rotherham, A. (2008). *Achieving teacher and principal excellence: A guidebook for donors*. Washington, DC: Philanthropy Roundtable.

Saltman, K. (2010). *The gift of education and venture philanthropy*. New York, NY: Palgrave Macmillan.

Schorr, J. (2013). A revolution begins in teacher prep. *Stanford Social Innovation Review.* Retrieved from http://ssir.org/articles/entry/a_revolution_begins_in_teacher_prep

Skinner, E., Garreton, M.T., & Schultz, B. (Eds) (2011). *Grow your own teachers: Grassroots change in teacher education.* New York, NY: Teachers College Press.

Sleeter, C. (2008). Preparing white teachers for diverse students. In M. Cochran-Smith, S. Feiman-Nemser, & D. J. Mcintyre (Eds), *Handbook of research on teacher education* (3rd ed., pp. 559–582). New York, NY: Routledge.

Sondel, B., Kretchmar, K., & Ferrare, J. (2014). Mapping the terrain: Teach for America, charter school reform, and corporate sponsorship. *Journal of Education Policy, 29*(6), 742–759.

Suggs, C., & deMarrais, K. (2011). *Critical contributions: Philanthropic investment in teachers and teaching.* Atlanta, GA: Kronley & Associates.

Sykes, G., & Dibner, K. (2009). *Fifty years of federal teacher policy: An appraisal.* Washington, DC: Center on Education Policy.

Turney, C., Eltis, K., Towler, J., & Wright, R. (1985). *A new basis for teacher education: The practicum curriculum.* Sydney, Australia: University of Sydney Press.

Valencia, S., Martin, S., Place, N., & Grossman, P. (2009). Complex interactions in student teaching: Lost opportunities for learning. *Journal of Teacher Education, 60*(3), 304–322.

Vick, M. (2006). "It's a difficult matter": Historical perspectives on the enduring problem of the practicum in teacher preparation. *Asia-Pacific Journal of Teacher Education, 34*(2), 181–198.

Weiner, L. (1993). *Preparing teachers for urban schools: Lessons from thirty years of school reform.* New York, NY: Teachers College Press.

Windschitl, M., Thompson, J., & Braaten, M. (2011). Ambitious pedagogy by novice teachers. *Teachers College Record, 113*(7), 1311–1360.

Zeichner, K. (1980). Myths and realities: Field-based experiences in pre-service teacher education. *Journal of Teacher Education, 31*(6), 45–55.

Zeichner, K. (1996). Designing educative practicum experiences for prospective teachers. In K. Zeichner, S. Melnick, & M. L. Gomez (Eds), *Currents of reform in pre-service teacher education* (pp. 215–234). New York, NY: Teachers College Press.

Zeichner, K. (2009). *Teacher education and the struggle for social justice.* New York, NY: Routledge.

Zeichner, K. (2010a). *The importance of strong clinical preparation for teachers.* Testimony presented at a US Congressional Briefing organized by the American Association of Colleges for Teacher Education, US Senate Office Building, Washington, DC. Retrieved from aacte.org.

Zeichner, K. (2010b). Rethinking the connections between campus courses and field experiences in college and university-based teacher education. *Journal of Teacher Education, 89*(11), 89–99.

Zeichner, K. (2010c). Neo-liberalism and the transformation of teacher education in the US. *Teaching and Teacher Education, 26*(8), 1544–1552.

Zeichner, K. (2011). Assessing state and federal policies to evaluate the quality of teacher preparation programs. In P. Earley, D. Imig, & N. Michelli (Eds), *Teacher education policy in the US: Issues and tensions in an era of evolving expectations* (pp. 75–105). New York, NY: Routledge.

Zeichner, K. (2012). The turn once again toward practice-based teacher education. *Journal of Teacher Education, 63*(5), 376–382.

Zeichner, K. (2013). Two visions of teaching and teacher education for the 21st century. In X. Zhu & K. Zeichner (Eds), *Preparing teachers for the 21st century* (pp. 3–20). Heidelberg, Germany: Springer.

Zeichner, K. (2014). The struggle for the soul of teaching and teacher education. *Journal of Education for Teaching, 40*(5), 551–568.

Zeichner, K., & Conklin, H. (2005) Teacher education programs. In M. Cochran-Smith & K. Zeichner (Eds), *Studying teacher education* (pp. 645–746). New York, NY: Routledge.

Zeichner, K., & Conklin, H. (2008). Teacher education programs. In M. Cochran-Smith & K. Zeichner (Eds), *Studying teacher education* (pp. 645–746). New York, NY: Routledge.

Zeichner, K., & Melnick, S. (1996). The role of community field experiences in preparing teachers for cultural diversity. In K. Zeichner, S. Melnick, & M. L. Gomez (Eds), *Currents of reform in preservice teacher education* (pp. 176–198). New York, NY: Teachers College Press.

Zeichner, K., & Payne, K. (2013). Democratizing knowledge in urban teacher education. In J. Noel (Ed.), *Moving teacher education into urban schools and communities* (pp. 3–19). New York, NY: Routledge.

Zeichner, K., Payne, K., & Brayko, K. (2015). Democratizing teacher education. *Journal of Teacher Education, 66*(2), 1–14.

Zeichner, K., & Peña-Sandoval, C. (2015). Venture philanthropy and teacher education policy in the US: The role of the New Schools Venture Fund. *Teachers College Record, 117*(6). Retrieved from www.tcrecord.org/content.asp?contentid=17539

8

ENGAGING AND WORKING IN SOLIDARITY WITH LOCAL COMMUNITIES IN PREPARING THE TEACHERS OF THEIR CHILDREN

Kenneth M. Zeichner, Michael Bowman, Lorena Guillen, and Kate Napolitan

> Teachers often see parents' goals and values as impediments to students' academic accomplishments. Parents in turn believe that teachers are antagonistic toward them and fail to appreciate the actual conditions that shape their children's lives. This lack of trust between teachers and parents—often exacerbated by race and class differences—makes it difficult for these groups to maintain a genuine dialogue about shared concerns. The resultant miscommunications tend to reinforce existing prejudices and undermine constructive efforts by teachers and parents to build relational ties around the interests of children.
>
> *(Bryk & Schneider, 2002, p. 6)*

It is very clear from the literature in education (e.g., Bryk & Schneider, 2002; Comer, 2009; Murrell, Strauss, Carlson, & Dominguez, 2015) that teachers need to know about the communities where their students grow and develop, how to develop respectful and trusting connections with students' families and other adults in their students' communities, and how to make use of this knowledge and these relationships in ways that support their students' learning. It is also very clear from the literature in teacher education that while learning to work with families and in communities has been articulated as an important goal of teacher education for more than 50 years (e.g., Flowers, Patterson, Stratemeyer, & Lindsey, 1948; Hodgdon & Saunders, 1951), there has been only minimal attention to both the preparation of teachers to work with families and communities (Graue, 2005), and to community field experiences as a source for teacher candidate (TC) learning (Cochran-Smith & Villegas, 2017).

This lack of attention to communities and community field experiences in teacher education has been the case in both early entry and college recommending programs as well as in many of the new hybrid teacher residency programs

(Zeichner, 2014). In the highly visible and widely discussed 2010 report of the Blue Ribbon Panel of the National Council for Accreditation of Teacher Education (NCATE), "Transforming Teacher Education Through Clinical Practice" (NCATE, 2010), no substantive attention is given to the role of clinical experiences in local communities. Despite the lack of emphasis on community-based learning and working with families and communities in teacher preparation programs, there have been a number of isolated and often temporary efforts to address these issues in teacher preparation programs in the US.

This chapter analyzes a programmatic effort in teacher education to engage members of a local community as mentors of TCs in a large research university in the Pacific Northwest, and to examine the impact of this work on the perspectives and practices of the TCs. Although the issue of accessing community-based knowledge in the preparation of teachers applies to all education settings, our focus here is on preparing TCs in a predominately white university to teach in schools serving non-dominant families and communities highly impacted by poverty.

What follows is an argument in three parts. The first part organizes previous teacher–family–community efforts within teacher education into a three-tiered typology: involvement, engagement, and solidarity. We do this to parse the rhetoric in education around "community" (Philip, Way, Garcia, Schuler-Brown, & Navarro, 2013) and distinguish the epistemological groundings, the educational purposes, and the implementation requirements of each approach.

The second part examines Mountain City University's (MCU's) "Community Teaching Strand" (CTS),[1] a curriculum co-constructed by teacher educators and members of a multicultural, education-focused, community-based organization (CBO). Using individual and focus group interview data with elementary and secondary TCs, cooperating teachers (CTs), and university coaches, as well as survey data from elementary and secondary TCs, we argue that the CTS is a case of attempting to move a teacher education program toward engagement and solidarity approaches to teacher–family–community relationships built on mutual benefit and trust. Although our data revealed a positive impact on TC learning and their actions within classrooms, extending in the few cases examined into the first year of teaching, the final part of the chapter discusses some of the programmatic tensions that arose from the CTS and the features of the work that supported and obstructed TC learning. We conclude the chapter by discussing some of the implications of this work for teacher education programs.

Teacher–Family–Community Relations in Teacher Education

The idea that teachers should interact with families and in neighborhoods and communities has a long history in modern American education. The movement to create "schools as social centers" during the Progressive Era recognized "the necessity of getting better teamwork between the school and the home" (Perry,

1916, p. 47). Historical case studies have depicted a range of different rationales for developing this "teamwork" over the course of the twentieth century: from paternalistic and racist attempts to sanction and correct parental child-rearing strategies (e.g., Reese, 1986) to truly collaborative attempts to build humane educative spaces, especially by non-dominant groups within the segregated schools and society of the Jim Crow South, North, and West (e.g., Donato, 2007; Walker, 1996). As Epstein and Sanders (2000) contend, since the 1960s, federal educational policies and programs such as Head Start and Title I have "legislated the involvement of low-income parents" (p. 285) in their children's education.

Over the past two decades, educational researchers and policy makers have attempted to organize and formalize local teacher–family–community practices into frameworks, standards, and professional development curriculum that promote interaction and partnership as a means of increasing academic achievement, especially in Title I schools (see Epstein & Sanders, 2000; Ferguson, 2009).

Teacher education programs, too, have adopted an understanding that teacher–family–community relationships are important to teaching, albeit in fits and starts and to varying degrees (see Boyle-Baise & McIntyre, 2008; Broussard, 2000; Epstein & Sanders, 2006; Zeichner & Melnick, 1996; Zygmunt & Clark, 2016). Building on and extending earlier work that distinguishes community and family involvement from engagement (e.g., Calabrese Barton, Drake, Perez, St. Louis, & George, 2004), we propose a typology for understanding the myriad approaches to teacher–family–community relationships in both K–12 schools and in teacher education. Our typology consists of three approaches that we name as follows: teacher–family–community *involvement*, teacher–family–community *engagement*, and teacher–family–community *solidarity*.

Rather than seeing these approaches as static and totalizing, we understand that schools, districts, and teacher education programs can move between approaches. However, as we discuss below, significant epistemological, pedagogical, and political differences exist between the three approaches. We argue that these differences are intrinsically linked to conceptions about the causes of educational inequity and how teacher–family–community relationships might address them. These differences can—and did, in our program—result in misunderstandings, miscommunications, and tensions related to (a) the goals of teacher–family–community relationships, (b) the people invited to participate, and (c) the terms of participation.

Teacher–Family–Community Involvement

When many educators think of teacher–family–community interaction, they think about activities that we identify as belonging to the involvement approach: family curriculum nights, Parent Teacher Association (PTA) meetings, family–teacher conferences, student homework assignments that include family–home connections, and, increasingly, events that include community service providers such as local CBOs and social service agencies. These involvement activities create opportunities for school staff to share their knowledge and expertise with families and community providers about school expectations, specific school curriculum, ways to support children's learning outside of school, effective communication with teachers, and ways that families and CBOs can support teachers and the school as a whole.

Many school districts around the country have adopted Epstein's (2002) Six Types of Involvement framework, which details practices related to parenting, communicating, volunteering, learning at home, decision making, and collaborating with the community. The ultimate goal of this approach is to increase academic performance. In Evans's (2013) review of the empirically based literature in teacher education, he argued that if the subject of teacher–family–community interaction is addressed in teacher education programs, the involvement approach remains the most common.

This kind of coursework reflects a particular tendency to understand teacher–family–community interaction as a technical matter that can be enhanced through skill development. Yet, at its core, it is an important acknowledgment that families and out-of-school-time providers are important to the educational development and outcomes of students. It recognizes that increased teacher–family–community communication is important and attempts to create and maintain school-based policies that encourage communication and collaboration. Schools and teacher education programs that adopt this approach are trying to develop teachers who have the disposition and skills to talk with families and providers, although most of the talk is often done by the teachers and is limited to curriculum or student academic progress.

The literature in teacher education cautions that when family–community activities in field placements are unmediated or lightly mediated, they are often "superficial" (Baumgartner & Buchanan, 2010), and sometimes have negative effects, including the reinforcement or production of stereotypes about race, culture, families, neighborhoods, and communities (McDiarmid, 1992).

Although the involvement approach predominates, Evans's (2013) review also suggests "a slight shift" and "a new emphasis on relationship building [that] is slowly starting to replace more technical approaches" (p. 125). This is what we refer to as the engagement approach.

Teacher–Family–Community Engagement

The engagement approach attempts to "flip the script" from the involvement paradigm. Instead of teachers and school staff as the knowledgeable participants, this approach stresses the knowledge that families, CBO staff, and community mentors can impart to teachers. The goal of this approach is to create opportunities where teachers can develop an understanding of students', families', and communities' "funds of knowledge" (Gonzalez, Moll, & Amanti, 2005) to help them better serve and see their students. In K–12 schools, the engagement approach can take various forms, including home visits (Schlessman, 2012), neighborhood walks led by families and community leaders (Henderson & Whipple, 2013), and "listening sessions" where teachers and administrators listen to stories from families and students about desired educational environments.

This approach has found its way into teacher education programs through curricular and experiential inclusions in multicultural education and social foundations coursework and in TC placement in non-school community settings (e.g., Boyle-Baise, 2005; Buck & Sylvester, 2005; McDonald, Bowman, & Brayko, 2013). In an early article on this kind of work in teacher education, Haberman and Delgadillo (1993) coined the term "interprofessionals" to describe the development of TCs "who look beyond what happens in the classroom to what happens in the child's school, family, and community which can make an impact on improved teaching and learning practices" (p. 2).

Subsequent reviews in the teacher education literature (Boyle-Baise & McIntyre, 2008; Sleeter, 2001; Zeichner & Melnick, 1996) echo the potential in such an approach. Coursework and community experiences grounded in the teacher–family–community engagement approach can increase awareness of personal prejudices; increase knowledge of, and attention to, cultural diversity and within-group diversity (McDonald et al., 2011); can encourage teachers to approach communities as learners (Buck & Sylvester, 2005; Mahan, Fortney, & Garcia, 1983); can disconfirm stereotypes (Sleeter, 2001); can foster confidence about making community connections (Boyle-Baise, 2005); and, on some occasions, can be used to improve instruction (Evans, 2013). However, Sleeter (2001) notes that the engagement approach in teacher education takes significantly more time and attention and, therefore, runs the risk of being undermediated, which can reinforce stereotypes and cause candidates to sour on the idea of family and community engagement in their future practice. In addition, our research on community mentors suggests that this approach requires families and community participants to do the majority of the work: work that is often un(der)compensated and mentally and spiritually exhausting (Guillen, 2016).

Teacher–Family–Community Solidarity

Underlying the solidarity approach is an understanding that educational inequalities (e.g., opportunity and/or achievement gaps) are part and parcel of broad, deep, and racialized structural inequalities in housing, health, employment, and intergenerational transfers of wealth. Over the past two decades, community organizing efforts that foreground educational concerns have received renewed attention in the literature. Some of this work has focused on the participation of families and community activists in high-profile experiments in community- and site-based control within large urban school districts such as Chicago (e.g., Bryk & Schneider, 2002; Hong, 2011), New York (e.g., Fabricant, 2010), and

Philadelphia (e.g., Fine, 1993). Other work has presented individual empirical cases from across the country that show how families, community activists, teachers, and teachers unions have joined forces to create "bottom up" educational and social reform proposals in the midst of a market-oriented and "top down" policy environment (e.g., Warren & Mapp, 2011).

However, there exist few scholarly articles on this kind of approach to teacher–family–community interaction within the teacher education literature. Hyland and Meacham's (2004) work on Community-Knowledge-Centered (CKC) teacher education programs makes the case for basing programs "on the assumption that colleges of education have an ethical responsibility to systematically work towards educational justice and take a lead in this effort" (p. 124). They rightly identify the CKC approach to be "explicitly political" and urge teacher education to "model for students and teachers how to organize collectively to incorporate subjugated knowledge and marginalized community perspectives in their own practice" (p. 124). This work mirrors the more general effort to encourage schools to incorporate the lived experiences, untapped insights, and knowledge of non-dominant parents and families in public schools (Baquedano-López, Alexander, & Hernandez, 2013; Barajas-Lopez & Ishimaru, 2016; Tatto et al., 2001).

Although small, the "Grow Your Own" (GYO) teachers' initiative in Chicago discussed by Hong (2011) is a promising example of teacher preparation programs grounded in the organizing/solidarity approach. Created as a partnership between a community/neighborhood organization in a low-income neighborhood and local universities, this GYO initiative seeks to recruit, prepare, and support the development of bilingual teachers and teachers of color who have deep connections with these communities, families, and schools. There are few other examples of teacher education programs that have developed coursework or experiences that explicitly link "social justice teaching" to broader and deeper community organizing efforts or social movements.

In sum, the literature on approaches to teacher–family–community relationships in both K–12 education and teacher education provides the field with a number of possibilities for including family and community members' voices and perspectives in their work. We argue that in each of the three approaches there are differences in who is considered "appropriate" for inclusion and under what terms. Under an involvement approach, we might imagine a group of mothers attending a class session in teacher education to role-play parent–teacher conferences or an assignment that asks TCs to assess their own partner school's practices using Epstein's involvement framework. These very well could be beneficial practices, but they are invitations to work on teacher–family relationships from a school-centric frame.

Under an engagement approach, we might imagine family or community members coming into teacher education programs to share their knowledge about, and experiences with, teachers and schools, and/or TCs going into their partner school's neighborhood to do asset mapping and interviews with residents. In these cases, families and community mentors are viewed as having valuable knowledge to share, and TCs are tasked with developing the dispositions and skills to find and "tap into" that knowledge.

Under a solidarity approach, we might imagine sustained engagement, wherein family and community members become mentors to, and co-collaborators with, both teacher educators and TCs for the purposes of transforming the curriculum and learning environment in both teacher education and K–12 schools. In such a case, parts of the teacher education program curriculum open up for negotiation and joint work; teacher educators and family/community mentors together struggle over pedagogical, content, and assessment issues related to their work.

Below, we examine an attempt at one university to move the teacher–family–community curriculum in its teacher education program toward engagement and solidarity approaches.

The Setting

MCU's elementary teacher education program (ELTEP) and secondary teacher education program (STEP) are cohort-based four-quarter graduate programs that offer a master's degree in teaching. The university is located in a city with a population of about 650,000. In the spring of 2012, both programs faced a curricular decision. For a number of years prior, both ELTEP and STEP TCs were placed in CBOs as sites for teaching learning. Although research on these efforts suggested that there was some benefit in the CBO placements for elementary TCs, it was understood by TCs, faculty, and mentor teachers to have limited relevance to TCs once they moved into the classroom for student teaching and the project was ended (McDonald et al., 2011). The question in the spring of 2012 became, how could ELTEP and STEP continue to acknowledge the importance of learning about local communities and building relationships with families and community educators while also deepening and extending the relevance of this work?

The CTS began as a proposal by the then teacher education director as a response to this question. Over the first year, the CTS developed into a variety of scaffolded actions TCs could take in their clinical placements to get to know students, families, and neighborhoods. Over the second year, STEP and then ELTEP connected with the Family Community Mentor Network (FCMN)—a multicultural, education-focused, CBO—to co-plan CTS curriculum and coursework with faculty and instructors. This connection with FCMN was an explicit attempt, according to programmatic materials, to give those who have the most at stake in the effects of teacher preparation—and in public education in general—a substantial say in its operation (Guillen, 2016). This was an initial move toward deeper engagement and solidarity with local community members in the preparation of teachers.

As an umbrella organization, FCMN serves as a vehicle for Mountain City's youth, families, and community members to share their knowledge, concerns, and proposals with local community organizations, individual schools, and entire districts. The two leaders of FCMN identify their work as advocating for individuals and groups within particular educational settings as well as helping to build a more comprehensive education justice movement. Through their work, they have consistently challenged local schools and districts by asking the question, whose voice matters when it comes to educating our children? (Guillen, 2016). The two FCMN leaders, who were the co-planners of the work described here, describe what they do "as connecting the grassroots to the grass tops" (Guillen, 2016). FCMN's work with MCU's teacher education programs was its first sustained effort at "connecting the grassroots" to university-based teacher education.

With FCMN's leadership, more than 70 community mentors worked with TCs in 2013–2014 in a variety of settings and formats. From the perspective of the faculty and instructors involved in the CTS and the leaders of the FCMN, the goal of their joint work was to develop, through numerous "touches" (as the community mentors often called interactions), opportunities for TCs to see family members and community elders as having deep knowledge about children, communities, and education, and that this knowledge was vital for building equity-oriented classrooms and schools.

The CTS: An Approach to Teacher–Family–Community Relations

The faculty/instructors of the CTS and the leaders of the FCMN grounded their joint work in two concepts. First, Murrell's (2001) concept of the community teacher pointed toward the importance of identity work in teacher education:

> Community teachers draw on richly contextualized knowledge of culture, community, and identity in their professional work with children and families in diverse urban communities. … Community teachers have a clear sense of their own cultural, political, and racial identities in relation to the children and families they hope to serve. This sense allows them to play a central role in the successful development and education of their students.
>
> *(p. 4)*

Second, Cochran-Smith's notion of "learning to teach against the grain" located teacher identity work and the act of teaching in broader contexts of educational and social change.

> Prospective teachers need to know from the start that they are a part of a larger struggle and that they have a responsibility to reform, not just replicate, standard school practices. … Teaching against the grain stems from, but also

generates, critical perspectives on the macro-level relationships of power, labor, and ideology-relationships that are perhaps best examined at the university, where sustained and systematic study is possible. But teaching against the grain is also deeply embedded in the culture and history of teaching at individual schools and in the biographies of particular teachers and their individual or collaborative efforts to alter curricula, raise questions about common practices, and resist inappropriate decisions.

(Cochran-Smith, 1991, p. 280)

These foundational concepts appeared in programmatic materials (e.g., course descriptions, syllabi) and often structured decisions about the readings/materials assigned to TCs, the kinds of interactions between TCs and community mentors, and the forms of assessment within the CTS. In addition, these concepts informed the essential questions for the CTS work, which were presented to TCs at the beginning of the academic year:

1. What is a community teacher and why would I want to be one?
2. How can I develop a clear sense of my own cultural, political, and racial identities in relation to the children and families I hope to serve?
3. How do I build alliances and take part in this work to help me understand, engage, and respond to students and their communities?
4. How can I sustain myself, and the practices that are part of being a community teacher, during this program and in my own practice?

Although the CTS contained a number of curricular and experiential elements, for the purpose of this article we focus on TC learning and programmatic tensions related to the three most prominent ways that TCs and FCMN community mentors interacted within the CTS: panel presentations and debriefs, geographically based small group conversations, and field-based seminar course content and connections.

Panel Presentations and Debriefs

FCMN preferred panels for particular topics; they felt it was a good way to introduce a topic as a first "touch." FCMN advanced several topics for panels and then planned the panels with university teacher educators. The panels included "FCMN Family Panel: Hopes and Dreams," "Mountain City Civil Rights and Education Panel," "Teaching Against the Grain," "The School to Prison Pipeline, Prisoners' Perspectives Panel," and a screening and discussion of the PBS documentary "American Promise." Typically hosted off campus, with both secondary and elementary TCs required to attend, panels sought to connect FCMN community mentors to certain scholarly texts assigned in the social foundations course and the field-seminar.

Either immediately following the panel or in the subsequent seminar class session, TCs were given opportunities to discuss the issues raised in the panel and to make sense of what they were learning and observing. These discussions were mediated by one or two of the FCMN leaders, one or more FCMN community mentors, and CTS faculty/instructors.

Geographically Based Small Group Conversations

Because Mountain City's teacher education program places TCs in schools throughout the city and in several nearby districts, and because CTS faculty/ instructors recognize that teacher–family–community relationships differ depending on context, FCMN leaders organized small group discussions around issues of concern to candidates for each of the four school placement regions. They sought to create opportunities for TCs to engage in conversations about their teaching and teacher–family–community relationships with families who lived in that geographic region, but logistically this was not always possible.

One-Credit Field-Seminar Course and Course Connections

In both the elementary and secondary programs, a one-credit field-seminar course was the most consistent space for the CTS-FCMN work. In the elementary program, the field-seminar course met weekly in the summer and fall and operated under a reduced schedule in winter and spring. In the secondary program, the seminar met weekly in the spring and fall quarters, with only a few meetings during the winter quarter. The instructors of the field-seminar and the leaders of the FCMN also tried to make curricular connections with other courses.

For example, in ELTEP, the summer social foundations course had a "place-conscious" orientation, meaning that a number of course texts and course experiences focused on the social, historical, and educational geographies of the Mountain City area (Bowman & Gottesman, 2013). As such, and in connection with the CTS, the local indigenous tribe hosted a session with texts and cultural teachings by tribal members. Also, when the entire ELTEP cohort participated in a 3-week summer program at a local elementary school, families from the neighborhood took TCs on a neighborhood walk, introducing them to residents and people employed in the community and pointing out assets such as the community center, the library, and the community garden.

Also in ELTEP, the "Culturally and Linguistically Responsive Teaching" and the "Classroom Management" courses each included a class session that FCMN helped to organize: "Talking About Race and Difference With Children" and "Race, Discipline and Equity in the Classroom: Community Perspectives." In addition, the "Differentiated Instruction" course hosted a family panel organized by FCMN that involved multicultural family members talking with TCs about learning disabilities and instructional accommodations. In the "Teaching and

Learning" course, four mothers who identify as Latinas and biracial from a partner elementary school talked with the TCs about their experiences as parents in schools generally and in parent-teacher conferences specifically. This course also devoted a session and a course assignment to parent-teacher conferences, along with the connections to the CTS Strand readings and class discussions.

In STEP, the field-seminar instructor organized field trips to local sites that are historically, politically, and educationally significant as sites of community, identity, resistance, and (re)building for non-dominant groups in the area. For example, one of these visits in 2013–2014 was to El Centro de la Raza, a CBO that advocates for the Latino community in the region.

Taken together, the CTS-FCMN work significantly expanded—and we will argue deepened—Mountain City programs' curriculum and commitment related to teacher–family–community relationships. Using the three-category typology discussed above, we argue that many TCs viewed these panels and debriefs, small group conversations, and coursework as promoting, at various points, engagement and solidarity approaches to teacher–family–community relationships. This work also caused tensions within the programs (e.g., Napolitan, 2016), as some TCs and teacher educators questioned the qualifications, purpose, and extent of FCMN's participation in teacher preparation.

Research Methods and Research Questions

Our study focused on the 2013–2014 elementary and secondary teaching cohorts. During this year, there were 65 TCs in ELTEP and 64 in STEP. We employed qualitative methods of interviews, focus groups, observations, document reviews (e.g., program documents, TC inquiry projects), and surveys of the entire cohorts several times during the year. Data included in this article are from individual interviews with 12 case study teachers in May and June 2014, 5 in ELTEP and 7 in STEP, and from 7 focus groups conducted throughout 2013–2014 with volunteers from the ELTEP and STEP cohorts that included a mixture of 16 case study and non-case study teachers (https://education.uw.edu/zeichnerprotocols-jte). Some of these 16 participants were involved in more than one focus group. The case study teachers were selected from among those in both programs who appeared early on to be taking up the ideas surrounding community teaching and represent the range of race/ethnicity and gender existing in the programs.[2]

We also briefly refer to data from surveys (https://education.uw.edu/zeichner-surveys-jte) completed by TCs in the two cohorts during and at the end of their program. These six surveys (four in ELTEP and two in STEP) asked TCs to comment on particular aspects of their experience during the year including the CTS, and to provide specific examples of their connections with families and communities. The response rates for these surveys ranged from 53 to 98 percent.

Finally, we conducted interviews with four of the ELTEP case study TCs and three of the seven STEP case study TCs in January 2015 during their first year of teaching to gain a beginning understanding of to what extent, and how, these graduates were utilizing the CTS work in their new schools.

Three primary research questions are explored in this research:

- *Research question 1*: What do TCs learn through their participation in the CTS?
- *Research question 2*: To what extent and how do TCs bring community teaching into their classrooms during the program and as first-year teachers?
- *Research question 3*: What programmatic features encouraged and/or constrained TC learning from the community mentors?

Data Analysis

Our research team consisted of a senior faculty member—who also served as the teacher education program director at the beginning of the CTS work—and three advanced graduate students who served as instructors in various courses of the teacher education programs, including the field-seminar course.

The research team transcribed and coded the individual and focus group interviews and met together on a regular basis during 2013–2014 to discuss the data that were collected. We first analyzed the interviews in relation to each of the three research questions using open coding and then looked for specific patterns within data for each question that led to a second round of analysis focused on the types of claims we could make from this information. We checked our claims and addressed rival explanations by examining other sources such as surveys and course-related "exit tickets" and interviews with university coaches, community mentors, and CTs that provided additional feedback on all TCs. The findings reported below represent the central themes that emerged related to TC learning and the features of the program that supported and obstructed that learning.

Findings Related to TC Learning

Repositioning Families: From Barriers to Resources

Across interviews, TCs reported a shift in their understandings about the role of families in the education of children and youth, the responsibility of teachers to communicate with families, and the possibilities of collaboration with families. We identify this learning outcome as "repositioning families."

Consistent with Waller's (1932) assertion, and based on either their own experiences or what they heard from others, several case study and focus group interviewees came into the teacher education program with the belief that parents and teachers were "natural enemies." This belief shifted as a direct result of the CTS work, especially the structured interactions with FCMN mentors.

> [Families] are such an important and valuable resource. ... They're totally not barriers. They have a right to let me know what their *hopes and dreams* are for their children and what I can do to guide them. My perspective on the role of parents and families has completely shifted due to the CTS work.
>
> *(Nancy, May 20, 2014)*[3]

Importantly, in this interview, conducted near the end of the program, the TC used the very language at the heart of the first FCMN panel of the year: that parents and families have "hopes and dreams" for their children that teachers need to know. This candidate added emphasis to her statement by arguing that such a discussion of "hopes and dreams" was not merely a good idea, but it was a fundamental *right* that families should have in contemporary schools.

The "FCMN Family Panel: Hopes and Dreams" encouraged TCs to consider relationships with families and students as a necessary dimension of equitable instruction.

> It was explicitly said that you can't effectively teach all of the kids in your class if you're not reaching out to parents, or trying to find out what they do outside of school or the different ways that they learn. Because if you teach one style, what you've been raised with, you're giving preference to a certain group of kids who are going to be able to succeed, who already have what they need to succeed, and you're just choosing not to see or meet the needs of a large group of your kids. That's something that I don't think that we would have been able to understand if we didn't have a family panel first thing. I came to education with an idea of why I wanted to be a teacher, but then experienced a really powerful paradigm shift to hear what parents want for their kids.
>
> *(Rainee, May 18, 2014)*

We might understand this TC's "paradigm shift" as the realization that her "apprenticeship of observation" (Lortie, 1975) as a successful student would not necessarily translate into successful teaching. Instead of replicating the "style" of her favorite teachers or imitating the practices that were successful with her as a student, this candidate credits the initial family panel with teaching her that "effective" and equitable teaching is reliant upon relationships with parents as well as interest in children's lives outside of the classroom.

The initial family panel, the geographically based conversations with FCMN mentors, and the FCMN-organized session titled "Talking About Race and Difference With Children" placed the practice of teacher–family communication in a socio-historical context marked by ethno-racial and social class distrust. That is, FCMN mentors were often explicit in arguing that teachers and families had developed into "natural enemies" because of ethno-racial and class differences. On several occasions throughout the year, FCMN mentors of color discussed their own negative experience with white teachers in hopes that these experiences would help TCs understand potential distrust as well as encourage them to build trust through conversations about their child. One TC reflected on what she learned:

> That was really eye opening in thinking about how to talk to parents about their child's education and how important it is to be really positive and approachable for parents so that even if they didn't have a good school experience you get to change that for their child.
>
> *(Lisa, May 19, 2014)*

Importantly, FCMN mentors and CTS instructors discussed teacher–family communication as something that is most effective when it is frequent and its content varied. In addition to the FCMN family panels and small group discussions, the CTS included several trainings on "positive phone calls home" and "family visits"—a less intimidating form of a "home visit" where a teacher and parent/guardian meet at a mutually agreeable location. Adamant that teacher–family relationship and trust building could not occur if communication begins only after a negative event or only at a parent–teacher conference, TCs were encouraged to repeat the mantra, "My first communication with families should always be positive." Several TCs noted this approach as one of their key points of learning:

> The most important thing that I've taken from the strand is interacting with parents frequently in a positive way and having them be involved in their kids' learning. Just like starting with positive emails or phone calls home and opening that into "Hey would you like to come into the classroom to observe or to help, or to be a part of a lesson, or to teach us something or read a book aloud," and just continuing that the whole year. I think this has really stood out to me.
>
> *(Aditi, May 19, 2014)*

One candidate summarized what she learned through the CTS about teacher–family communication this way: "It really never crossed my mind that it should be a part of what a good teacher does" (Lisa, May 19, 2014). The repositioning of the family from a barrier to a resource also impacted how TCs viewed their own role as teachers. For example, some began to express a view of teachers as a part of a larger constellation of effort in their students' lives to help them learn and develop.

> I'm now thinking of the role of teacher as something less than an expert. There's so much wisdom coming from other places in my students' lives that I'm really, their secondary or tertiary educator. My role is not to transmit my

knowledge and expertise, but to help develop them in tandem with all of the other parts of their lives. I'm not the sole steward of their learning.

(Padma, May 18, 2014)

As opposed to much of the popular educational discourse, Mountain City TCs articulated a vision of both families and broader communities as positive influences on student achievement and as holding "wisdom" that should be recognized and understood. For some, this acknowledgment that teachers are "not the sole steward" of students' learning meant that teaching, parenting, and caring for young people did not have to be an isolating practice. Padma continued,

It gives power to the students and the families in the community, but I also feel empowered as a teacher ... to have all these other ways to try and navigate and try to find a solution ... it opens up so many doors and just stops that feeling of helplessness.

(Padma, May 18, 2014)

For another TC, seeing families as resources and as potential sources of empowerment required an examination of her own experiences and ways of interpreting the actions of others. As a white TC who admitted to having little cross-cultural knowledge and experience, the small group conversations with FCMN mentors allowed her the opportunity to ask questions and at least begin "walking the road" of community teaching (Cochran-Smith, 2004).

[The CTS] got me really thinking about the way I see other people and how I view myself in relation to them. I think it has been a big takeaway for me in my life, not just in teaching. ... Not making assumptions of people based on the way they act and really taking the time to get to know and understand why they do the things they do has been a big change for me in my life. ... I think the chance to ask the open and honest questions that I've never had the opportunity to ask and get honest answers from people who don't view it in a bad way. That was a big change for me I think as a person. ... It influenced my practice and I'm more open to families. I think getting to understand the reason for things, not just assuming. I would say that it has been more beneficial for me as a person because I was never exposed to institutional racism as a kid. I always had the opportunities and I never realized that there's people who didn't have the same opportunities as me.

(Tessa, June 2, 2014)

Translating Knowledge into Action

Data collected from analysis of TC coursework products, interviews, and surveys, both during the year of the program and in case study teachers' first year of teaching, indicate that some TCs translated their repositioning of families and their repositioning of their own vision of teaching into actions in their classroom and/or in their school. Some of the TC actions were driven by assignments and requirements in the program—such as the requirement that they conduct an action-oriented inquiry project on a CTS-related issue or by a particular course.

For example, the end of the program survey of elementary TCs indicated a range of actions taken by TCs during the program because of course assignments or the inquiry project: making family visits, observing students in their after-school programs, attending student soccer games after school and on the weekends, surveying parents or students about what they do after school and on the weekends, interviewing parents about their child's strengths, surveying students who had been sent out of classrooms for behavioral reasons, and involving parents in the curriculum or asking them to come into the class to share something they know with the students.

One elementary TC referenced both the FCMN panels and the CTS training on "positive phone calls home" as she discussed the actions she began to take when she assumed greater instructional responsibilities in her school placement classroom.

> The parents in all of the panels have told me that I need to be calling parents and having positive connections with them. I knew that I needed to call and engage with them positively. That was one of the things on the top of my list. It's hard and I'm still scared of doing it, but I found a way to make it something I could do. That involved calling to introduce myself and invite parents to an event in our class, and compliment their kid. That went over really, really, really well. I mean they really liked to hear that. Made even the parents who felt a little standoffish feel a little more comfortable with our class and happy about their kids. That really had an effect on our class. I took a classroom survey before and after our event, which also included calling parents and it changed. I don't know how statistically significant it is, but the bar went up … I think this is really huge.
>
> (Olivia, June 3, 2014)

This TC admitted that calling families was hard and scary for her, but she noted both the immediate and long-term impact of the practice. For her, the positive impact could be found both in families' comfort level with her as a teacher and in their positive view of their child's participation in school. Another TC discussed communication with families as a strategy to improve student performance in the classroom:

> Recently, I had this little girl who hates science, anything that has to do with bugs. I reached out to her mom and said "I can't get her to do this, what do I do?" Mom responded within half an hour. "Do this, this, and

this." I did it and the little girl is looking at worms the next day. How powerful is that to use the voice that knows this kid better than anyone else to help her with her education.

(Miriam, May 18, 2014)

Another TC gave us an example of how her positive reaching out to a family of one of her students immediately resulted in a change in the student's behavior.

One student never turned in homework for the whole year and after I made that positive phone call home, that Monday he turned in his homework and said that his dad was working with him for the weekend. It was really cool. I definitely saw an impact right away.

(Rubi, June 4, 2014)

The First Year of Teaching

The conceptual positioning of families as holders of wisdom and knowledge *as well as* the actual experience of talking, consulting, and collaborating with families during their teacher education program influenced the ways in which our case study candidates began their first year of teaching. Coincidentally, three of the elementary case study participants secured teaching positions at the same elementary school—a high poverty school serving many recent immigrant families and English learners. Partially attracted to the school because of the principal's talk about greater family and community involvement, they quickly realized that they were the only or part of a small minority of teachers who actively worked to connect with their students' families, and learn about their communities and lives outside of school.

Although these teachers described the pressures that they were facing to have highly controlled classrooms, they engaged in a number of activities they used while in the program, such as making positive phone calls to parents and guardians, making family visits in students' homes or in other places in the community, bringing students' cultures into the curriculum, attending to issues of social and emotional learning, and so on. Echoing the finding related to teacher empowerment discussed earlier, these teachers met regularly to support one another and to figure out ways to do the community teacher work they wanted to do without raising concerns among their colleagues. They talked about being pulled in two separate ways (high classroom control vs. community teaching) and about how they regularly justified the community teacher work using the district's inclusive language, its instructional framework, and state standards. Similar to Cochran-Smith's notion of "teaching against the grain," they identified this strategy as working "undercover" to be community teachers and about how easy it would be for them to just comply.

You've really got to finesse it. You've got to know our principal, who is all about data and [the] Danielson [framework] and certain things that work for her. ... It's kind of like we have to infiltrate the system. We have this hidden agenda where we could say we're collaborating because of reading buddies and we're going for Distinguished on Danielson. Really we are trying to push for community and we can do that better if we're working together.

(Rubi, January 16, 2015)

The sheer number of students that high school teachers work with on a daily basis made the task of communicating with their families seem more daunting to some secondary TCs. Yet, even 5 months into her first year of teaching, one STEP graduate discussed how she continued to prioritize teacher–family communication precisely because of her experience in a FCMN panel:

I often think about the parent panel we had during spring quarter last year and how parents were very passionate about wanting to know what was going on with their students and that it is important that the communication is culturally appropriate and that it starts out positively. To me that means making an effort early on to make a connection with parents, with all parents if possible, but most especially with those parents or guardians of those students who might have a harder time meeting academic and behavioral expectations. ... So I try to do phone calls twice a week. I schedule it into my Outlook calendar. I don't always get to it, but I try. ... Overall, I find parent communication to be essential to the success of my work as an educator and to students' academic work.

(Jackie, February 22, 2015)

Although less frequent, the CTS also impacted graduates' curriculum development in their first year of teaching. A white secondary graduate cited the FCMN panel on the school-to-prison pipeline as an influential moment that caused her to think about how she could incorporate contemporary social and political content into her English Language Arts classroom. After graduation from the program, she accepted a position at Mountain City's "least white high school," which had been designated as "persistently low-performing" by the state in 2011, prompting a group of parent, teachers, community members, and district officials to agitate for significant academic reforms, including the introduction of an International Baccalaureate program. In her first weeks in the school, recognizing the frustration and outrage of many of her African-American students in the wake of the August police shooting of Michael Brown and the ongoing conversations about race, (in) justice, and "the New Jim Crow," she planned a new unit with these themes at the center.

The school-to-prison pipeline panel that we did. ... We went to it in the evening...but we talked a lot about race relations and it was so interesting to hear so many community members that went over and talked about how our African-American students are underserved and how a lot of them end up going to jail and that is something we need to teach. ... To see these community things that we talked about reflected in my school ... I did a mini unit, a week-long thing on the Ferguson case. ... Let's analyze what happened, look at the documents, talk about why people are upset, what does all of this mean, kind of the critical analysis aspects of it. ... I asked my kids at the end of the semester what was the most valuable thing that they learned this semester. A ton of them said that unit. They were so glad as a teacher I was willing to talk about these things that they care about and that they talk about and that I was acknowledging that there is a problem of race in our society. ... I feel that if you asked me two years ago if I would ever teach something like that in a language arts class, I'd have been "No, it's not a book. You teach books, right? Yeah." I feel like the CTS classes are particularly to thank.

(Moira, February 5, 2015)

Although outside the scope of this chapter, we recognize the need for additional research on how teacher–family–community relations work within teacher preparation programs influences the kinds of schools that graduates choose to work in, the extent to which they continue to use strategies and content learned in the program, and the ways in which they adapt their community teaching practices to the district or institutional contexts they find themselves in.

In the following section, we link TC learning and actions to some of the programmatic features and tensions that emerged because of the CTS and the joint work with the FCMN. It is this line of analysis that benefited from the earlier distinction between teacher–family–community *involvement, engagement,* and *solidarity.*

Findings Related to Programmatic Features

"All of those Panels" Provided a Space for Emotion in the Room

As noted above, the participation of FCMN mentors in panels, small group conversations, and several courses was an important feature of the CTS to many TCs. Several stated that there is a big difference between reading something or discussing complex and sensitive issues with a professor, and hearing it and discussing it with community mentors. For example, one candidate said, "There's a different conversation that you tend to have with a community member than with a faculty member" (Hannah, February 24, 2015). Another TC spoke to the same issue "I think that using outside people made it resonate stronger, absolutely.

… Seeing how strongly parents really feel about it, made it inspiring" (Aditi, May 19, 2014).

Although a minority of survey participants indicated that they had at times felt attacked or criticized when the mentors talked about experiences with racist or uncaring teachers or placed schools within a historic system of racism and oppression, case study and focus group participants reported that they believed that community mentors genuinely wanted to help them become better teachers because they wanted their children to get a good education in public schools.

> Besides the words that they're saying, there's the emotion in the room. There's more meaning conveyed there than anything that you can read on paper or hear about from someone telling you they heard it.
>
> *(Sachi, May 18, 2014)*

> Their real-life experience, what they or their kids have experienced, is very effective.
>
> *(Nabila, May 18, 2014)*

> I think unfortunately I always had the feeling that they really didn't care about their kids, that they weren't there and maybe they wouldn't come in because they didn't care about their kids, really care. I think that there's been a really big shift in my thinking, just hearing stories from people who are in those positions.
>
> *(Tessa, June 2, 2014)*

Two elements related to programmatic features stood out in our interviews. First, participants mentioned the "emotion in the room" in FCMN panels and conversations, and placed this in contradistinction to much of their experience in coursework and in their student teaching placement. We argue that connecting TCs with this "emotion"—variously described in interviews as "passion," "care," and "personal stories"—is foundational to the work of teacher–family–community relations. We also argue that creating authentic spaces for TCs (as well as practicing teachers and teacher educators) to listen to parents, extended family members, and community mentors can help the former realize just what is at stake in education. This is an especially important argument for us, as we witness a number of school districts and teacher preparation programs around the country experiment with forms of teacher–family–community relations that stress "high-leverage practices" through simulation or role playing rather than participation in authentic and "emotional" conversations about the problems and possibilities of education (e.g., Khasnabis, Goldin, & Ronfeldt, 2015).

Second, case study and focus group participants stressed that repeated contact— "all of those panels"—with FCMN mentors helped them realize the importance of teacher–family–community relations to good teaching. Yet, several TCs also leveled a critique of what they perceived to be a disconnect within MCU's program:

> I feel like they (the meetings with community mentors) were not as frequent as they should have been … you really had to hit it hard during the year instead of just doing it. … It wasn't as often as it should have been.
>
> *(Tiffany, June, 12, 2014)*

> I think that it would have been helpful to see the parents right away from day one and not have it disconnected—being there one day on that first day when you were welcoming the new cohort, then disappearing until a panel or something. Having the constant presence of parents from these panels … just so the student teachers get the impression that they (the parents) should be in the schools too. … If you want us to believe that you should have parents welcome in the school, then they should be welcome in the teacher education program as well.
>
> *(Nabila, March, 19, 2014)*

Of course, detached pockets of attention to particular issues are nothing new in teacher preparation. The literature in the field is replete with curricular divides between foundations and methods (e.g., Grossman, Hammerness, & McDonald, 2009), pitfalls between methods instruction and classroom experience (Feiman-Nemser & Buchmann, 2011), and barriers to integrating culturally relevant and discipline-based teaching and learning (e.g., Hand, 2012; Turner & Drake, 2015). Over the course of our interviews, TCs identified a number of places where the CTS work and experiences could be better integrated with instructional methods coursework and experiences.

Spaces for Curricular Integration: Methods Courses and School Contexts

Consistent with Turner and Drake's (2015) and Dutro and Cartun's (2016) findings that teacher preparation programs often fail to integrate TCs' learning about cultural funds of knowledge and attention to learning practices to teach subjects such as literacy and math, MCU TCs often pointed to missed opportunities for integration of the CTS and field-based methods work. As a result, some TCs felt that they were asked to figure out on their own how to translate what they learned about their students' communities and from the interactions with their families into teaching strategies.

> For the amount of time that we spend in schools, it could have been a lot more focused on [community teaching] methodologies and teaching practices so that we can have them at our disposal and you can apply what

you know about this student and their family and their learning styles and where they come from. ... We are forced to connect those and how they weave together on our own.

(Nadir, June 2, 2014)

Some TCs felt that they had clinical placements where their CTs served as models and reached out to families in positive ways and tried to make them feel welcome in the school as well as used these interactions to learn more about their students.

I think that my CT is really good about working with families. She really makes an effort to reach out to families so I've had a good model ... In the beginning, it was very hard to get to the level she was with the families because I wasn't there much in the beginning. ... I think that it has been a good experience for me to sec the way she keeps in contact with families.

(Tessa, June 2, 2014)

Other TCs stressed either the negative attitudes that they experienced in their placements about strengthening connections to families or the disconnect that they felt between the emphasis on the CTS strand in certain courses and experiences and the lack of knowledge about this alleged program emphasis by CTs.

I always see positive interactions when they are planned and required. Then behind the scenes ... a very begrudging reluctance to communicate with parents. The message I get is that I should be warned that they will ruin everything if I'm not careful.

(Sachi, May 19, 2014)

As we know from decades of research in the field, integration across courses and between programs and placements are perennial issues (e.g., Hammerness, 2006). Importantly, we believe that the integration of the teacher–family–community work is not merely technical or logistical in nature. We argue that the movement toward collaborating with educational organizing groups, families, and community mentors—represented by MCU's initial collaborations with the FCMN— presents teacher preparation programs with a distinct epistemological and political challenge. At its core is the understanding that a more just, humane, and responsive education is possible. Yet, such an education cannot be achieved *only* through the attainment of "ambitious" or "high leverage" teaching practices or *only* through greater exposure to learning theories or socio-historical ways of seeing classrooms and schools. Such an education is only possible when teachers are also prepared through engagement and in solidarity with the hopes, dreams, and visions of the families and communities with whom they work. This requires both TCs and teacher educators to listen, learn, question, and plan in solidarity with local community members.

Conclusion

Preparing teachers to work in respectful ways with, and learn from, their students' families and to learn about the communities in which their students live are important parts of the mission of teacher education programs. The findings of our research into the role of local community members mentoring TCs indicate that the planned and purposeful mentoring of TCs by local community members in a few courses in their program contributed to helping some TCs begin to see that developing relationships with their students' families and learning about their communities can serve as resources to help teachers succeed in educating their students. Our data also show some evidence of student teachers and first-year teachers acting on their newly developed appreciation for the expertise of families and their knowledge of their students' communities even in situations when their actions were not driven by course assignments, and even when this kind of effort was not common in their schools. The mentoring of TCs by local community members appeared to be a critical factor in the development of these perspectives by these novice teachers.

Fundamentally, the CTS work has been one part of an attempt to further shift the center of gravity in teacher education (Cuban, 1969) toward schools and local communities while maintaining the important contribution that can be made by colleges and universities or other program providers (Zeichner, Payne, & Brayko, 2015). Although this work has been complex and filled with tensions, we think that our findings related to TC learning suggest the potential contribution that community-based teacher educators can make to preparing teachers who are committed to working with and for communities instead of on them.

Despite the difficulties that we experienced in this early stage of our work in achieving the engagement and working in solidarity with community members beyond the small groups of university and community-based teacher educators who planned and taught together, we believe that the effort to figure out how to engage local families and communities in the education of the teachers who will teach their children program-wide is an important element of preparing teachers to better serve the needs and aspirations of everyone's children. Continuing to parachute well-intentioned teachers from university and non-university teacher education programs into public schools who know little about their students, their families, and communities, and who are not committed to engaging families and communities in schooling, will continue to widen the opportunity and learning gaps that have persisted. The mission of teacher education is not to try to "save" students from their communities, but to work with and for communities to help build on their strengths and develop greater community capacity.

Although developing more "Grow Your Own" programs (e.g., Skinner, Garreton, & Schultz, 2011) that prepare teachers who live in communities to become teachers in their own communities is an important part of what needs to be done, most teachers are going to continue to teach in communities in which they do not live. Given the demographic profile of teachers and of the students who attend public schools, the big challenge before us is to learn how to better prepare and support teachers who are committed to the families and communities of their students as they go in to teach "other people's children" in communities that are often unfamiliar to their own life experiences. It is ironic that so little of this work goes on in teacher education programs across the US when so many of them have claimed the mantle of social justice as the basis for their work.

The work at MCU has been difficult for all participants for a variety of reasons and on a variety of levels. TCs, as we note above, sometimes found it difficult to translate the CTS work into their own student teaching contexts and sometimes were forced to confront difficult topics about race, racism, privilege, and schooling that they did not always want to examine.

Although family and community mentors worked well with a number of the university teacher educators, on a number of occasions, they felt disrespected by programmatic representatives or TCs, and some found it difficult to learn that many TCs had yet to be exposed to some of the topics and relationships that they valued. Some teacher educators and programmatic representatives appeared to have difficulty seeing the value of community and family participation in the programs and, at times, they criticized the work of the community mentors by, for example, complaining that mentors "just tell stories" or suggesting that they are not pedagogically skilled enough to teach TCs. This tension between professional autonomy and community participation is common in educational reform efforts that have attempted to bring community members and professional educators together as equal partners (Dyrness, 2011). It is important that continuing to figure out ways to engage and work in solidarity with local communities in preparing the teachers of their children becomes a central part of the work in teacher education programs that claim to want to contribute to greater social justice.

Authors' Note

The CTS work and the writing of this paper were carried out in collaboration with our community partners. Dawn Bennett, Jolyn Gardner, and Kerry Cooley-Strom.

Notes

1   All the names of people and organizations are pseudonyms.
2   More detailed analyses of the experiences of some of the individual elementary teacher education program (ELTEP) case study teachers are available in other reports of this research (e.g., Napolitan, 2016b).
3   All the interview quotes in this article are from ELTEP unless otherwise noted.

References

Baquedano-López, P., Alexander, R. A., & Hernandez, S. J. (2013). Equity issues in parental and community involvement in schools: What teacher educators need to know. *Review of Research in Education, 37*, 149–182.

Barajas-Lopez, F., & Ishimaru, A. (2016). Darles el lugar: A place for nondominant family knowing in educational equity. *Urban Education*. Retrieved from http://journals.sagepub.com/doi/abs/10.1177/0042085916652179 on March 31, 2017.

Baumgartner, J., & Buchanan, T. (2010). "I have HUGE stereotypes": Using eco-maps to understand children and families. *Journal of Early Childhood Teacher Education, 31*(2), 173–184.

Bowman, M., & Gottesman, I. (2013). Why practice-centered teacher education programs need social foundations. *Teachers College Record*. Retrieved from www.tcrecord.org

Boyle-Baise, M. (2005). Preparing community-oriented teachers: Reflections from a multicultural service learning project. *Journal of Teacher Education, 56*(5), 446–458.

Boyle-Baise, M., & McIntyre, D. J. (2008). What kind of experience? Preparing teachers in PDS or community settings. In M. Cochran-Smith, S. Feiman-Nemser, & D. J. McIntyre (Eds), *Handbook of research on teacher education* (3rd ed., pp. 307–329). New York, NY: Routledge.

Broussard, C. A. (2000). Preparing teachers to work with families: A national survey of teacher education programs. *Equity & Excellence in Education, 33*(2), 41–49.

Bryk, A. S., & Schneider, B. L. (2002). *Trust in schools: A core resource for improvement.* New York, NY: Russell Sage.

Buck, P., & Sylvester, P. (2005). Preservice teachers enter urban communities: Coupling funds of knowledge research and critical pedagogy in teacher education. In N. Gonzalez, L. Moll, & C. Amanti (Eds), *Funds of knowledge: Theorizing practices in households, communities, and classrooms* (pp. 213–231). Mahwah, NJ: Lawrence Erlbaum.

Calabrese Barton, A., Drake, C., Perez, J. G., St. Louis, K., & George, M. (2004). Ecologies of parental engagement in urban education. *Educational Researcher, 33*(4), 3–8.

Cochran-Smith, M. (1991). Learning to teach against the grain. *Harvard Educational Review, 61*(3), 279–310.

Cochran-Smith, M. (2004). *Walking the road: Race, diversity and social justice in teacher education.* New York, NY: Teachers College Press.

Cochran-Smith, M., & Villegas, A. M. (2017). Research on teacher preparation: Charting the landscape of a sprawling field. In D. Gitomer & C. Bell (Eds), *Handbook of research on teaching* (5th ed., pp. 439–538). Washington, DC: American Educational Research Association.

Comer, J. (2009). *What I learned in school: Reflections on race, child development, and school reform.* San Francisco, CA: Jossey-Bass.

Cuban, L. (1969). Teacher and community. *Harvard Educational Review, 39*(2), 253–272.

Donato, R. (2007). *Mexicans and Hispanos in Colorado schools and communities, 1920–1960.* Albany: State University of New York Press.

Dutro, E., & Cartun, A. (2016). Cut to the core practices: Toward visceral disruptions of binaries in PRACTICE-based teacher education. *Teaching and Teacher Education, 58*, 119–128.

Dyrness, A. (2011). *Mothers united: An immigrant struggle for socially just education.* Minneapolis: University of Minnesota Press.

Epstein, J. L. (2002). *School, family, and community partnerships: Your handbook for action.* Thousand Oaks, CA: Corwin Press.

Epstein, J. L., & Sanders, M. G. (2000). Connecting home, school, and community. In M. T. Hallinan (Ed.), *Handbook of the sociology of education* (pp. 285–286). New York, NY: Springer.

Epstein, J. L., & Sanders, M. G. (2006). Prospects for change: Preparing educators for school, family, and community partnerships. *Peabody Journal of Education, 81*(2), 81–120.

Evans, M. (2013). Educating preservice teachers for family, school, and community engagement. *Teaching Education, 24*(2), 123–133.

Fabricant, M. (2010). *Organizing for educational justice: The campaign for public school reform in the South Bronx.* Minneapolis: University of Minnesota Press.

Feiman-Nemser, S., & Buchmann, M. (2011). Pitfalls of experience in teacher education. In S. Feiman-Nemser (Ed.), *Teachers as learners* (pp. 167–180). Cambridge, MA: Harvard Education Press.

Ferguson, C. (2009). *A Toolkit for Title I Parental involvement.* Austin, TX: The Southwest Educational Development Laboratory.

Fine, M. (1993). [Ap]parent Involvement: Reflections on parents, power, and urban public schools. *Teachers College Record, 94*(4), 682–710.

Flowers, J. G., Patterson, A., Stratemeyer, F., & Lindsey, M. (1948). *School and community laboratory experiences in teacher education.* Oneonta, NY: American Association of Teachers Colleges.

Gonzalez, N., Moll, L., & Amanti, C. (2005). *Funds of knowledge: Theorizing practices in households, communities, and classrooms.* Mahwah, NJ: Lawrence Erlbaum.

Graue, E. (2005). Theorizing and describing preservice teachers' images of families and schooling. *Teachers College Record, 107*(1), 157–185.

Grossman, P., Hammerness, K., & McDonald, M. (2009). Redefining teaching, re-imagining teacher education. *Teachers and Teaching, 15,* 273–289.

Guillen, L. (2016). Partnering with teacher education programs: The community mentor experience (Unpublished doctoral dissertation). University of Washington, Seattle.

Haberman, M., & Delgadillo, L. (1993). *The impact of training teachers of children in poverty about the specific health and human services offered to the students in their classrooms.* Milwaukee: University of Wisconsin-Milwaukee. Retrieved from ERIC database. (ED36775 l).

Hammerness, K. (2006). From coherence in theory to coherence in practice. *Teachers College Record, 108*(1), 1241–1265.

Hand, V. (2012). Seeing culture and power in mathematical learning: Toward a model of equitable instruction. *Educational Studies in Mathematics, 80,* 233–247.

Henderson, A., & Whipple, M. (2013). How to connect with families. *Educational Leadership, 70,* 44–48.

Hodgdon, E., & Saunders, R. (1951). Using the community in teacher education. *Journal of Teacher Education, 2*(3), 216–218.

Hong, S. (2011). *A cord of three strands: A new approach to parent engagement in schools.* Cambridge, MA: Harvard Education Press.

Hyland, N. E., & Meacham, S. (2004). Community knowledge centered teacher education: A paradigm for socially just educational transformation. In J. L. Kincheloe, A. Bursztyn, & S. R. Steinberg (Eds), *Teaching teachers: Building a quality school of urban education* (pp. 113–134). New York, NY: Peter Lang.

Khasnabis, D., Goldin, S., & Ronfeldt, M. (2015, April). Using simulated parent-teacher conferences to assess interns' abilities to partner with families. Paper presented at the American Educational Research Association Annual Meeting, Chicago, IL.

Lortie, D. (1975). *Schoolteacher*. Chicago, IL: University of Chicago Press.

Mahan, J., Fortney, M., & Garcia, J. (1983). Linking the community to teacher education: Toward a more analytical approach. *Action in Teacher Education, 5*(1–2), 1–10.

McDiarmid, G. W. (1992). The arts and sciences as preparation for teaching (Issue Paper No. 92–93). East Lansing: National Center for Research on Teacher Learning, Michigan State University.

McDonald, M. A., Bowman, M., & Brayko, K. (2013). Learning to see students: Opportunities to develop relational practices of teaching through community-based placements in teacher education. *Teachers College Record, 115*(4), 1–35.

McDonald, M. A., Tyson, K., Brayko, K., Bowman, M., Delport, J., & Shimomura, F. (2011). Innovation and impact in teacher education: Community-based organizations as field placements for preservice teachers. *Teachers College Record, 113*(8), 1668–1700.

Murrell, P. C., Jr. (2001). *The community teacher: A new framework for effective urban teaching.* New York, NY: Teachers College Press.

Murrell, P. C., Jr., Strauss, J., Carlson, R., & Dominguez, M. (2015). Community immersion teacher development: Pragmatic knowledge of family and community in professional field-based practice. In E. Hollins (Ed.), *Rethinking field experiences in preservice teacher education* (pp. 151–166). New York, NY: Routledge.

Napolitan, K. (2016a). Showing the seams: Teacher candidates' experiences with programmatic tensions in community-focused teacher education (Unpublished doctoral dissertation, Part 2). University of Washington, Seattle.

Napolitan, K. (2016b). You have to reach before you can teach: A study of teacher candidates' journeys of community teaching (Unpublished doctoral dissertation, Part I). University of Washington, Seattle.

National Council for Accreditation of Teacher Education. (2010). *Transforming teacher education through clinical practice: A national strategy to prepare effective teachers.* Washington, DC: Author.

Perry, C. A. (1916). *Educational extension.* Cleveland, OH: Survey Committee of the Cleveland Foundation.

Philip, T., Way, W., Garcia, A., Schuler-Brown, S., & Navarro, O. (2013). When educators attempt to make community a part of classroom learning: The dangers of (mis)appropriating students' communities into schools. *Teaching and Teacher Education, 34*, 174–183.

Reese, W. J. (1986). *Power and the promise of school reform: Grassroots movements during the Progressive era.* Boston, MA: Routledge & Kegan Paul.

Schlessman, E. (2012). When are you coming to visit? Home visits and seeing our students. *Rethinking Schools, 27*(2). Retrieved from www.rethinkingschools.org/archive/27 02/27 02 schlessman.shtml

Skinner, E., Garreton, M. T., & Schultz, B. (Eds). (2011). *Grow your own teachers: Grassroots change for teacher education.* New York, NY: Teachers College Press.

Sleeter, C. E. (2001). Preparing teachers for culturally diverse schools: Research and the overwhelming presence of whiteness. *Journal of Teacher Education, 52*(2), 94–106.

Tatto, M. T., Rodriguez, A., Gonzalez-Lanz, D., Miller, C., Busscher, M., Trumble, D., … Woo, A. (2001). The challenges and tensions in reconstructing teacher-parent relations in the context of school reform: A case study. *Teachers and Teaching, 7,* 315–333.

Turner, E., & Drake, C. (2015). A review of research on prospective teachers' learning about children's mathematical thinking and cultural funds of knowledge. *Journal of Teacher Education, 67,* 32–46.

Walker, V. S. (1996). *Their highest potential: An African American school community in the segregated South.* Chapel Hill: University of North Carolina Press.

Waller, W. (1932). *The sociology of teaching.* New York, NY: Wiley.

Warren, M. R., & Mapp, K. L. (2011). *A match on dry grass: Community organizing as a catalyst for school reform.* New York, NY: Oxford University Press.

Zeichner, K. (2014). The politics of learning to teach from experience. In V. Ellis & J. Orchard (Eds), *Learning to teach from experience* (pp. 257–268). London: Bloomsbury.

Zeichner, K., & Melnick, S. (1996). The role of community field experiences in preparing teachers for cultural diversity. In K. Zeichner, S. Melnick, & M. L. Gomez (Eds), *Currents of reform in preservice teacher education* (pp. 176–196). New York, NY: Teachers College Press.

Zeichner, K., Payne, K. A., & Brayko, K. (2015). Democratizing teacher education. *Journal of Teacher Education, 66*(2), 122–135.

Zygmunt, E., & Clark, P. (2016). *Transforming teacher education for social justice.* New York, NY: Teachers College Press.

9

DEVELOPING PROFESSIONAL CAPITAL IN TEACHING THROUGH INITIAL TEACHER EDUCATION

Comparing Strategies in Alberta, Canada and the US

Kenneth M. Zeichner and Jesslyn Hollar

In this chapter, we contrast the approaches to improving teacher quality through initial teacher education (ITE) in the Canadian province of Alberta, a consistently high-performing system on international comparisons, to the approach taken in the US,[1] which has consistently fared less well than the average country in these comparisons. The difference in the policies and practices in these two education systems with regard to ITE's contribution to improving teacher quality can be understood by drawing from Hargreaves and Fullan's (2012, 2013) contrast between education systems that invest in building business capital and those that focus on building professional capital.

In systems that emphasize the development of business capital, the focus is on greater deregulation and market competition as the way to achieve high teacher quality. For example, there has been a growth in some countries like England and the US (e.g., Furlong, Cochran-Smith, & Brennan, 2009) in alternative fast-track preparation programs where teachers complete most of their preparation on the job as teachers of record. In many of these programs, teaching is viewed as the implementation of a series of discrete techniques, and there is little concern with developing teachers' adaptive expertise and careers in teaching (Zeichner, 2014). Bringing academically talented individuals into teaching is seen as desirable even when they do not stay long and contribute to teacher attrition rates, particularly in schools serving low-income and minority communities (Phillips, 2015; Zeichner & Hutchinson, 2008).

Despite research that indicates that the increased reliance on young underprepared teachers who only stay for a few years in schools in communities highly impacted by poverty has undermined the quality of learning for students (Ronfeldt, Loeb, & Wyckoff, 2013) and has cost school districts millions of dollars for replacing teachers who only stay for a few years (National Council on Teaching and America's Future, 2007), in a business capital approach, an inexperienced, itinerant teaching staff is desirable because labor costs are reduced in the short run, and there is a steady supply of individuals to enroll in entrepreneur-developed alternative teacher training programs.

In contrast, in education systems that focus on the development of professional capital, teacher candidates complete an ITE program prior to independent practice in a classroom. In these systems, colleges and/or universities play a central role in ITE (Moon, 2016). For Hargreaves and Fullan (2012) professional capital consists of three elements: human capital, social capital, and decisional capital. Hargreaves and Fullan (2013) define human capital as the talent of individuals; social capital as the collaborative power of the group; and decisional capital as the wisdom and expertise—developed over time—to make sound judgments. In this approach, there is a focus on developing teachers as professionals who are able to exercise their judgment in the classroom, and on developing social capital in schools where the collective impact of highly collaborative work by teachers who stay over time enhances the learning of students. Investing in strengthening teacher professional learning is valued in this perspective, and there is a desire to support long-term careers in teaching.

Recent Developments in ITE in the US

Although historically there have been a variety of pathways into teaching and providers of programs in the US, from about 1960–1990 colleges and universities held a virtual monopoly on the preparation of teachers (Fraser, 2007; Zeichner, 2016). During this time, state and federal policies focused on building professional capital, and teaching was considered a career. For example, the building of a national framework for the development of state teacher standards for beginning teachers by the Council of Chief State School Officers and the development of career ladders for teachers in many states communicated a strong message that teaching was a profession (Darling-Hammond, Wise, & Klein, 1995). With the exception of emergency licenses that were granted to individuals in subject and geographic areas where there were teacher shortages, all teachers in US public schools completed either an undergraduate or post-graduate college or university program that met state teacher licensing requirements.

Investment in building business capital in ITE can be traced to the early 1980s, when new alternative preparation programs began to emerge in New Jersey, Texas, and California, with some programs administered by districts, states, or independent providers, including networks of charter schools (Stitzlein & West, 2014). The emergence of fast-track teacher preparation programs came at the same time as a shift in US policy toward public education generally that promoted deregulation and market competition in K–12 education (Cochran-Smith et al., in press). The disruption of the dominant system of college and university teacher education and its replacement by new entrepreneurial developed programs reflects the business capital approach to reform that has been adopted by the federal government, business community, and philanthropy.[2]

The emergence in 1990 of Teach for America, the largest and most influential fast-track program in the country, brought with it a change in financial investments in ITE programs. The federal government, private foundations, and individual venture capitalists began to provide large sums of money to promote the development and scaling up of non-university fast-track programs and turned away from investing in innovation in university teacher education (Hess & Henig, 2015; Zeichner & Peña-Sandoval, 2015). For example, Teach for America has sent over 32,000 teachers into public and charter schools since 1990 with the aid of huge philanthropic support (e.g., about $180 million from the Walton Foundation alone) plus over $200 million of support from the US Department of Education and millions of dollars of additional support from individual states and districts (Zeichner & Peña-Sandoval, 2015).

Philanthropic investment in entrepreneurial ITE programs continues to increase. Recently the Bill and Melinda Gates Foundation, the largest foundation in the US, initiated a new funding program for teacher education.[3] As a part of this initiative, almost $8 million was awarded to a group of non-university programs to fund "teacher education transformation centers." The group is led by the Relay Graduate School of Education, an independent school of education that legally awards master's degrees in New York state although they are not an accredited college or university. The Bill and Melinda Gates Foundation also recently donated $12 million to The New Teacher Project (TNTP). TNTP is a national independent teacher education organization whose Teaching Fellows programs are currently based in eight school districts. TNTP Teaching Fellows programs have prepared over 34,000 teachers since their beginning in 1997. As a fast-track program, TNTP expects its teacher candidates to master a set of generic teaching and classroom management skills and has a narrow mission to raise student standardized test scores.

As philanthropists and the US Department of Education reduced financial support to college and university programs and increased financial support for the development of alternatives, many states have followed suit and have changed their policies to support the growth of fast-track programs (Crowe, 2011). States have also withdrawn a large amount of their financial support for the public universities while these universities continue to educate about two-thirds of the nation's teachers (Zeichner & Peña-Sandoval, 2015).

Beyond the increased monetary investment in alternative preparation programs, the explosion of non-university fast-track programs has been helped by a process of knowledge ventriloquism (Zeichner & Conklin, 2017), where carefully selected research supporting deregulation and greater market competition has been used to develop and support exaggerated narratives of failure about university teacher education and exaggerated narratives of success about entrepreneurial programs. This in turn has led to constant repetition of these narratives by the media and an expansion of non-university fast-track programs often serving the needs of the growing number of charter schools.

Relay Graduate School of Education provides one clear example of the rapid and unwarranted growth of a fast-track program through knowledge ventriloquism. Despite the lack of any empirical evidence that it has accomplished even its own narrow goals in preparing teachers to raise test scores, there are now 14 Relay Graduate School of Education sites throughout the US. Relay began in New York City in 2007 as an independent program ("Teacher U") within Hunter College that was started by the leaders of three charter school networks. In 2011, "Teacher U" separated from Hunter College and changed its name to Relay GSE. A $10 million gift from hedge fund operator Larry Robbins provided initial funding for the program. This was followed by a $30 million gift from the Robin Hood Foundation where Norm Atkins (the director of Relay) served as co-executive director from 1989–1994. Relay has since attracted substantial funding from major philanthropists including the New Schools Venture Fund, and the Carnegie, Dell, Fisher, Bill and Melinda Gates, Schusterman, and Walton foundations.

In the business capital approach, teaching is technically simple and does not require much in the way of advanced training, university coursework, or clinical practice. The teacher education programs at Relay fit this model. Relay offers 2-year, part-time programs available to full-time teachers teaching with provisional certification. About 40 percent of the program is delivered through online instruction. Its curriculum consists mainly of content designed to help its teachers master Lemov's (2010) strategies to "Teach Like a Champion." Relay now operates programs in New York City, Newark, Chicago, New Orleans, Houston, Memphis, Philadelphia, and Camden. Relay intends to continue expanding its franchise. Caperton and Whitmire (2012) stated that "the vision is to keep expanding so that in a decade from now, 10,000 teachers in cities around the country are enrolled in an umbrella of Relays" (p. 80).

US federal education policies are also indicative of the increased investment in the business capital approach to teacher education. In particular, federal education policy positions ITE through university teacher preparation programs as a barrier to be overcome through what are called "teacher preparation academies." In the recent 2015 reauthorization of the federal education law in the US, the US Congress approved the use of federal funds to support "teacher preparation academies." The policy places several restrictions on states that choose to fund the academies and ultimately lowers standards for teacher education. For example, states choosing to use federal funds to support these academies must agree to allow fast-track academies. States using federal funds to support academies must also not place any restrictions on undergraduate or professional course work of teacher candidates enrolled in the academies or require faculty to hold advanced degrees.[4]

The rapid expansion of both non-university and fast-track teacher education programs and declining enrollments in college and university programs in the US is a clear example of a business capital approach to developing teacher quality. It is a result of: increased monetary investment in non-university and fast-track ITE and disinvestment by philanthropists, states, and the federal government in colleges and universities; the production of narratives that position college and university teacher preparation programs as failures and entrepreneurial start-up teacher preparation programs as successes through the use of carefully commissioned and selected research; and educational policies that actively work to incentivize the expansion of non-university and fast-track ITEs.

Despite opposition to these trends among many college and university teacher educators and some teacher unions, this expansion is the outcome of over three decades of investment in a business capital approach to teacher preparation. It has come at the expense of building professional capital and has led to a common perception among policymakers that teacher education programs are obstacles to be minimized. For example, Sean Corcoran claims that:

> A naïve approach to raising the quality of the teaching workforce would be simply to impose higher barriers to entry by raising minimum standards for certification. Higher entry standards by definition raise the *minimum* level of quality, but may in fact result in a drop in average quality if higher quality candidates are disproportionately dissuaded by these costs. ... Teacher preparation programs are an important example of barriers to entry into teaching.
>
> *(Corcoran, 2009, p. 43)*

It should be noted that, in addition to efforts to deregulate and privatize the system from the outside, enduring weaknesses in the college and university teacher education system have contributed to the focus on developing business capital. There is a long history of critique of these systemic weaknesses from both inside and outside the system (e.g., Goodlad, 1990; Chubb, 2012). Still, the view that university and college teacher preparation programs are barriers to overcome underscores the broader view by proponents of a business capital approach that teaching is simple work that requires lots of tenacity but little in the way of rigorous course work or clinical practice.

ITE and Teacher Quality in Alberta

One of the international jurisdictions that emphasizes a different strategy of teacher preparation and development from that of the US is the Canadian province of Alberta. As Canada's fourth most populated province, Alberta consistently ranks in the top tier in the Program for International Student Assessment (PISA) in science, numeracy, reading, and mathematics. Unlike some other high-performing education systems, Alberta has a multilingual and ethnically diverse population of about four million people. Immigrants account for about 18 percent of the total population.

Alberta also boasts plentiful natural and nonrenewable resources, including large oil and oil sand deposits, gas, bountiful forests, and agriculture. Alberta's natural resources include more than 60 percent of Canada's conventional crude oil reserves and all of its heavy oil and oil sands reserves. Due to the fluctuating nature of oil prices, however, the revenues obtained on an annual basis can be unpredictable. Even so, Alberta's revenue from oil plays a large role in its education budget. For example, Alberta's general revenue funded 68 percent of the 2014–2015 budget (Alberta Education, 2014). As such, the education system in Alberta is affected by the price of oil and gas (in what is referred to as a "boom and bust economy"), and funding for schools varies with the condition of the economy. Even with these fluctuations, Alberta is one of the wealthiest provinces in Canada.

This brief case is based on a 2-year study of policies and practices related to teaching and teacher education in the province (Zeichner, Hollar, & Pisani, in press). It illustrates the effort to build professional capital in teaching through ITE—a common strategy in several high-performing education systems like Finland, South Korea, Germany, Ireland, and Singapore.

As a high-performing province adjacent to the US, Alberta makes for a compelling comparative case. In many ways, and despite the size differences, Alberta and the states in the US have much in common, including a diverse population with significant indigenous communities and many immigrants and refugees. With a combination of historically conservative government and progressive social ideologies, Alberta has managed to maintain a delicate balance between top-down policy directives and teacher agency. Much of this balance is the result of a longstanding culture of mutual trust between the teaching profession, teacher education institutions, school administration, and the government. This trust is the result of a long-term investment in developing the professional capital of teachers.

The success of Alberta's education system is a result of a variety of cultural, economic, and political factors and policies both inside and outside the education sector. One of the factors behind educational success in Alberta is the social safety support provided to students and their families. For example, Alberta has a strong healthcare system, awards up to a year of job-protected maternity leave and 37 weeks in parental leave, provides childcare subsidies to low-income families, has a higher minimum wage rate than the US federal minimum wage rate when converted to US dollars, and provides rent support to low-income families. In general, the social supports that exist for children and families provide stronger social preconditions for learning than in many countries.

A second factor in Alberta's success is the political stability that has existed until recently in the province, with over 90 years of Progressive Conservative leadership that has prevented some of the shifting and turning that is associated with constant changes with party leadership in some other systems. Even though this stable leadership has been relatively conservative on a number of issues, it has provided strong and consistent support for both public education and teachers that outmatches many systems including some that are politically more liberal. This strong public and government support has translated into very generous salaries and benefits for teachers that exceed the compensation provided for teachers anywhere else in North America.

A third factor supporting Alberta's educational success has been the unusual degree of trust and collaboration that has existed across the various education stakeholder groups such as the Ministry of Education, the teachers' association, teacher education institutions, and school administrators. The fact that school principals belong to the same professional association as teachers has supported a collaborative rather than adversarial relationship between teachers and principals. Also the common practice of individuals being seconded for periods of time from one sector of education to another (e.g., teachers who spend time working at the Ministry or in the teachers' association) has also supported the culture of trust and collaboration.

This is not to say that Alberta has been totally immune to attempts to place more emphasis on a business capital approach. For example, as Hargreaves and Shirley (2012) point out, Alberta was the first Canadian province to experiment with charter schools, and efforts have been made to establish a pay for performance system for teachers. Alberta also has introduced more system-wide standardized testing of students than some other leading education systems like Finland.

Still, one consequence of the trust and collaboration across education stakeholder groups is the emphasis on teachers' professional learning rather than on teacher evaluation. For example, following the rejection of a teacher pay-for-performance plan that was proposed by a staff member in the ministry, the government invested over $80 million CAD a year for 12 years to support inquiry-based school improvement projects by teachers and others at the local school level (Hargreaves et al., 2009; Hargreaves & Shirley, 2012; Parsons, McRae, & Taylor, 2006). The Alberta School Improvement Initiative was the direct result of this huge investment in teacher-led learning and lasted for a 12-year period. In general, Alberta's education system invests in teacher learning rather than in teacher evaluation.

As in the US, the work of teaching has intensified in Alberta. Teachers, overall, spend a relatively high number of hours per week teaching and grading and meeting with students and have relatively little time during the school day for collaboration with their colleagues (e.g., Alberta Teachers' Association, 2012a). Despite work intensification, however, Alberta's teachers generally feel respected and valued by the public and government and are very well compensated. This is in stark contrast to the US where teachers are under attack on a daily basis in the media and where their morale and job satisfaction is in decline (e.g., Metlife, 2012).

Another important factor in Alberta's education success is the insistence on strong ITE before individuals can serve as a teacher of record in the classroom. In an interview with Paul MacLeod, a former director of the Professional Standards Branch, it was made clear to us that Alberta values a strong foundation in coursework and clinical experience before individuals become teachers of record.

> We often talk about cardiologists. I really prefer he [complete] his program before he opens me up. I would prefer he's not learning on the job. We know there's an internship process. We know he's going to be going through that but we prefer the [degree is] in place before he actually decides to split me open. Same with teachers. We know that they're going to grow. We know that you never stop learning professionally, but you've got to have that degree or some form of meeting a certification standard.
>
> *(Paul MacLeod, June, 2014)*

These values are at odds with those in many parts of the US, where the proportion of "early-entry" teachers who begin teaching fulltime after only a few weeks of preparation continues to grow, and where many of those prepared in alternative certification programs feel unprepared to begin teaching (American Federation of Teachers, 2012).

Alternative certification, specifically emergency or conditional certification, is something that does not, with two exceptions, happen in Alberta. In the late 1960s and 1970s, there were special certificates to allow teachers to start teaching with 2 years' experience; these standards have since been raised. Alberta currently has two "bridging programs": one for career and technical education and the other for teachers with certification from outside of Canada. These programs offer teacher candidates some credit for their expertise and then require that candidates complete a program (about 1 year in duration) where they receive additional credit hours. Essentially, by combining the candidate's work experience and a year of schooling, the candidate has completed half of his/her teacher education requirements. In this alternative bridging program, an individual can begin teaching prior to completing his/her teacher education program and without an Interim Professional Certificate if he/she has expertise in an area and has made substantial progress on his/her teacher education course work.

Even with the bridging programs—similar to conditional certificates granted to teachers in the US—nothing like the fast-track programs exists in Alberta. Even the Teach for Canada program that has recently emerged in the country requires those admitted to be already licensed as teachers. This is in sharp contrast to the 45 "Teach for" programs around the world that allow individuals to be teachers of record with no more than a few weeks of pre-service preparation.

A strong university system of teacher preparation is certainly a significant factor in Alberta's educational successes. Alberta's teachers are well educated. Individuals wanting to become teachers in Alberta first need to have a Bachelor's of Education degree from a post-secondary institution, or possess a recognized bachelor's degree supplemented by an approved post-graduate teacher preparation program. In order to teach in Alberta one must first graduate from a university teacher education program and hold a valid teaching certificate called an Interim Professional Certificate. To earn their initial teaching certification, individuals must provide evidence of at least 4 years of university education, the completion of a minimum of 48 semester hour credits in professional teacher education coursework, and a minimum of 10 weeks of supervised student teaching (practicum). Despite the minimum 10-week practicum requirement, the Director of the Professional Standards Branch in the Ministry explained that the actual length of student teaching in Alberta's programs is at least 14 weeks. The Director also noted that many teacher education programs are moving toward a 20-week practicum.

In contrast to the explosion of alternative teacher preparation program providers in the US, Alberta has nine approved teacher preparation institutions— all of which are housed in universities or colleges and taught by faculty members within the school of education therein. Online teacher certification programs and narrowly defined skill-based programs (Zeichner, 2014) on the rise in the US are not accepted as teacher preparation programs in Alberta. Furthermore, school-based or employment-based teacher training programs are also not recognized for certification purposes.

The Professional Standards Branch in the Ministry of Education holds memoranda of agreement with the nine teacher preparation institutions. In so doing, staff of the Professional Standards Branch meet with the deans of the institutions on a fairly regular basis and receive annual updates regarding any programmatic changes to the teacher preparation program(s). Then, every 5 years, the Professional Standards Branch completes an efficacy report, similar to an audit of the program, ensuring that the institution meets the Teaching Quality Standard. This process includes surveys of current students, alumni, and employers of program graduates. While the Professional Standards Branch may encourage and recommend that teacher education programs make some adjustments to their programs, such as more closely aligning parts of their programs to provincial vision documents such as Inspiring Education, for example (Alberta Education, 2010), they do not issue mandates. Instead, they rely on a high degree of mutual trust between the governance system and teacher education system.

Teacher preparation program degree requirements for students in Alberta are similar across programs. In general, students complete between 120 and 150 semester credits of college coursework either as undergraduates or post-baccalaureate students. The teacher preparation institutions offer Bachelor's of Education undergraduate programs. Some teacher preparation institutions also offer 5-year combined-degree (concurrent) programs, which result in a Bachelor's degree in a content area and a Bachelor's of Education. Select teacher preparation institutions also offer 2-year "after degree" or post-baccalaureate (consecutive) programs leading to a Bachelor's of Education degree and teaching license.

Admission to teacher certification programs in Alberta is somewhat, but not overly, competitive. For example, in Fall 2013, there were 5,363 applicants for places in teacher education programs in the nine teacher education institutions. In total, 3,453 were qualified for admission, 2,695 were offered places, and 2,123 accepted and enrolled in a program. Although minimum requirements for program admission and program completion are the responsibility of the post-secondary institutions that have teacher education programs, admission requirements to the teacher preparation programs are similar across programs. Most programs require at minimum a 2.3 GPA on a 4-point scale, previous documented experience working with students and/or children, a teaching philosophy statement, and an interview with the faculty of education.

In undergraduate and combined-degree programs (concurrent), prospective candidates are required to take an orientation to teaching course or series of courses around the teaching profession with or without a field experience in the schools before applying to the teacher preparation program. Additionally, various documented checkpoints along the way must be completed satisfactorily in order to remain in the program.

Overall, admission requirements in Alberta's institutions for teacher preparation are not particularly noteworthy, especially when held up against admissions requirements for teacher candidates in countries like Finland, South Korea, and Singapore. However, these requirements (particularly the interview component), combined with checkpoints along the way to counsel students out of the program, if needed, broaden the scope of the definition of selectivity beyond academic criteria alone and provide the ability to monitor and control who enters the profession in ways that take both academic and professional performance criteria into account.

This approach is in sharp contrast to the business capital approach, which strives to "bring the best and the brightest" into teaching. For example, a report by McKinsey (Augste, Kihn, & Miller, 2009) that advocates admitting the top third of graduating students into teacher education programs has had a huge influence in different countries. As Paine (2013) points out, however, while this report has a lot to say about bringing the best and the brightest into teaching, it has very little to say about the kind of preparation for teaching they should receive. In this business capital approach there is a desire to attract academically proficient people from elite universities into teaching. However, lack of attention to the nature and quality of initial teacher preparation and an absence of concern with the issue of teacher retention reinforces a view that teacher preparation and retention do not matter. Instead an inexperienced teaching force with high turnover is perceived as beneficial when the ranks of the inexperienced teaching force are filled with smart, passionate young teachers from prestigious institutions.

All of the teacher preparation programs in Alberta advance an "educating the whole teacher" approach instead of taking candidates with strong academic backgrounds and providing crash courses in tips and tricks of the trade. Teacher preparation programs first prioritize or build upon a strong academic foundation. They then expand coursework to focus in-depth on how children learn and the practice of teaching. In general, teacher preparation programs focus on coursework in the foundations of education (i.e., child development, orientation to teaching, history of education, learners in a diverse society, literacy) followed by advanced coursework in practice (i.e., assessment, teaching methods, advanced lesson planning, etc.) culminating in a supervised field experience. Practicums and field experiences are woven throughout the programs of study.

In the US, there is a push to increase the duration and intensity of clinical field experiences, privileging the view that the real practice of teaching occurs in the field and undermining the value to be gained from foundational coursework. This instrumental view of clinical experience in the US that is disconnected from any theoretical foundation in coursework is vastly different from the approach taken to clinical practice in Alberta.

The length and structure of clinical experiences in teacher preparation programs in Alberta differ according to the institution of higher education and the program type but range between 14 and 21 weeks of clinical practice. In Alberta, there does not appear to be anything noteworthy about the length or intensity of the clinical field experience that differentiates Alberta's programs from university programs in other OECD countries.

As is the case in the US, Alberta, too, has had to deal with teacher shortages in hard-to-staff schools in the rural northern part of the province. In fact, one aspect of the inequities that do exist is the unequal access to experienced teachers in these more remote communities. The Ministry is engaged in several initiatives to increase teacher retention in the rural north (e.g., in indigenous "band" schools). There continues to be a serious problem in attracting teachers to teach and then stay in these remote schools. Still, rather than resorting to a service-oriented business capital approach to human resource management, the government is focused on preparing more people who live in these communities to be teachers. For example, it funds an aboriginal teacher education program at the University of Alberta called the Aboriginal Teacher Education Program or ATEP. The government also funds a rural practicum for teacher candidates to experience the rural north, and it provides financial incentives to teachers who agree to teach for a specified number of years in some northern districts.

In summary, two of the factors that help explain the overall success of the education system in Alberta have been a strong commitment to public education and to a college and university system of teacher education. Although there are various pathways into teaching in Alberta (concurrent, consecutive, and post-baccalaureate programs), there is one high standard of preparation that must be met by all programs and by teacher candidates regardless of the pathway. It is also apparent that the legitimacy of college and university teacher education programs in Alberta is not questioned as is the case in the US, England, and several other countries where university teacher education has been declared a failure by leading policymakers and by the media (e.g., Zeichner & Peña-Sandoval, 2015). In addition, Alberta's teacher education programs do not need to prove their worth by meeting punitive accountability requirements, as is the case in the US and England.

Also, unlike in the US, and some other countries, the preparation of teachers in Alberta is not validated by cross-institutional comparative performance assessments, and the content knowledge of teacher candidates is not measured by standardized proficiency examinations. Teacher education programs in Alberta are fairly typical of traditional college and university-based programs in the US with campus and field components and prepare all teachers to meet a rigorous set of standards that reflect a professional view of teaching. There is nothing exotic in Alberta's teacher education system that would differentiate it from other strong college and university systems in high-performing education systems.

As in many education systems around the world, problems exist in Alberta in preparing and retaining teachers to teach in remote and rural areas. However, rather than initiating US-style fast-track programs that insert young and enthusiastic missionaries into these communities for a brief stay and thereby deliberately maintain a revolving door of underprepared temporary teachers in these communities, Alberta has invested in funding community-based programs and incentives in the regular college and university programs for teachers to teach over time in rural communities.

In addition to the strong support for public education and college and university teacher education, the presence of strong social supports for children, the high compensation and respect for teachers in the society, strong cooperation and collaboration on education across stakeholder groups, access to high-quality professional development for teachers, and emphasis on teacher learning and development contribute to Alberta's strong education system. These types of conditions are preferred to external teacher evaluation as the way to achieve high teacher quality. There are no magic bullet policies or practices related to teacher education that can be adopted by other systems to replicate Alberta's success. It is the whole package of providing the social preconditions for learning together with the policies and practices that support public education that is crucial. Teachers and teacher education make a major contribution to Alberta's reputation as a leading education system.

Conclusion

In contrasting Alberta with the US, it becomes apparent that Albertans' long-standing faith and trust in the public education system, its teachers, and institutions preparing public school teachers is a critical factor in the success of Alberta's education system. By contrast, in recent decades in the US the public and government's faith and trust in its public educational institutions and those working in them has been undermined and eroded.

In fact, the professional capital that used to exist for teachers and teacher preparation in the US is being systematically stripped away. Many public school teachers in the US have limited decisional capital to make their own preferred judgments. They have limited options to choose or design curricula or develop high-quality classroom assessments to assess student learning. In the drive to encourage market competition, punitive evaluation systems for teachers, rather than investment in teacher development and teacher learning, drive teachers to compete against each other rather than learning from and alongside each other. This has been accompanied by a lack of access to high-quality professional development. Most of what is now called professional development in the US is top-down and aimed at getting teachers to conform to directives. Although a recent study (TNTP, 2015) shows that districts spend a lot of money on professional development for teachers in the US, teachers do not highly value much of it because it often consists of short one-shot events focused on compliance with external directives rather than on the more teacher-driven professional development that exists in high-performing education systems like Alberta's.[5]

The revolving door of fast-track prepared teachers, particularly in poor urban and rural schools, has undermined the ability of US school systems to build social capital in terms of preferred collaboration. Ironically, this decimation of the social capital of the school system has strengthened other kinds of social capital enabling fast-track teaching missionaries to pursue more lucrative policy advocacy and consultancy positions in the entrepreneurial education market. In an effort to increase teacher quality, the US positions university and college teacher education program as unnecessary burdens and barriers to attracting high-quality candidates and thus undermines public legitimacy for such programs. And rather than paying teachers salaries on par with other professionals as in Alberta, many teachers in the US remain chronically underpaid.

Through the deregulation of teacher education in an effort to encourage market competition, the US is investing in the expansion of fast-track teacher preparation programs, which narrowly conceive of and measure successful teaching as the ability to raise test scores and say nothing about successful teaching as the ability to incite curiosity, develop a love of learning, or cultivate empathy and compassion for others. Fast-track programs are also undermining a deeper and broader view of human capital, which moves beyond undergraduate grade point averages and the selectivity-rankings of undergraduate institutions to ensure that teachers not only have deep knowledge of their content area, but also understand the social, historical, and cultural contexts of education, have strong pedagogical content knowledge, and are able to adapt their teaching to the diverse learners in their classrooms.

Instead, the decision by philanthropists, business and corporate interests, and the federal government in the US to invest in the business capital approach and ignore the successes of other countries' decisions to adopt a professional capital approach has led to the growing privatization of public education. Indeed, businesses are capitalizing on this opportunity: from charter schools and entrepreneurial teacher preparation startups to the corporations and businesses involved with test development and test administration.

By contrast, Alberta's system has decided to invest in building "the whole teacher." Alberta has strong public and governmental support for public education, teachers, and teacher education institutions. Alberta pays its teachers well with competitive salaries and benefits. There is a lack of fast-track teacher education programs and there is consistent support for university teacher education. Alberta provides access to high-quality and teacher-driven professional development, reinforcing the view of teaching as a career, of teachers as professionals, and of teacher learning as a continuum across their careers. The US would do well to learn from Alberta's continued investment in the professional capital of teachers and its resultant effects on student achievement.

Notes

1   We are aware that there are conceptual issues involved in comparing a province of about four million people with a country of over 300 million people. Although it is possible to describe dominant trends in US policy and practice because of the growing role of the Federal Education Department, it makes less sense to discuss Canada as a country because of the absence of a Federal Ministry of Education and the significant variability among provinces.
2   For example, see www.brookings.edu/blogs/brown-center-chalkboard/posts/2016/01/27-essa-teacher-prep-innovation-arnett?rssid¼brown+center+chalkboard
3   Seewww.gatesfoundation.org/Media-Center/Press-Releases/2015/11/Teacher-Prep-Grants
4   Seewww.washingtonpost.com/news/answer-sheet/wp/2015/12/05/the-disturbing-provisions-about-teacher-preparation-in-no-child-left-behind-rewrite/
5   See www.youtube.com/watch?v¼8FCtDHWowkc&feature¼youtu.be&list¼UU88 i6dfMrRI5AZ PIrHVtGmQ

References

Alberta Education (2010). *Inspiring education: a dialogue with Albertans.* Retrieved from http://ideas.education.alberta.ca/media/80898/inspiring_education.pdf

Alberta Education (2014). *Education Funding in Alberta.* Retrieved from http://education.alberta.ca/media/8309883/education%20funding%20in%20alberta%20handbook%202014-2015%20v2.pdf

Alberta Teachers' Association (2012a). *The new work of teaching: A case study of the work life of Calgary public teachers.* Edmonton: Alberta Teachers' Association.

American Federation of Teachers (2012). *Raising the bar: Aligning and elevating teacher preparation and the teaching profession.* Washington, DC: American Federation of Teachers.

Auguste, B., Kihn, P., & Miller, M. (2009). *Closing the talent gap: Attracting and retaining top- third graduates to careers in teaching*. Retrieved from http://mckinseyonsociety.com/closing-the-talent-gap/

Caperton, G., & Whitmire, R. (2012). *The achievable dream*. New York, NY: The College Board.

Chubb, J. (2012). *The best teachers in the world: Why we don't have them and how we could*. Palo Alto, CA: Hoover Institute Press.

Cochran-Smith, M., Maker, M., Burger, S., Carney, M., Chang, W., Fernandez, B., Keefe, E., Miller, A., Sanchez, J. & Stern, R. (in press). Teacher quality and teacher education policy: The US case and its implications. In M. Akiba & G. Le Tendre (Eds), *The Routledge international handbook of teacher quality and policy*. London: Routledge.

Corcoran, T. (2009). "Human capital policy and the quality of the teacher workforce." In D. Goldhaber & J. Hannaway (Eds), *Creating a new teaching profession* (pp. 29–52). Washington, DC: The Urban Institute.

Crowe, E. (2011). *Race to the top and teacher preparation*. Washington, DC: Center for American Progress.

Darling-Hammond, L., Wise, A., & Klein, S. (1995). *A license to teach: building a profession for 21st century schools*. Boulder, CO: Westview Press.

Fraser, J. (2007). *Preparing America's teachers: A history*. New York, NY: Teachers College Press.

Furlong, J., Cochran-Smith, M., & Brennan, M. (Eds) (2009). *Policy and politics in teacher education*. London: Routledge.

Goodlad, J. (1990). *Teachers for our nation's schools*. San Francisco, CA: Jossey Bass.

Hargreaves, A., & Fullan, M. (2012). *Professional capital*. New York, NY: Teachers College Press.

Hargreaves, A., & Fullan, M. (2013). The power of professional capital, *JSD: The Learning Forward Journal*, *34*(3), 36–39.

Hargreaves, A., & Shirley, D. (2012). *The global fourth way: A quest for excellence*. Thousand Oaks, CA: Sage.

Hargreaves, A., Crocker, R., Davis, B., McEwen, L., Sahlberg, P., Shirley, D., & Sumara, D. (2009). *The learning mosaic: A multiple perspective review of the alberta initiative for school improvement AISI*. Alberta Education, Edmonton. Retrieved from http://education.alberta.ca/

Hess, F., & Henig, J. (2015). *The new education philanthropy*. Cambridge, MA: Harvard Education Press.

Lemov, D. (2010). *Teach like a champion: 49 techniques that put students on the path to college (K-12)*. San Francisco, CA: Jossey-Bass.

Metlife (2012). *Survey of the American Teacher*. Washington, DC: Metlife. Retrieved from www.metlife.com/assets/cao/foundation/MetLife-Teacher-Survey-2012.pdf

Moon, B. (2016) (Ed.). *Do universities have a role in the education and training of teachers? An international analysis of policy and practice*. Cambridge: Cambridge University Press.

National Council on Teaching and America's Future (2007). *The high cost of teacher turnover: A policy brief*, National Commission on Teaching for America's Future, Washington, DC. Retrieved from http://nctaf.org/wp-content/uploads/2012/01/NCTAF-Cost-of-Teacher-Turnover-2007-policy-brief.pdf

Paine, L. (2013). Exploring the interaction of global and local in teacher education: circulating notions of what preparing a good teacher entails. In X. Zhu & K. Zeichner (Eds), *Preparing teachers for the 21st century* (pp. 119–140). Berlin: Springer.

Parsons, J., McRae, P., & Taylor, L. (2006). *Celebrating school improvement: Six lessons from Alberta's AISI projects.* Edmonton: School Improvement Press.

Phillips, O. (2015). *Revolving door of teachers costs schools billions every year.* National Public Radio, Washington, DC. Retrieved from www.npr.org/sections/ed/2015/03/30/395322012/the-hidden-costs-of-teacher-turnover

Ronfeldt, M., Loeb, S., & Wyckoff, J. (2013). How teacher turnover harms student achievement. *American Educational Research Journal, 50*(1), 4–36.

Stitzlein, S. M., & West, C. K. (2014). New forms of teacher education: connections to charter schools and their approaches. *Democracy and Education, 22*(2). Retrieved from http://democracyeducationjournal.org/home/vol22/iss2/2/

TNTP (2015). *The mirage: Confronting the hard truths about our quest for teacher development.* Washington, DC: TNTP.

Zeichner, K. (2014). The struggle for the soul of teaching and teacher education. *Journal of Education for Teaching, 40*(5), 551–568.

Zeichner, K. (2016). The changing role of universities in US teacher education. In B. Moon (Ed.), *Do universities have a role in the education and training of teachers? An international analysis of policy and practice* (pp.107–126). Cambridge: Cambridge University Press.

Zeichner, K., & Conklin, H. G. (2017). Beyond knowledge ventriloquism and echo chambers: Improving the quality of the debates in teacher education. *Teachers College Record, 119*(4), ID No. 18148, Retrieved from www.tcrecord.org

Zeichner, K., & Hutchinson, E. (2008). The development of alternative certification policies and programs in the United States. In P. Grossman & S. Loeb (Eds), *Alternative routes to teaching: Mapping the new landscape of teacher education* (pp. 15–29). Cambridge, MA: Harvard Education Press.

Zeichner, K., & Peña-Sandoval, C. (2015). Venture philanthropy and teacher education policies in the US. *Teachers College Record, 117*(6), 1–44. ID No. 17539. Retrieved from www.tcrecord.org

Zeichner, K., Hollar, J., & Pisani, S. (in press). Teacher policies and practices in Alberta. In C. Campbell & K. Zeichner (Eds), *Developing teachers and teaching in Canada: Policies and practices in Alberta and Ontario.* San Francisco, CA: Jossey-Bass.

10

ADVANCING SOCIAL JUSTICE AND DEMOCRACY IN TEACHER EDUCATION

Teacher Preparation 1.0, 2.0, and 3.0

Kenneth M. Zeichner

Currently, about two-thirds of teachers in the US are prepared in college and university programs while the other one-third are prepared in relatively new non-university programs run by school districts, nonprofit and for-profit private providers, and by various combinations of different stakeholders (National Research Council, 2010). Regardless of the type of teacher preparation program and who runs it, most teacher educators make claims that their programs focus on issues of social justice and equity. This chapter raises concerns about the degree to which teacher educators' claims about their programs focusing on social justice and equity are reflected in their practices.

Teacher Preparation 1.0 and 2.0

Over the last decade, teacher education programs in colleges and university have come under increasing attack from a variety of critics including the former US Secretary of Education, Arne Duncan (Keller, 2013). The criticisms of these programs focus on the issues of their intellectual rigor and practical relevance (Wilson, 2014). There have been criticisms of teacher education programs in colleges and universities throughout the history of university teacher preparation (Fraser, 2007). What is new about the current critiques, as Wilson (2014) points out, is the fact that these criticisms have, with the help of philanthropists, think tanks and advocacy groups, the US Department of Education, and policymakers (Zeichner & Peña-Sandoval, 2015), been coupled with the emergence of a new set of non-college and university programs that are intended to "disrupt" the teacher education field and stimulate innovation. Many of these programs (e.g., Schorr, 2012) are fast tracks where teachers complete most of their certification requirements as teachers of record after a few weeks of pre-service teacher education, and many of them focus very narrowly on the technical aspects of teaching and raising pupils' standardized test scores, and ignore other aspects of teaching as professional work such as teachers learning how to exercise their judgment in the classroom and to adapt their teaching in response to the changing needs of their students (Zeichner, 2014). Many of these programs are also linked with charter school networks and serve as the suppliers of teachers to these networks (Stitzlein & West, 2014). Some of these programs, like the Relay Graduate School of Education, which recently opened its fifteenth location in Dallas-Fort Worth, are expanding very rapidly nationally and preparing more teachers each year (Zeichner & Conklin, 2016).

The new programs that have been brought into the field by social entrepreneurs to stimulate innovation in teacher education have been proclaimed as 2.0 programs (Gastic, 2014) and, by implication, college and university programs (teacher education 1.0) have been declared to be obsolete. For example, Gastic (2014) predicts:

> The next decade will see the proliferation of teacher prep 2.0 models as the benefits of their collective approach to teacher education become better known and more widely recognized.
>
> *(p. 105)*

> Those programs that fail to join this learning community will soon reveal their obsolescence and find themselves struggling to justify their existence. Demand will shift to more relevant, affordable and flexible programs where teachers are held to high professional standards of knowledge and skill under advisement of strong instructors and coaches who are committed to improving a teacher's effectiveness.
>
> *(p. 109)*

It is my contention that, although most teacher educators in 1.0 and 2.0 programs state that they focus on issues of social justice and equity in preparing teachers, very few programs in both categories have enacted in their practices some of the key values of social justice teacher education.

The Absence of Culturally Responsive Teacher Education

Two examples of how 1.0 and 2.0 teacher education programs have failed to actualize in their education of teachers the values they espouse are related to issues of power and knowledge, and to issues of cultural responsiveness.[1] First, it is very clear in studies of the experience of teacher candidates of color in predominately white college and university programs that there is often a lack of recognition and responsiveness in programs to the linguistic and cultural attributes that teacher candidates of color bring to their preparation for teaching, and the preparation of teachers in these institutions frequently ignores the needs of teacher candidates of color and focuses on the preparation of white teachers to teach students of color (Villegas & Davis, 2008).

While college and university teacher education programs, in part because of state standards and national accreditation requirements, now include coursework in multicultural education and clinical placements in schools highly impacted by poverty, research has continued to show an overwhelming bias of whiteness that frames discourse and practices in many college and university programs (Sleeter, 2001). While there are exceptions to this problem in teacher education institutions and programs that are not predominately white (e.g., Irvine & Fenwick, 2011; Skinner, Garreton, & Schultz, 2011), most 1.0 programs encourage their teacher candidates to teach in culturally responsive ways in their elementary and secondary school classrooms while not teaching in culturally responsive ways themselves.

From what is known about the 2.0 programs that began to emerge in the US in the early 1990s with the beginning of Teach for America, they too ignore the cultural and linguistic capital that their teacher candidates bring to their programs and teach a standard set of knowledge and skills to everyone in the program with little or no accommodation of the different assets and needs of their students (Kretchmar & Zeichner, 2016). A number of these new programs like Relay focus very narrowly on teaching teacher candidates a set of classroom management skills (e.g., Lemov, 2010) to implement with fidelity, and do not address the issue of culturally responsive teaching in elementary and secondary school classrooms. Their theory of action is that if teachers use the teaching and management techniques they are taught they will be able to raise student test scores and social justice and equity will be achieved. Typically, neither the outcomes of schooling beyond test scores nor the costs of obsessively focusing on raising test scores are discussed in the 2.0 program literature (Kretchmar & Zeichner, 2016).

Most of the research on the experiences of students of color in teacher education programs is based on experience in college and university programs. The conclusion that 2.0 programs are guilty of the same problem of "colorblindness" in pedagogy as 1.0 programs is inferred from the total absence in the 2.0 program literature of any discussion of culturally responsive teacher education pedagogy and from the dominance of a discourse of "helperism" where the emphasis is to save students from their broken communities rather than recognizing and building on the strengths and funds of knowledge that exist in these communities.

Knowledge and Power in Teacher Education Programs

A second issue that reflects the frequent contradiction between an expressed commitment to social justice in teacher education and the realities of program practices is concerned with the question of whose knowledge counts in the education of teachers. One would expect teacher educators in programs that espouse a social justice mission to take a democratic approach to the issue of whose knowledge counts in the education of teachers. In such an approach, teachers in the elementary and secondary schools that serve as sites for clinical placements in programs and local community members who provide educational and other services in communities outside of schools and the families who send their kids to the local public schools would be engaged in equitable collaboration with teacher education programs and programs would work to incorporate the expertise in schools and communities into their work with prospective teachers.

Here, despite the pervasive rhetoric in the literature on college and university teacher education about the importance of genuine and equitable partnerships with schools in preparing teachers (Goodlad, 1998) and the emergence of movements to establish professional development and partner schools as sites for teacher education (Zeichner, 2007), for the most part these partnerships have been very university-centric and have replicated the power–knowledge relationships that existed in traditional forms of university teacher education (Duffy, 1994; Murrell, 1998; Zeichner, 2009).

On the other hand, many 2.0 programs have constructed a false dichotomy between theory and practice and have uncritically glorified the teaching practices that are a part of their already established frameworks (e.g., Farr, 2010) while they demonize theory as irrelevant to daily practice in classrooms. This uncritical glorification of practice within particular frameworks is not the same thing as valuing and accessing knowledge and expertise from schools. It is a very program-centric approach, which does not open the programs up to challenge and critique, nor does it engage K–12 educators in significant decision-making about programs. Furthermore, the marginalization of what is referred to as "theory" in many of these programs narrows the preparation of teachers too far and minimizes the importance of context and culture in teachers' work. This lack of attention to culture and context in preparing teachers will negatively impact teachers' work (Zeichner, 2009).

Also, despite the unquestioned importance of the relationships among teachers, schools, families, and communities in the education of students (Cuban, 1969), and the call in the literature for more attention to preparing teachers to work in respectful and equitable ways with the families and communities of their students and for programs to access the knowledge and expertise in local communities in service of this goal (Zeichner & Melnick, 1996), there has been little attention to these issues in both 1.0 and 2.0 programs (Zygmunt & Clark, 2016). Despite isolated examples to prepare teachers to *involve* families in the education of their children (i.e., to get them to listen more to what the school has to tell them), there are even fewer examples of efforts to *engage* or *work in solidarity with* families and communities (Zeichner, Bowman, Guillen, & Napolitan, 2016).

Continuing to parachute well-intentioned teachers from university and non-university teacher education programs into public schools who know little about their students, their families, and communities and who are not committed to engaging families and communities in schooling will continue to widen the opportunity and learning gaps that have persisted. It is ironic that so little of this work goes on in teacher education programs across the US when so many of them have claimed the mantle of social justice as the basis for their work.

Practicing the Values and Commitments of Social Justice and Democracy in Teacher Education: Teacher Education 3.0

Unfortunately, current debates about teacher education in the US are mostly about which is the better vision: teacher preparation 1.0 with a greater focus on clinical practice or teacher preparation 2.0 with a focus almost exclusively on "training" teachers to engage in a set of teaching and classroom management practices that will supposedly raise student test scores. Both teacher education 1.0 and 2.0 claim the mantle of teacher education for social justice although, in reality, neither approach practices it. In order to realize in practice the values and commitments that are espoused in relation to social justice and equity, teacher education programs need to be transformed in ways that model the culturally responsive teaching that they advocate for teacher candidates and that disrupt the power-knowledge hierarchies that have marginalized the voices and expertise of teachers and local community members in preparing teachers.

Teacher education 3.0 rejects the choice that is now being provided in current policy debates, and offers a model that is built on a new more democratic architecture where responsibility for educating teachers is more equally shared by different stakeholders (i.e., schools, universities, local communities) who collaborate in equitable ways (Zeichner, Payne, & Brayko, 2015). In some cases, additional stakeholders such as local teacher unions and nonprofits are also involved in helping to shape a program. In this approach the epistemology of the program brings together knowledge and expertise from the university, schools, and local community in more democratic ways, and the focus is on working with and for communities rather than to save students from them. Here teacher education becomes a part of a larger project of community development and teachers see their work in classrooms as a part of a larger struggle for social justice through a more democratic process of deliberation and collaboration across institutional structures.

Zeichner (2010) and Noel (2013) provide examples of current work in US teacher education programs that show movement toward the kind of democratic epistemology that is a crucial element in teacher education 3.0. Some teacher educators have also advocated the teacher residency model as a structure for a program that is more inclusive of different forms of expertise located in universities, schools, and local communities (e.g., Berry, Montgomery, & Snyder, 2008). While I believe that the cross-institutional collaboration that is included in teacher residencies offers the potential to represent a 3.0 stance toward teacher education, in reality teacher residency programs vary in the ways that they include the knowledge and expertise of different stakeholders and in their ideological and political commitments (Zeichner, 2014).

For example, few of the existing teacher residency programs genuinely include the knowledge and expertise of local community educators, leaders, and families in the curriculum and employ local community members as mentors of teacher candidates. Additionally, some of the existing residency programs that involve the collaboration of universities and a local nonprofit and prepare teachers for a specific set of charter schools in a district do not collaborate with districts. Finally, some residency programs that on the surface involve the collaboration of universities, only include them in superficial ways (Zeichner, 2014). We need to look beyond the organizational charts at the ways in which knowledge and expertise from the different partners are accessed and used.

Once university, school, and community partners are brought together in equitably collaborative ways, the issue of culturally responsive teacher education pedagogy begins to become more visible in programs and its presence or absence in different parts of the program becomes an issue for discussion (Zeichner et al., 2016).

Finally, it is important to note that teacher education 3.0 is not particular to any specific program structure. While the hybrid teacher residency model offers the potential to incorporate the central elements of the approach, it is also possible for existing 1.0 and 2.0 programs to move in this direction as well. In the end, it is the substance and quality of teacher education programs rather than the labels tacked on to programs that make the most difference in preparing culturally responsive community teachers. It is time that teacher educators in all camps own up to how teacher education programs have fallen short in practice in modeling the ideals and commitments they tell their teachers to use in schools.

Note

1   There are also other ways in which many programs have fallen short of practicing what they preach including their failure to deliver on their promises to diversify the racial and ethnic composition of teacher candidate cohorts. With this issue, like the ones discussed here, there are promising examples of success in isolated programs, but a general lack of accomplishment in the field as a whole (Sleeter, Neal, & Kumashiro, 2015).

References

Berry, B., Montgomery, D., & Snyder, J. (2008). *Urban teacher residency models and institutes of higher education: Implications for teacher preparation.* Washington, DC: NCATE.

Cuban, L. (1969). Teacher and community. *Harvard Educational Review, 39*(2), 253–272.

Duffy, G. (1994). Professional development schools and the disempowerment of teachers and professors. *The Phi Delta Kappan, 75*(8), 596–600.

Farr, S. (2010). *Teaching as leadership.* San Francisco, CA: Jossey-Bass.

Fraser, J. (2007). *Preparing America's teachers: A history.* New York: Teachers College Press.

Gastic, B. (2014). Closing the opportunity gap: Preparing the next generation of effective teachers. In R. Hess & M. McShane (Eds), *Teacher quality 2.0.* Cambridge, MA: Harvard Education Press.

Goodlad, J. (1998). *Educational renewal: Better teachers, better schools.* San Francisco, CA: Jossey-Bass.

Irvine, J. J., & Fenwick, L. T. (2011). Teachers and teaching for the new millennium: The role of HBCUs. *The Journal of Negro Education, 80*(3), 197–208.

Keller, B. (October, 2013). An industry of mediocrity. *New York Times.* Retrieved October 20, 2013 from www.nytimes.com/2013/10/21/opinion/keller-an-industry-of-mediocrity.html?_r=0 on

Kretchmar, K., & Zeichner, K. (2016). Teacher education 3.0: A vision for teacher education to impact social transformation. *Journal of Education for Teaching, 42*(4), 417–433.

Lemov, D. (2010). *To teach like a champion: 49 techniques that put students on the path to college.* San Francisco, CA: Jossey-Bass.

Murrell, P. (1998). *Like stone soup: The role of professional development schools in the renewal of urban schools.* Washington, DC: American Association of Colleges for Teacher Education.

National Research Council. (2010). *Preparing teachers: Building evidence for sound policy.* Washington, DC: National Academies Press.

Noel, J. (2013) (Ed). *Moving teacher education into urban schools and communities: Prioritizing community strengths.* New York: Routledge.

Schorr, J. (2012). A revolution begins in teacher education. *Stanford Social Innovation Review* www.ssireview.org/articles/entry/a_revolution_begins_in_teacher_prep

Skinner, E. A., Garreton, M. T., & Schultz, B. D. (2011). *Grow your own teachers: Grassroots change for teacher education. Teaching for social justice.* New York, NY: Teachers College Press.

Sleeter, C. (2001). Preparing teachers for culturally diverse schools: Research and the overwhelming problem of whiteness. *Journal of Teacher Education, 52*(2), 94–107.

Sleeter, C. E., Neal, L. I., & Kumashiro, K. K. (Eds). (2015). *Diversifying the teacher workforce.* New York: Routledge.

Stitzlein, S. M., & West, C. K. (2014). New forms of teacher education: Connections to charter schools and their approaches. *Democracy and Education, 22*(2). Retrieved December 1, 2014 from democracyeducationjournal.org/home

Villegas, A. M., & Davis, D. E. (2008). Preparing teachers of color to confront racial/ethnic disparities in educational outcomes. In M. Cochran-Smith, S. Feiman-Nemser, & D. J. McIntyre (Eds), *Handbook of research on teacher education* (pp. 583–605). New York: Routledge.

Wilson, S. (2014). Innovation and the evolving system of US teacher preparation. *Theory into Practice, 53*, 183–195.

Zeichner, K. (2007). Professional development school partnerships in a culture of evidence and accountability. *School–University Partnerships, 1*(1), 9–17.

Zeichner, K. (2009). *Teacher education and the struggle for social justice.* New York: Routledge.

Zeichner, K. (2010). Rethinking the connections between campus courses and field experiences in college and university-based teacher education. *Journal of Teacher Education, 89*(11), 89–99.

Zeichner, K. (2014). The struggle for the soul of teaching and teacher education. *Journal of Education for Teaching, 40*(5), 551–568.

Zeichner, K., & Conklin, H. (2016). Beyond knowledge ventriloquism and echo chambers: Improving the quality the debate on teacher education. *Teachers College Record, 118*(12), 1–38.

Zeichner, K., & Melnick, S. (1996). The role of community field experiences in preparing teachers for cultural diversity. In. K. Zeichner, S. Melnick, & M. L. Gomez (Eds), *Currents of reform in preservice teacher education* (pp. 176–196). New York: Teachers College.

Zeichner, K., & Peña-Sandoval, C. (2015). Venture philanthropy and teacher education policy in the United States. *Teachers College Record, 117*(5), 1–44.

Zeichner, K., Payne, K., & Brayko, K. (2015). Democratizing teacher education. *Journal of Teacher Education, 66*(2), 122–135.

Zeichner, K., Bowman, M., Guillen, L., & Napolitan, K. (2016). Engaging and working in solidarity with local communities in preparing of the teachers of their children. *Journal of Teacher Education, 67*(4), 1–14.

Zygmunt, E., & Clark, P. (2016). *Transforming teacher education for social justice.* New York, NY: Teachers College Press.